SHOOTING *MIDNIGHT COWBOY*

SHOOTING

FARRAR, STRAUS AND GIROUX   NEW YORK

MIDNIGHT COWBOY

ART,

SEX,

LONELINESS,

LIBERATION,

AND THE

MAKING

OF A

DARK

CLASSIC

GLENN FRANKEL

Farrar, Straus and Giroux
120 Broadway, New York 10271

Grateful acknowledgment is made for permission to reprint the following material:
Excerpts from *The Diary of Anaïs Nin: Volume Five, 1947–1955*, copyright © by Anaïs Nin, and *Volume Six, 1955–1966*, copyright © by Anaïs Nin. Used by permission of Houghton Mifflin Harcourt Publishing Company. All rights reserved.
Excerpts from *Trapeze: The Unexpurgated Diaries of Anaïs Nin*, edited by Paul Herron (Sky Blue Press/Swallow), copyright © by the Anaïs Nin Trust. This material is used by permission of Ohio University Press, www.ohioswallow.com.
Excerpts from the Anaïs Nin Papers, Charles E. Young Research Library, UCLA. Permission granted by the Anaïs Nin Trust.
Excerpts from the published works, letters, and other writing of James Leo Herlihy, copyright © Jeffrey Bailey. Used by permission of Jeffrey Bailey.

Library of Congress Cataloging-in-Publication Data
Names: Frankel, Glenn, 1949– author.
Title: Shooting Midnight cowboy : art, sex, loneliness, liberation, and the making of a dark classic / Glenn Frankel.
Description: First edition | New York : Farrar, Straus and Giroux, 2021. | Includes bibliographical references and index.
Identifiers: LCCN 2020034903 | ISBN 9780374209018 (hardcover)
Subjects: LCSH: Midnight cowboy (Motion picture)
Classification: LCC PN1997.M43686 F73 2021 | DDC 791.43/72—dc23
LC record available at https://lccn.loc.gov/2020034903

Designed by Abby Kagan

Our books may be purchased in bulk for promotional, educational, or business use. Please contact your local bookseller or the Macmillan Corporate and Premium Sales Department at 1-800-221-7945, extension 5442, or by email at MacmillanSpecialMarkets@macmillan.com.

www.fsgbooks.com
www.twitter.com/fsgbooks • www.facebook.com/fsgbooks

10 9 8 7 6 5 4 3 2 1

Dedicated to the memory of

Alan Finder, Gregory Katz,

and Nick Redman

For me, for the filmmakers I came to love and respect . . . cinema was about revelation—aesthetic, emotional, and spiritual revelation. It was about characters—the complexity of people and their contradictory and sometimes paradoxical natures, the way they can hurt one another and love one another and suddenly come face to face with themselves.
—Martin Scorsese

No one should come to New York to live unless he is willing to be lucky.
—E. B. White

CONTENTS

SHOOTING *MIDNIGHT* COWBOY

INTRODUCTION

I like the surprise of the curtain going up, revealing what's behind it.
—John Schlesinger

John Schlesinger was looking forward to a triumphant entry on his first visit to Hollywood. *Darling*, the British director's third professional feature film, had been a surprise hit on both sides of the Atlantic, winning three Academy Awards and introducing international audiences to twenty-five-year-old Julie Christie, whose fresh looks and exuberant energy embodied the naughty spirit of Swinging London. She played Diana Scott, a thoughtless and predatory supermodel who broke up marriages, yawned her way through orgies, and generally set new records for narcissism and duplicity, yet radiated an irresistible charm and vulnerability that made you feel sorry for her even as you cheered her downfall. It was only Christie's second major film, yet with Schlesinger's careful direction, she gave such an adept and nuanced performance that she won the Oscar for Best Actress.

The year was 1966 and Hollywood loved new talent, especially when it came with a British accent. The moviemaking capital of the world had recently embraced Peter O'Toole, Albert Finney, Sean Connery, Julie Andrews, and Michael Caine, and now it loved Julie Christie and the thoughtful filmmaker who had recognized and captured on film her seductive charisma.

Suddenly, after a decade-long apprenticeship making short, spirited documentaries for BBC Television and low-budget black-and-white feature films, John Schlesinger was the hot new thing, a movie director of wit, irony, and substance. Everyone wanted to meet him, and powerful people were pushing substantial projects toward him, including *Funny*

Girl and *Fiddler on the Roof*, both of which he turned down. Best of all, studio heads were asking, "What do *you* want to do next, John?" And when John said what he wanted to do next was a big-budget adaptation of Thomas Hardy's Victorian novel *Far from the Madding Crowd*, starring Christie, Alan Bates, Peter Finch, and Terence Stamp—among the cream of British acting talent—MGM said yes.

He spent six months slogging with cast and crew through the quaint market towns and ancient, picturesque fields of rural Dorset and Wiltshire in southwest England. When the film was finished, the studio flew three hundred journalists to London, housed them at the Savoy, and treated them to a week of free food, royal welcomes to Windsor Castle and Buckingham Palace, boat rides and bus trips through Thomas Hardy country, and a star-studded preview at the Marble Arch Odeon. Movie premieres were planned for New York and Los Angeles, with another one squeezed between them at the last minute for Washington, D.C. Success was a foregone conclusion.

Then the reviews started arriving. *Far from the Madding Crowd* bombed. Despite its lush visual beauty and fine acting, the film was too modern to feel authentic, yet too traditional to feel youthful, and Christie's curiously underwritten character careened from headstrong, independent woman to swooning fool for love, a modern material girl trapped in a nineteenth-century soap opera. *The New York Times'* chief film critic, Bosley Crowther, usually a sucker for sincere classical epics, mournfully branded it "sluggish, indecisive, and banal."

John Schlesinger, who thought he was coming to America for a coronation, instead found a wake.

At the New York premiere, he could sense members of the audience slipping into a coma. There was utter silence at the end. "It *was* frightfully slow," he would later admit. "We were too much in awe of Thomas Hardy."

A lavish premiere party had been planned for after the screening at the Grand Ballroom of the Plaza Hotel. When John walked in, he noticed there were only three full tables. The handful of intrepid guests applauded wanly. "It was an absolute disaster," he recalled. Even his parents slipped out early.

By the time he awoke the next morning, the Washington premiere had been canceled. Instead, he flew directly to the West Coast, escorted by the head of publicity for MGM. The man asked gingerly what John was planning for the future, then offered a piece of advice: "Be very careful what you do next—you can't afford to make something which is really not right for you."

Despite his sudden belly flop as a big-time director, John Schlesinger had no intention of doing anything other than what he thought was right for him. And what was right for him, he had decided, was to make a film out of a novel that was so bleak, troubling, and sexually raw that no ordinary film studio would go near it.

Midnight Cowboy, written by James Leo Herlihy and published in 1965, tells the story of Joe Buck, a handsome but not overly bright dishwasher from Texas who buys himself a cowboy outfit and hops a bus to New York City to seek his fortune by becoming a male hustler selling sexual favors to frustrated older women. Joe's business plan fails miserably and he winds up squatting in a shabby and deserted apartment building with Ratso Rizzo, a disabled, tubercular con man and petty thief. Ratso becomes Joe's host, pimp, adviser, and, ultimately, his friend. Joe ends up turning tricks with men in Times Square, and savagely beats and robs one older customer to buy bus tickets to Florida for himself and his desperately sick friend, who wets his pants and dies just before the bus arrives in Miami. The book contains scenes of heterosexual and homosexual intercourse, sadomasochism, fellatio, gang rape, prostitution, and illegal drug use.

Trapped inside the straitjacket of Hollywood's old Production Code system of censorship—under which even a husband and wife couldn't be seen sleeping together in the same bed, and a toilet could never be shown, let alone flushed—*Midnight Cowboy* could not have been made just a few years earlier. But by 1968, the year after the disastrous release of *Far from the Madding Crowd*, the motion picture industry was in deep trouble. Ticket sales had been steadily falling for more than two decades, and most of the studios were sliding toward insolvency. The genres that had sustained Hollywood during its long golden age—westerns, musicals, romantic comedies, biblical and historical epics—had grown stale and predictable, and many of the highly paid stars and filmmakers who worked in them had lost the magical power to attract increasingly younger audiences. In a time of political upheaval and changing social mores, Hollywood seemed less relevant than ever.

The studio heads, cognizant of their economic precariousness, had recently scrapped the old code and replaced it with a ratings system designed to allow for more adult stories, themes, and language. Not everyone embraced the new system; church groups, parental activists, and local politicians in small-town America—the backbone of the moviegoing public for generations—feared a loosening of moral standards and a threat to the well-being of children.

Just as there were deep divisions and uncertainty inside the film industry over box office receipts and freedom of expression, so the country was torn by political unrest at home, a protracted and self-destructive war in Vietnam, the murders of Martin Luther King and Robert F. Kennedy, the betrayal of the hard-won victories of the civil rights movement in school desegregation, voting rights, and social justice, and the demands for equality and recognition by the women's liberation and gay rights movements. Richard Nixon, a conservative Republican, captured the White House in November 1968 in a narrow electoral victory over liberal Democrat Hubert Humphrey, while a third-party insurgency led by former Alabama governor George Wallace helped awaken and inflame the populist demands and racial fears of white working-class voters. The election capped a pivotal year when, according to social historian Charles Kaiser, "all of a nation's impulses toward violence, idealism, diversity, and disorder peaked to produce the greatest possible hope—and the worst imaginable despair."

The birthplace and battleground for many of these conflicts was New York City. Emerging from World War II as the world's greatest metropolis, New York by the late 1960s was on a downward path to seemingly terminal decline, fueled by economic hardship, rising crime, political violence, and government repression and ineptitude. Yet it was also the incubation chamber for daring and innovative experiments in popular culture and sexual expression, including film, art, literature, theater, and music. Thousands of young people still poured into the city each year, seeking not just a job or an education but a sense of identity and adventure. New York was never a refuge—the city's embrace was far too noisy, edgy, chaotic, and dangerous for comfort or reassurance. But it was exhilarating. "The city arouses us with the same forces by which it defeats us," wrote literary critic Alfred Kazin, who spent a lifetime walking its streets.

The architect and filmmaker James Sanders argues that while New York is a great literary city with nearly two centuries of novels, short stories, plays, essays, poems, and songs exploring its inhabitants, landmarks, and enduring myths, it's an even more perfect movie city because of its anxious restlessness and adventurism—"ideal for the constantly moving images that make up a film." Movies, he writes, are "the city's true mythic counterpart."

The city was a vast film school for moviemakers and moviegoers. Repertory film houses like the Cinema Village and Bleecker Street Cinema, in Greenwich Village, and the Thalia, Symphony, and New Yorker, on the Upper West Side, offered the equivalent of a full-scale, constantly repeating film history course at bargain prices. In the early sixties, future director Martin Scorsese and auteurist critic Andrew Sarris shared office space in a second-floor walk-up at Eighth Avenue and Forty-second Street, the butt end of Times Square, to be near the shabby movie houses where for a quarter they could catch double features and new films from Europe. Folksinger Phil Ochs and his pal Marc Eliot, the future author of a book about the rise and fall of Times Square, saw John Ford's *Fort Apache* and *The Searchers*, both starring John Wayne, while Bob Dylan, newly arrived from Minneapolis and pining for Suze Rotolo, his as-yet-unattainable girlfriend, took in *Atlantis: The Lost Continent* and *King of Kings* in a marathon double bill that temporarily dulled his pain. And the future cultural critic Phillip Lopate cut high school classes to see Jean Renoir's exquisite drama *Rules of the Game* "with my legs dangling over the Apollo balcony" at 223 West Forty-second Street, the most successful art house for foreign films in the United States.

"Each art breeds its fanatics," recalled Susan Sontag. "The love that cinema inspired, however, was special. It was born of the conviction that cinema was an art unlike any other: quintessentially modern; distinctively accessible; poetic and mysterious and erotic and moral—all at the same time. Cinema had apostles. Cinema was a crusade. For cinephiles, movies encapsulated everything."

Like so many young artists and cinema buffs, Jim Herlihy and John Schlesinger had each ventured to New York for fame and fortune. Otherwise, they seemed to have little in common. Herlihy was the son of working-class Catholics raised in a slowly deteriorating neighborhood of Detroit, and he barely made it through high school. He worked strenuously to keep his homosexuality a secret from his family, and found home a suffocating environment that he escaped by enlisting in the navy as soon as he reached eighteen. An aspiring novelist, playwright, and actor, the arc of his career reflected the unprecedented opportunities and turbulence of the times in which he lived. He used the G.I. Bill to attend Black Mountain College, an experimental school of the arts in North Carolina. Once he made it to New York he joined the periphery of the lively and influential gay arts community that emerged from the shadows after World War II. *Blue Denim*, his best-known play, ran for six months on Broadway and was made into a successful feature film. His three novels all garnered critical praise, and two of them were made into Hollywood movies.

John Schlesinger, by contrast, grew up in a family of sophisticated, upper-middle-class Jews in a wealthy suburb of London, surrounded by great literature, classical music, and theater. After serving in the British military during World War II, he attended Oxford University. Early on, his parents knew of and tacitly accepted his sexual orientation even while they worried about how their high-energy, high-maintenance firstborn child would find happiness and fulfillment.

Both were men of great personal charisma who could be generous friends and mentors, yet each was uncomfortable in his own skin— Herlihy coped all his life with self-diagnosed manic depression, while Schlesinger's moods rose and plummeted almost daily. Each was a spirited, seemingly guilt-free gay man whose sexuality was well-known to friends and close companions, yet each remained in the closet publicly for many years out of fear of ostracism and the potential damage to his career. And each found his ultimate artistic expression among the cracked, garish canyons of Times Square and its lonely, ruined denizens.

The *Midnight Cowboy* film project that Schlesinger and his producer, Jerome Hellman, ultimately cobbled together seemed like an especially risky gamble. Besides the rawness of the source material, the director was a chronically insecure and temperamental worrier who didn't want to hire either of the leading men; the actors themselves were relatively untested newcomers; the producer was coming off a mediocre comedy—*A Fine Madness* (1966)—and undergoing a painful divorce; the formerly blacklisted screenwriter was a brilliant but self-destructive alcoholic; the cinematographer was a newly arrived Polish immigrant making his first feature film. No one involved—not the actors, the director, the producer, or the film company that financed it—expected the movie to make a dime's worth of profit.

More than fifty years later, *Midnight Cowboy* remains a bleak and troubling work of novelistic and cinematic invention, floating far above most other books and films of its era. The novel has long been out of print, the novelist largely forgotten. The film hovers around the upper middle in polls of Hollywood's one hundred greatest movies, but John Schlesinger's name is usually missing from the lists of New Hollywood's celebrated auteurs, such as Scorsese, Spielberg, Coppola, Polanski, and Altman. Yet *Midnight Cowboy* remains one of the most original and memorable novels and movies of its era, a cutting-edge portrait of love and loneliness, compassion and squalor among the most unlikely of people in the most unlikely of places—"so rough and vivid," wrote the *New York Times* film critic Vincent Canby, "that it's almost unbearable."

This book tells the story of this dark, difficult masterpiece and the deeply gifted and flawed men and women who made it. It is a book about New York in a troubled era of cultural ferment and social change. It's about the rise of openly gay writers and gay liberation—the movie was released in May 1969, just a month before the Stonewall riots fired their ringing symbolic shot. And it's about the coming of age of Hollywood in the brief but fertile interregnum between the eclipse of the old studio system and the rise of a new one, a time when original, risk-taking movies flourished, old rules were shattered, and a new breed of filmmakers took on adult themes and characters that had never been seen in mainstream movies before.

It begins with a darkly handsome young man from Detroit with aspirations to be a writer and a closetful of secrets about his sexuality, his restless solitude, his periodic bouts of depression, and his taste for emotionally damaged characters who reflected his own labyrinthine conflicts.

1. THE WRITER

None of us feels that he's entirely normal. We're all moving along hoping we're getting away with an image of normality—but our secret is that we've got this sweet little place that isn't quite like anybody else's.
—James Leo Herlihy

Tall, thin, and stylishly dressed, Anaïs Nin arrived at Black Mountain College, in Eden Lake, North Carolina, from her home in New York on a warm autumn day in October 1947 to lecture about her new novel, *Children of the Albatross*, and meet with writing students. Nin was forty-four years old and virtually unknown outside of her immediate circle of avant-garde novelists and poets—it would be almost twenty years until she published the first of the intimate seven-volume diary that would establish her as one of the most celebrated and notorious writers of the twentieth century. In 1947 she was just an obscure author with an overabundance of self-regard and a dearth of readers; her books sold few copies, her name was on no one's lips. She had a wealthy, dutiful, and long-suffering husband in New York and an ardent young lover in Los Angeles with whom she planned to liaise once her book tour was completed. And she had an intriguing presence. "There was an aura about her, a sense that she was holding a séance," wrote the literary critic Anatole Broyard, who met her in Greenwich Village.

She was not expecting much from her visit. Black Mountain was a small, experimental college where teachers, many of them refugees from prewar Europe, held classes in the liberal arts and sciences including art, drama, music, photography, writing, and most anything else proposed by themselves or their students. The student body, recalled Alfred Kazin, who taught there briefly, consisted largely of "waifs, psychic and intellectual orphans, children of agitated professional families in agitated New York, Cambridge, and Chicago," plopped down in a woodsy, communal setting where they were expected to help build their own classrooms and grow their own food. But one student stood out for Nin, a handsome, dark-haired, talkative young man with piercing blue eyes and intense nervous energy.

His name was James Leo Herlihy. He was twenty years old and recently discharged from the U.S. Navy, and he had arrived at the college just a few weeks earlier from his home in Detroit. He told Nin he was desperate to become a writer. She looked at him and was captivated. "He had laughing Irish eyes, a swift tongue, and seemed outwardly in full motion in life," she would recall. They had a long conversation about art and literature—"phosphorescent talks because of his responses, his quick displacements, a quality born of American restlessness and migratory habits."

Still, she also noted a dark side to his infectious enthusiasm. He showed her a chart he kept in his journal that recorded daily the ups and downs of his moods. Pointing to the lowest ebb, he told her, "The day it goes below that point I will commit suicide."

"He said it smiling, defiantly," she later wrote. "It was as if he wore the mask of youth, alertness, gaiety even, and that this dark current was so far below the surface it had not yet marked his face or his voice or invaded his eyes. Yet I believed him."

As for Herlihy, he had never met anyone who looked or talked like the Paris-born Nin. "She had her face beautifully painted with lovely delicate mascara," he would recall. "And she wore beautiful clothes. She had marvelous little high heel slippers. Her clothing was feminine and enticing and romantic and stylish." The effect on Jim and his fellow students was magical. "Picture, if you will, youngsters who were just developing from the drab grayness of war-time, and who saw this sparkling, tinkling creature as perfection itself. When she told us that we too could live out our dreams, well—we were converted, to say the least."

Nin asked him what kind of writer he wanted to be. He cited Upton Sinclair's politically radical, muckraking novel *The Jungle* as a model. He wanted "to write a book about how cruel we are to one another, a book that tells that in such a way that the whole world will cry."

And what about you? he asked her in return. Her answer stunned him: "I want to contribute to the world one fulfilled person—myself."

"And that was the beginning of—for me—a life-long double-mindedness," Jim later recalled. "There was the part of me that wanted to do something for the world, and part of me that wanted to understand what it meant to be a fulfilled individual." Nin's message had gotten through. "If you want to affect the world, first of all you have to affect yourself."

He was smitten. There was nothing sexual about it—he was gay and, by his own account, "paralyzed with self-consciousness." But for him, she embodied a place where artists exchanged confidences, supported one another, aspired to greatness. It was a world he longed to be a part of, and an identity he desperately craved. And although they were worlds apart, she seemed to understand how hungry he was, perhaps because beneath all of her carefully constructed artifice she was hungry, too.

"She gave me all the attention that anyone could ever hope for at that age . . . and when she left, I thought about her forever," he recalled more than thirty years later. Her visit "was just the most glamorous thing that ever happened to me."

There had not been much glamour in Jim Herlihy's young life. He was the middle child of five in a working-class family of German and Irish background. His father, William, a strong, quiet man, was a construction engineer and building inspector for the city of Detroit; his mother, Grace, blond and statuesque, was a housewife and former amateur singer. They lived in a modest two-story house in a run-down neighborhood north of downtown and attended mass every Sunday.

Before he turned five, Herlihy's family moved to a cheaper house on South Sugar Street in Chillicothe, Ohio, his mother's hometown, after his dad injured his leg and could no longer work. It was the heart of the Depression; his father and a neighbor stole chunks of coal from a nearby railroad yard to burn in the stove. His parents sent him to Catholic school, where, as he recalled, "nine of the ten nuns that I studied under were insane."

When he was seven, his parents gave him a toy typewriter made of cheap tin for Christmas—he would laboriously turn a dial to a letter and hit a button to record it on a piece of paper. He used it to compose imaginary scenes for puppet shows. Later, as a teenager, his older sister, Jean, joined the Book of the Month Club, and he got his first access to novels by Thomas Wolfe, F. Scott Fitzgerald, and Upton Sinclair. "From the first time that I was aware there were words I knew I wanted to write," he would recall, but "how could anybody growing up on 76 South Sugar Street be a writer?"

He also knew from an early age that he was attracted to boys, although it took him until his mid-teens to figure out what that meant. One thing was for sure: he knew he had to hide his feelings—not just from his parents and his siblings but from the church. "I never really believed sex was bad," he would recall, "only that you shouldn't get caught at it by persons who thought it was."

After the family returned to Detroit, Jim attended John J. Pershing High School while also working long nights and weekends as a drugstore clerk. He later claimed he was thrown out of school for a bit for playing hooky. "School paralyzed me," he recalled. "I slept in every class. I thought of professors as bloodless monsters with enormous heads, thick glasses, and tiny, damp penises."

He felt isolated. Perhaps it was those absurd teachers, or perhaps it was his demanding father—who drank too much, spent most of his time at home in self-imposed isolation in his basement lair, and viewed his good-looking but somehow off-kilter son through a miasma of disappointment. Or perhaps it was his own uncomfortable sexuality and rapid-fire mood swings that at times threatened to engulf him. Later in life he would diagnose himself as manic depressive. But for now, Jim Herlihy was developing and coping with a sense of how grotesque and lonely the world could be. He had a big secret—his sexuality—that he didn't dare share with anyone. Being a writer was perfect—he could be the observer, the outsider, engaged yet protected. God's lonely man.

He graduated high school in December 1944 and a few weeks later, a month shy of his eighteenth birthday, enlisted in the navy. He was too late to see action overseas, but the navy gave him an important mentor: an ensign named John Lyons, who in civilian life had taught English at Loyola University and who worked with him on writing short stories and introduced him to books by Henry James, Willa Cather, and Katherine Mansfield. It was Lyons who pointed him toward Black Mountain College. The cost of annual tuition was sixteen hundred dollars, which he paid for out of the G.I. Bill and his own savings. He stopped by home in Detroit long enough to pack his things and was on his way to the Smoky Mountains. Suddenly, becoming a writer didn't seem so completely out of reach.

Black Mountain had opened its doors in August 1933 with twelve faculty members, twenty-two students, outsized ambitions, and a minuscule budget. It called itself a "log cabin college," but the main building was a three-story southern-style mansion with a wide portico and a broad, yawning lobby, which housed a philosophy grounded in European modernism and self-induced democratic principles, with plentiful space for large, noisy egos to clash.

Jim Herlihy was immediately enthralled. He signed up for eleven courses, not just writing but drawing, painting, sculpture, Greek drama, English grammar, piano, and singing. "It was understood if there was something you wanted to learn about you could get someone to teach it even if it wasn't an established course," he recalled.

He was especially fond of his first writing teacher, Mary Caroline Richards. She was a poet, essayist, potter, and painter, a premature hippie mystic in flannel shirts and blue jeans, who kept her hair in a long ponytail and preached the gospel of unselfish communal living. She was widely admired for her "warmth and vulnerability, her compassion for others," wrote Martin Duberman in a history of the school. She and Jim forged an intimate friendship that would last the rest of their lives.

The school had an excellent pedigree; among those who would teach or study there over its twenty-four-year existence were John Cage, Robert Creeley, Merce Cunningham, Elaine and Willem de Kooning, Buckminster Fuller, Francine du Plessix Gray, Walter Gropius, Robert Rauschenberg, Robert Motherwell, Charles Olson, Ben Shahn, and Cy Twombly. Herlihy shared a makeshift dormitory space with photographer Lyle

Bongé and future filmmaker Arthur Penn, and he took Penn's course on the Stanislavski method of acting. "They had me in mind when they opened that place," said Herlihy. "No exams, you choose what you want to take, and no one interferes with your sex life."

But there were constant factions and endless internecine battles over funding and control, and Jim began to see clear obstacles to creativity. "The drawings all began to look alike, and the paintings all began to look like they had the same sort of teachers," he would recall. "There was an intolerance of other styles, anything that wasn't a member of the cult."

One of his teachers, the novelist and critic Isaac Rosenfeld, a well-respected member of the New York literary establishment, demolished Herlihy's half-completed first novel and a short story. "He said he didn't see any reason for me to ever continue in writing, that I might well find some way to get into some other field," Jim recalled, "because he just didn't find that there was any merit at all there." By delivering this bitter news, Rosenfeld claimed "he was doing me this great colossal favor." Jim was crushed.

He dropped out of Black Mountain after just one year, and returned home to Michigan. But the aptitude test he took at the University of Michigan confirmed that writing and acting—another of Jim's boyhood ambitions—were in fact the occupations he was best suited for. Soon after, he boarded a Greyhound bus for Los Angeles. He talked his way into the dramatic arts program at the Pasadena Playhouse School of the Theatre, a training ground for hundreds of young performers over the years, including Dana Andrews, Tyrone Power, Eleanor Parker, Gene Hackman, Angela Bassett, Al Pacino, and—a half dozen years after Jim departed—a scruffy recent dropout from Santa Monica City College named Dustin Hoffman.

Under the direction of Gilmor Brown, a sixty-two-year-old Shakespearean thespian of the old school, Pasadena offered an exhaustive range of courses in acting, play production, voice and speech training, history and literature of the theater, costume design, set dressing, and makeup. There was even a required course in fencing. "This training affects practically every muscle in the body," the school's brochure insisted. "It quickens the eye. It promotes mental alertness."

Jim Herlihy had the dark, beguiling looks, deeply resonant voice, and low-flamed charisma to succeed as an actor. "He had these beautiful shoulders," recalls Jeffrey Bailey, a writer and teacher who met him many years later. "Graceful, and he knew how to walk. A very straight back. Most writers wouldn't think of themselves as having an instrument, as they called the body. [Jim] did."

But Pasadena Playhouse–style acting bored him. "The kind of roles I would get in plays were the ones in which I stick my hands in my pockets and say 'Gee, Mr. Jones, I'd like to marry your daughter,' while I shifted my weight," he recalled. He quickly resolved to write his own.

His first play to reach the stage was *Streetlight Sonata*, a two-act, full-length "modern tragedy," as he called it, "dedicated to people who encourage others." Its main character is a doomed young novelist named Joe who stands under a streetlamp observing damaged people tell their stories and who falls in love with a prostitute victimized by a cruel lover. It was a fairly typical first work: sincere, a bit ponderous, humor-free. But the seeds of *Midnight Cowboy*, with its parade of wounded souls, were surely planted here.

The play received a brief run in June 1950 at the Playbox, a small experimental theater that Gilmor Brown had built and operated in his backyard. When the actor who played Joe couldn't make it one night, Herlihy played the part himself. He also played small roles in other students' plays and worked on a novel and an array of short stories.

None of which paid the rent at the small, depressing rooming house in a seedy section of Sunset Boulevard in West Hollywood where he lived for six months. For that he worked late afternoons and evenings washing dishes at the lunch counter of the local Woolworth's; later he traded it for a clerk's job at Gordon's Satyr Bookstore at Hollywood and Vine, a Bohemian hangout for book lovers. His salary was thirty dollars a week. When she was in town Nin would stop by to pick up her mail and chat with her young friend.

Soon he was restless and homesick. In August 1949 he set out to visit his family by the cheapest means possible—hitchhiking. In a note to Mary Caroline Richards he made it sound sarcastically romantic. "I'm going to Detroit tomorrow night," he wrote, "walking across the desert at 8 pm with my thumb and praying to the sagebrush and cactus and stars for a ride from some kind traveler into the sunrise at Las Vegas and from there through the mountains of Nevada into Salt Lake City, et cetera, through Cheyenne and Chicago. Papa sent me enough money to put chili sauce on the dead jack-rabbits that will sustain me along the way, and I'm looking forward to a great adventure."

When he returned to Los Angeles a few weeks later his high spirits crashed. The novel he was working on, *Strangers from Home*, wasn't jelling, as he explained to Nin in a despairing letter. "I write a lot these days, not good work; I cling to the surface like a dying man, afraid to submerge into the real lake of conflicts and sources; it is like a fear of drowning." A new love affair had gone sour as well, and he told Nin he fantasized about being "deathly ill and thinking how Bob would feel at my bedside." But thanks to her, he said, he had snapped out of longing for death: "I think of you and with the thought comes all of the miracle and excitement of being alive, like a kind of tidal wave burying the charm of death."

Nin had settled in for several months with Rupert Pole, her twenty-eight-year-old lover, at Sierra Madre, in the foothills above the San Gabriel Valley, where she was accumulating rejection letters from New York publishers for her latest novel, *A Spy in the House of Love*. She empathized with Jim Herlihy's black mood. She introduced him to the expatriate British novelist Christopher Isherwood and other members of the small but lively gay literary set in Los Angeles, and she sympathized with his restlessness. She encouraged him to start keeping a diary, as she did; he had his doubts, but she said it would help his writing, and he did it to please her. She would always insist that his diary contained his best writing. When she headed back to New York they regularly kept in touch.

He was deeply grateful for her sympathy and support. "I wonder if you know that you have shown to me and given to me in every conceivable way a kind of love which I have never known before in my life," he wrote to her.

Still, nothing in Los Angeles seemed to be working for him. And so he did what he often would do when reality became too hard for him to cope with. He packed his bags and left town. "Come to New York," Nin told him. "We will find a way."

"The residents of Manhattan are to a large extent strangers who have pulled up stakes somewhere and come to town, seeking sanctuary or fulfillment or some greater or lesser grail," wrote E. B. White in 1949. He warned that New York "can destroy an individual, or it can fulfill him, depending a good deal on luck. No one should come to New York to live unless he is willing to be lucky."

Jim Herlihy arrived in New York City in March 1952 at the height of its post–World War II glory. While many of the world's great cities were still recovering from the war's devastation, unscathed New York was on a growth spurt. Midtown Manhattan was experiencing an unprecedented building boom of monumental glass-and-steel office towers, including the new United Nations headquarters complex on the East River; the master builder Robert Moses was in the process of completing the vast network of highways, bridges, tunnels, parks, playgrounds, and public housing that would remake and, all too often, deface the city. Wall Street outstripped the City of London as the center of finance, while Broadway overshadowed London's West End as the capital of theater and music, and the Upper East Side overtook Paris as the heart of the art world.

It was for New York a "moment of grace," wrote social historian Jan Morris. "Never again would it possess the particular mixture of innocence and sophistication, romance and formality, generosity and self-amazement, which seems to have characterized it in those moments of triumph." New York, wrote cultural historian David Reid, was "the capital of the Twentieth Century."

Metropolitan New York's population of 12.5 million made it for a brief period the world's largest city. Its two million Jews outnumbered the Jewish populations of Tel Aviv, Jerusalem, London, and Warsaw combined. It had more Black people than any other American city, more Germans than anyplace outside of Germany, almost as many Italians as Rome, and as many Irishmen as Dublin. It was America's largest factory town and shipping port and the center of national media and popular culture. "New York had never been so attractive," wrote Anatole Broyard. "The post-war years were like a great smile on its sullen history."

It was also reputedly the city with the world's largest gay population. Gays and lesbians participated in and sometimes dominated the worlds of theater, art, music, dance, fashion, and literature. Those who were gifted, adept at self-promotion, or just plain lucky might find wealth, celebrity, and a sense of community among friends and fellow travelers. "From all over the country, homosexuals had converged on New York," wrote Gore Vidal in his landmark 1946 novel, *The City and the Pillar.* "Here, among the indifferent millions, they could be as unnoticed by the enemy as they were known to one another."

Aspiring artists, gay and straight, arrived from all over: Jonas Mekas from Lithuania; Andy Warhol from Pittsburgh; Jasper Johns from Sumter, South Carolina; William Inge from Independence, Kansas; Harper Lee from Monroeville, Alabama; Lorraine Hansberry from Chicago, Illinois; Nina Simone from Tryon, North Carolina; William Styron from Newport News, Virginia; Jack Kerouac from Lowell, Massachusetts; Allen Ginsberg from Paterson, New Jersey; Michael Harrington from St. Louis, Missouri; Gay Talese from Ocean City, New Jersey. Slum housing was ubiquitous and rents were cheap. In "Bleecker Street," songwriter Paul Simon's ode to the scrappy main artery of Greenwich Village:

> A poet reads his crooked rhyme
> Holy, holy is his sacrament
> Thirty dollars pays your rent
> On Bleecker Street

Jim Herlihy arrived by bus—the cheapest mode of public transportation and one he came to prefer even after he could afford more comfortable alternatives. On buses, he could observe not just the passing countryside but also his fellow travelers, their quirks, dilemmas, and aspirations. He came east with a dubious job offer from a book publisher that turned out to consist of reading cheesy genre fiction novels for two dollars per manuscript. "You can imagine how long I lasted," he wrote to his friend and former roommate Ed Mitchell back in California. He had no regular place to stay. He crashed for a bit with Hugh Guiler, Anaïs Nin's husband, in their West Ninth Street apartment in Greenwich Village, then took a spare room offered by his fellow playwright Bill Noble, a former teacher from the Pasadena Playhouse, in his apartment on West Seventy-third Street.

Although Herlihy was far from naïve, New York confronted him in ways he found rudely memorable. On one of his first days in the city, he asked a woman on the street how to get to the Statue of Liberty and got shut down immediately. "It's up in Central Park taking a leak" was her astringent reply. More than a decade later, he would incorporate that line in *Midnight Cowboy*, as part of Joe Buck's introduction to Manhattan.

At first he found the city even more daunting than Los Angeles. "New York is impossible to live in, filthy, expensive, etc., but in many ways very stimulating," he wrote to Mitchell. "Already it is too warm here and I may crack up from the filth; I shower twice daily and still itch from dirt and dust. . . . Don't have any intimate friends here, but many many people I've known from other parts, old teachers, actors and show people I've known from California, etc.; although I'm not lonesome, I am lonely."

He wasn't alone for long. Sometime that summer he ran into a young man he had first met in Los Angeles. Dick Duane was a nightclub singer and piano player with soft brown eyes, delicate features, a three-octave vocal range, and the lung power to fill a cavernous ballroom. Born in Seattle, Duane had a raw musical talent that had landed him a spot in Hollywood at the MGM school for gifted children, alongside Roddy McDowall and Jane Powell. After a few years of training and polish in drama, music, and dance, he set out on his own for San Francisco, where he landed gigs at hotels and clubs, before heading east to New York. The high points of his early career included bookings at the Copacabana, a spot on *The Ed Sullivan Show*, and some memorable recordings. Although virtually uneducated, Dick was smart, witty, and easy on the eyes, and he quickly made his way into New York café society at places like Johnny Nicholson's on Fifty-seventh Street and various watering holes in the Village. By 1950 he knew the chilly, insouciant Gore Vidal, the charming, flamboyant Tennessee Williams, the gifted, malicious Truman Capote, and the dark, brooding William Inge, plus Dorothy Parker, Tallulah Bankhead, Carson McCullers, the writer and producer

John Van Druten, and the director Joshua Logan. "There were playwrights and writers coming out of the woodwork," Duane recalls.

These were gay or bisexual artists who thrived in the largely open, somewhat tolerant atmosphere of New York, yet at the same time they maintained a protective wall around themselves and their friends. Sodomy was a crime in forty-nine states, police raids on gay bars and other hangouts were regular events, and muggings and other crimes of violence were a real threat. When he first came to New York, the novelist Edmund White would recall, a plainclothes police officer entrapped him in the men's room of a movie theater and threatened to arrest him. "At last he'd let me go, but I had grasped the lesson—gay desire was illegal. The most fundamental thing about me—my desire to sleep with other males—was loathsome to society."

Dick Duane introduced his new friend Jim to his old friends. Many were highly regarded and well-connected in their fields, like Van Druten, a gentle, friendly soul who dabbled in Eastern mysticism. He wrote *I Am a Camera*, the award-winning play that he adapted from Christopher Isherwood's *Berlin Stories* and that later became the basis of the hit musical *Cabaret*. Like Tennessee Williams, Van Druten took an early interest in Herlihy and encouraged his playwriting. So did George Freedley, an author, critic, and, for more than thirty years, the influential head of the Theater Collection at the New York Public Library; and Leo Lerman, a writer and editor at Condé Nast, whose Sunday evening open houses at his town house on Lexington Avenue on the Upper East Side were a place to meet and be met. And so did a set of younger men who were Herlihy's contemporaries, such as novelist Evan H. Rhodes, playwright James Kirkwood, producer Walter Starcke, author Darwin Porter, and interior decorator and travel book writer Stanley Haggart, all of whom welcomed the handsome newcomer to their social circle.

Jim Herlihy mesmerized these friends with his ability to turn all of his attention to the person he was talking to, giving that person the sense that he valued their opinion and honored their worth. "His gaze was intense," recalled his Black Mountain College friend Lyle Bongé, a Mississippian. "My maid once said that no one had ever paid her such close attention when she spoke. When you conversed with him you felt he was concentrating his entire being on what you had to say."

Dick Duane was more than just an entry point for Herlihy into New York's gay world. He was also an antidote for the loneliness and sense of isolation that had been eating at Jim all of his young life. "I've met someone here, Ed, and we're planning to make a life together," Jim wrote to Mitchell back in Los Angeles.

Dick was smitten as well. "Jamie was so charming and so good-looking and so original," he recalls. "There were times when he was so sweet. But he also scared me because he could go from being that wonderful, loving man to this extreme temperament. There were dark moods that would creep up on him. He always had a depressive side where he'd say, 'I hate life.' But when he was at his best it was rhapsodic."

Toward the end of that first year in New York, Herlihy invited Duane to join him for Christmas back home in Detroit. There Dick took the measure of Jim's family. He found Grace, Jim's mother, charming and welcoming, with a deep affection for her creative son. His father, Bill, was more remote. "The father was a sweet man, but he sort of created a world for himself in the basement and he would sit down there and get progressively drunker," Duane recalls.

As for Dick, the family embraced him as Jim's close friend, no questions asked. "You had to be a real cuckoo not to know who I was, but they would just leave it aside," Dick recalls. Still, he had the impression that Grace had developed a sense of her son's sexuality and was quietly accepting of it.

Finally, there was his older brother, Billy, who worked construction and whom everyone in the family, including Jim, seemed to worship. "Billy was the charmer of all time," Duane says. "He wasn't as good-looking as Jamie, but he was more macho. I had the feeling the brother was the father's ideal man, the macho guy living in a trailer somewhere."

For all his discomfort with his family, Jim was proud of his working-class roots and he seemed both fascinated and repelled by the sad, disconnected folks in his hometown and in his own family. He had one foot in their world, thought Dick, and the other in New York. Still, at times it seemed like Jim Herlihy didn't truly belong in either one.

2. THE LAZIEST BOY

I live in England because in many ways I'm a little scared. I don't trust success and I don't trust failure.
—John Schlesinger

While Jim Herlihy was seeking to make a new life for himself in New York in the early 1950s, John Schlesinger was returning to an uncertain one in London. He had just come home from some fifteen months on the road, first with an acting troupe in Australia and New Zealand, followed by six months in Scotland with another theatrical company. The ostensible purpose of these excursions was to polish his performing skills and his theatrical résumé. But he was also seeking to mend a broken heart. His first true love, Alan Cooke, a fellow aspiring young actor whom he'd met at Oxford University and with whom he had made two low-budget black-and-white feature films, had ended their romance after expressing shame over being gay. When Winifred Schlesinger, John's no-nonsense mother, picked him up at the train station, the first thing she said to him was "I hope you've gotten over Alan Cooke."

While Jim Herlihy trod carefully with his family about his homosexuality, being gay was not an issue for John Schlesinger and his parents. They knew about it and more or less accepted it. What they were deeply worried about was his future.

They had their reasons. Ever since childhood, their oldest son had been prone to fits of melancholy and despair. He suffered from migraines, was afraid of the dark, hated loud noises and couldn't stand firearms and fireworks, had an inordinate fear of rats and insects, and didn't learn to ride a bicycle until he was eleven. He seemed to lack direction, and his lingering desire to work as an actor, a profession that offered few golden opportunities and a dismal host of pitfalls, served to confirm their worst fears.

"I knew I didn't fit in, and I regretted that terribly, and it probably informed everything in my life," Schlesinger would recall many years later. He was acutely sensitive to "the idea of failing in the eyes of other people," he said, and felt underappreciated for the things he could do and ashamed for the ones he couldn't. He desperately wanted to exceed expectations, especially those of his critical but loving parents, but was never confident he could. "I've been dogged by that all my life," he said. It was surely one of the things that attracted him to stories about people who were outsiders, dreamers, and failures. He felt like he was one of them.

He had compensated in part by becoming the family impresario. Long before John Schlesinger directed Alan Bates, Julie Christie, and Dustin Hoffman, he directed his siblings, cousins, and family friends in small productions in the sitting room of their elegant home in Hampstead, one of London's most affluent neighborhoods, using the small 9.5-millimeter home movie camera his grandmother had given him. These little films were melodramas, song-and-dance revues, and adaptations of macabre German fairy tales. "We never played, you understand," his sister Hilary told William Mann, his biographer. "We were always directed by John right from the moment we could walk."

Still, there were times he drove his parents to despair. In August 1940, when John was fourteen, Winifred Schlesinger wrote a letter to her husband in which she called their eldest child "the laziest, most selfish & feckless boy I have ever come across. He is not interested in the world's affairs & seems quite unaware that there is a war on. He sits in an armchair all day unless forcibly evicted & listens to rubbish on the wireless. I'm afraid I must sadly say that our eldest son is a washout."

Bernard Schlesinger, a distinguished pediatrician who served as a senior medical officer in the British military in two world wars, shared his wife's lament. In his own written reply, he bemoaned John's "spinelessness & inertia."

At the time John had just completed a miserable first year at Uppingham, his father's alma mater, an austere and thoroughly stereotypical

English boarding school for boys founded in 1584. He was bored, bullied, and lonely, and ran away more than once. He was a mediocre student and absolutely no good at sports. He was also gay and Jewish—not a winning combination in a society deeply hostile to both, although the gay part was tacitly more acceptable in the all-male dormitory, where it was not uncommon for two boys to quietly crawl into bed together after the lights went out.

The Schlesingers were upper-middle-class Jews, the children of wealthy German and Dutch immigrants, highly assimilated and enamored of all things English. They loved classical music—Bernard played the cello, Winifred the violin—ballet, literature, Shakespeare, Wagner, and Brahms. They had a cook and an undercook, a parlor maid, nursery maid, chauffeur, and governess. They dressed each evening for dinner.

They were charming, tolerant, and highly principled people who didn't attend synagogue, yet were proud of their ethnic background and well aware of the casual anti-Semitism that pervaded English society. They saved the lives of twelve German Jewish children by sponsoring their resettlement in London in 1939, a few months before war broke out, and paid for their housing and schooling throughout the rest of their childhoods. But when it came to John, Bernard and Winifred's empathy had its limits. They insisted that he return to Uppingham to complete his education, despite the obvious discomfort it was causing him.

John Schlesinger survived Uppingham, as well as two years in the British army at the end of the war. Unlike his father, he detested military life but managed to transfer from the Royal Engineers in Singapore to the Combined Services Entertainment Unit, a haven for gay men that tolerated flamboyance and cross-dressing so long as it was confined to the stage. After his tour of duty ended, he went on to Oxford, where he studied English literature at Balliol College. But his most memorable experiences there centered around his involvement as an actor and director at the Oxford University Dramatic Society, another safe gathering place for gay men.

Still, discretion in public was an absolute necessity. After the more permissive sexual practices of wartime, a cloud of antigay repression descended upon British society in the late forties and early fifties. Although the Wolfenden Report of 1957 advocated the abolition of laws criminalizing homosexuality, it remained a "crime against nature" for another full decade. Many gay men and women had served with distinction during the war, but the public image of homosexuals as perverts and subversives was reinforced after Guy Burgess and Donald Maclean, British spies who defected to Moscow, were outed. Alan Turing, the brilliant mathematician who had helped crack the Enigma codes during the war, was convicted of "gross indecency," forced to submit to hormone therapy—in effect, chemical castration—to "cure" him of homosexuality, and eventually driven to suicide. The great Shakespearean actor John Gielgud was arrested in a public lavatory in 1953; four years later Brian Epstein, a prominent young Liverpool businessman later to become the manager of the Beatles, was arrested and fined for "persistently importuning" outside a men's room at the Swiss Cottage underground train station in London. John Schlesinger openly paraded his sexuality among his social circle of friends, artists, and collaborators, but to the outside world his closet door remained sealed. When asked publicly about it, his usual response was "I think that's my affair and no one else's."

John was small, pudgy, and prematurely balding; his weight wandered up and down, as he himself put it, "like a whore's drawers." He armed himself with a coat of irony, an abiding pessimism, and a loathing of pretentiousness and authority. He also had a wicked sense of humor—playful, camp, vulgar, sly, and mischievous.

Even more revealing was the morning ritual of self-flagellation and despair that John would repeatedly enact on his film sets. Running his fingers absentmindedly through the long blond hair of Ann Skinner, his devoted aide-de-camp, he would announce, "The rushes I saw last night are awful. We are making a piece of shit here, why are we doing this?" And then, with the help of his bemused cast and crew, he would talk himself back down to something equivalent to normal.

"That was his way of fishing for reassurance," says Schlesinger's devoted nephew, the writer Ian Buruma, who interviewed his uncle extensively in the years before his death. "He was a drama queen when he wanted to be, but there was a lot of steel behind his dramatic insecurity."

He couldn't bear not working. He had something to prove—to his parents, to his colleagues, to the world—and he was eternally restless to get on to the next thing. While he loved the security of working in England with actors and crews he felt comfortable with, he hated the cramped budgets and small thinking of those who controlled the purse strings of British cinema. The United States, by contrast, was rude, crude, and materialistic, yet it offered the creative challenges and opportunities he craved.

His life revolved around "the three F's," or so he proclaimed: films, fucks, and food—but as his nephew put it, "not necessarily in that order." He loved actors and formed deep emotional ties with Christie, Bates, Glenda Jackson, and many others. Yet he could explode in anger at their perceived shortcomings. Often on a film set he would single out a handsome young actor for special abuse. He openly humiliated Terence Stamp during the making of *Far from the Madding Crowd* (1967) for failing to recite his lines with what Schlesinger deemed the necessary gusto, and he beat Murray Head with a stick when the twenty-four-year-old actor failed to memorize his lines before filming a crucial scene for *Sunday Bloody Sunday* (1971), one of John's most enduring and personal works.

He admitted succumbing to "black despair" at times. "I often get angry and then express my rage very fast almost to anyone who happens to be there," he explained. "I have a short fuse and I like to blow it quickly and then I get on with life. I've always been a demon for getting enormously involved in whatever I'm doing.

"I don't just make a film. I fuck a film, day and night."

During the first half of the 1950s, Schlesinger continued to pursue his acting career, performing in nearly twenty plays and five feature films, plus various radio and TV gigs, including several episodes of *The Adventures of Robin Hood*, a British television series that became a hit on both sides of the Atlantic. But he was nearing thirty and still spinning his wheels, and he eventually concluded that his future lay in making films rather than appearing in them. In postwar Britain, the state-run British Broadcasting Corporation held a virtual monopoly over broadcast media, but Schlesinger couldn't land a regular job at the Beeb or a position in its filmmakers training program. Finally he got a temporary gig as a researcher and assistant director for a BBC documentary film about cheese making. It led to a low-level position on a new topical news program called *Tonight*. There he got the chance to make a number of creative short films but quickly fell out with the man in charge, who found him cheeky and undisciplined. Pushed out the door the following year, he latched on at *Monitor*, a new Sunday afternoon television series devoted to the arts.

This proved to be the break he needed. Working for Huw Wheldon, the program's smart and innovative producer, Schlesinger learned the basic film grammar of editing and montage, and how to work fast, cheap, and carefully on deadline. Wheldon "taught me to go out and quickly sum up a situation and to use my observation and first impressions and put them down very rapidly," he recalled. "It afforded me the chance to fail. If something didn't work awfully well there was always the next *Monitor* program to do something for."

He made more than two dozen documentary pieces over a three-year period. Among his colleagues were Ken Russell, Humphrey Burton, and Melvyn Bragg, all of whom went on to creative success and fame in the U.K. His films got longer and better and more entertaining. He did programs on the creative methods of an acting teacher, on children's art, and on the fad for high-fidelity stereo equipment, all of which benefited from his natural curiosity, humor, and keen eye for quirky stories and intriguing characters—gifts that would serve him well in making *Midnight Cowboy* a decade later. Then British Transport Films came along and offered him the chance to do a thirty-three-minute, black-and-white film about Waterloo, London's busiest train station.

Terminus (1961) presented a day in the life of Waterloo from sunrise to midnight. It's a sympathetic portrait of disconnected people: a stationmaster struggling to keep the trains running on time; a pretty young woman with a bouquet of flowers waiting expectantly for someone who never arrives; an uncomfortable pair of newlyweds waiting for the train to take them on their honeymoon; dour convicts in handcuffs being transported to Dartmoor prison; a five-year-old boy sitting on a suitcase crying because he's been separated from his mother; a homeless woman scavenging through trash bins—all of them presented with understated grace and humor. In Schlesinger's skillful hands, the station symbolized Britain and its people in mid-century, having survived a second devastating world war but facing an uncertain future.

The movie showed Schlesinger's growing sense of confidence and willingness to do whatever it took to get what he needed on film. His ruthless determination knew few bounds. "We got the boy to cry by giving him a bar of chocolate and then taking it away from him," he confided to the film critic Alexander Walker.

The film was given nationwide theatrical distribution and won a Venice Film Festival Golden Lion and a British Academy Award. And it brought an ambitious, stylish, and impetuous Italian-born movie producer knocking on John Schlesinger's door.

Part Italian, part English, part Persian, and all Jewish, Joseph Janni had studied industrial engineering at Milan University in the mid-1930s but quickly gravitated to the school's *cine* club, where he fell in love in with movies and met such future icons of Italian cinema as Vittorio De Sica, Nino Rota, and Carlo Ponti. Janni left Mussolini's Italy for London in August 1939 fully expecting to go on to the United States and a prospective job in the film business. Five days later, Hitler invaded Poland, World War II began, and Janni was taken into custody along with hundreds of fellow Italians suddenly categorized as enemy aliens. After several months in a British internment camp, he was released and offered a job writing propaganda in Italian for the BBC. He eventually went to work as a line producer for the Rank Organisation, one of two giant entertainment conglomerates that together wielded a stranglehold over British commercial cinema. There he learned the fundamentals of feature film production but despised Rank's bureaucratic mindset, especially when the heads of various departments sent him little memos with unsolicited and, so far as he was concerned, unhelpful suggestions. "I told my secretary if one of these ever gets on my desk, you're fired," he later recalled.

After five years he walked out and launched Vic Films, his own production company.

A vain and volatile man and an inveterate womanizer, Joe Janni pushed his way into the cozy, self-contained world of British cinema like a gate-crasher at a garden party. "He was well-dressed and blustery and he spat a lot when he talked," recalls Ann Skinner, whom he hired as a secretary. When he didn't like reality, Janni would simply alter it to fit his needs. On one production, he was late for an evening film shoot, picked up Skinner in his Jaguar convertible, and shot off ignoring all street signs and traffic lights. "At one point I said, 'Joe, we're going the wrong way down a one-way street,'" recalls Skinner, "and he said, 'No, this is the only way I know to go.'" Another time when a policeman pulled him over for speeding, saying, "I've been watching you," Janni shot back, "In that case I hope you've learned something."

Janni moved into independent film production at a pivotal moment in modern British popular culture. Despite playing an important role in the American-led victory over the Axis powers, Britain had emerged from the aftermath of the war shorn of most of its empire and with a battered, outdated, industry-heavy economy. The south of England slowly climbed out of its deep hole of war-imposed austerity. But the north, birthplace of the original Industrial Revolution, whose prosperity and social system were tied to rust-belt textile mills, factories, and coal mines, had entered a painful and seemingly irreversible decline. The Suez Crisis of 1956, a military intervention mismanaged by a coterie of smug, out-of-touch mandarins, revealed the decay at the heart of government and marked the death knell of Britain as an independent global power. The ruling class was losing its grip. In May of that same year, John Osborne's play *Look Back in Anger*, directed by a young upstart named Tony Richardson, opened at London's Royal Court Theatre. Its hostile, working-class antihero, Jimmy Porter, was deeply alienated from British society and his own bleak circumstances, ranting bitterly at his estranged wife and friends about the limitations of life, class, and poverty. The play touched a nerve and became a major hit. Other playwrights, novelists, and filmmakers soon followed, their stories set in the damaged and decaying corners of London and the long-neglected north. The Royal Court became their theatrical home, with Richardson and his fellow director Lindsay Anderson searching out and producing socially meaningful plays for a new generation of angry young men and women.

One of the first feature films to acutely capture this simmering class struggle was *Room at the Top* (1959), based on John Braine's bestselling novel. Joe Lampton, a wounded war veteran who comes to a small northern town for a low-level managerial job, is hungry for money and power. He craves the privileges previously reserved for the aristocratic elite, and he strives to acquire them by impregnating and marrying the boss's daughter. Along the way, he feels compelled to dump an older woman with whom he has forged a loving and erotic relationship. Their smoldering sexuality shocked readers and moviegoers at the time, as did Joe's reptilian coldheartedness. The film, directed by Jack Clayton, was a hit in both Britain and the United States. Laurence Harvey, in his first major starring role, captured all of Joe's lust and avarice, and Simone Signoret won an Oscar for Best Actress as his vulnerable and sensual mistress.

Room at the Top's success helped set off a wave of "kitchen-sink dramas"—novels, plays, and movies that replaced the drawing room settings and clever cocktail party repartee of Noël Coward and his generation with raw, sexual, sometimes violent characters and working-class locations. Suddenly the best new British films were full of sneering, foulmouthed, oversexed young men on the make and the wives and lovers they used and abused along the way. "There didn't seem any point in going on with all those pictures about country homes with comic servants or stiff-upper-lip officers and Cockney conscripts," recalled film director Karel Reisz. "We felt our pictures should reflect more of what was in the air."

Reisz was one of the three most recognized leaders of this austere but powerful neorealist movement, alongside Richardson and Anderson. Much like John Schlesinger, all three started out by making small black-and-white documentaries about working-class people in hardscrabble cities and towns. Anderson was the oldest and most dour of the group, a compact, curly-haired Oxford graduate who wore red shirts and lectured his fellow filmmakers about ideology, ethics, and aesthetics like a university don. His early subjects included residents in a bleak north England factory town; children at the Royal School for the Deaf, and workers at the vegetable, flower, and fruit market in London's Covent Garden. Richardson, another Oxford alum and the son of a Yorkshire pharmacist, and Reisz, a middle-class Jewish immigrant from Czechoslovakia, made *Momma Don't Allow* (1956), about jazz enthusiasts at a local dance hall. The three of them, along with Lorenza Mazzetti, put together a documentary series at the National Film Theatre in London in February 1956—the same year as the Suez Crisis—under the umbrella title "Free Cinema." It became an annual event.

The Free Cinema–ists had no overarching cinematic philosophy, just a commitment to authentic characters and settings and a vaguely left-wing ideology. "Implicit in our attitudes," they declared in their 1956 manifesto, "is a belief in freedom, in the importance of people, and in the significance of the everyday."

The French New Wave film director François Truffaut had once haughtily dismissed British cinema as "a contradiction in terms." The *New Yorker* film critic Pauline Kael, never one to mince words or feelings, judged that "the English can write and they can act, but they can't direct movies. They never could." (She graciously issued to Alfred Hitchcock and Carol Reed, two directors of undeniable stature, a reprieve from facing her rhetorical firing squad.) But suddenly young British filmmakers were creating their own compelling, indigenous stories, following in the footsteps of Italian postwar neorealists like De Sica, Roberto Rossellini, Luchino Visconti, and Federico Fellini.

Tall, thin, and charismatic, Richardson was the most adventurous and entrepreneurial of the group. Early on he had taken two Osborne plays—*Look Back in Anger* and *The Entertainer*—and turned them into feature films starring, respectively, Richard Burton and Laurence Olivier and produced by Woodfall Films, a company founded by Richardson, Osborne, and Harry Saltzman (later one of the founders of the James Bond series). Woodfall's first cinematic hit, produced, directed, and co-written by Richardson, was the groundbreaking *A Taste of Honey* (1961), based on a play by nineteen-year-old Shelagh Delaney, about a seventeen-year-old schoolgirl who flees her reckless, overbearing mother, becomes pregnant with a Black sailor's baby, and moves in with a supportive gay friend in an ultimately fruitless search for emotional stability. It starred Rita Tushingham, a wide-eyed, awkward, yet soulful nineteen-year-old actress who looked like she'd just stepped off the sidewalks of her native Liverpool for a quick cup of tea. Richardson's financial backers had advised him to offer the part to a known star like Audrey Hepburn, but he refused. With its unconventional female protagonist, unblinking realism, and pessimistic narrative, *A Taste of Honey* is in many ways the most daring of the kitchen-sink dramas. The film "peeled away a lot of layers," Tushingham told an interviewer thirty years later. "We had this ridiculous class system—we still have it—and people were saying, 'Who would be interested in seeing what people do in their kitchens?' And suddenly yes, people *did* want to see it and were quite shocked at times. It broke down a lot of barriers."

Richardson followed up with *The Loneliness of the Long Distance Runner* (1962), based on an Alan Sillitoe short story about a rebellious young man sent to a reformatory, starring another talented newcomer, Tom Courtenay. Richardson, who could sound both complimentary and condescending in the same sentence, pronounced that Courtenay "could have a great future, I feel, provided he doesn't get his teeth fixed."

But Richardson was getting at something important. These different kinds of stories required a different breed of actor: passionate, hungry, with strikingly different faces and regional accents—Courtenay, Tushingham, Alan Bates, Albert Finney, Richard Harris, Oliver Reed, Michael Caine, Rachel Roberts, Shirley Anne Field, and a host of others. "In my day Tom Courtenay wouldn't have carried a spear," said the director Bryan Forbes, who helped push for the changes.

They were the British version of an American generation of more naturalistic and compelling film actors—Dustin Hoffman, Robert De Niro, Al Pacino, Gene Hackman, Jack Nicholson, Robert Duvall. But the British got there first. "The nature of actors has changed," boasted Bates, who grew up in the northern town of Derby. "The affected way of acting, the affected way of speaking—all that stuff about losing the accent you came to London with—all that's finished. Actors *use* their backgrounds now. And although there's not much glamour around, there's a lot more excitement."

Eager to join and cash in on this new cinematic movement, Joe Janni bought the rights to *Saturday Night and Sunday Morning*, a Sillitoe novel about a young worker in a bicycle factory who is determined to squeeze as many thrills out of life as possible. Arthur Seaton has a virginal girlfriend and an older mistress; he drinks, screws, and brawls his way through each weekend, and swears he will never become like his parents who are, in his assessment, "dead from the neck up." Janni couldn't persuade the Rank Organisation or other traditional distributors to finance the movie and wound up selling the rights to Woodfall for the equivalent of fifty-six hundred dollars. A frustrated Janni vowed he would never let it happen again.

Richardson hired Karel Reisz to direct the film. Reisz took the cast and crew to the factories and mines around Nottingham and cast the inflammatory Albert Finney as the rowdy, pugnacious Arthur. It was, wrote the film historians Sue Harper and Vincent Porter, "the first time in British cinema [that] the working class were shown not to care about the disapproval of their betters, and to have a culture of their own—hedonistic, abrasive, volatile—which was perfectly competent for the job at hand."

The film was a big hit in England and established the handsome, twenty-four-year-old Finney—himself from Salford in the north of England—as a sexy new star, the British equivalent of James Dean. In 1999 it was ranked fourteenth in the British Film Institute's list of the one hundred best British movies.

The adult themes of films like *A Taste of Honey* and *Saturday Night and Sunday Morning* made clear that the sexual revolution had invaded the shoreline of British popular culture despite the best efforts of government censors to keep it out. In October 1960, the same month that *Saturday Night* premiered, D. H. Lawrence's novel *Lady Chatterley's Lover*, banned in Britain for three decades for its depiction of sexual intercourse and adultery, went on trial at the Old Bailey. The prosecution counted thirteen scenes of sexual intercourse in the book, as well as lavish use of shocking words like *fuck, cunt, balls, shit, arse, cock,* and *piss*. But several dozen distinguished writers, critics, and politicians signed petitions on behalf of the novel and dozens more attended the trial in sympathy—the American poet Sylvia Plath got a press ticket from the British poet Stephen Spender. The surprise verdict of "not guilty" in early November was hailed by *The Guardian* as "a triumph of common sense," and opened the gates for far more permissive policies for books, movies, theater, and art. Just as in the United States, these works appealed to postwar audiences eager for more sophisticated and adult entertainment.

Joe Janni soon acquired two more kitchen-sink properties—Stan Barstow's first novel, *A Kind of Loving*, and a West End play called *Billy Liar*. The son of a Yorkshire coal miner, Barstow was a sales manager by day and aspiring novelist by night. *A Kind of Loving* is about Vic Brown, a talented young draftsman working in the office of a Manchester factory who gets his pretty girlfriend Ingrid pregnant and agrees to marry her. Vic isn't as ruthless and amoral as Joe Lampton in *Room at the Top* nor as unruly and self-destructive as Arthur Seaton in *Saturday Night and Sunday Morning*, but he feels restless and trapped. Despite her beauty, Ingrid bores him, and they both know it. The book is about settling for less than you want, and trying to make do. "The way I see it is this," a resigned Vic concludes. "The secret of it all is there is no secret, and no God and no heaven and no hell. And if you say well what is life about, I'll say it's about life, and that's all." The novel was the English equivalent of John Updike's groundbreaking American classic *Rabbit, Run* (1960), published that same year.

Janni made a deal with Anglo-Amalgamated, a small independent distributor, to help finance and distribute both films. Now he needed to hire a director he could work with. He was a regular viewer of *Monitor* and had especially enjoyed John Schlesinger's piece on a small Italian opera company trying to find its way in London's West End theater district. Then, after seeing *Terminus*, he sent Schlesinger a copy of Barstow's novel and summoned the director to his office.

"He said to me, 'I liked the observation in your film and I liked the humor,'" Schlesinger would recall. "'I would like to discover you.'"

And John, who was insecure but no wallflower, replied, "Well, be my guest."

3. TWISTED APPLES

Writing is so lonely. It's like sentencing yourself to solitary confinement.
—James Leo Herlihy

Becoming a successful writer in New York City, Jim Herlihy soon discovered, was no simple task. At Black Mountain College or the Pasadena Playhouse you could take courses in writing and convince yourself you were learning the craft and getting somewhere. But in New York, he was just another suffering young writer—one of life's unfortunate clichés—with a blank page staring coldly back at him from a black metal typewriter. As for his fiction, there were many stops and starts and detours—novels abandoned after twenty pages, short stories that no magazine seemed interested in publishing. *Flight from Home*, his latest attempt at a novel, was turned down by three publishers. "The stories are still attracting lavish rejection letters," he wrote to Ed Mitchell. "They all seem to think 'he writes well enough' but no one buys a word. What to do! I'm living on unemployment compensation . . ."

His playwriting career wasn't going much better. When he came East he brought with him *Moon in Capricorn*, a fantasy about a girl who has a star lodged in her heart. By following her natural impulses, she winds up destroying herself and causing others to suffer as well. Herlihy managed to get the play a brief run at a community theater upstate in Chestertown, but his efforts to interest the New York crowd of agents and producers into taking it on got exactly nowhere.

He lived for a time on thirty dollars a week in unemployment insurance, but when the checks ran out he was forced to take a series of low-paying, starving-artist gigs: clerk-typist in a public relations firm for $1.50 an hour; editor of a house organ for a charitable organization;

sweeper of floors at a recording studio; dishwasher in Woolworth's basement; and, finally, picnic-plate wrapper for a paper products company. He once calculated that by the time he reached thirty he had held forty-three different odd jobs, for mostly pitiful pay.

Anaïs Nin, his guardian angel, was a constant source of support. Eventually she helped him make a breakthrough, convincing her friend Thomas Guinzburg, an editor at *The Paris Review*, the new, avant-garde literary magazine he had founded with Harold L. Humes, Peter Matthiessen, and George Plimpton, to publish one of Herlihy's more disturbing short stories.

"The Sleep of Baby Filbertson" (later retitled "Crazy October") is a grim and somewhat confusing tale about a corrosive mother and her nineteen-year-old son, Daisy and Rudy Filbertson, two obese and self-destructive barbiturate addicts, set in New York on a hot and hazy October afternoon. "The entire island seemed to have been submerged in an ocean of hot light and walking through it required a swimmer's effort," Herlihy writes. "Women invented parasols made of newspapers to blind them from the sun, and men blotted their foreheads with handkerchiefs and squirmed inside their suits."

Mother and son trade insults. When he calls her a "sonofabitch," she slaps him hard across the face. Rudy flees their stifling West Side apartment to catch a Ginger Rogers movie, but when he emerges from the theater after the film he is hit by a car. A kindly young Black man helps him to his feet and into a taxi but refuses his offer of a ride uptown. When he gets home his mother tries to bully him into kissing her. He resists, takes another phenobarbital, and slips into a dream. The piece concludes viciously: "His bed was like a slab on which lay the corpse of some giant foetus." Sweet dreams, Rudy.

"A Summer for the Dead," a surreal, Nathanael West–style novella published in *The Paris Review* two years later, is equally bleak but more skillfully drawn. It is set in a boardinghouse in Pasadena occupied by a collection of lonely, love-starved misfits. The main character is Wesley Stuart, a carpenter who builds sets for a Los Angeles television station. Wesley's sexual preferences are unspoken, but he has a visceral aversion to Faye, a flirtatious, unemployed, and half-unhinged actress who lives in the room next to his, and to Mrs. Kromer, his religion-obsessed landlady. But he finds himself strangely attracted to Earl Walker, a self-possessed deaf and blind salesman. Wesley cooks dinners for Earl and takes him on walks. Then Wesley discovers that Earl has been sleeping with Faye. When she comes on to Wesley as well, he pummels her violently, shocking the landlady and causing her to die of heart failure. The fragile, lopsided little community in the boardinghouse shatters.

There is sympathy in these despairing narratives, but no redemption, just a heavy, insistent sorrow. Herlihy's characters come in two varieties: people either crushed by their own virulent neediness, or so fiercely isolated they should be wearing NO TRESPASSING signs around their necks. No one escapes these stories with their soul intact, let alone their dignity. Not unlike many of the dedicated losers he would later create for *Midnight Cowboy*.

"In its pages are worlds within worlds, a kind of mania of vision, a burning heat, and an almost transcendental bubbling over of desire that eventually explodes in violence," wrote the *Paris Review* editor Christian Kiefer in a 2017 appreciation. "There is an undercurrent of sexuality in Herlihy's work, or perhaps *over*current, since it often seems to flow right across the surface of the text with its scent of sexual funk and frustrated pheromones."

Besides getting him critical attention, the published pieces gave Herlihy entrée to a lively little corner of New York literary society. *The Paris Review* threw him a cocktail party—forty serious people smoking pipes and sipping scotch on the rocks, including Plimpton, Matthiessen, and the up-and-coming young novelist William Styron. Herlihy basked in the attention but claimed to be ambivalent about it. "It was nice to be the center of attraction, but they are not my world," he wrote Nin. Still, "it sounds egocentric, but I sensed a very real reverence for my work." The shy working-class kid from South Sugar Street was starting to arrive.

Flawed as Herlihy's two early pieces are, they show the strong gothic influence of Carson McCullers and Tennessee Williams, both of whom were reaching the height of their popularity and success as Jim was launching his writing career. But his true literary father was Sherwood Anderson, and his focus was fixed on the twisted forms of humanity that

Anderson himself depicted so intimately in *Winesburg, Ohio*, his most enduring and disturbing book.

Like Jim Herlihy, Sherwood Anderson was a restless, troubled son of the Midwest. Born and raised in small-town Ohio, he worked various odd jobs and didn't finish high school until he was twenty-four. He wrote ad copy, then managed a paint and roofing supplies company until 1912, when, at the age of thirty-six, he suffered a nervous breakdown, walked out on his wife and three children, moved to Chicago, and started writing fiction. *Winesburg, Ohio*, dedicated to his late mother, is a linked collection of twenty-four small pieces that aren't fully constructed short stories but briskly sketched scenes and portraits of tortured, troubled people—Anderson calls them "grotesques"—residing in a town where death, failure, and thwarted sexuality are the principal features of life. Perhaps the most famous piece is "Hands," about a lonely and timid old man named Wing Biddlebaum who has lived for twenty years in the town barely speaking to anyone and befriending only a young newspaper reporter. Wing's real name, it turns out, is Adolph Meyers; he had been a popular schoolteacher in a small Pennsylvania town before he was forced to flee after allegations he had fondled his male students. It was his hands that had betrayed him, caressing the shoulders and heads of his young charges with such passionate intensity that inevitably one of them became sexually aroused.

Jim Herlihy loved Anderson's writing, and he would continue to model many of his flawed and damaged characters in his fiction after Anderson's dislocated souls. But he was also still determined to succeed as a playwright. *Moon in Capricorn* finally got a gig in New York in the fall of 1953, at the celebrated Theatre de Lys in Greenwich Village, soon to gain fame for its long-running revival of *The Threepenny Opera*. Brooks Atkinson, the chief drama critic of *The New York Times* and the voice of God for struggling playwrights, praised Herlihy's play as "an odd and interesting drama . . . imaginative, stimulating, and worth taking seriously."

Others were less encouraging. "It didn't bore me," declared Richard Watts of the *New York Post*, who refused to take the play seriously. ". . . Anyway, no real harm is done to anyone, not even to the drama critics."

Things were looking up, albeit slowly, but steadily enough that Herlihy would declare 1955 "the happiest year of my life." He finally was able to quit the paper-plate job and devote himself full-time to writing. "I have everything I can rationally expect," he told Nin. "The basics, like food, etc., relief temporarily from economic pressures, a handsome lover, new short novel appearance, play in preparation for Broadway, etc."

By the following spring, he felt broke again—so poor he couldn't afford needed dental work. "My cavities were so numerous I was unable to chew meat and was consigned to a diet of soft food," he recalled.

Still, he received a prestigious Yale University Fellowship in Drama that allowed him to commute by train for six months to New Haven, where he studied under the theater arts professor and drama critic John Gassner and helped revise drafts of several plays. One of them, *Box 704*, an earnest but pedestrian family drama, was bought and broadcast on NBC television. Around the same time, the famed movie producer David O. Selznick, who had met Herlihy in New York, invited him to write an outline for a planned film about Mary Magdalene for Selznick's wife, the actress Jennifer Jones, with the idea that he might hire Herlihy to write the screenplay as well. Jim got three thousand dollars for the work, but Selznick then killed the deal. As a lapsed Catholic writing for a Jewish film mogul about a New Testament icon, he found the circumstances mildly amusing. But "there was a queasy feeling in my belly. Wasn't this what selling out was all about?" He took the money nonetheless.

While his writing was going well, life with Dick Duane was anything but tranquil. Both men could be high-strung and temperamental. Duane's outbursts of anger were dramatic but short-lived, while Herlihy's went deeper and lasted longer. And he was more restless sexually. "He wanted to live that wilder life, and that was not for me," Dick recalls. "More partners, more risks. To keep alive. He was terribly afraid of growing older.

"And it was hurtful. I was not looking for monogamy, but I wanted my life to be a little more controllable."

For his part, Herlihy felt suffocated by Duane's longing for something approaching fidelity. "I do love him more than I've loved anyone else," Jim wrote to Nin, "but I am so sorry why he can't understand that I need freedom. It's not just freedom to be unfaithful, as you know, but a need to believe that I can make at least the small decisions without conditioning and impediments."

Nin herself was inevitably dismissive of Herlihy's new partner. "The boy is a little too pretty and too commercial and too much like meringue and cellophane packages (dressed to the hilt in white silk ties and talking about 'selling sex' with his singing)," she wrote in a diary entry. "But they are happy so that is all that matters."

Duane found Herlihy talented and tender but often hard to read. "He could go from being that wonderful loving man to this extreme temperament," Duane says. "At dinner parties, if he felt threatened or uncomfortable, he would immediately go into a character, tell a joke, break out a good story, give a performance." He could imitate any voice, impersonate his new gal pals like actresses Tallulah Bankhead and Joan Blondell, and just about anyone else. It was a protective wall that Herlihy could hide his true self behind.

In 1956 he and Dick finally moved in together, renting an apartment on West Fifteenth Street in the Chelsea district, which was occupied by damp, aging warehouses, a forlorn part of town that Herlihy condemned as "a Campbell's Soup and Kraft Cheese neighborhood. Trucks back in and out of the Port Authority all day long, just across the street." But Herlihy and Duane were unfazed. They used colorful wallpaper, plaster, and paint to transform their shabby apartment into "a place of beauty" for a party in honor of Nin, who was suitably impressed.

Even for two young guys constantly short of cash, New York in the mid-fifties offered exquisite pleasures. There were trips to Coney Island and visits to the Downbeat, one of the Fifty-second Street jazz clubs where Miles Davis, Dizzy Gillespie, Billie Holiday, Art Tatum, and Charlie Parker regularly performed. "The people at the bar were lovely; drunken and rapt, like angels with amnesia," Herlihy reported. "I felt cleansed." He and Duane also attended the annual female imperson-ation ball at the Rockland Palace in Harlem—"a really stunning event—funny and painful, macabre and beautiful." And when things in New York got too tense or hectic, as they often did, there was Key West.

Although both are islands, it would be hard to imagine a place less like Manhattan than Key West, the southernmost tip of the United States, located almost halfway between Miami and Havana. No building there was taller than three stories, most of the houses were wooden cottages, basements didn't exist, and neither did rush hour. There were just thirty thousand people spread over eight square miles. Except when revelers hit the Old Town bars at sundown, the island's loudest noise was the sound of the ocean breeze whispering through the palm trees. "You got tired of those New York winters, and for ninety-five hundred dollars you could buy a house here," recalls Kirby Congdon, a poet and painter who moved to Key West from New York in 1959, around the same time that Jim Herlihy started buying property there. Both of them ended up owning cottages on the same quiet lane.

Key West had been a naval base ever since it was claimed for the United States in 1822 by Lieutenant Commander Matthew C. Perry, who later, as commodore, led the opening of Japan. Sailors, ship wreckers, fishermen, professional gamblers, and Cuban cigar makers all wound up there, and the streets at night outside the bars and cheap hotels were often filled with hustlers of both sexes. The island had been a tropical refuge and playground for writers and artists for nearly a century. The poet Wallace Stevens came to visit in 1922, to escape the harsh winter back home in Hartford, Connecticut. "The place is a paradise," he wrote of the Florida Keys to his wife, Elsie, that January. "Midsummer weather, the sky brilliantly clear and intensely blue. We must come together as soon as we can and every winter afterwards." Stevens would come for the next eighteen years, until Key West became so "furiously literary" he felt compelled to flee.

Many writers would follow over the years, ranging from the poets Robert Frost, Richard Wilbur, Elizabeth Bishop, James Merrill, and John Ciardi to the novelists John Dos Passos, Ralph Ellison, John Hersey, Alison Lurie, and Thomas McGuane. Novelist David Kaufelt attributed the love of writers for Key West to what he called the Peter Pan theory. "Freud said that we are at our most creative when we are in our very early youth," Kaufelt told an interviewer for National Public Radio. "That's where we are here. We wear shorts, we ride bicycles, we have the water, a great symbol of the unconscious, and we're free to be children here and let our spirits go. There's nobody in suits and ties telling us what we have to do."

Ernest Hemingway, the great writer as eternal adolescent, started coming in the 1920s. He and his second wife, Pauline, moved into a two-story Spanish Colonial at 907 Whitehead Street in 1931, one of the largest residences on the island, a wedding gift from her rich uncle. Hemingway wrote some of his finest books there, including _To Have and Have Not_, _For Whom the Bell Tolls_, and _Green Hills of Africa_. But when the couple divorced in 1940, after he took up with war correspondent Martha Gellhorn (who would become wife number three), he fled the area, seldom to return.

Tennessee Williams arrived the following year, after suffering the disastrous Boston premiere of _Battle of Angels_, one of his earliest plays. Williams loved Key West's loose frontier atmosphere—including the handsome young sailors and Cuban street boys—its heat and its isolation, and the fact that he could swim in the warm, sultry ocean almost every day of the year. He would have his breakfast at a Cuban restaurant, spend his day at the typewriter in a one-room shack, then ride a rented bicycle down the flat, sunburned streets, and dance in the evenings with his landlady at Sloppy Joe's, one of Hemingway's old joints and one that Pauline herself still frequented.

Williams liked being surrounded by a worshipful crowd, and he quickly attracted a lively group of friends and followers from New York, including Gore Vidal, Christopher Isherwood, Truman Capote, and Carson McCullers. They would join him in the late afternoons in the front parlor of the Trade Winds hotel for drinks and gossip. Dick Duane quickly slotted in when he first visited Key West. At Duane's urging, Jim Herlihy first came down in the mid-fifties—on a Greyhound bus, of course.

Duane introduced Herlihy to Williams, whose work Jim had admired with "total awe," he would recall. "From the moment of my first encounter with _The Glass Menagerie_, I was in a bag, slung over his shoulder."

Before Williams had a pool installed in his backyard, he and Herlihy went swimming off the Monroe County pier at the end of White Street at twilight most evenings. "It was inexpressibly comforting to have the daily company of a kindred spirit," Herlihy told an interviewer. "Just knowing we were both engaged in the same sort of lunatic pursuit provided some essential ground that meant everything to me."

Williams grew very supportive of Jim's work, praising his early short stories and novels. But although Jim was never in Williams's weight class as a playwright, a certain rivalry developed that Dick Duane could feel at the dinner table whenever the two writers got together. "There were times when it was loving and times when it wasn't so loving," Duane says. "When people started talking about [Jim] and Tennessee was at the table, there was that envy. There can only be one star in a room."

Still, Herlihy came to love Key West, largely for the same reasons that had attracted Williams: the combination of being part of an exclusive unofficial club of gay artists who supported each other—at least when they weren't engaged in byzantine feuds—and of having an escape route from the grime, pressure, and occasional hostility of New York's hyperbolic scene.

"The town excited me too much," Herlihy told author Lynn Mitsuko Kaufelt. "I spent all my time exploring, walking the streets. The place was mysterious, funky, indescribably exotic. It had much of the charm of a foreign country, but you had the post office and the A&P and the phone worked, so life was easy. The town had a kind of beauty that did not know about itself: it just was."

Herlihy started spending more and more time away from New York, and when he started making money as a writer, he used some of the royalties to buy real estate in Key West, where prices were stunningly low, especially when compared to Manhattan. The place he loved best was a nineteenth-century cottage at 709 Bakers Lane in the Old City. He also made friends with some of the local talent, including Henry Faulkner, an eccentric artist from Kentucky who showed up every winter with a car full of cats and dogs and had a habit of standing on restaurant tables to denounce eating meat or yelling "Hey girls!" at the cops as he cruised past the Key West police station.

Williams remained Key West's main literary attraction for four decades. His presence helped attract hangers-on and tourists with money to spend. Still, not everyone appreciated the gay crowd that collected around him like moths to a flame. When a local family opened a nightclub called Raphael's, Williams and his entourage came by one evening to check it out. As they were leaving, one of the owners took Williams aside. According to the author William McKeen, she told Williams, "I hope you enjoyed yourself, but we would rather you not come back. Don't get me wrong, but we don't want this place to get a reputation as a homosexual hangout."

"Good luck with the place," replied Tennessee Williams, hiding behind a frozen smile.

Blue Denim, Jim Herlihy's next play, cowritten in the mid-fifties with his friend and former drama teacher Bill Noble, took up similar themes as *Box 704*, but with more sharply drawn characters and more bite. Set in a middle-class home in Detroit, the play centers on Arthur Bartley, a soon-to-be high school grad who gets his girlfriend Janet pregnant, then steals ninety-two dollars from his parents to pay for an abortion. The parents, Major and Lillian, are well-meaning but clueless about the emotional and psychological needs and dilemmas of their son—each time Arthur tries to talk to them about his girlfriend's delicate condition, they rush to change the subject. When Major finds out about the stolen money, he slaps Arthur hard across the face. But Major's anger loses steam as he learns the truth about Arthur's sincere and unselfish attempts to help Janet. The play ends all too neatly: Arthur and Janet declare their love for each other, while Arthur is reconciled with his parents. In white suburbia of the 1950s, apparently, all's well that ends well.

At first, no one would consider *Blue Denim* for Broadway because of its controversial subject matter. But the director Arthur Penn, Jim's fellow Black Mountain College alumnus, found backers to mount a brief run in Bridgeport, Connecticut. Penn's gun-shy producers insisted on deleting any direct reference to abortion. "The subject of abortion is taboo in this country," Penn told actress Patricia Bosworth, who played Janet. "It's a crime, it's a sin, so the play will be controversial." The line "Janet has had an abortion" was changed to "She's just had a dreadful operation."

Bosworth had been called back for three additional auditions before getting the role. She recalled Jim Herlihy as "a tall shambling man with a handsome ruined face" who watched her intently each time she performed the scene in which Janet reveals she is pregnant. "When it was all over, Herlihy ran up to the footlights to shake my hand and say I'd read the scene exactly as it should be read."

The reviews of the Bridgeport production were reasonably positive. As a result, Joshua Logan, one of New York's hottest directors, agreed to bring the play to Broadway. But Logan was tied up directing the movie version of *South Pacific*, which meant that *Blue Denim*'s Broadway run was put off for nearly a year.

It finally opened at the Playhouse Theatre on February 27, 1958, to excellent reviews and surprisingly little controversy. Brooks Atkinson declared the new play "original [and] overwhelmingly dramatic. The basic theme is not the terrible consequences of a love affair but the awful barriers that divide parents and children." Atkinson loved the acting and Josh Logan's direction, but he had harsh words for Herlihy and Noble. "It needs richer writing than its authors have brought to it," he scolded. "*Blue Denim* is so sparing that it is more like an outline of a clinical study than a fully resolved drama."

Still, Eleanor Roosevelt admired its social relevance and gave it her seal of approval in her nationally syndicated newspaper column, and the Catholic press generally was supportive. *Blue Denim* ran for 166 performances, then was optioned by 20th Century-Fox, which made it into a film starring Brandon deWilde and Carol Lynley that cost $980,000 to make and earned $2.5 million at the box office. But before that happened, the censors in charge of Hollywood's Production Code had ordered one last excruciating deletion: the abortion itself. Instead, the screenwriters— Hollywood veterans Philip Dunne and Edith R. Sommer—were compelled to impose a very 1950s solution: Arthur accompanies Janet on the train to her aunt's house in another city, where she will stay until she has the baby. What will happen next—will they get married and keep the baby or will Janet put it up for adoption?—is left unresolved.

Jim capitalized on the success of *Blue Denim* to mount a production of his comedy, *Crazy October*, featuring once again the grotesque, barbiturate-addicted twosome of Daisy Filbertson and her lazy, obese son, Baby. Only this time he took them out of the claustrophobic New York apartment of his original short story and planted them in a roadside café in West Virginia that Daisy manages, and he introduced an aspiring young ingénue, her abusive fiancé, and a handful of other tediously stock characters. Besides his duties as playwright, Jim also directed the play, which starred Tallulah Bankhead—the hard-drinking, pill-popping Broadway legend who, at age fifty-six, had lost much of her allure but none of her outrageousness—and the veteran actresses Estelle Winwood and Joan Blondell. It was set to open on Broadway at the Alvin Theatre on November 3, 1958, but never made it. After tryouts in New Haven and Washington, Jim announced he was suspending the production pending revisions to the script. Bankhead, for one, was deeply disappointed. "I'm sorry it isn't coming to play New York," she told the *New York Post.* "I've never heard so many laughs in a play. But the author himself says the first act promises something that the second act doesn't fulfill." Nonetheless, she and Jim remained close friends until her death a decade later.

He had better luck the following year, when E. P. Dutton finally published the original short story version of *Crazy October* and four other pieces in a collection entitled *The Sleep of Baby Filbertson and Other Stories.* In a tribute to Sherwood Anderson, Jim chose as the book's epigraph an excerpt from *Winesburg, Ohio*, about walking in an apple orchard in the fall:

> On the trees are only a few gnarled apples that the pickers have rejected. . . . One nibbles at them and they are delicious. Into a little round place at the side of the apple has been gathered all of its sweetness. One runs from tree to tree over the frosted ground picking the gnarled twisted apples and filling his pockets with them. Only a few know the sweetness of the twisted apples.

The twisted apples were Jim's metaphor for his characters. "It seems to me that the fundamental experience of being alive on this planet is a gothic and grotesque experience," he would later tell an interviewer. "It's really a frightening place. None of us feels that he's entirely normal."

His short story collection was praised as "robust, humorous, and original" by *Time* magazine. Its anonymous reviewer placed the stories squarely "in the tradition of Eugene O'Neill, Carson McCullers and Tennessee Williams in focusing on 'the twisted fruits of humanity.'"

Jim was even more heartened by the appraisal of novelist Nelson Algren. "The world of James Leo Herlihy is that of the useless and unzipped, the loveless and defrauded, lost multitudes shut off from the living whose cries are never heard," Algren wrote in *The Nation*. "Herlihy writes with an edge of iron that Steinbeck lost and Saroyan never had, a real indignation at humiliation of the human spirit."

There was, however, one aspect of the human spirit that Jim couldn't explore candidly in his fiction. Three of the protagonists in that first collection of stories are clearly gay, but Jim never says so explicitly on the page. Other novelists had been more direct in exploring gay sexuality. Gore Vidal's *The City and the Pillar* (1948), Truman Capote's *Other Voices, Other Rooms* (1948), and James Baldwin's *Giovanni's Room* (1956) all had gay themes or characters but managed to find mainstream publishers. But by being open about the homosexuality of their characters, each author had risked paying a price in terms of commercial and critical success. It was a chance Jim was not willing to take.

"Don't forget, when we talk about the fifties, we're talking about the Dark Ages," he later explained to an interviewer. "No publisher would have risked bringing out a book in which two men actually touched one another sexually. They could go into the bedroom, but once they got the door closed, the chapter had to end. A lot of my work in those days had to do with the effects of all that repressiveness."

There are no gay characters, open or hidden, in the novel he had been working on for several years and finally published in 1960. *All Fall Down* focuses on the Williams family of Cleveland. The father, Ralph, a former left-wing radical turned second-rate real estate broker, spends most of his time in the basement polishing off bottles of bourbon and reminiscing about the good old days. His wife, Annabel, is a neurotic and overprotective mother. Their fourteen-year-old son, Clinton, has skipped high school for fifty-seven straight days, unbeknownst to his parents, spending most of the time at a local candy store filling dozens of notebooks with overheard conversations and adolescent fantasies and pining for his wandering, ne'er-do-well older brother, Berry-berry, to return home.

Berry-berry (an unfortunate name redolent of a character in a bad Tennessee Williams play) is the hole in the heart of this emotionally stunted family. A handsome, charismatic vagabond and serial sexual predator, he loves to seduce, abuse, and abandon women who are helplessly attracted to his fugitive kind. He has been arrested several times for assault, yet his family always posts bail and sends money for a bus ticket, hoping he will return home. His father sees his oldest son as an archetypal male and much-hoped-for drinking companion; the mother has an incestuous longing for her exciting older son; and Clinton yearns for his brother's companionship. Berry-berry "was like some drug to which the family—he and Ralph and Annabel—were all addicted," writes Jim.

Once Berry-berry finally does return, however, he makes clear his contempt for the family, and most especially for Mom. He kisses her full on the lips, but later tells Clinton, "I suppose you know I hate her guts. She makes my flesh creep." It's also clear that the feelings behind Berry-berry's misogyny extend beyond women to include himself as well. "You know something?" he tells his younger brother. "I hate life."

Berry-berry's ultimate act of contempt is to seduce and abandon Echo O'Brien, an attractive but emotionally fragile family friend whom Clinton has a crush on. She becomes pregnant with Berry-berry's child and dies soon after in a one-car accident that may well be suicide. At that point, Clinton finally faces the awful truth about his malevolent brother, rejects his friendship, and determines to flee the family home.

All Fall Down is James Leo Herlihy's most autobiographical work. The fictional family members are caricatures of Jim's own father, mother, and older brother. And Clinton, the sensitive, wounded, hyper-observant teenager, is a stand-in for Jim himself. "Life was a thing that took place out of his presence," Herlihy writes of Clinton, summing up nicely the alienation and frustration felt by generations of white, middle-class American adolescents. "It went on in a room just before he entered it and took up again after he left."

Despite his lack of formal training as a writer or editor, Dick Duane was an essential helper for *All Fall Down*. Duane knew Jim Herlihy intimately and he knew Herlihy's family as well, and he had an instinctive feel for what Jim was trying to accomplish. He developed a strategy for dealing with Jim's insecurities as a novelist: "Don't tell a writer what they're doing badly, because they already know. Just tell them how wonderful they are. I think that was the most helpful thing I did for him."

In return, Duane extracted a promise that Jim would not go back each day and linger over the words he'd already written. "When he rewrote something it didn't have the same energy, so I made him promise not to do it. I know he wasn't always pleased, but by doing this it let him get on with the work."

Herlihy clearly understood the value of Dick's tutelage. He dedicated the book "For Dick Duane, for his help."

All Fall Down was applauded by fellow writers and reviewers. Tennessee Williams contributed a warm and generous blurb. "There is something very wonderful about this book," he wrote. "It has a luminous thing . . . The dialogue and the writing are so true and so perfect."

Orville Prescott of *The New York Times* called it "a deft and superior novel." The *New York Herald Tribune* compared it favorably to the work of Capote, Inge, and McCullers, adding, "Herlihy sheds a mourning light on the dark nights of the adolescent soul, and does it with humor and tenderness." *Time* magazine said the book contained "as splendid a set of odd-balls as has appeared in U.S. writing since J. D. Salinger's more eccentric creations."

All Fall Down went on to respectable sales and a paperback edition that sold even better. The novel was optioned by MGM. It got the full Hollywood treatment—direction by newcomer John Frankenheimer, at the beginning of a distinguished career, from a screenplay by William Inge, a new friend of Jim's who was one of the most prominent playwrights and screenwriters of the era. It starred Warren Beatty, twenty-five years old and just off his first leading role, as Bud in Elia Kazan's *Splendor in the Grass*, also written by Inge. Plus Eva Marie Saint, Karl Malden, Angela Lansbury, and Brandon deWilde, again playing the eternal baby-faced teenager. The movie was dense, melodramatic, and deeply implausible.

Critics for the most part scorned it, most especially the Berry-berry character. Herlihy blamed Beatty. In the novel, Jim noted, "Berry-berry . . . was a bad, bad boy but he was lovable and charming. How else could his family have liked him? Beatty played him contemptuously. He was no good at all."

Nonetheless, *All Fall Down* had been an extraordinary experience for a first-time novelist. The glowing reviews, the book sales, and the movie deal all heralded the arrival of a new author worthy of public attention.

Herlihy's friends were delighted. All except for one, and she was the most important of them all.

All through those trying early years in New York, Anaïs Nin had been a rock of support for Herlihy. She had loaned him money, helped him find places to stay, occasionally paid his rent and his medical bills, introduced him to magazine editors, book publishers, and theatrical producers, and praised his writing, especially the journals that she had insisted he keep.

Her diaries make no effort to conceal her infatuation for him. "Everyone likes him," she wrote in the winter of 1951–52. "He has the Irish gift of the tongue, the laughing blue eyes. His atmosphere is playful, but he has a serious core. He tightens his belt around a neat slender waist, and has an equally neat and slender delivery. His nimbleness permits him to enter any world at all, and handle it with dexterity. He is the superior, the talented, creative, self-created man."

Every now and then, she let spill her sexual longing for him, and even confessed that she would prefer him to Rupert Pole, her West Coast paramour. "Jim is the only one who is alive by my definition of aliveness. If Jim and I had had the sensual contact, I would have been happier with him than with Rupert."

He, in turn, sang her praises in letter after letter. The younger and less confident of the two, he was desperate to maintain their ties of affection and respect. "It has thrown me into a panic of fear that I may have lost you or failed you in some way," he wrote to her.

Nin knew she needed him, too, to assuage her own sense of jealousy and alienation from the literary establishment she couldn't seem to crack. Her own writing was intimate, subjective, erotic, and elusive—easily dismissed by mainstream critics of that era. "[Jim's] enthusiasm sustains me, keeps me from suffering from my ostracism from the American writing scene," she wrote in 1952. "I am left out of every anthology, every poetry reading, every magazine. The world is silent."

But as it did with other young writers, Nin's fascination with Jim Herlihy began to fade in direct proportion to his growing success. The problems had started in 1953, with the favorable newspaper reviews for *Moon in Capricorn*. "Relationship with Jim Herlihy endangered because I cannot love his play *Moon in Capricorn* and he needs my total admiration," she wrote in her diary. "The slightest hint of unacceptance disturbed him deeply. The dialogue ceased to be sincere."

The warm critical reception for *Blue Denim* five years later also had left her cold. She couldn't understand why he was wasting his time on such banal, trivial work, and expressed resentment that he now seemed to believe he no longer needed her.

Nothing could be further from the truth, he told her. He still needed her love and support, and he pleaded with her not to let his newfound success come between them. "I love the theater for giving me my freedom," he told her, "but it wouldn't be worth much if I'd lost you."

But he *was* losing her. In one diary entry, she abandoned the pretense that she was selflessly seeking to help him write better, and admitted that what she really wanted was his undivided loyalty. "I behaved very badly toward Jim," she confessed, "like a parent who expected his child to bear a strong resemblance. His writing turned out to be so different than I expected. I rejoice over his success, because it will make his life easier; I am sad that I cannot respond to it."

Herlihy tried desperately to win her back. His basic strategy was to lavish more and more praise on her work. He lauded what he called "your faith in your voice," comparing it to "the essential strength of Shakespeare and Dostoevsky and D. H. Lawrence and Tennessee Williams—their fidelity to their own voice."

"Why is it that with you everything becomes illuminated and exciting?" he asked her. "That's the secret of your seduction. You create an intimacy, an atmosphere in which one has an intense feeling of exciting."

The crisis came to a head when he sent her a draft of *All Fall Down*. When she wrote back to him after reading it, her tone was remorseful but merciless. "Because I love you so deeply, I cannot lie to you," she told him. The story left her cold. The characters, she complained, were small and coarse—not the noble figures she herself wanted him to focus on. "From the beginning, you remember, we had a discussion about your putting yourself inside of little people. This is what you have done now in this novel, and even though I know the theme of the brother's love is deeply felt by you, I still could only regret that it should be imbedded in such limited, shrunken, inarticulate, almost subnormal people. The characters seem stunted and half-alive."

Her criticism devastated him. According to Dick Duane, he immediately stopped writing. "He went into total depression," Duane recalls. "I said, 'We've got to finish the book,' and he said, 'I can't.' It was heartbreaking to watch."

Herlihy conceded as much in an interview some fifteen years later. "I hadn't realized 'til now how deeply my creativity was entwined with her approval," he recalled. "My work lost a lot of its thrust and authority."

Herlihy knew Nin had pulled this same withdrawal of support from other writers as they became successful, including Henry Miller, Lawrence Durrell, Tennessee Williams, and Gore Vidal, and he felt he had no choice but to move out from under her suffocating shadow. "I could not choose Anaïs over my career," he later told Noël Riley Fitch, one of her biographers. "I was hurt by it—*she can't be saying these things about me.* Yet I knew that it followed the pattern."

Both he and Nin regretted the rift that inevitably ensued, but each was too proud to surrender to the other. It would take a decade before they patched up their differences. Meanwhile, his dark moods continued to haunt him. In one of his last letters to Nin before their correspondence ceased, he said he had been reading about the Swedish writer Stig Dagerman, who had killed himself at age thirty-one because he felt he couldn't write anymore. Herlihy, who was thirty-two, had "experienced a moment of terrible identification with him," he wrote. Still he woke up the next morning in a state of elation. "I've been having a difficult time understanding the fluctuations of my spirits, and am still uncertain whether to attribute it to the flu, or vice versa."

He'd failed to write anything for five months. "It is a long process for me," he wrote, "and God knows where it is leading to."

Where it was leading was back to some of his most troubling themes: broken families, loneliness, twisted sexuality, impoverished lives and souls. Only with a new set of characters, a more raw and explicit sexuality, and a setting where his work had never gone before.

James Leo Herlihy had discovered Times Square.

4. DARLING

Bastard, bastard, bastard.
—Julie Christie

O n the first day of shooting his first feature film, *A Kind of Loving*, John Schlesinger had what would become a classic John Schlesinger moment.

The director and his leading man, Alan Bates, pulled up in a hired car at the location in a suburb of Manchester, the once-thriving heart of the Industrial Revolution now in a terminal state of decay, to an assemblage of trucks, cameras, lighting equipment, platforms, and crew, all of them waiting for Schlesinger to take command. It was too much. He longed to tell the driver, "Turn 'round, let's go back to the hotel." But he knew he couldn't. Sink or swim, this was it. He gritted his teeth and stepped out of the car.

His fears were not unfounded. The director of photography was a deeply experienced but bad-tempered veteran who would constantly complain that his first-time director didn't know what the hell he was doing—"which I didn't," Schlesinger would later concede. There were endless disputes over the outdoor lighting and the wasted afternoons when the sun got lost behind dark clouds and refused to reappear. Meanwhile, Joe Janni hovered like an anxious prep school headmaster, constantly whispering in Schlesinger's ear, "Come on, you must be quicker."

Still, while he knew dreadfully little about the mechanics of feature filmmaking, Schlesinger knew exactly what kind of movie he wanted to make. He used his journalistic and documentarian sensibility, honed during nearly five years at the BBC, to capture details and nuances other filmmakers might not have bothered with or even noticed. He observed, for example, that when eating at social events like weddings, Mancunians hunched over their plates, holding their knives and forks above their shoulders and spearing their meat as if it were still squirming. He ransacked a hotel cloakroom with June Ritchie, the local actress he picked to play the female lead, to find just the right overcoat that an aspiring young Manchester woman might covet. Outside a church he recruited three local women in scarves for the wedding scene that kicks off the movie.

"What would you say if this were a real wedding and you knew the girl?" he asked them.

"She looks lovely!" and "She's done all right for herself, hasn't she?" came the replies.

"Fine! Now say it like that when we turn the camera on you."

For the lead character, he and Janni had chosen Bates, a tall, dark, and handsome man with a dreamy choirboy's face that betrayed every emotion he harbored inside and every brazen thought as well. Bates was already a star onstage—Janni had had to slap down ten thousand dollars to buy out his contract for Harold Pinter's *The Caretaker* playing on Broadway—but not yet in films. Bates's soft features gave off an air of sexual ambiguity. Schlesinger immediately fell in love with him, but he settled for a close and lasting friendship after he found out Bates was sleeping with Ritchie. It was an affair that John, showing his ruthless side, quietly encouraged because he thought it might help both of their performances.

Whether on location in Manchester or back at Shepperton Studios, west of London, Schlesinger and Janni snarled over the script, the casting, and the budget. "You ridiculous faggot!" Janni would exclaim. "You Italian cunt!" Schlesinger would bark in reply.

"They were always fighting, Joe and John," says Ann Skinner, who started out as a secretary in Janni's office but eventually transferred to Schlesinger's. She recalls Janni knocking on her hotel room door late one night during the film shoot and ordering her to take urgent dictation. It was a letter firing John for some minor infraction that Skinner can no longer remember. Janni never sent it. The two men wound up making six films together. It was a deep, noisy, affectionate partnership.

Skinner wound up working on virtually all of Schlesinger's movies as a "continuity girl"—the assistant tasked with keeping track of every shot in every scene. "All you have to do," he told her, "is remember what I say about takes and always laugh at my jokes." Although she only had a high school education and no background in cinema, John listened to her and made her feel her opinions mattered, and he passed on to her his passion for movies. "There was an inclusiveness in his attitude toward film and his attitude toward me," says Skinner, who went on to become a highly respected television and movie producer.

A Kind of Loving is a quieter, less polemical film than most of the kitchen-sink dramas of its era, but in many ways it is even more despairing. The large industrial firm that Vic Brown and Ingrid Rothwell work for is not a heartless sweatshop, just a clean, gray, regimented place where young people's dreams are put permanently to sleep. Neither character is rebelling against their working-class families, but just trying to create some breathing room for themselves. Which makes their predicament all the more poignant—two young lives in the process of being wasted and inevitably dragging each other down. "It was absolutely life as it was lived," Bates said later. "It wasn't about exceptional folk, it was really about everyday people and their struggles."

Although both Bates and Ritchie do excellent work, the best performance in the film belongs to the veteran actress Thora Hird, who plays Ingrid's hard-boiled, shrewish mother. After Vic and Ingrid marry, he moves into Ingrid's bedroom in the family's cramped row house. Vic is an intruder, spoiling Mrs. Rothwell's relationship with her only child, whom she dominates. Mrs. Rothwell won't even give him a house key. A frustrated Vic goes drinking one night with his mates, comes home, and throws up on the rug in her spotless, preciously arranged living room. Her anger and utter contempt erupt. Denys Coop, the irritable director of photography, hated the scene, according to Schlesinger, complaining that it was vulgar. John, of course, couldn't have cared less what Coop thought.

Hird, who was fifty, had grown up in Morecambe, a seaside town in the Lancashire region sixty miles northwest of Manchester. Mrs. Rothwell was a dramatically different role for Hird—not just the rawness of the character's emotions but the fact that she was an authentic north-erner. When Hird had first come to London nearly three decades earlier to work at the city's renowned Ealing Studios, she had been told to lose her northern accent if she wanted to get acting roles. She did so with alarming speed. "I was never asked to play anyone from Lancashire," she would recall. But with *Loving*, "finally, I was asked if I could manage a northern woman's part and I thought at first it was sarcasm. When I told them I was from Lancashire, they were surprised. They hadn't known."

At the Berlin Film Festival, while the jury watched the movie down-stairs, Schlesinger paced upstairs and ranted at Janni. "Why did we ever bring this film here? It will never win! Everyone will hate it! You stupid Italian cunt, what were you thinking?" It won the Golden Bear for best picture. Suddenly, John Schlesinger and Joe Janni had a hit.

A Kind of Loving went on to become the sixth-most-popular film in Britain in 1962. It cost the equivalent of $460,000 to make and earned nearly three times that amount.

At first the general public and the critics assumed John Schlesinger was a close comrade of Tony Richardson, Lindsay Anderson, and the other Free Cinema filmmakers because his directorial style, north of England setting, and working-class characters seemed so akin to theirs. In truth, he found the Free Cinema comrades arrogant, left-wing pseudo-intellectuals, while they saw him as a shallow, apolitical entertainer with no ideological anchor. "I was considered an outsider, even though I'd been at Oxford with several of them," said Schlesinger, who seemed to need enemies like a fire needs fuel and was quite willing for these self-styled social critics to fill the role. "They rather looked down their noses at me." After all, he had learned his trade doing television, a medium many of them despised. "I remember Lindsay Anderson saying once, 'You've got to set your sights higher than television,'" Schlesinger told an interviewer. "I felt resented, quite frankly." As for his own political views, he said, "The objective is to make a good film and not to moralize like a social worker."

But if Schlesinger was unwilling to remain within the narrow confines of kitchen-sink drama, so was Tony Richardson, whose commercial ambitions were just as intense as John's. Richardson's next film, *Tom Jones* (1963), an adaptation of Henry Fielding's eighteenth-century picaresque novel, was an audacious affair, filmed in color and flush with cheeky contemporary humor, boisterous sexual innuendo, and Brechtian-style direct addresses to the audience from its spirited, randy hero. It cost just one million dollars to make and ultimately earned thirty-seven times that amount at the box office in Britain and the United States—one of the biggest and most surprising hits of the decade. It won Oscars for Best Picture and Best Director for Richardson, Best Adapted Screenplay for John Osborne, and Best Musical Score for John Addison; swept the British Academy Awards as well; and made Albert Finney an international star.

That same year John Schlesinger made a more modest but no less iconoclastic comedy. *Billy Liar* was the tale of a compulsive young fantasist in a small north of England city working as a clerk in an undertaker's firm. Billy's work life toggles between incompetence and larceny—he dumps in a garbage bin the 260 holiday calendars he was supposed to mail to customers and pockets the postage. While dreaming of becoming a comedy writer in London, he lives at home with his parents and grandmother and juggles two jealous girlfriends—each of whom believes he's engaged to her—while pursuing a third. He invents for himself a host of wild fantasies in which he plays the hero—the imperious president of the Republic of Ambrosia, a bush-jacketed guerrilla leader, a pretentious Churchillian orator. Tom Courtenay is adept at the loose, anarchic comedy bits and evokes sympathy for Billy despite his clueless and self-destructive behavior; he's a lovable loser whom we root for even though we realize his dreams are doomed.

Once again Schlesinger took his cast and crew up north, to the industrial cities of Manchester, Bradford, and Leeds, places where prewar slums were finally being bulldozed and soulless public housing projects were rising in their place. The film's tone is lighter, more high-spirited, and far less bleak than *A Kind of Loving*. And for the first time Schlesinger paints the corners of many of the scenes with satire and media mockery. The film opens with a series of shots of dull council flats against the soundtrack of a fictional morning radio program called

Housewife's Choice, in which the announcer sends birthday greetings to a local mom who "likes to sing while she does the housework." Later on, there's a supermarket opening emceed by an idiotic local television personality.

But the film's true lightning bolt strikes halfway through with the introduction of Liz, the young woman Billy longs for, played by a fresh and irrepressible Julie Christie. She arrives to a cool beat on a high-hat cymbal, swinging her purse and sashaying down the cracked pavement like a floating exclamation point, stopping to check herself out in the shiny reflection of a shop window and smoke a cigarette, admiring her own self-confident sexuality. She is blond, natural, accessible, and uninhibited—in short, something new in British movies, and every Angry Young Man's wet dream.

Christie, twenty-three, had been born in India, the daughter of a tea plantation manager. After her parents split up, she came to England with her mother and trained for the theater at the Central School for Speech and Drama at the University of London, whose alumni included Laurence Olivier, Vanessa Redgrave, and Judi Dench. She got small parts on television and two low-budget movie comedies. It was reported that she didn't get the role as the first Bond girl, in *Dr. No*, because the producer deemed her breasts too small (they hired the statuesque Ursula Andress instead). Schlesinger and Janni at first rejected her for *Billy Liar*, hoping for a more voluptuous actress for what they believed was an earth mother role.

They quickly changed their minds, and Schlesinger reconfigured the character's opening scene into a star-making turn. Christie is only in *Billy Liar* for eleven minutes, but they are memorable ones. Liz loves Billy and tries to convince him to leave his dead-end life and board a night train with her to London. He agrees to go, but at the last minute backs out, resigning himself to his fantasy world because he lacks the courage to risk taking a chance in the real one.

The film was both a critical and box-office success. Along with *Tom Jones* it marked the decline of the somber, austere kitchen-sink movies and the ascendancy of more vivid and entertaining comedies and dramas, including *The Knack . . . and How to Get It* (1965) and, in 1966,

Georgy Girl, *Alfie*, *Morgan—A Suitable Case for Treatment*, and *Blow-Up* (made by the Italian director Michelangelo Antonioni but filmed in London). These new films were the cinematic equivalent of the Beatles, whose vivid, anarchic iconoclasm was captured in their own movie debut, *A Hard Day's Night* (1964), directed by Richard Lester. Their move from Liverpool to London in November 1963 helped launch Swinging London, the new mod capital of music, film, art, photography, fashion, and celebrity culture, which *Time* magazine, in an April 1966 cover story, would later celebrate as "Camelot-on-Thames." The drab gray suits, bowler hats, and buttoned-up cardigan austerity of Britain's postwar era were being kicked aside by rich, bold, clashing paisley colors, bell-bottoms, wide lapels, long hair, and newfound sexual freedom. Teenagers, a relatively new economic, sociological, and cultural phenomenon in Britain, whose tastes and spending habits were being shaped by radio, television, and glossy magazines, were emerging as their own distinct demographic. The movie business responded accordingly. "When Julie Christie boarded that train south at the end of *Billy Liar*," wrote the film critic Alexander Walker, "she brought the British cinema along with her."

Becoming famous was fun, and John Schlesinger was never suspected of being a monk. He reveled in his new status as a celebrity film director and basked in the glamour, high living, and sexual license of the London scene. He invested in Le Carrosse, a hip new restaurant in Covent Garden opened by his pal Geoffrey Sharp, and he loved the good food and fine wine, easy access to handsome young men, and decadent country house weekends that came with his fame and stature. But Schlesinger was too much the restless outsider to stay comfortable for long. The new London had its own pretensions, moral corruption, and soulless beautiful people on the make. "He had a clear vision of how people are led astray by their own illusions," says his nephew Ian Buruma.

Darling was his first film project not adapted from a novel or play. The original story flowed out of a conversation Schlesinger had on the set of *Billy Liar* with the journalist Godfrey Winn. He told Schlesinger about a call girl hired and shared by several wealthy businessmen who set her up in a flat on London's posh Park Lane for their personal use and exploitation. After several months of this sordid arrangement she threw herself off the balcony in despair.

Schlesinger was intrigued. Joe Janni knew a socialite who had been through her own set of similar sexual experiences, minus the suicide, and he dispatched the director along with the screenwriter Frederic Raphael to meet her and record her story. There were several bumps and detours—the woman was in the midst of divorce proceedings and feared their script might divulge too much, so at one point she obtained a legal injunction against them. Raphael had to scrap his initial draft altogether and, working closely with Schlesinger in a prickly and tempestuous partnership, eventually emerged with a bitingly satirical account of a fictional character named Diana Scott, a beautiful young model who navigates the splashy, morals-free world of fashion, advertising, and journalism using her wit, intuition, and seductive beauty to build a career as a celebrity without any detectable talent beyond her smashing good looks. She becomes, in the time-honored phrase, famous for being famous. By focusing his story on her, John Schlesinger not only moved his storyteller's lens from the north of England to London, but from working-class protagonists to an ultra-decadent branch of the bourgeoisie.

When we first meet Diana, she's telling her life story to a women's glamour magazine, narrating a self-portrait of a sincere and dedicated working girl in marked contrast to the heedless, predatory narcissist we are seeing act out on the screen. Diana uses her uninhibited sexuality to get the men in her life to give her what she wants. There are strong overtones of the Profumo affair of 1963, when a senior Conservative Party cabinet secretary was brought down and publicly shamed by his sexual antics with a young call girl named Christine Keeler. Diana destroys her own early marriage by initiating an affair with a married television journalist named Robert Gold (played by Dirk Bogarde), who leaves his family for her only to find that her idea of fidelity is, as he puts it, "not having more than one man in bed at the same time." While still living with Robert, she takes up with Miles Brand (Laurence Harvey), an avaricious and cold-blooded advertising executive who is as self-involved as she is. He helps her get the lead part in a sleazy horror movie and the plum role of "The Happiness Girl" for a corporate ad campaign selling bonbons to the masses.

Diana changes partners as frequently as she changes her mod wardrobe, always hoping that the next man she sleeps with will provide her with the fame, riches, and fulfillment she craves. "I always feel as if there's one more corner to turn and I'll be there," she tells Miles.

He takes her to a kinky party in Paris where a man and woman engage in intercourse in front of a group of jaded voyeurs. People dance, take off their clothing, make out with strangers. Diana seems more bored than aroused. Later, she meets Malcolm, a gay photographer, played by Roland Curram, whose work helps make her famous. He's her only real pal, perhaps because he's immune to her sexual charms but no threat to her self-esteem. There's a sly scene of Malcolm picking up a handsome young waiter at an outdoor café in Capri, while Diana, who is also cruising the waiter, jealously looks on. Sex is a commodity, a source of power and entertainment, a way for beautiful people to exert control over others. The Royal Board of Film Censors didn't approve of this depiction of rampant promiscuity and ordered cuts that render some of *Darling*'s more risqué moments puzzling at best because the more explicit parts have been excised. Nonetheless, the film casts an unblinking eye on debauchery and its consequences. It has one other striking attribute: it treats homosexuality in an adult and matter-of-fact way—not too hot, not too cold; Malcolm is one of the film's more sympathetic characters and, according to the film historian William J. Mann, perhaps the first unapologetic, sexually active gay man in a mainstream movie.

Diana winds up marrying a much older Italian prince, a widower with seven children who is a bobsled enthusiast and accomplished philanderer. She spends her days cooped up in a remote palace, with no playmates, no excitement, and no sex, while he goes off to Rome to tend to his mistresses.

Throughout the film, Schlesinger sprinkles in scenes that underscore the hypocrisy of the world he is depicting. An older woman picks meat from a sandwich while a member of Parliament discourses on the problem of third-world malnutrition. A man being interviewed on the street rattles on mindlessly about "how rife homosexuality has become in

London—I think it's gotten considerably worse over time." Diana attends the funeral of a famous novelist she met through Robert, but when challenged by a journalist, she can't name a single book the man wrote.

The thread that holds the film together is Christie's bold, naturalistic performance. Diana is willful, ignorant, greedy, and blatantly dishonest, yet also vulnerable and seductive. As we watch her hop from bed to bed screwing up the lives of everyone she meets, including her own, we become another unwitting victim of her charm and charisma.

"It was probably the easiest part I've done!" Christie told an interviewer in 1994. "I understood a lot of what that silly girl was going through. I did despise that vacuous, empty-headed part of her. But the rest—all that ruthless selfishness and superficiality—I understood very well indeed."

Schlesinger gave Christie the confidence to go as far as she had to without worrying about whether she would look good or bad. He made no attempt to excuse Diana's behavior or compromise on depicting her amorality, and he made sure Christie didn't, either.

"I suppose John and I really bonded on *Darling*," she recalls. "He pushed me and pushed me and pushed me and I, spoilt brat that I was, screamed at him. So he pushed me more!" There were times, she says, when "we were like gladiators fighting it out between us."

At times he bullied her into doing what he wanted. There is a scene toward the end of the movie when a frustrated Diana, trapped in the palace of her faithless husband, shuffles from room to room of her bedroom suite crying and stripping off her clothing one piece at a time. At first Christie wore pasties over her nipples, but when she complained they were uncomfortable, John allowed her to peel them off. But he ignored her pleas that she not be filmed naked.

"Get your knickers off, darling."

"Oh, John, do I have to?"

"'Course you do, you're an actress."

"Bastard, bastard, bastard!"

Schlesinger oversaw the mod-style outfits Christie wore for the film—the "Chelsea Girl Look" of tartan skirts, jumpers, knee-high socks, head scarves, and hair bands. He dictated to costume designer Julie Harris the various wardrobes he wanted Christie to wear in Rome ("very Vidal Sassoon"), Paris ("very Mary Quantish"), and London. The casual, uninhibited clothes became very much a part of the character and helped make Christie a mod fashion icon for young women on both sides of the Atlantic. As the British cultural critic Christine Geraghty put it, the emphasis of Christie's clothes was "not so much on following a sixties style but creating it."

"It's not at all what I myself liked," Christie recalls. "I thought it was so artificial. But they went ahead and I rather rumblingly acquiesced. After all, this was *Darling* by John Schlesinger, and it was *not* Julie Christie."

Darling has generally been dismissed by critics over the years for its artifice and supposed superficiality. Schlesinger himself called it "one of my least favorite films," and said he didn't believe its jumpy camera work and arch dialogue had aged well. It's a cold movie, almost as cynical as its characters. But it captures the empty hedonism of its time and place with savage accuracy. What was originally conceived as a tragedy of a young woman in over her head emerges as something more unique and troubling; not a comedy, nor a drama, nor a morality play, although it has elements of all three. It is, instead, that rare creature, a wholly original piece of filmmaking. Its lacerating critique of Swinging London and its beautiful inhabitants set a tone that John Schlesinger would return to again with New York City in *Midnight Cowboy*.

The *New York Times* film critic Bosley Crowther called *Darling* "a slashing social satire and also a devastating spoof of the synthetic, stomach-turning output of the television-advertising age—it is loaded with startling expositions and lacerating wit. The screen never put forth types and dialogue more purple and frank than those here." It was, Crowther concluded, "a film that will set tongues to wagging and moralists to wringing their hands."

Darling got excellent reviews and made money on both sides of the Atlantic, and it got Schlesinger his first Academy Award nomination for Best Director. He didn't win, but Christie was a surprise winner for Best Actress; Frederic Raphael won for Original Screenplay, and Julie Harris for Costume Design.

The movie brought Schlesinger the same kind of international acclaim that *Tom Jones* had brought his old kitchen-sink rival Tony Richardson. But Schlesinger was reluctant to do what Richardson and just about every bankable British filmmaker and performer had done since the dawn of movies—set out across the Atlantic for the center of the filmmaking universe. For now, perhaps, it was safer to remain at home. And so instead of going to Hollywood for the money, he and Joe Janni searched for a way to make the Hollywood money come to them.

5. THE GAY METROPOLIS

Times Square is the magnet for all the lonesome exiles jammed into this city.
—John Rechy, *City of Night*

Dotson Rader, tall, baby-faced, and just shy of eighteen, arrived at the Port Authority Bus Terminal in New York City from his home in Minnesota on a warm June afternoon in 1960 looking for a fresh start after fleeing military school and a nervous breakdown. He stashed his bag in a coin-fed locker, then wandered out onto Forty-second Street dressed in a madras shirt and tight khaki pants with a few coins in his pockets. His first stop was the lunch counter across the street at Whelan's Drugstore, where he asked the waitress how much food a nickel would buy. She eyed him incredulously. "Two slices of bread," she replied. But when she saw him spreading mayonnaise and ketchup on the bread, she brought him some meat to make a sandwich. "I felt like I'd found a home," he recalls.

Rader, who would become a prominent journalist, New Left activist, author, and close companion of Tennessee Williams, walked the streets around Times Square all afternoon and into the evening. He wandered past ten fading movie houses, a half dozen fleabag hotels, porn shops with grimy plate-glass windows, hard-faced bars, the Playland arcade, featuring Hubert's Museum and Flea Circus, and the twenty-four-hour Nedick's, selling coffee, doughnuts, and a fruit drink of uncertain provenance for fifteen cents. He navigated sidewalks jammed with tourists, office workers, kids ducking school, hookers, hustlers, and their prospective customers. In the evening he settled down on a bench in Bryant Park, behind the majestic New York Public Library. Around midnight, a man tapped his leg.

"What are you doing here?" the man asked.

"Trying to sleep," he replied.

"Wanna make five bucks?"

"It was the first time," Rader recalls, "that I realized the connection between money and sex."

Money and sex were the essential ingredients of the "cheerful vulgarity," in the author Jan Morris's phrase, of Forty-second Street between Seventh and Eighth Avenues. On the eastern end of the block was Times Square—known to promoters and admirers as "the crossroads of the world"—with its legitimate theaters, celebrity restaurants, and breathtakingly garish electric billboards. On the western end was the Port Authority—just ten years old but already a tarnished haven for junkies, petty criminals, and denizens of the "meat rack" near the departure gates, where young men liaised with older ones, steering them to men's room toilet stalls or a nearby back street dubbed "Vaseline Alley."

Still, for all the dangers, Forty-second Street was a surprising mixture of innocence and sleaze. It was Sodom without Gomorrah—half wicked, half tame. You could be mugged or propositioned the minute you emerged from the Seventh Avenue IRT or wander the streets for weeks and never encounter anything untoward. When it came to Times Square, New York pleaded nolo contendere.

Jim Herlihy never spoke about what he might have been doing in Times Square in the early 1960s, even to friends, partly out of his innate sense of discretion and partly from self-protection. But even while he was living with Dick Duane, Jim was in constant motion. When he wasn't taking Greyhound buses home to his family in Detroit or on cross-country excursions to California and Texas, he was prowling the streets of Manhattan. His restless energy inevitably propelled him to Times Square. "He was attracted to the dark side in a big way," says Bob Thixton, the ex-navy man who became Duane's partner after Dick and Jim broke up permanently. "He was very experimental in his private life and went to all the dens of iniquity that existed in New York at that time."

Those who knew Jim well have no doubt he was an enthusiastic participant in the area's seedier delights. "I can readily picture the curious, exuberant and libidinous young actor he must once have been occasionally costuming himself in boots and bandana to go off and shoot the bull with the boys in Times Square," writes Jeffrey Bailey, a close friend of Jim in later years. "I remember what he once said to me about his sex life: that he never said no when he wanted to say yes."

Like a rite of passage, Forty-second Street lured countless New Yorkers to its coarse corridors in the 1960s. But one constant throughout the street's steady rise and prolonged decline was its attraction to gay men. Along with Harlem and Greenwich Village, the area was a more-or-less safe haven for what the social historian George Chauncey calls "an organized, multilayered, and self-conscious sub-culture," largely invisible to the straight world but hidden in plain sight for gays who were drawn to it.

The Depression had attracted scores of young men to New York from withered small towns looking for economic opportunities and social adventure, who ended up working the streets servicing a largely middle-class male clientele. Many of these hustlers were "trade"—neither they nor their customers thought of them as gay. In fact, their sexual ambiguity was part of their appeal.

"I didn't mind being known as a Forty-second Street hustler, but I sure did not want to be known as a 'faggot,'" wrote Herbert Huncke, a drug addict, petty thief, and convicted felon who haunted the area for three decades. "Faggots have a hard way to go—they're everyone's property."

World War II brought a flood of soldiers and sailors to New York City, many of them looking for excitement before shipping off overseas. "I never saw anything like it in my life," recalled Woody Allen, whose father took him to Times Square on Sunday afternoons during the war from their home in Brooklyn just to take in the sights. "It was just one movie house after another, all lit up, a number of them with stage shows, and the streets were jammed with soldiers and sailors, 'cause it was during the war. It was just what a choreographer would choose to exaggerate if he was choreographing a ballet about New York."

Straight or gay—and many gay servicemen from small-town America discovered for the first time in their lives that they were not alone in their sexual orientation—they descended upon Forty-second Street like

packs of wolves. In his memoirs, Tennessee Williams recalls cruising the
area with his friend the novelist Donald Windham, making "abrupt and
candid overtures" to groups of sailors and GIs, and bringing them back
to Windham's Greenwich Village pad or Williams's room at the YMCA.
One night they brought two sailors back to a room at the nearby Clar-
idge Hotel. After "the brutal sex-bit," as Williams called it, the sailors
ripped the phone cord from the wall, beat up Windham, knocking out
a few of his teeth, then set upon Williams. Both men wound up being
treated by a young doctor at the YMCA. "Thus ended for quite a while
our Times Square cruising together," wrote Williams.

Gore Vidal, just nineteen and finishing up his service in the army
in 1945, found the Hotel Astor bar at West Forty-fifth and Broadway
the city's most exciting place to cruise for soldiers, sailors, and marines
on the prowl. "Few civilians, and no woman, ever dared intrude on these
male mysteries," he wrote. "At any time of day or night, hundreds of men
would be packed six-deep around the long oval black bar." Vidal recalled
the researcher Alfred Kinsey—"a gray-faced man who always wears a
polka-dot bow tie"—setting up shop at a table on the mezzanine, where
he interviewed Vidal and other willing male subjects for his landmark
study of male sexuality.

Kinsey also hung out at the L-shaped bar at the Angle, a seedy drinking spot on Eighth Avenue between West Forty-second and Forty-third
Streets, where Huncke, who called himself "Kinsey's pimp," introduced
him to some of the avatars of the Beat Generation: Allen Ginsberg,
William Burroughs, and Jack Kerouac. Besides the omnipresent prostitutes, Huncke writes, "there were burglars and thieves and muggers,
people of that nature. They'd let you hang around the bar if you had
enough to buy yourself a drink. You could stand at the bar and someone
would approach you."

Forty-second Street was a magnet for all kinds of aspiring writers.
The novelist Edmund White cruised for male hustlers while the future
authors John Rechy, Jim Carroll, and Samuel Delany worked the streets
in the sixties. Marlon Brando, James Dean, and Montgomery Clift—
who was arrested for soliciting a male hustler on Forty-second Street
in 1949, just weeks after he was nominated for an Academy Award for

Best Actor for *The Search*—were in the vanguard of a vast community of theater people who roamed the jazz clubs and all-male bars. Lenny Bruce and Diane Arbus patrolled Hubert's Museum for midgets, the three-legged man, and a character known as the Pinhead. "Forty-second Street was dangerous," recalled Arbus's friend Emile de Antonio, an art dealer and documentary filmmaker. "We'd pass a sea of empty beer cans, broken bottles, druggies, pimps, and then we'd go to Grant's for clams and French fries." It was just scary enough to be edgy, a good story to take back uptown to your civilized social circle.

In March 1960, a few months before Dotson Rader arrived, *The New York Times*, whose sober, dignified headquarters were just a block away, published a front-page report by Milton Bracker headlined "Life on W. 42d St. A Study in Decay." Using the classic *Times* flat-affect, irony-free narrative voice—the newspaper equivalent of an undertaker reading from a price list of coffins—Bracker sketched a portrait that was half police blotter and half Dante's *Inferno*. "Homosexual males converge in the area and are most prevalent at the Eighth Avenue end of the block," he wrote. "The clergy, the police, merchants, and business organizations generally agree that homosexuality has increased in the area over a period of several years.

"In two weeks of studying the area, at virtually all hours, this reporter encountered several of the most extreme types. One was a Negro who wore fluffed-up hair and heavy black makeup on his brows and lashes. Another obvious deviate was a white youth with thick blond hair and handsome features who wore makeup on his eyebrows."

The IRT and IND subway stations, Bracker cautioned demurely, "are not the most inviting places in the world for sensitive people." Homeless people lurked in the underground arcades, he warned. "The drifters are like eternal reminders of the inner anguish of any metropolis. They are apt to have bad complexions and matted heads of hair."

Dotson Rader found Forty-second Street less alarming and predatory than did *The New York Times*. He hustled on the street for sex and money for a spell and quickly made friends with other hustlers. One of the first he met was a beautiful boy from Indiana named Cartwright. Homosexuality and prostitution were both illegal—the former potentially a more serious offense than the latter—and Cartwright helped Rader learn the rules of the game. How to discreetly connect with customers. How to talk to cops. Where to safely go and where to avoid.

"Most of the street hustlers I knew were nice guys," Rader recalls. "They were good kids but they were lost boys, and they couldn't go home again. If you offered them a little kindness and human decency, they responded with decency."

Samuel Delany had his first gay sexual experience in the balcony of the once-ornate New Amsterdam Theater in 1960 at the age of eighteen, when a man pressed up against his thigh. Delany, who grew up in Harlem, did little hustling—"I couldn't go off with somebody I'd never seen before and get an erection on cue," he recalls ruefully—but he spent a lot of time having sex in the balconies and men's rooms of the New Amsterdam and a half dozen other movie grindhouses. Sometimes, after sharing a six-pack of beer or a bottle of vodka, a man would fall asleep and wake to find his pants pockets had been slit with a razor and his empty wallet left on the seat beside him. But the general atmosphere, Delany insists, was benign, not scary.

"It was a twenty-four-hour street and a very lively place," recalls Delany, who was to become a popular and much-honored fantasy and science fiction writer. "I met opera singers and carpenters and actors and janitors and a window washer from the Empire State Building. There were married guys and working guys. Some were interesting and some were sad. Some you saw just a few times and some you saw again and again."

Sometimes, the sex would spill over to other parts of Forty-second Street. The poet and diarist Jim Carroll, who grew up on Manhattan's Lower East Side, recalled in *The Basketball Diaries* how the men's room at Grand Central Terminal at five-thirty on weeknights was full of male commuters about to head home to the suburbs. They lined up at the urinals with "the usual seedy dudes, hustlers, etc. and all these eyes peeking down at the guy next to me who's peeking down at me along with the guy on my other side and jacking off like madmen, forty pistons pumping back and forth at incredible rates." Carroll, a thin, wispy, and baby-faced teenager, said the frenzied scene made him wonder if he was "the only person in the place that came down just for normal body functions."

The experiences as a young gay man of the novelist Edmund White, who first arrived in New York in 1962, were less frenzied but no less anonymous. "Much of my spare time was devoted to sex—finding it and then doing it," writes White in his evocative memoir *City Boy*. "In those days before online hookups and backroom bars and outdoor sex, when there weren't even very many gay bars, we had to seek out most of our men on the hoof. Back then people glanced back over their shoulders . . . Then we had to look back or we'd spend the night alone. The whole city was awash with desire and opportunities to satisfy it. . . .

"There was no 'gay pride' back then," adds White. "There was only gay fear and gay isolation and gay distrust and gay self-hatred. I didn't even feel part of 'homosexual society'—we didn't think like that back then. The term would have made us laugh: 'Homosexual society? My dear, I'm not even a queer deb.'"

Despite various court rulings and gradual liberalization, the anti-sodomy laws would remain on the books in New York until 1980, when the state court of appeals struck them down. Up until then, the authorities would wield those laws like a club, staging a series of raids at gay bars and other notorious hangouts, and the New York State Liquor Authority would follow up by suspending the liquor licenses of establishments deemed unsavory. Police officials argued that the raids were for the benefit of gay customers otherwise being preyed upon by the criminal element. Deputy Police Chief James B. Leggett told the *Times* that "the rise of organized young hoodlums and the patent increase of homosexuals on the city's streets has brought a wave of rape, muggings, and other crimes of violence often culminating in murder."

Mayor Robert F. Wagner, a liberal Democrat, had presided over a crackdown on illegal drugs, prostitution, and vagrancy in the summer of 1954 that resulted in fifteen hundred arrests over four weeks but no noticeable reduction in either crime or sin. Indeed, the raids helped force out many small independent retailers who were then replaced by mob-connected ones. This meant more prostitution and the rise of dirty bookstores, yet at the same time provided more insulation for gay customers because patrolmen on the take were less inclined to harass the mob's lucrative clientele.

Still, public attitudes remained intensely antigay, as reflected in a December 1963 *New York Times* front-page article headlined "Growth of Overt Homosexuality in City Provokes Wide Concern," by Robert C. Doty. It began, "The city's most sensitive open secret—the presence of what is probably the greatest homosexual population in the world and its increasing openness—has become the subject of growing concern of psychiatrists, religious leaders, and the police."

Open secret or not, the *Times* article explored what it characterized as the two conflicting viewpoints in the contemporary discussion of homosexuality. On one side was the "organized homophile movement—a minority of militant homosexuals that is openly agitating for removal of legal, social, and cultural discriminations against sexual inverts." This group argued that gay people should be treated like any other minority group because homosexuality was "an incurable, congenital disorder"— although the *Times* report insisted "this is disputed by the bulk of scientific evidence." On the other side was the psychiatric community, which was pressing for "an end to what it calls a head-in-sand approach to homosexuality." This group cited "overwhelming evidence" that homosexuals were not born but created—generally and inadvertently by emotionally ill-adjusted parents. Fortunately, a cure was at hand: "sophisticated analytical and therapeutic techniques."

The story proceeded to somberly assess the number of gay people in New York, describe where they lived and how they socialized with each other, and track the rise of gay publications and political organizations. It cited "evidence" from Dr. Irving Bieber of New York Medical College, who had directed a nine-year study of gay men. "In virtually every one of the cases they studied, they found evidence of a dominant, intimate mother and a hostile or detached father." The inevitable result: the child's "capacity for normal erotic expression has been crippled psychically."

Bieber cautioned against treating gays like any other minority because their group status was based on illness rather than race, ethnicity, or culture. His fellow psychiatrist Charles W. Socarides warned that the nascent campaign by fledgling gay rights groups for social acceptance was worrisome because "the homosexual is ill, and anything that tends to hide that fact reduces his chances of seeking and obtaining treatment."

The *Times* article was written during the postwar heyday of psychoanalysis, when it seemed like virtually every Manhattanite of sufficient income and social class was in analysis, and psychiatrists were the social and moral equivalent of the priesthood during the Middle Ages. "There was an inevitability about psychoanalysis," wrote the *Times* literary critic Anatole Broyard. "It was like having to take the subway to get anywhere." After their anointment as evidence-based experts by the *Times*, Bieber and Socarides would go on to become publicly recognized authorities in the now-discredited field of sexual "conversion"—how to turn long-suffering homosexuals into responsibly straight husbands and fathers.

Gay Talese, author of *The Kingdom and the Power* (1969), the definitive history of the *Times* of that era, reported that A. M. Rosenthal, the paper's ambitious new metropolitan news editor, had commissioned the Doty piece because he noticed there seemed to be a lot more gay people on the streets of New York than when he had last worked there. "This led to a superb article that was, by old *Times* standards, quite revolutionary," wrote Talese with unblushing admiration.

"It was just the worst kind of *New York Times* article," says the historian Charles Kaiser, author of *The Gay Metropolis*, a landmark work. "It cited all of this so-called scientific evidence and expert opinion to support the deepest prejudices and preconceptions of its editors."

CBS News broadcast its own version of the *Times* piece in March 1967, with Mike Wallace as lead reporter and interviewer. "The Homosexuals" presented the same claims that homosexuality was a deeply harmful yet curable disease. It featured a question-and-answer session with Socarides before an audience of concerned college students, an interview with Inspector James Fisk of the Los Angeles Police Department, who asserted that homosexuality threatened civil society, and chilling footage of the arrest of a nineteen-year-old man caught propositioning an undercover police officer in a men's room in a public park in L.A.

"This will ruin me," the man told the arresting patrolmen.

"What if a child walked in?" one of them replied. "It would ruin him for life."

The program cited a Louis Harris survey finding that 65 percent of Americans believed homosexuality was "more harmful to society than adultery, abortion, or prostitution" and looked upon homosexuals with "disgust, discomfort, or fear."

But the broadcast also ran interviews with a federal judge and a city district attorney in Boise, Idaho, who argued that laws prohibiting private sexual behavior among consenting adults should be eased or repealed altogether, and it quoted two clergymen—one Catholic, the other Protestant—expressing sympathy and compassion for gay people. Perhaps most important, the program opened with a handsome and seemingly well-adjusted twenty-eight-year-old man named Lars Larson who declared to Wallace and forty million viewers, "I am a homosexual." Larson was smart and articulate, and, most of all, he seemed perfectly normal.

For Charles Kaiser, then a seventeen-year-old high school student struggling with his own sexuality, and for millions of others, the program was a revelation. "The basic problem was the compete denial in the culture that homosexuality even existed," Kaiser recalls. "So to have a healthy, attractive young man declare 'I'm gay and I exist, I'm gay and it's okay,' was a huge breakthrough."

Another arena patrolled with increasing alarm by the media watchdogs was the performing arts. *The New York Times* weighed in in 1961 to express concern about the prominence of gays in the theater world with a piece by the theater critic Howard Taubman that began: "It is time to speak openly and candidly of the increasing incidence and influence of homosexuality on New York's stage—and, indeed, in the other arts as well."

Taubman's tone was more sorrowful than angry. But his thesis was clear and toxic: homosexuals were corrupting the American theater in subtle but meaningful ways, whether it was a male costume designer dressing women to make them look unappealing, or two clearly "mannish females" walking across a stage in a drama for no particular reason.

Even worse, wrote Taubman, was the depiction of women in plays by gay authors: "the unpleasant female of the species . . . exaggerated into a fantastically consuming monster."

Four years later, the novelist Philip Roth rang the same themes in a nasty attack in *The New York Review of Books* on Edward Albee's play *Tiny Alice*, which Roth called "a homosexual daydream." Roth's piece, entitled "The Play That Dare Not Speak Its Name," blasted *Tiny Alice* for "its tediousness, its pretentiousness, its galling sophistication . . . [and] its ghastly pansy rhetoric and repartee." But the real problem, Roth declared, was Albee's purported dishonesty—his unwillingness to come clean and admit he was writing about homosexuality, which is why the play is "so unconvincing, so remote, so obviously a sham."

Roth, perhaps the greatest American novelist of his generation, was known as a passionate political liberal and human rights advocate, which makes the virulence of his antigay assault all the more stunning in retrospect. He would later deny that his article was an attack on homosexuals, but his language was mocking and demeaning. The tone was contagious, unleashing lesser writers to be even more vicious. Wilfrid Sheed, reviewing a cross-section of new plays in *Commentary* three months later, pleaded to see "the homosexual sensibility asserted openly in one play rather than sneaked into twenty. It would, if nothing else, leave a cleaner smell."

The *New York Times* theater critic Stanley Kauffmann rang the same bell the following year in a piece headlined "Homosexual Drama and Its Disguises." Kauffmann declared, "I, like many others, am weary of *disguised* homosexual influence" in the theater, and he singled out three of "the most successful American playwrights of the last twenty years" as the chief culprits. He didn't name them, but everyone on and off Broadway knew he was referring to Tennessee Williams, William Inge, and Albee. Kauffmann expressed some sympathy, saying the three writers were forced to disguise their gay and lesbian characters as heterosexuals because of societal norms. Nonetheless, he declared, "We have all had very much more than enough of the materials so often presented by the three writers in question: the viciousness toward women, the lurid violence that seems a sublimation of social hatreds, the transvestite sexual exhibitionism . . ."

Jim Herlihy, having had only one successful play produced on Broadway, was too small a fish to merit such brutal attention from these vigilant guardians of sexual morality in the theater, but their attacks surely were one of the reasons his plays and his first novel tiptoed around these issues and featured no openly gay characters.

By uncritically reporting established homophobic views without skepticism or rebuttal, mainstream media institutions were effectively endorsing them. And it wasn't just *The New York Times*. In 1969, *Time* magazine, in a two-page essay entitled "The Homosexual in America," covered much the same ground as Kauffmann, but minced even fewer words. The story concluded with a ringing condemnation of homosexuality in the magazine's patented Voice of God: "It is a pathetic little second-rate substitute for reality, a pitiable flight from life. As such it deserves fairness, compassion, understanding and, when possible, treatment. But it deserves no encouragement, no glamorization, no rationalization, no fake status as minority martyrdom, no sophistry about simple differences in taste—and, above all, no pretense that it is anything but a pernicious sickness."

Time focused its bloodshot eye especially on popular theater and movies. On Broadway, it reported, "it would be difficult to find a production without homosexuals playing important parts, either onstage or off." As for gays in Hollywood, "you have to scrape them off the ceiling," claimed the Broadway producer David Merrick. *Time* went on to allude to a "Homintern," or homosexual mafia, in the arts that dictated who got hired or fired and what tastes prevailed. The notion, *Time* conceded, was exaggerated, "but in the theater, dance, and music world, deviates are so widespread that they sometimes seem to be running a kind of closed shop."

"Homintern" was a derogatory term used by anti-Communist crusaders in the early 1950s, during congressional hearings into alleged Communist and homosexual infiltration of the U.S. government. It was a play on the word "Comintern," the shortened name of the Soviet-controlled Communist International, tasked with spreading Marxism around the globe. The Wisconsin senator Joseph McCarthy, the leading Red Scare demagogue, claimed that "Communists and queers" were secretly conspiring to undermine America's moral fiber, corrupt its young people, and create the conditions for Red conquest. Thousands of suspected gay people were singled out and fired from their government jobs at the federal, state, and local levels, just as thousands more purported Communist sympathizers lost theirs. *Time*'s revival of the term nearly a decade after McCarthy's death was a particularly odious slur.

No one expected extravagantly homophobic institutions like the Catholic Church (despite the sexual proclivities of many of its leaders and priests) and evangelical Christians to do anything other than consign gays and lesbians to the deepest and most creatively imagined circles of hell. But the condemnation of those in supposedly open-minded New York City, with its liberal media and progressive politicians— groups that might have been expected to express sympathy, or at least understanding—was a bitter blow. Instead, they helped validate public fear and hatred of gays and lesbians and keep them stripped of civil rights. The role of the psychiatric community was in many ways key. Its insistence that gay men and women could readily choose to seek treatment and a cure for their so-called disease led logically to the conclusion that those who chose not to were responsible for their own misfortune. Worst of all, their unshakable loyalty to homosexuality served as clear proof of their perversion. Those who wallowed mindlessly in gay promiscuity were a threat to vulnerable young people, whom they would surely seek to recruit to their ranks. They were not only sick themselves, so the argument went, they were spreading their disease to healthy innocents.

This was the dark side of progressivism, the certainty that so-called human defects could be diagnosed and cured scientifically—the same belief that underlay the sterilization of so-called mental defectives and the mutilation through lobotomy of the purportedly mentally ill. Bad science led to bad "cures." Too many analysts, concluded Kenneth Lewes in his landmark study *The Psychoanalytic Theory of Male Homosexuality*, "have violated basic norms of decency in their treatment of homosexuals."

Jim Herlihy didn't know it at the time, but Anaïs Nin also held homophobic views. In a handwritten diary entry in late October 1953, she wrote, "Relationship to Jim came to the same standstill as with other homosexuals. You strike the bottom, the limitations. He did not absorb enough, he could not go deeper, he was facile, adaptable, gave illusion of receptivity but behaved childishly."

In a later journal entry, she went further. Two related and destructive trends were strangling American literature, she wrote: the worship of youth and homosexuality; she linked the two in a way that reflected her devotion to psychoanalysis. Many psychiatrists argued that homosexuality in its essence was the result of retarded maturity—men who chose not to outgrow their childhood fixation on male genitalia. "The true degenerates are not the homosexuals for being homosexual," she wrote, "but those who by a process of stunted growth continue to exhibit at fifty all the symptoms of awkward, aggressive, dissonant, unstable adolescence."

The writer Merle Miller, who was gay, experienced the social consequences of this kind of attitude when a friend called from New York on a Friday before getting on a train to come up to Miller's Connecticut home for the weekend. The friend said he had changed his mind about bringing along his sixteen-year-old son. "I've always leveled with you, Merle, and I'm going to now. I'm sure you understand."

Miller said, No, I don't understand. Please explain it to me.

The man replied that his son "is only an impressionable kid, and while I've known you and know you wouldn't, but suppose you had some friends in, and . . . ?"

Miller had never molested a child in his life, nor had any of his gay friends. Moreover, he had heard many accounts of how people came to realize they were gay, and none of them ever claimed it was the result of seduction. "But then maybe it is contagious, floating in the air around me, like a virus," wrote Miller. He told his friend to stay home.

Miller said he was confident that the laws discriminating against gay people would eventually be scrapped. But private acceptance would take much longer. Unlike with Black people, Miller believed, homosexuals would never benefit from any guilt feelings on the part of white liberals. "So far as I can make out, there simply aren't any such feelings."

Tennessee Williams, despite his celebrated success, felt much the same. Dotson Rader recalls accompanying Williams to a party thrown by the theater producer Irene Selznick, daughter of Louis B. Mayer, the former head of MGM, at the Pierre hotel. Cary Grant was there as well as many other luminaries, and Rader, deeply impressed by all the celebrity firepower, had a great time. Waiting for the elevator on the way out, he gushed to Williams about how wonderful everyone had been and how they should come to these parties more often. Williams said nothing, but when the door closed, he shoved Rader against the side of the elevator and snarled, "Baby, don't you ever forget, when you walk out that door, you're the cocksucker who just left the room. They like you because you're useful to them, and when you're not, they won't have anything to do with you."

Martin Duberman's own coming-of-age story, sharply, poignantly, and self-critically recounted in his memoir *Cures: A Gay Man's Odyssey*, illustrates one of the most startling features of the era of gay repression: many gay men accepted and internalized the condemnation and opprobrium directed their way.

Duberman, who was born in 1930, is a prizewinning historian and playwright and one of the most respected public intellectuals to have emerged from the gay liberation movement. He is known for his radical views and willingness to express them strongly in public. Yet throughout the 1950s and '60s, even as he was developing a left-of-center critique of American society, Duberman resisted his own sexuality. He was a good-looking young man attracted to other good-looking young men, but he saw gay relationships as ultimately hopeless and disappointing and feared he had condemned himself to a life of empty, loveless promiscuity. He sought out psychotherapists who promised to "cure" him of his gay affliction if only he would cooperate with their program. He kept trying and failing, and each therapist wound up accusing him of moral failure. Perhaps the most embarrassing moment came during a marathon group therapy session where the leader insisted that he go off to a private area and fondle two naked women from the group. When he failed to get an erection, the leader accused him of "pussyfooting" and hiding his true feelings.

Duberman eventually saw through the fraudulent analytical constructs and bullying of each of his psychotherapists. Still, even after the Stonewall riots of June 1969 and the subsequent rise of gay liberation, it took several years for him to embrace the movement.

By the summer of 1962, Jim Herlihy and Dick Duane had stopped living together. Jim's devouring need for freedom and his feelings of suffocation had combined with Dick's jealousy and fears that Jim could veer out of control, and the conflicts made their life together unbearable. Still, he and Dick would remain in close contact for at least another decade. Dick would serve as editorial adviser for Jim's next two novels and later presented *Stop, You're Killing Me*, a collection of three short Herlihy plays, at the State 73 theater in Manhattan.

After he and Dick split, Jim moved to a fifth-floor walk-up in the East Village, at 68 East Seventh Street. It was small and cheap—a practical place he could stay when he came to New York from Key West, which had become his principal home. He watched the neighborhood slowly transition from grim poverty to an early hippie invasion. "The neighborhood freaked out around me," he would recall. "This flow of long hair began taking place at my doorstep and I loved it. I thought these kids had such wonderful energy and such great direction and I also felt they bore within them the seeds to survival of the world."

Still, it remained a high-crime, high-drug zone, with cracked sidewalks and broken windows. "When I finally located his building, I was astonished by its miserable state—surely a published writer like Herlihy didn't have to live like this in New York," recalled his friend Jamake Highwater, who visited him there in the mid-sixties. But when Highwater stepped inside, "Abruptly the world changed. [The] apartment floated above the filth and gloom: gleaming white walls, posters and paintings, candles burning on ledges and tables, plants filling the incensed air. Once you plunged through the surface of New York, you found yourself in an inner sanctum where people used imagination and ingenuity to transform hovels into places to live." Pride of place in the living room went to a bronze statue of his pal Tallulah Bankhead, cast in 1927 by the English sculptor Frank Dobson and given to Jim and Dick by the actress in a curious gesture of narcissistic generosity.

The apartment reflected Jim's personality—cautious and wary on the outside, concealing the lively and imaginative spirit within. His sense of discretion was part of his moral code. In the mid-1960s he had become friends with Martin Duberman and had warmly encouraged Duberman to write a history of Black Mountain College. But when the book came out, in 1972, Jim wrote a review in *The Village Voice* that Duberman said "sent me reeling." The review criticized Duberman for revealing the fact that Bob Wunsch, the school's rector, had been arrested for alleged homosexuality in the late 1940s, an incident that helped poison relations between the avant-garde school and the conservative rural North Carolina community that surrounded it. "What I want," Jim concluded, "is for each of us to mind his own sexual business, historians included."

Duberman, who had disclosed his own homosexuality for the first time in the book, conceded that he should have been more sensitive about Wunsch's privacy. He later wrote, "I was unable to throw off the baleful feeling that that I hadn't sufficiently thought through all the moral implications involved." But Jim Herlihy had.

The final split with Anaïs Nin over Jim's novel *All Fall Down* a few years before had crushed his spirit and left him tethered to that dark corner where his mind sometimes wandered. When he tried to start writing again, he couldn't stand his own work. He started three novels, none of them any good. "I got scared," he recalled. "I shoved all three into a drawer and thought, 'Well, how am I going to make a living?'" That's when he decided to go back into acting.

His timing was fortuitous. His fellow playwright Edward Albee had recently completed an hour-long, one-act, two-character play called *The Zoo Story*, slated for a weeklong summer-stock production at the Everyman Repertory Theater in Rockport, Maine, in August 1962. Jim managed to snag the meatier of the two roles, playing Jerry, a hostile and deeply troubled gay provocateur living in a cheap West Side boardinghouse for the mentally ill. He meets a publishing executive named Peter on a bench in Central Park, tells him a long, twisted tale of how he poisoned his landlady's dog, then attacks Peter with a knife. But Jerry falls on it himself in a final act of self-destruction. It is a physically and emotionally demanding role—Jerry's incendiary monologue in the middle of the play lasts eighteen nonstop minutes—and Herlihy did it beautifully, reaching deep inside himself to find the anger and despair at the heart of Jerry. "In the shifty, neurotic performance by James Leo Herlihy, Jerry is unforgettable," wrote *The Boston Globe*'s theater critic. "Jerry as played by Mr. Herlihy will linger in your mind from year to year." He played the role again in Paris in January 1963 and the following summer at the Theatre Company of Boston, a testing ground for promising but unknown young actors, including, a few years later, Dustin Hoffman and Jon Voight.

Herlihy took on other, smaller roles: in a summer stock production of Harold Pinter's *The Caretaker*; in an episode of the hit television series *Route 66*, in which he played a soulful newspaper reporter covering a murder trial in a small southern town; and in a trifle of a romantic comedy called *In the French Style*, filmed in Paris, as one of Jean Seberg's four lovers—the one who marries her in the end. The roles helped restore his confidence that he could make a living as an actor and allowed him to ease back into writing after a break of some eighteen months.

A famous, outspoken woman helped nudge him along the way, but it wasn't Anaïs Nin. During *The Zoo Story*'s Paris run, Herlihy met Marlene Dietrich at a party. Although she was an actress, Dietrich had no respect for her own profession; she only did it, she insisted, because she had no choice—it was all she knew how to do. She told him she'd read and admired his work, and she bluntly inquired of him, "What is a writer like you doing here, starring in a play and going to cocktail parties? Why aren't you writing books?"

Jim gave her a long-winded answer that he knew was an evasion. Dietrich knew it, too, and scolded him for not doing what he surely knew he must. "She hit the ceiling," he would recall. "She was marvelous! She said she thought that was the silliest thing she'd ever heard." It was time, Dietrich demanded, that he get back to work.

A few months later he finally did.

6. "A TOUCH OF THE FLICKS"

The film industry knows less about itself than any other major industry in the United States.
—Eric Johnston, president of the Motion Picture Association of America

For all the excitement that the kitchen-sink dramas and their celebrated successors like Tony Richardson's *Tom Jones* and John Schlesinger's *Darling* had created, British cinema was in deep trouble by the mid-1960s. It was dominated by two giant companies, the Rank Organisation and Associated British Picture Corp, owners of the country's major cinema house circuits. Their tastes were stodgy and their appetite for risk-taking virtually undetectable, yet no British-made feature film could hope to succeed at the box office without the backing of one or the other. Ticket sales were dropping every year, while the cost of production kept rising. There simply wasn't a large enough moviegoing audience in Britain to support the industry. By 1967, American companies were financing nearly 90 percent of all the movies made in the United Kingdom. The biggest international successes, like *Lawrence of Arabia*, the James Bond series, *A Hard Day's Night*, *Alfie*, *Georgy Girl*, and a handful of others, were almost totally paid for with money from America, which is where most of the profits ended up.

Worse, perhaps, the industry seemed worn out and wary. Michael Caine once remarked that "the British make pictures, while the Americans make movies." "He said pictures are static things which you hang on the wall, whereas movies *move*," recalls the actor Glenda Jackson.

John Schlesinger was just as critical of his peers and compatriots. Praising French New Wave directors like Jean-Luc Godard and François

Truffaut, he told an interviewer that "the sheer exuberance and inventiveness of these directors staggers one. They are unhampered—they have freshness, and this seems one of the most difficult things to do in the British cinema as it is today." He added, "We are a nation of conformists and this is difficult to escape from."

Slowly but inevitably the new wave of promising young British actors left for America—Caine, Jackson, Christie, Bates, Peter O'Toole, Sean Connery, Richard Harris, Oliver Reed, and many others. Some of them maintained homes in the United Kingdom, but almost all of them made their living in Hollywood.

This flight to California was about money, of course, but it wasn't *just* about money. Many British actors and directors perceived a lack of respect for their work back home. Even David Lean, perhaps the greatest classical British filmmaker of them all, complained to Kevin Brownlow, his biographer, about the way his films were dismissed by the British elite. He described how during the reception at the December 1962 royal premiere of *Lawrence of Arabia*, Lean's masterpiece, Prince Philip, the Duke of Edinburgh, came up to him and said, "Ah, good evening. Good flick?" Lean replied, "I hope so, sir."

"Now, he had no intention of being insulting, or talking down," Lean recalled. "But we were 'the flicks.' And that is still the way the English Establishment feels about the movies. Wherever I now go in the world, I am absolutely astounded by the immediate respect I get for being a film director. But in England it's still a good old touch of the flicks. And it's a shame."

In truth, Hollywood, although far larger and richer than its British counterpart, was also slouching toward a financial and artistic reckoning. The studio system that had ruled the motion picture industry for more than three decades had been in a slow but steady state of decline since the end of World War II due to a variety of factors, including the landmark 1948 Supreme Court antitrust decision that stripped the studios of their lucrative theater chains; competition from television and other new forms of entertainment; and the flight of urbanites to the suburbs and subsequent decline of downtown movie palaces. Weekly ticket sales had plummeted from ninety million during World War II to forty-three million by 1965 and were continuing to fall. While most of the old studios still existed, their function had changed dramatically; they still financed and distributed movies, along with television programs, but they no longer created many of them. They laid off thousands of employees, including actors, directors, writers, artisans, and crew members, and leased their facilities to independent filmmakers and TV production companies. Lost was "the genius of the system," as the French film critic André Bazin had once described the Hollywood dream-making machine: the old, reliable method of making decent movies at an industrial rate and a high level of competency that sometimes ascended to art.

The essayist, novelist, and screenwriter Joan Didion once knowingly wrote that "much of what is written about pictures and about pictures people approaches reality only occasionally and accidentally." A twenty-five-page cover story in *Look* magazine in March 1965, headlined "The Big Flick Kick," offered an inadvertent illustration of Didion's judgment. After interviewing "the moguls of today," *Look* managed to convince itself that a "new movie boom" was under way that would capture a new and younger audience—"the irreverent millions between seventeen and twenty-two," as the magazine warily described them—as well as "Mr. and Mrs. Average Citizen." "The creative side is taking over," declared one anonymous studio executive. "New blood has a chance as never before."

Look, which would itself soon fall victim to the some of the same forces choking Hollywood and go out of business in 1971, offered some avuncular words of wisdom for filmmakers. It warned them to "heed reality. We are a wiser people, who have been through a lot of wars and living, and tasted every kind of entertainment." An article on cinematic nudity insisted, "For sex appeal, put on clothes. To destroy it, bare the bodies." Two articles on movie stars featured celebrities who were at or near the end of their bankable years: the first, entitled "The Pro," was about Bette Davis, who was fifty-six that spring, smoked four packs of cigarettes a day, and drank scotch from a tumbler at night; the second, "King and Queen," focused on Richard Burton and Elizabeth Taylor, whose charmless on-screen performances and chaotic off-screen dalliance during the making of *Cleopatra* (1963) had disrupted the production, bloated its cost by millions, and nearly bankrupted 20th Century-Fox.

No problem, *Look* declared. Hollywood "is riding the range of the reliable: larger-than-life musicals, Biblical epics, super-Westerns, shockers, war dramas, adventure-travel comedies, and opulent versions of literary classics and best-sellers."

Some of these old reliable genres indeed still worked occasionally. *The Sound of Music*, released in 1965, was a huge success. Made for a budget of eight million dollars, it hit the one-hundred-million-dollar mark in ticket sales by the end of 1967, saving Fox from the open grave *Cleopatra* had dug for it. MGM scored big in 1967 with *The Dirty Dozen*, a violent and unconventional World War II fantasy. But many traditional genres were running out of steam. The same *Hollywood Reporter* article that disclosed *The Sound of Music*'s profits also reported that the team behind the picture—veteran director Robert Wise, producer Saul Chaplin, and star Julie Andrews—were in the final stages of filming *Star!*, a musical biopic about the late British stage actress Gertrude Lawrence, for Fox. The budget was said to be around fifteen million dollars. Richard Zanuck, in charge of production at Fox, also revealed that the company's next big road-show picture would be *Doctor Dolittle*, opening Christmas week of 1967. Both films turned out to be massive flops. So did *The Bible* (1966), a lumbering epic directed by John Huston. Old Hollywood was buckling under its own weight.

Two years later, the illusions of "The Movies: The Big Flick Kick" were largely dead and buried. Hollywood was in trouble and knew it, although it hadn't figured out exactly what to do about it. The studio execs were especially puzzled by the new generation of sophisticated young filmgoers whose politics and tastes seemed dramatically different from those of their parents. "It's hard to convey now how much insecurity and anger there was about the counterculture," recalled Paul Schrader, who got his start as a screenwriter during this era. "Hollywood was angry, Sinatra was angry, they're all angry. They thought, 'It's not our world anymore. And we have no idea how to sell what we sell to those kids.'"

Schrader became part of a generation of rebels knocking at Hollywood's gates, among them maverick studio system veterans like Robert Altman, Sam Peckinpah, and Dennis Hopper, and New Yorkers trained in theater and television like Sidney Lumet, Mike Nichols, and Arthur Penn, Jim Herlihy's fellow Black Mountain College alum. Influenced by foreign filmmakers like Jean-Luc Godard, François Truffaut, Federico Fellini, and Ingmar Bergman—the same directors who were inspiring Tony Richardson and John Schlesinger in Britain—the new American rebels set out to make more personal, character-driven films that either defied or ignored the old genres, appealed to younger and more sophisticated audiences, and explored adult themes and sexuality.

One of the walls they sought to breach was the Production Code, the self-censorship system that had forced the producers and screenwriters of Jim Herlihy's *Blue Denim* to change its story line to eliminate any mention of abortion. The code had been established in the early 1930s under pressure from the Catholic Legion of Decency and its puritan allies. It had banned vulgar language, upheld "the sanctity of the institution of marriage and the home," and barred "lustful kissing" and "passion that stimulates the baser emotions." Adultery, premarital sex, homosexuality, and abortion were not allowed or even mentionable, nor was anything else that might "lower the moral standards of those who see it." The code was successful in calming the nerves of the legion and defanging some of the dozens of local and state censorship boards that had sprung up around the country armed with the power to ban or mutilate any film that offended their brittle sensibilities. Under Joseph Breen, the strong-willed ex-newspaperman who administered the code until 1954, the office was feared and loathed in equal measure by studio executives and filmmakers. But the Supreme Court ruled in 1952 that movies were a form of free speech covered by the First Amendment. The decision, known as *Burstyn v. Wilson*, had limited impact because it allowed states and localities to continue to ban movies they judged obscene. Still, independent filmmakers became more willing to challenge Production Code restrictions. Otto Preminger, an autocratic producer-director who delighted in thumbing his nose at Hollywood authority, defied the Breen office after it refused to approve *The Moon Is Blue* (1953), a light romantic comedy starring William Holden, David Niven, and Maggie McNamara—the office wanted to delete words like "seduction" and "virginal" from the screenplay—and *The Man with the Golden Arm* (1955), a dark drama about drug addiction starring Frank Sinatra and Kim Novak. Both pictures were distributed by United Artists, which quit the Motion Picture Producers and Distributors of America and released the films without a seal of approval. And both made good money at the box office, helped, no doubt, by Preminger's highly publicized battles against censorship.

The biggest challenge yet came in 1964 with *The Pawnbroker*, a low-budget, black-and-white film about a Holocaust survivor who runs a pawnshop in Harlem and is haunted by memories of his dead wife and two children, all of whom were murdered by the Nazis. It was directed by Lumet, starred Rod Steiger, a brilliant and corrosive method actor, and was independently produced by Ely Landau. The Production Code office, which had been denied the opportunity to review the screenplay ahead of the filming, objected to a fifteen-second scene in which a prostitute bares her breasts to the Steiger character, who then flashes back to a memory of his wife with her breasts forcibly exposed by concentration camp guards. Landau argued that the nudity was essential to the story and anything but prurient. The appeals board of the Motion Picture Association of America, the organization run by and for the heads of the seven major studios, was swayed by an impassioned argument for the movie by the distinguished producer-director Joseph L. Mankiewicz, former head of the Director's Guild, and granted it an exception provided that Lumet shorten the nude scene. Although the Legion of Decency issued a "C" for Condemned, the movie won enthusiastic reviews when it was released the following year, grossed almost three million dollars, and earned Steiger an Oscar nomination for Best Actor.

The Pawnbroker was also notable for its innovative use of subjective flashbacks. Following a path first blazed by the French director Alain Resnais in *Hiroshima mon amour* (1959), Lumet and the film editor Ralph Rosenblum constructed a series of "flash cuts"—lightning-quick images of the suffering of the pawnbroker's wife and children and his own helplessness to protect his loved ones that Steiger's character remembers from the brutal past. Some of the flash cuts came and went so rapidly that audiences could barely tell what they were seeing, but the cumulative impact was to depict visually the traumas that haunted Steiger's character. We saw what he had seen, and felt something of the horror he had experienced.

In 1966, Jack Valenti, a charismatic, smooth-talking former Texas public relations man and presidential aide to Lyndon Johnson, took over as president of the MPAA. Valenti was keenly aware that he hadn't been hired because of his superior knowledge of the movie business—he knew very little about it, as he constantly reminded his audiences. Instead, the studio heads picked him for his acute political antennae, to guide the industry through one of the most tumultuous eras in American political and cultural history, a time when, as he himself put it, "there were stirrings of insurrection at all levels of society." Valenti understood that the movies, which had dominated popular culture ever since the controversy over D. W. Griffith's racist epic *The Birth of a Nation* fifty years earlier, were anything but immune to the current upheavals.

Early on in his tenure as president, Valenti came face-to-face with the unpleasant absurdities the outmoded Production Code trafficked in. The director Mike Nichols had recently completed filming his first movie, a screen adaptation of Edward Albee's incendiary Broadway play *Who's Afraid of Virginia Woolf?*, starring Elizabeth Taylor and Richard Burton as a bitter, self-destructive married couple. Just ten days after taking office, Valenti and his new vice president, the celebrated New York lawyer Louis Nizer, flew to Los Angeles to the palatial office of Jack Warner, head of Warner Bros., the film's distributor. To Valenti's dismay, he and Nizer found themselves negotiating with Warner over specific language in the screenplay, agreeing they would leave in a reference to an imaginary game called the "Hump the Hostess," but delete three instances of "screw you" while leaving a fourth intact. "By today's standards, the movie might be a training film for a nunnery," wrote Valenti in his memoirs, "but in the sixties it was controversial." He found the entire exercise demeaning and "even absurd, that grown men could be spending their time on such a puerile discussion." Like *The Pawnbroker*, *Virginia Woolf* was granted an exemption based upon its artistic merit. So too was *Alfie*, a British import that was cleared to discuss a character's abortion. It was quickly evident to Valenti that the exceptions were becoming the rule.

A few months later he was confronted with another controversy, over the Italian director Michelangelo Antonioni's *Blow-Up*, which included some fifteen seconds of female nudity and sexual intercourse. Production Code administrators insisted on cutting the scene. Here too MGM, the film's distributor, got around the censors—and mocked them as well—by releasing it under the label of an MGM subsidiary.

At first Valenti toyed with the idea of killing the code outright and replacing it with a simple warning label: "For Mature Audiences." But this proved unacceptable to politicians and community leaders who saw adult-themed movies as a threat to America's moral fiber. It was the artists versus the puritans in a struggle for America's cultural soul, a battle that neither Valenti nor the studio heads he worked for wanted to be caught in the middle of. They chose instead to replace the code with a ratings system designed, at least in its early days, to offer wider artistic latitude for filmmakers willing to accept an R or even an X rating, restricting audiences to those aged seventeen and over. In his press statement announcing the change, Valenti boldly declared, "We believe the screen must be as free for filmmakers as it is for those who write books." But a few paragraphs later he contradicted himself by warning producers and directors that "freedom without discipline is license, and that's wrong too." It was Jack Valenti's tacit acknowledgment that the battle over censorship was far from over. The new system was enacted on November 1, 1968, and went into effect just in time for the MPAA to review *Midnight Cowboy* before its release the following May.

Throughout the heated public debates over movie censorship, one taboo was seldom mentioned: homosexuality. The Production Code had effectively banned any depiction of gay men and women in movies. Even the word itself was forbidden. But just as other adult themes started to seep into mainstream American films and other cultural realms in the early sixties, cinematic homosexuals took their first steps out of the closet—although only in roles that depicted them as singularly depraved, unhappy, and self-destructive.

William Wyler's *The Children's Hour* (1961), based on a play and screenplay by Lillian Hellman, told the tale of two women teachers at a private girls' school who are falsely accused of lesbianism (another banned word that is never uttered in the film). In the play Hellman makes clear that one of the women, Martha (played in the film by Shirley MacLaine), realizes she has fallen in love with Karen (Audrey Hepburn), although the movie is much less explicit. In an agonized confession filled with self-hatred, Martha reveals her true feelings to Karen. "I feel so damn sick and dirty I just can't stand it anymore!" she cries. Later, she hangs herself. As the gay film historian Vito Russo points out, "It is not a lie that destroys Martha; it is the awful truth."

In Otto Preminger's *Advise and Consent* (1962)—adapted from Allen Drury's bestselling novel about Washington politics—a handsome young senator from Utah is blackmailed about his brief affair with a fellow male soldier during World War II. The senator, played by Don Murray, goes to New York to track down his former lover and finds him at Club 602, a gay bar jammed with grotesque men, many of whom are holding their cigarettes at effeminate angles while leering at the anxious stranger in their midst. Bongo drums begin to beat, Frank Sinatra croons on the jukebox about "a secret voice," and the senator flees in panic and disgust. When his former lover—a muscular blond in a tight polo shirt—follows him outside, the senator shoves him into a puddle of dirty water and races back to Washington, where he slits his own throat with a straight razor.

The two films helped establish a delicate pattern. From here on out, gay characters could appear openly on-screen but only in situations that made clear their misery and depravity and that resulted in dire consequences for all involved: prison for Jo (Barbara Stanwyck), the lesbian whorehouse madam in *Walk on the Wild Side* (1962), after one of her thugs accidentally kills the beautiful young prostitute she loves; an arrest for homicide for Major Penderton (Marlon Brando), who shoots a young soldier (Robert Forster) he lusts after in *Reflections in a Golden Eye* (1967); and suicide for Sergeant Callan (Rod Steiger) in *The Sergeant*

(1968) after he reveals his perverted nature by planting a drunken kiss on the lips of a handsome male private (John Phillip Law). None of these films did terribly well either with critics or at the box office.

"There was a body of work emerging in the sixties, but it was not quite there yet," says the film historian Ronald Gregg of the Columbia University School of the Arts. "Most Hollywood films with gay characters were social problem films that treated homosexuality like alcoholism or some other disease. Because Hollywood wanted to appeal to a general audience, it couldn't get past the social problem approach. At the same time, the Production Code, with its outright censorship, was coming to an end."

Things were somewhat different in the United Kingdom. While homosexuality remained against the law until 1967, gay characters were depicted with more sympathy and less panicky opprobrium in movies like *A Taste of Honey* (1961), *The L-Shaped Room* (1962), *The Leather Boys* (1964), and John Schlesinger's own *Darling* (1965). But perhaps the most empathetic of all the mainstream films with gay themes was one of the earliest. *Victim* (1961) was directed by Basil Dearden and starred Dirk Bogarde, one of Britain's biggest film stars and himself a closeted (at that time) gay man. Bogarde plays Melville Farr, a married lawyer who is about to take a high-ranking position as a queen's counsel when he is contacted by Barrett, a young gay man whom he had been seeing socially, who is looking for legal help because he's being blackmailed. After Barrett is arrested for theft and commits suicide in jail, the blackmailers turn their attention to Farr, who must choose between surrendering to extortion or having his secret life as a gay man exposed and his distinguished career ruined.

In one of the film's most revealing moments, Farr seeks to enlist the help of other gay blackmail victims—including a celebrated actor and a wealthy businessman—to catch the extortionists. None of them are willing to get involved. "Bring them down and we go with [them]," one of them warns Farr. "Just pay!"

Farr's fragile relationship with his devoted wife, Laura, is depicted with sensitivity. He had sworn off sleeping with men and promised he would be faithful to her when they got married. He tells her he's kept his word but confesses that he had lusted after Barrett, which is why he had stopped seeing him. "You understand?" he tells his shocked wife. "Because I wanted him!"

With the help of a sympathetic police detective, Farr ultimately unmasks the bad guys, who are arrested. But he has no illusions about the damage to his reputation. "My friends will lower their eyes," he tells Laura, "and my enemies [have already] guessed."

Victim was critically acclaimed in Britain for its humane handling of a sensitive subject, but it was shunned in the United States because it was deemed too sympathetic to gay people. The film was denied a Motion Picture Association of America seal for distribution because it used the word "homosexual." *Time* magazine self-righteously condemned it for its "coyly sensational exploitation of homosexuality as a theme—and, what's more offensive, an implicit approval of homosexuality as a practice."

Russo, in his landmark 1981 study *The Celluloid Closet*, compiled what he called a "necrology": a list of thirty-nine American feature films in which gay or lesbian characters either are murdered, commit suicide, or cause the death of others. Those films should have posted a surgeon general's warning: homosexuality, like cigarette smoking, could be fatal to one's health.

Although he longed to make a film that treated homosexuality in a more straightforward and sympathetic fashion, John Schlesinger had no intention of stepping out of the closet either personally or cinematically. Instead, he and Joe Janni searched for another sophisticated story about contemporary Britain that would pursue the same adult themes of sex, power, and betrayal that *Darling* had ruthlessly captured. They came to focus on *A Severed Head*, a shrewd, witty, and hyper-observant Iris Murdoch novel that satirized the sexual and social mores of a set of upper-crust bourgeoisie in London, dissecting their empty lives, promiscuities, and adulteries. "Of all the lots-of-people-screwing-lots-of-other-people novels this is probably the best, and certainly the weirdest," wrote the British novelist William Sutcliffe.

Janni pitched the idea to the executives at MGM, because they had expressed keen interest in working with him and Schlesinger. But the studio execs were still clinging to the dubious comforts of old-fashioned genres. Dazzled by David Lean's success with *Lawrence of Arabia*, they were interested in funding a major road-show picture based in the U.K. They proposed a remake of *Tess of the D'Urbervilles*, a Thomas Hardy novel that MGM had first made into a film in 1924. Schlesinger responded by suggesting a different Hardy novel, *Far from the Madding Crowd*, about a beautiful, headstrong young woman in nineteenth-century rural England and her three male suitors. MGM offered a four-million-dollar budget; Janni knew he could raise another million from backers in England. Still, by Hollywood standards this was a serious bargain—the big studios were spending twice as much in America for far less ambitious work. Janni and Schlesinger leapt at the offer.

After making three films shot in contemporary urban settings, Schlesinger was intrigued by the idea of creating a full-scale, Technicolor historical epic with a big enough budget for a first-rate British cast and locations in the halcyon Dorset countryside. Hardy, he said, "was such a visual writer with a sense of drama and dramatic irony." And while he never said so in an interview, it seems likely that Schlesinger also hoped to impress his beloved parents, who surely felt more comfortable with a movie adapted from a Thomas Hardy novel than with *Darling* and its casual and corrosive sexuality.

John wanted to cast Vanessa Redgrave, not yet thirty but already highly experienced on stage and screen, to play the lead role of Bathsheba Everdene, the young beauty who takes over running her rich uncle's farming estate after his death. But Janni had signed Julie Christie to a five-film contract after *Billy Liar* and was keen to use her, and Schlesinger, always one of her biggest fans, was more than willing. Bathsheba is determined to establish her independence and rely on her own judgment to succeed in a male-dominated world. To keep her farm, she is forced to battle stormy weather, fire, and disease, and cope with the ardent attentions of three very different men. Who better than Christie to take this on? "She's playing a modern girl—I mean that was the whole point of casting her," the director would later recall.

He surrounded her with a fine collection of British actors: Alan

Bates, Peter Finch, and Terence Stamp as the suitors, and an impressive lineup of experienced stage and screen performers for the smaller roles. The cinematographer Nicolas Roeg—soon to launch his own distinctive career as a director—captured in gloriously vivid colors the rolling hills, dappled sunlight, and lush vegetation of southwest England's countryside.

The biggest obstacle proved to be the rain, which struck in early October and continued relentlessly through December, turning the bucolic rolling hills and dales of Thomas Hardy land into giant mud bogs and playing havoc with the shooting schedule. Schlesinger grew increasingly irritable and, as often was true, tended to single out for abuse one specific performer, in this case Terence Stamp, a dashing young icon of the new mod London. Stamp had the cruel good looks and heedless ego to play Francis Troy, the sergeant who lays siege to Bathsheba's infatuated heart and marries her but proves to be a reckless and self-centered rogue. Stamp came from a working-class background—his father was a tugboat stoker—and Schlesinger quickly came to feel that he lacked the discipline and technical skill as an actor to immerse himself in the role. "I didn't think Stamp was very good [and] he didn't like working with me, either," Schlesinger recalled many years later. "I remember we had to dub a lot of his performance because he just didn't have enough balls."

For his part, Stamp felt from the beginning that Schlesinger hadn't wanted him for the role and made little effort to work with him. "He wasn't the easiest man to get along with, and I didn't really have time to flatter him or be particularly nice to him," he would recall. "I was doing the best I could in spite of him."

Stamp said Schlesinger insisted that for the sake of authenticity he needed to learn to wield a Victorian military sword with his right hand—Stamp was left-handed—and then undershot the memorable scene where Troy seduces Bathsheba with a display of flashy swordsmanship on a deserted moor. Stamp says Roeg snuck off with him to the moor in the early evenings to shoot more footage without Schlesinger's knowledge.

Ann Skinner, who was on the film set every day serving in her usual capacity as John's devoted aide, believed he either underestimated or purposely denigrated the hard work that Stamp was putting in. "Terry had worked his butt off learning swordplay and horse riding for the part, but John gave him such a hard time," Skinner recalls.

Their worst clash came in the crucial climactic scene where Troy returns from a long absence to reclaim Bathsheba as his wife. Schlesinger blew up because he felt Stamp was failing to deliver his lines with the necessary conviction. But Ann saw an element of cruelty in John's temper tantrum. "John did take after take, and it was like he was punishing Terry," says Skinner.

By contrast, John never wavered in his loyalty to Julie Christie. Critics complained that she simply was not convincing as a nineteenth-century farm woman. She looked and sounded like someone who had parachuted in from Swinging London. In Frederic Raphael's all-too-faithful-to-the-novel screenplay, the sublime combination of self-assurance, mystery, and vulnerability that made Christie so intriguing in *Billy Liar* and *Darling* somehow got lost on the winding footpaths of Dorset.

Christie recalls feeling anxious about her acting. "I didn't have any confidence," she says. "I didn't think I was any good in the film, and I still don't." But Schlesinger worked hard to convince her that she could do it. "The director's job is to make the actor feel confident enough to forget their personal insecurities, and John never let me down in that area."

He wasn't above playing childish tricks to lighten the mood. Christie recalls a scene where Bathsheba enters a crypt and lifts the coffin lid of her husband's mistress. Instead of a fake corpse, Christie found a smirking prop man holding a large dildo between his legs. Everyone on the set burst into raucous laughter. "It was delightfully childish, like slipping on a banana skin," she says.

Schlesinger and his cast and crew slogged it out on location until February. "We threw our last dead sheep over a cliff yesterday lunchtime," he wrote to a friend, "and I managed to drive back—God knows how—in the afternoon. It's so long since I have seen double-lane traffic—can you imagine!"

There were hours and hours of footage to edit, along with color corrections to make, and a massive soundtrack to coordinate. The final cut ran three hours and twenty minutes—as promised, an old-fashioned road-show epic, complete with full orchestral score by the English composer Richard Rodney Bennett, whose film scores ranged from jazzy to majestic and who was nominated for an Academy Award for *Madding Crowd*. There was also an intermission with a lush entr'acte musical interlude.

Schlesinger was uneasy, as always, but for once he let his guard down, feeling confident that the film was a triumph. The first stop across the Atlantic was New York, and he was expecting a warm welcome there. Christie, Janni, and the film editor James Clark accompanied him, and his parents flew to New York separately.

The first critical British reviews didn't worry Schlesinger and Janni too much; John believed his films had always been underrated in his home country. But Bosley Crowther's negative review was a punch to the gut. The *New York Times* film critic, who had been warmly supportive of Schlesinger's previous work, said the movie looked ravishing but had no soul. He skewered it a second time the following weekend in a piece headlined "Magnificence Is No Longer Enough," writing as if Schlesinger's direction of the film had amounted to a personal betrayal. "How could John Schlesinger, who is one of the most brilliant of the group of young directors working in England, have let *Far from the Madding Crowd* become the pictorially excessive but dramatically barren film it is?"

Schlesinger arrived in Hollywood to find himself persona non grata. The PR people from MGM told him they had canceled the reception planned for that evening because they knew he'd be "tired." After that, they simply stopped talking to him altogether and didn't return his phone calls. In Britain, he later told an interviewer, when he had experienced failure "people tend to treat me like a bereaved soul. It's like death actually." In America, by contrast, "they're much less polite. They will actually turn on their heels when they see you coming and they don't call you up."

The suits at MGM did communicate their demand for a tighter version of the film. Working feverishly under Schlesinger's instructions, Jim Clark cut it by twenty minutes. It wasn't enough. The studio then assigned it to Margaret Booth, Hollywood's most esteemed female film editor, "who was cutting the film to ribbons," according to Schlesinger. He pleaded with MGM that he and Clark could make the cuts without doing damage to the story. In the end they brought it down to 169 minutes—thirty minutes shorter than the original. Audiences still stayed away.

It was a miserable experience and a huge comedown for Schlesinger. His first three feature films had been critically hailed and reasonably successful at the box office. All three had contemporary urban settings and spoke to the modern human condition. *Darling*, the last of the three, had been a bona fide international hit. But his fourth film, far more ambitious artistically, technically, and financially, had taken him out of his comfort zone and had failed.

All of his films addressed similar themes: they were about young people with aspirations, resisting compromise until they are forced to face the limits of their dreams and compelled to make hard choices. Often they have to settle for less than they want. Now Schlesinger faced a similar choice himself. He could go back home to England and reassert himself in the world that he knew best, a comfortable but ultimately suffocating environment operating at what he called "a sort of grey-beige level of mediocrity." Or he could stay on in America—brazen, crude, materialistic, rootless, scary-as-hell America—and take his chances. To do so, of course, he would need a great project—something daring and adventurous, and yet capable of attracting funding and, of course, an audience.

Fortunately for him, a striking new novel was available.

7. THE NOVEL

No matter where you're from, what your background, you come to the
city and you're alone here. It can be a cruel place, New York. It can be
a lonely place.
—Robert De Niro

Joe Buck felt like a different man as he walked out of the shoe store
in Houston in his new cowboy boots:

> Something snapped in the whole bottom half of him: a kind of power
> he never even knew was there had been released in his pelvis and he was
> able to feel the world through it . . . The world was down there, and he
> was way up here, on top of it. And the space between him and it was
> now commanded by a beautiful strange animal, himself, Joe Buck. He
> was exultant. He was ready.
> "I'm ready," he said to himself, and he wondered what he meant by
> that.

So begins *Midnight Cowboy*, James Leo Herlihy's most fully realized
work, the novel into which he poured all of his fragile talent, emotions,
and beliefs. He finally found a fully realized character in Joe Buck—a
man-child in the promised land, enamored by his own power and beauty,
yet riddled with uncertainty and haunted by loneliness.

Jim had a successful first novel, a Broadway play, and two Hollywood
movies behind him, all of which had skirted around or avoided altogether the incendiary subject of homosexuality. But this time all of the
walls and veils that he had erected in his previous work came down: he
was writing about sex, gay and straight, without blinking or hiding be-

hind flimsy metaphors. Part of this was surely the times: by 1964, when he wrote the bulk of the novel, gay fiction was standing on the banks of mainstream American literature and waving its arms. James Baldwin's *Another Country*, published in 1962, had explored the conflicts and passions of a Black bisexual jazz drummer and his troubled circle of friends. It was an instant bestseller. So was John Rechy's raw and disturbing *City of Night* (1963), the odyssey of a gay hustler from New York's Times Square to Los Angeles's Pershing Square, published by the small, famously libertine Grove Press. The following year, Simon & Schuster published Christopher Isherwood's *A Single Man*, an intensely moving account of a middle-aged gay man mourning the death of his longtime lover. Surely the stage was ready for *Midnight Cowboy*, a novel that depicts, in the words of its book jacket, "the dark underside of America from Texas to Times Square."

Joe Buck, six foot one in his new cowboy boots, handsome and twenty-seven and none too brilliant, has conceived a life-changing strategy and a business model: to use the one thing in life he believes he's good at to service for cash the desperate but affluent middle-aged women of Manhattan, tired of and disheartened by their boring, flaccid husbands. Joe wants to be a high-class, heterosexual stud employing his naked body and his bottomless well of good cheer to build a satisfied clientele in the bedrooms of America's greatest city. He's coming for money, sex, and fulfillment, seeking to connect with people in the only way he knows how.

After his arrival, it quickly all goes wrong. But before that happens, the novel drops back to tell us who Joe Buck is and where he comes from. He's a product of the American Southwest, not the rugged, starkly beautiful land of Hollywood's cinematic imagination, but the bleak, run-down collection of hot-baked, physically and spiritually stunted small towns and cities of modern Texas and New Mexico. Joe's unmarried mother deposits him at age seven with her mother, Sally Buck, a beauty shop owner in Albuquerque who divides her time between serving the impossible demands of her aging female customers and doggedly pursuing male companionship for herself, leaving little or no time to care for her solitary grandson. Fatherless, motherless, and on his own, Joe grows up skipping school, watching endless daytime television, and wolfing down peanut butter sandwiches and TV dinners while starved for companionship and affection. He tries to fill the gaping holes in his life with vivid fantasies. He dreams one night of "an endless chain of people marching across the side of the world . . . bus drivers, musicians, and soldiers and ten cent store girls; there were Chinamen and pilots, hillbillies and fat men and red-headed women . . . miners and bank clerks . . . millionaires and store detectives, swamis, babies, grand-mothers, thieves." But when he tries to join the parade, they all close ranks and make it impossible for him to break in. Even in his dreams, Joe is an orphan.

At sixteen he has his first sexual encounter, with Anastasia Pratt, the fifteen-year-old town slut, known to the guys as "Chalkline Annie," who finds him more passionate and solicitous than the other young men who have used and abused her. But it's only a brief respite of solace and com-panionship. She soon winds up being hauled off to a mental institution by her alarmed parents.

Joe is drafted, and while he's in the army his grandmother dies in a horse-riding accident. He has no home, no family, no friends. After the army, he moves to Houston and gets a job as a kitchen hand at the Sunshine Cafeteria, where he meets Perry, a slick sexual hustler with a predator's nose for neediness. Perry gets Joe stoned on marijuana one evening and seduces him, then takes him to a whorehouse outside of town, where Juanita and Tombaby, the proprietor and her obese "half-breed" son— shades of Daisy and Rudy Filbertson of "Crazy October"—set him up with a teenaged prostitute and spy on him making love to her, and when he catches them at it, they beat and rape him.

Joe sinks further into his own solitary confinement. But he recalls Juanita's description of New York as a place full of "fags and money and hungry women," and so he devises his escape plan. He buys himself a cowboy outfit and catches a Greyhound bus for New York City, fleeing Texas like a runaway stallion. When he first spies the Manhattan skyline from the bus, he grabs his crotch and declares, "I'm gonna take hold o' this thing and I'm gonna swing it like a lasso and I'm gonna rope in this whole fuckin' island."

But despite his new cowboy persona, Joe is clearly not suited for the task. His first sexual encounter with a woman, Cass Trehune, a middle-aged call girl on Manhattan's East Side, ends with her milking him for twenty dollars. Then, at a bar on Broadway near West Fortieth Street, he meets Rico Rizzo, nicknamed Ratso, a skinny, child-sized, "dirty, curly-haired, little blond runt" in his early twenties, with big brown eyes, incongruously large ears, a shriveled left leg, and a gait with "a kind of rolling motion to it, like the progress of a lopsided wheel."

Ratso moves in on Joe like a bird of prey. Unlike Perry, he isn't interested in exploiting Joe for sex but for money; he cons him out of another twenty, then sends Joe to a phony preacher named O'Daniel who, Ratso claims, can set Joe up with wealthy women. But O'Daniel is no pimp, just a religious fanatic preaching fire and brimstone from a fleabag hotel room. Joe's small nest egg is quickly devoured, and he is evicted from his cheap hotel, forfeiting his prized horsehide suitcase and virtually all of his possessions except the clothes on his back—his cowboy outfit—and his precious transistor radio.

He takes to the streets, wanders aimlessly for three weeks, keeping clean with soap, razor, and toothbrush, washing his private parts in the sinks of men's rooms and sleeping on the ruined balcony seats of Forty-second Street's all-night movie theaters, on the hard benches and floors of the Port Authority Bus Terminal, or in the backs of trucks parked below the West Side Highway. To stave off hunger he fills up on bowls of baked beans or macaroni and cheese for twenty cents each at the Automat or crams his pockets with raisins and carrots at the A&P for a quarter. When he looks into a mirror at the entrance of a building on Fifth Avenue, what stares back is "a big-eyed, handsome person, tall as a scarecrow and with the dark, purposeful look of a tireless hunter."

It's as if the city itself has smelled out Joe's vulnerability and pounced. "There was an awareness entering him too momentous to acknowledge: he was a nothing person, a person of no time and no place and no worth to anyone at all."

Desperate for cash, he joins the ranks of male hustlers on the corner of Eighth Avenue and Forty-second Street. After much hesitation, Joe snags a chubby, bespectacled schoolboy, no older then seventeen. The kid, after agreeing to pay him twenty-seven dollars—the sum Joe needs to redeem his suitcase—leads him through the streets of Hell's Kitchen to a rotting tenement. They climb the stinking stairwell to the roof, a haven of sweet smells and clean air. There, "on perhaps the most beautiful night of the year, under the pretty amber light of a harvest moon, an urgent and sorrowful labor took place while Joe Buck stood and waited, trying to concentrate on other matters."

After Joe ejaculates, the kid vomits. But the worst humiliation comes when the kid confesses he has no money. Joe threatens to beat him up and take his expensive-looking watch, but he ends up walking away, a gesture of both kindness and despair.

Just when things have hit bottom, Joe runs into Ratso at a Nedick's coffee shop on Eighth Street in Greenwich Village. At first Joe wants to throttle the little con man, but Ratso offers him a place to stay in a derelict building where he has made a nest. It's a simple transaction: Joe needs shelter, while Ratso, who is suffering from a lung condition that's worsening as the cold weather sets in, needs companionship. And he harbors his own dream: fleeing New York for the warm climes of Florida, where he hopes to regain his health amid the palm trees, orange groves, and sunshine.

The two wary companions are soon a familiar sight on the streets: "the little blond runt, laboring like a broken grasshopper to keep pace with the six-foot tarnished cowboy." Although the story lines are very different, there are overtones here of John Steinbeck's *Of Mice and Men* and the hapless partnership of the streetwise George and the hulking, innocent man-child Lennie.

Ratso mocks Joe's idea that he can make a living from servicing women. Still, he occasionally arranges for Joe to earn a quick five or ten dollars from lonely male customers in Times Square. But Ratso's health is rapidly deteriorating and Joe decides they need to get to Florida straightaway. He hits the streets around Times Square again and picks up Townsend Locke, a nervous, loquacious, middle-aged businessman from the Midwest who takes Joe back to his hotel room. There Joe demands fifty dollars. When Locke resists, Joe slaps him several times, and Locke encourages Joe to hit him again. "Locke cried out, but this time with pleasure." Then Joe looks down and sees "the evidence of the gratification Locke had received."

Joe ransacks Locke's wallet for $121 and starts to leave. But when he looks back he sees Locke picking up the phone. Joe goes back, pushes him to the floor, straddles him, and shoves the telephone receiver into his toothless mouth.

"You didn't kill him, did you?" Ratso asks him later.

"*Shut up, shut up, shut up!*" Joe replies.

Joe carries Ratso to the Port Authority, and they board a Greyhound for Miami. On the way, he discards his cowboy outfit in a trash can. "I'm no kind of a hustler," he confesses to Ratso. "I ain't even a good bum."

But Ratso is too far gone. He dies just as the bus reaches the outskirts of Miami. In a final act of tenderness, Joe "did something he'd always wanted to do from the very beginning, from the very first night he'd met Ratso at Everett's Bar on Broadway: He put his arm around him to hold him for a while, for these last few miles anyway."

Two desperate, lonely souls have found each other under the worst of circumstances in an urban jungle. But only one survives, and his fate is uncertain. *Midnight Cowboy* offers no easy answers nor a happy ending, just a question mark.

Where, exactly, did these characters come from?

On this subject, as on so many others, Jim Herlihy was always elusive. "I met Joe Buck in my head," he told an interviewer, "without ever having seen him in the flesh." There is clearly some of Jim himself in Joe, who is tall, broad-shouldered, and lean, with dark brown hair, same as Jim. They also wear similar clothing: One interviewer in Chicago recalled Jim showing up for lunch in a beige western suit, white shirt, string tie, and English-style Wellington boots. "The tall, slim author sauntered in as if he'd just tied up his horse below the awning on Goethe Street outside the Pump Room," she wrote.

"Yes, Joe Buck is Jamie," says Dick Duane, meaning spiritually. But

Joe is slow-witted and naïve—two characteristics no one would ever identify with Jim.

Dick suspects Jim encountered a Joe Buck figure during his many excursions to Times Square, but says Jim never discussed it with him. "I never asked him about that," says Dick, who helped edit the novel, which is dedicated to him. "He'd disappear for a couple of days. He was a very sexual man. [His disappearances] gave me great pain. But I understood it."

It's also clear that Ratso is, physically at least, an amalgam of people Jim knew. The curly hair, small stature, and gift of gab are somewhat reminiscent of Dick. Jim could have borrowed the limp from his own father, who had permanently damaged his leg in a workplace accident.

"Jamie was always fascinated by people who were slightly grotesque, and a lot of those people he amalgamated into Ratso," says Dick. "That character was so rich (and) vulnerable. . . . Somehow Ratso opened up Jamie to write things he never would have written."

When asked, Jim always remained coy in discussing the origins of the book and the characters. "I didn't want to write *Midnight Cowboy*," he told one interviewer. "I didn't want to write it at all. I thought of that story in 1963 when the character of Joe Buck started waltzing around inside my head, saying little things to me, being there when I closed my eyes. I knew that he could be written but I kept saying to myself, 'I don't want to write this.' Joe Buck wasn't going to have it any other way, so I wrote it."

To another interviewer he said, "I really dig that character, Joe Buck. I like him. I'd like to take a stick to him sometimes, and put my arms around him at others, but I really dig him. The saving grace: an ability to be committed. He has such a commitment to life that he cannot succeed in evil."

Wherever Joe comes from, one thing is clear: Jim Herlihy knew his way around Times Square. The poignant scenes of a homeless Joe surviving on the streets are full of the kinds of details that only a keen observer could have gathered.

Jim knows the art and psychology of cruising the streets for a john. "The trick was adjusting your mind and therefore your entire attitude, physical movements, eyes, etc., to just the right degree of interest-disinterest that would make them come up and talk to you: give them the nerve to, and yet not cause them to lose interest. At that point another skill entered into it: what to say, what not to say, when to close the deal, when to hold out for more."

Jim also understands that Joe is "trade"—a heterosexual man whose appeal to gay customers is his masculinity. Trade is expected to be the sexual aggressor—he can penetrate a customer but he never allows himself to be penetrated.

Jim also knows that the cowboy stud in suede jacket, jeans, and Stetson-style hat is one of the most iconic figures of gay fantasy. Virtually every issue of *Physique Pictorial*, a popular, cheap-paper, four-times-a-year illustrated booklet of black-and-white images of muscular, semi-clothed young beefcake in suggestive poses, displayed a handful of cowboys among its young studs. The back cover of volume 2, number 2 of the first year's set in November 1951 featured "Night in the Desert," a George Quaintance painting of two men lying naked together on the ground and two others stripped to the waist, facing each other provocatively behind a stone wall where two horses are tied to a hitching post. The cover of the first issue of volume 2 showed a naked man soaping up next to a cattle trough while three nearby cowboys watch with various expressions of interest and lust. Another issue that year depicted a bandit holding up a stagecoach and forcing two male passengers to strip off their clothes.

As the *Pictorial*s progressed into the sixties, the art was replaced by photos of young men with cowboy hats, pistols, and holsters, and eventually of men completely naked except for cowboy hats and small loincloths draped strategically over their genitals. By the early seventies the loincloths are gone altogether and a typical western photo has young men wearing just hats, holsters, and cowboy boots while prominently displaying their penises.

Similarly dressed young men, the crotch of their tight jeans stuffed with towels to suggest the bounty beneath, could be found cruising the sidewalks and hovering under the seedy movie marquees on Forty-second Street virtually every night of the week. Dotson Rader, who worked the streets in the early sixties, says the image of the cowboy not only worked for potential johns but also for the hustlers themselves. "When you do the street you think a lot about being a cowboy and about riding the goddam range with Big John Wayne on a horse and sleeping on a blanket with your buddies by a guttering fire with the sky above unblighted by Con Edison light and the muscles tired from honest work," Rader wrote in a semi-autobiographical novel.

He himself sported a black cowboy hat and leather jacket on his excursions to Times Square—it was the outfit he was wearing the first time he met pop artist Andy Warhol in the mid-sixties.

"Are you a real cowboy?" Warhol asked laconically. "Do you have a real six-shooter?"

When Rader said yes, Warhol perked up. "Can I see it?"

"We'll see," Rader replied.

Jim chose the cowboy for symbolic reasons as well. He embraced the idea of taking a quintessential character from the mythic American West of John Wayne and Gary Cooper movies and plopping him down amid the untamed squalor of New York. "The cowboy of American legend was a figure who rode into town tall and brave in his saddle, jaw squared in defense of the True and the Good and the Just," Jim wrote for a publicity brochure issued by his publisher, Simon & Schuster. "In his purity, this creature of high noon cast no shadow at all. But his legend did. And that's the story I hope I've told, of places where the shadow fell, and of the price a culture inevitably pays for the lies and half-truths it tells itself."

Jim entitled the first two drafts of the novel *Midnight Boy*. But one day in Key West Tennessee Williams shared with him his reaction when he first saw the young Marlon Brando rehearsing for *A Streetcar Named Desire* in 1948. Williams described Brando as an "earthy proletarian male" and a "regular midnight cowboy"—gay slang for a male hustler who works the night shift. Herlihy, who likely had heard the term before, proceeded to borrow it.

Jim Herlihy believed *Midnight Cowboy*, which was published in August 1965, was the best thing he'd ever written. But its raw sexuality shocked some readers, including his own mother. Grace Herlihy told her son she thought the book was pornographic. He bristled at her verdict.

Most critics were underwhelmed. *The New York Times Book Review* only gave *Midnight Cowboy* a capsule review and a quick kiss-off. It was as if the reviewer, Martin Levin, had a train to catch and thoughtlessly skimmed the second half of the novel. "Joe Buck is presented not as a caricature of the alienated man but as a sexy cipher exalted at finding someone more insignificant," wrote Levin. "For this revelation to touch the reader, however, Joe and his buddy would have to exhibit more than the eccentricities their author has given them."

But Stanley Kauffmann, the *New York Times* theater reviewer who was soon to become infamous within the gay literary world for his brutal critique of homosexual playwrights, was surprisingly sympathetic to the book. Kauffmann began his piece in *The New York Review of Books* by slamming gay writers who had romanticized "the theme of the young stud's search for communion in the nightworld. . . .

"Do we still need another dumb brute hero?" Kauffmann asked, or "another gallery of grotesques?" But he exonerated *Midnight Cowboy*, praising Jim's "hard and imaginative" prose, and his "unerring and witty sense of the way each of his people speaks." Finally, he praised the author for "the best vernacular-poetic descriptions of intercourse that I have read since Shelby Foote's *Follow Me Down*. . . .

"The accomplishment in this book is small, but it is admirable," Kauffmann concluded.

Emile Capouya, in the *Saturday Review*, announced at the start of his review that he didn't care for grotesque characters—"that literary plague loosened upon us by Sherwood Anderson." But he went on to describe *Midnight Cowboy* as "an appalling story, told with great skill, and important because Joe Buck is a characteristic product of the way we live."

The book's sales were even more lukewarm than the reviews, and Jim felt deeply disappointed. But in the gay literary world, *Midnight Cowboy* was noticed and talked about. By 1967, when a friend first introduced him to the novel, recalls the playwright Mart Crowley, "it was in the zeitgeist. Everybody I knew was reading it and talking about it."

Crowley was a thirty-year-old, unemployed screenwriter kicking around Hollywood, drinking too much and relying on the kindness of friends like the actress Natalie Wood to stay afloat emotionally and financially. He'd written a screenplay for Wood about twin sisters—one straight, the other lesbian—that she wanted to star in, but 20th Century-Fox shot down the idea. Then he wrote *The Decorator*, a television pilot for Bette Davis, with a part for a gay male sidekick to be played by the talented comedian Paul Lynde. ABC recast the sidekick role for a straight woman, then killed the show altogether. After another screenplay was rejected by Paramount, Crowley was dropped by the William Morris talent agency. He desperately needed a break.

Every Sunday around noon he'd buy a *New York Times* and make his way to the Swiss Chalet bar and grill on Rodeo Drive in Beverly Hills, where he'd down bullshots—beef consommé with vodka—order eggs Benedict, and read the newspaper. One Sunday he happened upon Kauffmann's piece "Homosexual Drama and Its Disguises," with its plea for a gay playwright to attempt "to write truthfully of what he knows, rather than to try to transform it to a life he does not know, to the detriment of others."

After struggling unsuccessfully to write and peddle something for a mainstream audience that had even a speck of honesty about gay life, Crowley took Kauffmann's column as a direct challenge. "A lightbulb went off," he recalls. "I thought, Why not?"

Crowley proceeded to write *The Boys in the Band*, perhaps the first openly gay mainstream play, part comedy, part drama, about a birthday party thrown by a bitter, hard-drinking writer named Michael for his good friend Harold. The setting was Michael's comfortable New York apartment, all the invited guests were gay men, and the surprise birthday present was a gay hustler. In his first draft of the play, Crowley had named the hustler Sailor and dressed him in navy togs. But after reading *Midnight Cowboy*, he changed the hustler's name and costume to Cowboy.

"It worked so much better," Crowley recalls. "I think I'd been thinking of Gene Kelly in *On the Town*, but making him a cowboy quickly morphed it into something sexier and darker."

Crowley and his friends in New York and Hollywood weren't the only ones talking about *Midnight Cowboy*. In London, a twenty-eight-year-old American artist named Kaffe Fassett read the novel and was intrigued. He took it to a new friend, John Schlesinger, and told him the story begged to be filmed. But when he rang Schlesinger two weeks later, the answer was no. "I can't get past the second page," John told him. "It's not interesting enough."

Guess I was wrong, Fassett told himself. But then John Schlesinger picked up the book again.

8. THE PRODUCER

Filmmaking, you know, is an enterprise in which ignorance is a tremendous asset.
—Jerome Hellman

John Schlesinger knew *Midnight Cowboy* was risky material. The subject was bleak, the sexual encounters well beyond frank, ranging from just plain sleazy to predatory and violent. The main characters were two unsympathetic losers—an emotionally crippled, not-very-bright faux cowboy from Texas and a slimy, tubercular con man from the Bronx. The novel was divided into two distinct and unwieldy parts—the first half took place in Texas and New Mexico, the second in New York—with Joe Buck the only overarching character. John knew it could be a nightmare to come up with a screenplay covering all that ground. Still, the more he thought about it, the more intrigued he became. He liked the idea of doing a story about a man trying to come to terms with a strange and dangerous new place. Joe Buck's journey was in some ways just like his own. "Even though I haven't had the same sort of fantasies and illusions as Joe Buck, I could sympathize," John said. "I know what it's like to be lonely, and to be a failure."

He first took the book to his longtime producing partner Joe Janni, figuring they would work together as usual. But Janni was appalled by the novel. Joe, a red-blooded Italian, had no problem with making sexy movies, but he felt the blatant homoeroticism of *Midnight Cowboy* would expose John's own homosexuality, subject him to anger and ridicule, and possibly destroy his career. "He thought the idea was terrible," John later recalled. "He said that I would ruin myself with it."

John was deeply disappointed. He and Joe had worked together for almost a decade and had done some exciting movies, and he felt Joe owed him a debt of loyalty. And he wondered: Without Joe, and with the debacle of *Far from the Madding Crowd* fresh in everyone's memory, how could he get any producer of note to work with him on developing *Midnight Cowboy*? Still, there was one man who came to mind, someone who might be both crazy and enterprising enough to go there with him.

Jerome Hellman had first met John in 1964, when Hellman had looked him up during a visit to London. Hellman was thirty-six and just launching a new career as an independent film producer after working for more than a decade as a talent agent. He had been impressed by John's first two features, *A Kind of Loving* and *Billy Liar*, and had hoped to interest him in *Promises in the Dark*, a film Hellman was developing about the romantic adventures of young working women in Manhattan. John liked the idea and he liked the brash, combative, what-the-hell attitude of the cheeky New Yorker who presented it to him, and they signed a contract in late September. But a year later, after finishing *Darling*, John pulled out abruptly, saying he felt the *Promises* script had too much in common with the movie he had just completed.

Hellman didn't argue or get upset, even though he'd waited a year for the chance to work with John. Instead, when John called again almost a year later to say he'd come up with another idea, this one based on a novel about a young man from Texas who comes to New York to seek his fortune as a male hustler, Jerry didn't hesitate. He read the book and gulped hard at its bleak, depressing subject matter and unmistakable gay subtext, but saw some of what John saw: an intriguing central relationship between the naïve young hustler, Joe Buck, and the low-life New Yorker, Ratso Rizzo. "Well, I don't really like the material, but if you want to do it we'll be partners," Jerry told John.

Because the book was full of raw, explicit sex scenes, several of them homosexual, Jerry wanted to be sure that he and John, whom he knew was gay, saw eye to eye about how to deal with the material. When they talked, it became clear that the two men shared a belief that the core of the story was the growing dependence of Joe and Ratso on each other, and that there was nothing sexual about the relationship. John insisted he was not interested in making a "gay" movie, but that he saw enough richness, humor, and intensity in the partnership between Joe and Ratso to make a powerful film. Jerry concurred. The two men also agreed that the Texas–New Mexico opening half of the book, which recounts Joe Buck's troubled childhood and sexual initiation, would need to be compressed as much as possible. Jerry still wasn't crazy about the story, but he jumped at the chance of working with someone with the obvious talent and intelligence of John Schlesinger. In March 1966 they took an option on the novel for five thousand dollars.

Jerry Hellman desperately needed a new project. After many marital battles, his wife of ten years had walked out on him, leaving their comfortable West Coast home in Bel Air and taking their two young children with her back to New York, where she eventually filed for divorce and became engaged to a man who promised the emotional and financial stability that Jerry seemed incapable of providing. His most recent film production, *A Fine Madness* (1966), starring Sean Connery, Joanne Woodward, and Jean Seberg, had flopped both critically and commercially, and he had had to sell the Bel Air house because he could no longer afford the payments. He was, by his own reckoning, "a lifelong depressive who expected everything to end badly," and he struggled some days just to get out of bed. That last morning in Bel Air, he says, "I remember packing my bags, for the last time in my own home, and watching the lovely house recede in the rear window of my taxicab" as he headed to the airport for a flight to New York. Emotionally speaking, Jerry Hellman was one of the walking wounded.

He was a compact man, just clearing five foot six, with a handsome, chiseled face, a pugnacious jaw, a fierce expression that he aimed like a weapon at people he didn't care for, and a well-muscled chest that arrived in a forward strut just before the rest of his body. The walk and the talk all seemed to say *Don't mess with me, I'm a tough customer.* But he carried around a deep secret: the tough guy act was indeed mostly just an act. Deep down, Jerry Hellman was the most insecure person in every room he entered. "I always had my own struggle with my feelings of inadequacy," he says. "That was a big problem in my life."

His other problem was women. He acted like he was catnip to the ladies, although many of the women who met him begged to differ. "I had a whole parade of women in my life," he says, looking back fifty years later at the difficult, hostile man he once was. "I think I was a real asshole."

Born in Brooklyn to working-class Jewish parents, Jerry had served two years in the Marine Corps and came home in 1947 to a twenty-seven-dollar-a-week job as a messenger boy at the New York office of the William Morris talent agency. It was the early days of television, which was largely headquartered in Manhattan, and he moved quickly to the L.A.-based Jaffe Agency, where he rose to become head of the New York talent department. An August 1952 list of his clients for radio and television included Humphrey Bogart (for radio only), Mary Astor, Lloyd Bridges, Farley Granger, Thomas Mitchell, Paul Muni, Merle Oberon, Jack Palance, and Shelley Winters. Jerry's other clients included the actors Hume Cronyn and Jessica Tandy, who became lifelong friends, and the directors George Roy Hill, John Frankenheimer, and Sidney Lumet, all of whom went on to great success, first in television and later in movies. Jerry opened his own office in 1957 and started producing television shows like *The Kaiser Aluminum Hour*, *The Philco Television Playhouse*, and *Goodyear Television Playhouse*, and later *Playhouse 90*. "It was a golden time in my life," he recalls. "Television produced a whole generation of writers, actors, and directors, and it was like working in the theater."

Six years later he sold the agency and became a full-time movie producer. His first feature film was *The World of Henry Orient* (1964), directed by Hill and starring the British comedian Peter Sellers. Two prep school girls in Manhattan develop a mad crush on a sleazy concert pianist and trail him around the city, making mischief while learning about the facts of life. The movie is a charming and humorous ode to a special kind of elite New York childhood as seen through the eyes of two budding adolescents, and it got good reviews and made a profit. Hill went on to become one of the most commercially successful directors of his generation, responsible for *Butch Cassidy and the Sundance Kid* (1969), *The Sting* (1974), and *The World According to Garp* (1982).

Hellman and Schlesinger shopped around *Midnight Cowboy* to various studios, starting with MGM, which contractually had the right of first refusal for John's next film. Someone there suggested that Joe Buck might be a great role for Elvis Presley, provided they could come up with some songs for him to perform and, of course, eliminate the gay overtones. Someone else suggested the gifted entertainer Sammy Davis Jr. for Ratso. John just shook his head in amazement: only in America. It was clear to him that MGM never could or would embrace a film project that genuinely reflected Jim Herlihy's bleak little novel.

Jerry and John discussed reaching out to some of the more independent producers in Hollywood and New York, including Joseph E. Levine at Embassy Pictures, Ray Stark at Seven Artists, and Ely Landau, who had produced *The Pawnbroker*. But Jerry figured that their best chance to get a deal to make *Midnight Cowboy* lay with David Picker, the thirty-five-year-old head of production and marketing at United Artists. Among the major film studios, UA was an outlier. It had been founded in 1919 by four of Hollywood's biggest celebrities: actors Charlie Chaplin, Douglas Fairbanks, and Mary Pickford, and famed director D. W. Griffith. The idea was for the artists themselves to control their own work and build a company that would make money and at the same time honor their artistic sensibilities. Or, as one observer put it at the time, "The lunatics have taken charge of the asylum."

From its earliest days, UA was a shaky enterprise, but the company hobbled along until 1951, when Arthur Krim and Robert Benjamin, two smart, well-connected New York lawyers, bought half of what was left of it for $1.5 million from Pickford and Chaplin, the surviving founders. UA was losing a hundred thousand dollars a week, and the two lawyers made a deal with the owners: if they could turn the studio around and make a profit during any one of their first three years, they could buy the other half of the company for the same price they'd paid for the first half. Thanks in large part to two back-to-back hits, *The African Queen* (1951) and *High Noon* (1952), they accomplished that feat the second year.

All of the major studios were starting to hit economic trouble in the early 1950s, due to shrinking audiences, bloated payrolls, and the vast acreage, buildings, and equipment they owned and maintained. But the reformulated UA had one major advantage over its competitors: it didn't actually own anything. No studio, no real estate, no long-term contracts with expensive movie stars, no equipment or crews. It was basically a middleman, putting up the money for those projects it took on and offering access to a distribution network to make sure the films it financed got into movie houses around the country. UA did individual deals with talented filmmakers and stars, one movie at a time. This vastly limited its financial liability while giving filmmakers freer reign over their work. At a time when the big studios were shedding staff and shrinking output, UA was able to attract some of the best talent in Hollywood, doing onetime contracts with the likes of John Wayne, Frank Sinatra, Burt Lancaster, and Billy Wilder, and distributing hit films like *Marty* (1955), *Around the World in 80 Days* (1956), *The Apartment* (1960), *Elmer Gantry* (1960), and *Irma la Douce* (1963).

The 1960s were a golden era for UA. Krim, Benjamin, and their third partner, Arnold Picker, grew to rely more and more upon David, Arnold's tall, Dartmouth-educated, movie-savvy nephew, and increasingly gave him the freedom to make decisions. With his guidance, the company had a series of hits, including the launch of the James Bond franchise, Tony Richardson's *Tom Jones*, and the two Beatles blockbusters, *A Hard Day's Night* and *Help!* David and his discerning bosses also did deals with Ingmar Bergman, Federico Fellini, François Truffaut, Louis Malle, Sergio Leone, Bernardo Bertolucci, and Claude Lelouch, bringing the work of some of Europe's best filmmakers to American audiences. UA insisted on tight budgets and final script approval, but otherwise its executives trusted the filmmakers they signed to deliver good work. It was a marked contrast to the heads of the big studios, who nervously oversaw each film project and intervened frequently, sometimes with catastrophic results. UA essentially became the *anti*-Hollywood film company. Krim, Benjamin, and Arnold Picker insisted on keeping the company based in New York and ventured to the West Coast as little as possible, leaving that onerous but necessary task to Arnold's enterprising young nephew.

"If we had wanted to make movies ourselves we would have done that, but this is not what this company did," says David Picker. "We reached out to filmmakers whom we were comfortable with and we were inclined to go along with them. We didn't bring them in to do the movies *we* wanted to make, we brought them in to make the movies *they* wanted to make. I did *Persona* because Ingmar Bergmann wanted to do *Persona*.

"We trusted our filmmakers. And we made plenty of mistakes, but quite often we were right."

Ever since he'd first seen *Billy Liar*, Picker had been intrigued by John Schlesinger. *Darling* only made him more eager to sign John. "You can only judge a filmmaker by the work," says Picker. "You look at Schlesinger and you know you're in the hands of a man who knows how to work with film." Picker wanted UA to be the company that financed John's first American film.

John told Picker he had "a dark little book" he was interested in and promptly sent over *Midnight Cowboy*. Picker thought it was hardly a promising prospect commercially. In fact, even before *Midnight Cowboy* had been published, in August 1965, a reader in the story department at UA had read the novel in galleys and done a critical report that concluded, "the action goes steadily downhill." UA, like every other studio or independent producer that had seen the book, took a pass. But having John Schlesinger's name attached made a big difference. Picker was willing to take a chance, provided Hellman and Schlesinger agreed to accept modest salaries and keep costs to a minimum. "We were inclined to go with their choice as long as it satisfied us that it would be made within a budget that he needed and could be cast in a way that worked for him and worked for us," Picker recalls.

Jerry and John agreed to a preliminary budget "not to exceed one million dollars," including fees totaling one hundred thousand dollars for the two of them. The two men would get 60 percent of the net profits if the movie happened to become a hit. The percentage sounded extremely generous except for the fact that no one believed the film would make a dime. Jim Herlihy would receive twenty-five thousand dollars in cash for the rights to his novel, with twenty-five thousand dollars more in deferred compensation, plus 5 percent of the net profits. The contract, which also stipulated that the movie would be filmed in black and white, was signed in November 1966. Picker added the film to his list of projects in development and sent Hellman and Schlesinger on their way to find themselves a scriptwriter.

It wasn't easy. John and Jerry made a short list of the writers they thought might be good. At the top were Gore Vidal and Truman Capote, two of the most celebrated gay novelists in the country, each of whom had experience writing plays and screenplays. John and Jerry's lunch with Vidal at the Plaza Hotel was disheartening. He began by telling them he thought *Midnight Cowboy* was garbage and that they ought to drop the book and instead make a film of his own—*The City and the Pillar*, a much better novel, in his exalted opinion. "We enjoyed a gossipy meal but he was clearly not our writer," John would recall. Capote was equally dismissive of the novel. Jerry and John batted around lots of other names, including Edward Albee, Charles Eastman, Arnold Schulman, and Francis Ford Coppola. Schulman said he liked the book but thought Joe Buck an uninteresting clod and not worth making a movie about. Most all of the others agreed.

One writer they didn't consider was James Leo Herlihy. Despite his playwriting experience, Jim had never written a screenplay. John and Jerry feared he would insist on faithfully preserving the Texas half of the book, something they believed couldn't work on-screen. John sat down with Jim at a Nedick's at Eighth Street and Sixth Avenue in Greenwich Village. Jim was amiable but said he felt the movie version of his novel *All Fall Down* had been a disaster and made clear he was skeptical that *Midnight Cowboy* would fare any better. Although John and Jerry both found Jim likable and sincere, they agreed it would be best not to start down that road.

A few days later they thought they had found their man. Jack Gelber was a personable young playwright who had had a major off-Broadway sensation in 1959 with *The Connection*, an avant-garde, jazz-infused drama about heroin junkies in New York. Produced by the Living Theatre, an experimental drama company, the play ran for 722 performances and was made into a movie directed by Shirley Clarke. *The Connection* was "exciting, dangerous, instructive, and terrifying, all the things theater should be," said Gelber's fellow playwright Edward Albee. These were precisely the qualities Hellman and Schlesinger said they were looking for. Gelber had never had another hit, but he was respected and well-liked around town, as both a writer and a drama teacher, and after a long, relaxed lunch, they decided to hire him. He signed a contract that paid him fifteen thousand dollars for a first draft and five thousand more for a revision if one were needed.

Jerry headed back to Los Angeles, where he moved into a drab rental at a place called the Mediterranean Village. With no work immediately at hand and few solid prospects, he began to slip back into depression—mourning the fact that his two children were in New York with his now ex-wife and her new fiancé. Just when things seemed bleakest, the independent producer Arthur Jacobs, an old pal, got in touch. Jacobs had just returned from London, where he had overseen the production of *Doctor Dolittle*, an old-school musical extravaganza financed by 20th Century-Fox. While working on the film set Jacobs, who was only forty-four, had suffered a heart attack, and his wife and doctors insisted he had to slow down or face lethal consequences. Jacobs said he needed a business partner he admired and could trust, and he offered Jerry a fifty-fifty deal. Jerry jumped at the prospect of having a savvy Hollywood pro to work with and an office on the Fox studio lot to go to every day he was in L.A. He now had time to return to New York and work with Gelber on the screenplay.

The first draft was a disaster.

It starts off with a series of events plucked from the book—Joe gets to New York and meets Cass, the tough New York broad, then meets Ratso, then experiences flashbacks to his traumatic childhood growing up in Texas. But halfway along the script switches gears by moving up a party scene from the book where Joe meets Shirley, a bored young socialite who agrees on a lark to pay him for sex. From that moment, Gelber's screenplay veers away from the novel. Shirley takes Joe to her luxury apartment. "Now Joe," she pleads, "don't hold it against me just because I am rich."

After spending the night with her, he comes back the next evening and she takes him to a Fifth Avenue dance party. While Shirley is in the ladies' room, Joe meets a young woman on the dance floor and tries to entice her to become his next paying customer. Shirley is furious. They go back to her place, where the dialogue begins to read exactly like a bad movie. "You know, I believe I'm getting fond of you," Joe tells her.

"That's a sweet lie, Joe," she replies. "I know this is not going to work out. You know it too."

Shirley sends Joe home to Ratso. But he comes back the next day and offers his exclusive and unlimited sexual services to her for a hundred dollars a week. Outraged and disappointed, she kicks him out. He goes on to meet the pimply kid in the movie theater and Towny, the middle-aged, masochistic businessman. Then Joe and Ratso board the bus for Florida and the novel's tragic conclusion.

John Schlesinger was still in the middle of the *Madding Crowd* film shoot when he got the Gelber draft, and he responded to Jerry with a scathing critique. Gelber had failed to chart Joe's slow decline over a series of challenging experiences in New York. Worse, his screenplay missed altogether the growing emotional dependence between Joe and Ratso. "It is the very essence of what I think the film must be about," John wrote to Jerry. "If this doesn't work, then we have nothing."

John was also very clear about what he *didn't* want. "The day has passed when people are really interested either in 'the swinging city,' seamy or otherwise, or in the mere sexual activities of a leading character. This is certainly not the reason I find the subject an interesting one."

Gelber, longing for further guidance, flew to London in early April of 1967, but John refused to see him, citing exhaustion from the *Madding Crowd* film shoot and the start of postproduction work. Instead he spoke by phone to Gelber, who suggested they eliminate the Ratso character altogether, or at least get rid of his limp—it was just a schmaltzy cliché, Gelber said. John cringed when he heard this, telling Gelber that Ratso had to stay in the story, limp and all. Still, he agreed that Gelber should go ahead with a second draft.

It arrived several weeks later, just as the edit of *Madding Crowd* was finally coming together, freeing John to focus on Gelber's work. He wrote a fifteen-page memo to Jerry coldly dissecting the new draft. While allowing that it was an improvement over the first one ("the order of events is less muddled"), John said, "But I feel we are still far away from the character of Joe Buck." He criticized Gelber's "bitty, meaningless use of dialogue," and various pointless, confusing, or "unfilmic" scenes. "Re-reading the novel at this area, I discovered how much is expressed about Ratso's and Joe's need for each other in their scene in the flat," wrote John. "Infinitely better done in the novel than in the script."

John's patience, never abundant, was at an end. He told Jerry that Gelber had to go. Jerry delivered the bad news in a letter dated July 24, 1967. He tried to let Jack down easy, thanking him for all his hard work but citing the production start date looming at the end of the year. Time was running out. "Under the circumstances," Jerry wrote, "I'm afraid we feel that we have no choice but to try again with a new writer in the hopes that a fresh perspective and a brand-new point of view may help us solve some of the remaining difficulties."

John went back to finishing work on *Madding Crowd*, while Jerry desperately reviewed his list of possible writers. "I felt that if we didn't get a writer soon, John would walk out," said Jerry, just as John had done two years earlier with their earlier project.

John and Jerry were an odd couple. There were times when they positively clicked, each one stoking the optimism, creative instincts, and goodwill of the other. Other times they fed each other's darkest fears about the project's weaknesses and their own inadequacies. "Whenever John was up, he loved I was doing this movie with him," Jerry recalls. "But when he was down he thought that Joe Janni was probably right and that I was leading him to disaster.

"Truth is, I was going through the same thing John was. I didn't know. I hoped people would pay to see this movie, otherwise I'd wasted a couple of years of my life."

George Litto, an aggressive, fast-talking talent agent with a long list of colorful clients and a studio pass that gave him permanent access to the Fox offices and backlot, kept bugging Jerry Hellman to meet one of his writers, a recovering alcoholic turned marijuana enthusiast named Waldo Salt. Jerry looked up Salt's credits—mostly A and B movies in the late thirties and forties, then a decade-long stretch on the Hollywood blacklist because of his Communist Party membership, followed by three confirmed flops in the sixties. Not a very promising résumé, and Jerry said no thanks. But Litto kept insisting. He barged in one day and slapped thirty-six pages of a partial script on Jerry's desk. "The Artful Dodger" was about a hip young dude living hand to mouth on the streets of New York while trying to avoid the draft. Litto begged Hellman to take it home. "Read it," he pleaded, "and if you don't want to meet Waldo Salt I promise I'll never set foot in your office again."

Jerry read it over the weekend and was impressed—as he recalls, it had "the same staccato, multilayered visual treatment I had heard John Schlesinger talk about." When he got back to his office the following Monday, he arranged to meet with Salt that same afternoon.

The man who walked through his office door looked to Jerry like the ancient mariner. Although he hadn't yet turned fifty-three, Salt came across as an elderly, strangely elfin figure, with a mane of wispy graying hair, puffy face, and impossibly large jug ears. "I kept staring at them without meaning to," Jerry recalled.

Litto had given Salt a copy of the book and Gelber's second draft in advance of the meeting, and Salt talked about how much he liked the novel, which immediately set him apart from Gore Vidal, Jack Gelber, and just about every other writer Schlesinger and Hellman had met with. Better still, Salt read aloud to Jerry from a ten-page memo he'd prepared about the book dissecting its main points and qualities, rejecting the approach Gelber's drafts had taken, and describing how Salt thought it could be more effectively adapted for the screen. In his "Notes on *Midnight Cowboy*," Salt started off by observing that "the screenplay seems to miss the exciting potential of the novel . . . primarily because the central character of Joe Buck has been completely lost somewhere in the transition from book to script." Salt proposed going back to the basic structure of the novel and emphasizing Joe's loneliness and his relief at connecting with Ratso, even though he remains deeply suspicious of the Bronx-born con man. "His disillusionment in this case is, in fact, the beginning of a relationship, not the end of it," Salt wrote.

The memo coolly found the beating heart of the novel. It "tells the story of a young man's search for love in the only world he knows, in the only way he knows, according to the values imposed upon him by his particular circumstances. The novel deliberately places Joe in the most corrupt and violent environment, allows him to choose the shabbiest narcissistic means of purpose—quite marvelously, I believe—using the very sordidness of Joe's existence to reveal the depth and desperation of his human need." Salt's memo showed great empathy for Joe and proposed restoring Joe's evolving partnership with Ratso as the emotional center of the film. The narrative structure that Salt proposed closely adhered to the book, starting with Joe dressing himself in his new persona as a cowboy, quitting his job as dishwasher, and heading for New York.

Jerry was hooked by both the man and the memo. He sent a copy to John in London with a note expressing his optimism about working with Salt. John sent back a cable the next day: "Much impressed Waldo Salt notes STOP would engage him immediately STOP off tomorrow love [signed] JOHN."

John Schlesinger and Jerome Hellman stood at a crossroads. Each of them felt he had hit bottom: John because of the embarrassing flop of his expensive new movie—"I was depressed out of my skull," he would recall—and Jerry because of the collapse of his marriage and his gnawing sense of guilt and despair. "I'm not a perfect man," Jerry says, with the benefit of fifty years of hindsight. "I wasn't a perfect producer. I did my best and I hoped that was gonna be good enough."

They didn't know it yet, but by adding Waldo Salt to their team they were taking on another desperate but deeply talented soul.

9. THE SCREENWRITER

A writer is someone to whom writing comes harder than to anybody else.
—Thomas Mann

Just about everyone who met Waldo Salt in the 1960s had the same response to his weathered face with impossibly heavy bags under two deep-set blue eyes, large, floppy ears, wispy graying hair, and crooked nose that looked like it had undergone an encounter with a barroom floor. Underneath the nose was a wary, sweet, almost cherubic smile and a quiet, gentle voice. "He's the sort of man who carries his history in his face," recalled Jim Herlihy.

He was a dedicated writer, a loyal friend, and a generous colleague. But his history was a melancholy one.

Salt grew up in Northern California in a well-to-do but deeply damaged family. His English-born father, a credit manager, was an abusive alcoholic, while his mother was a drug addict prone to writing suicide notes—including a note that young Waldo received one Christmas morning. He often described his harrowing childhood as something out of Eugene O'Neill's *Long Day's Journey into Night*. His parents dispatched him to a private grammar school in British Columbia and then to the San Raphael Military Academy (now known as Marin Academy) north of San Francisco. He attended Stanford University beginning at age seventeen, in 1931. By then he was himself an alcoholic in training—two years later he suffered his first attack of delirium tremens. He wrote and acted in local plays—"the prettiest girls at Stanford were there," he would confess—graduated early, and by 1936 had landed a job as a junior screenwriter at MGM for thirty-five dollars a week. It was still the early days of sound, a time when Hollywood, suddenly desperate for dialogue, dangled serious paychecks in front of writers such as George Bernard Shaw, William Faulkner, Dorothy Parker, Nathanael West, and Lillian Hellman. For a brief period Salt shared an office with F. Scott Fitzgerald.

Speaking of the East Coast writers who came to Hollywood, Salt would recall, "We used to say that it took about ten weeks, or the first option period on their contract, for them to go Hollywood and buy the convertible, the cashmere sports coats, the ascots, and, oh yes, an expensive record changer. That was a big thing then."

For a time he was the boy wonder of the MGM writers' unit, working under the producer Joseph L. Mankiewicz, who was just seven years older. The two men considered themselves young Turks. They didn't care for the industry's new dependence on spoken dialogue, insisting that the artistic essence of movies, whether silent or sound, wasn't words but images. "Dialogue can drive people right out of the movie theater," Salt warned.

Salt and Mankiewicz believed they were working in a revolutionary new art form where they should try to write, in Salt's words, "only in images, if possible, to use the dialogue as you use score, as you use sounds, and as you use the camera." Screenwriting, he insisted, "comes closer to the technique of poetry than to the technique of dramatic writing or novel writing."

One of his first screenplays was *The Shopworn Angel* (1938), a romantic comedy-drama starring James Stewart, Margaret Sullavan, and Walter Pidgeon, and produced by Mankiewicz. Stewart plays a naïve young soldier from Texas who falls in love with a cynical Broadway musical star he meets while in New York preparing to ship off to Europe with the first wave of American soldiers entering World War I. She and her wealthy boyfriend have grown tired of each other and seem headed for a breakup. But the soldier's sincerity and idealism awaken something in each of them and rekindle their love for each other. Still, she agrees to marry the soldier because she wants to give him something to live for, and the boyfriend reluctantly accedes to her plan. In the final scene they learn the soldier has been killed in combat, and they join onlookers in a morose but ultimately spirited rendition of "Pack Up Your Troubles in Your Old Kit Bag and Smile, Smile, Smile." Just reading the plot summary can inspire vertigo. But the jury-rigged little story packs a punch because it's grounded in surprisingly authentic feelings about the meaning of love and loss.

Which was the other part of Salt's artistry. He was fearless about zeroing in on the emotional truth of a scene or a character. "It's very hard to probe into yourself to make yourself face up to your responsibilities with the material," he once said. "To confront the things you don't want to confront. To make the people and the thing as real as you can make them."

He could have been talking about his writing or his life. "We're all born with essential needs, and the methods that we choose to pursue those needs are the things that make for drama."

In a town where integrity was a rare commodity, Salt's was not for sale. When he was assigned to improve a screenplay by his friend Bess Taffel, Salt insisted she get the sole screenwriting credit because, he said, she had done most of the work.

His other obsession was politics. Like a lot of idealistic young screenwriters during the Depression years, Salt veered left when he got to Hollywood. He joined the Communist Party in 1938, on his twenty-fourth birthday, recruited by fellow screenwriter Richard Collins, his closest friend. Collins served as best man at Salt's wedding, in 1942, to the actress Mary Davenport, whom Salt had met at party meetings. Salt was a true believer, recalled Davenport. Their small home on North Kings Road in Hollywood became a clubhouse for party members in the film industry. Even the Hitler-Stalin nonaggression pact, signed in August 1939, just a week before Germany invaded Poland, did not dampen their ardor.

After the United States entered the war, Salt joined the film bureau of the Office of War Information, writing documentaries for the army as a civilian consultant. When the House Committee on Un-American Activities launched its investigation into alleged Communist infiltration of the motion picture industry in 1947, he was one of nineteen "unfriendly witnesses"—current or former members of the party who pledged their refusal to cooperate with what they considered a witch hunt. He never made it to the stand during the committee's hearings in Washington that fall. After the first ten witnesses claimed they were protected by the First Amendment and refused to answer questions, the committee unexpectedly adjourned the proceedings. Salt was deeply disappointed not to be part of the Hollywood Ten—"it's like being on the battlefield and you're spared and the other guys are killed," Mary would recall. After exhausting their legal appeals, the ten went to prison for up to a year for contempt of Congress.

Soon after the hearings ended, representatives of the major studios got together in New York behind closed doors and signed a statement pledging not to hire anyone or retain any current employee who refused to cooperate with the committee's investigation. Once Salt's draft screenplay for MGM was finished, the studio head Dore Schary refused to renew his contract. For a while he got a few assignments quietly sent his way by friends in the business, including screenplays for two swashbuckling action flicks starring Burt Lancaster: *The Flame and the Arrow* (1950), for which he got screenwriting credit, and *The Crimson Pirate* (1952), for which he didn't. Salt brought great energy and a campy sense of humor to both these pictures, and was well paid. His last salary at Norma, Lancaster's independent production company, was $1,250 per week. But he worked under the constant threat of being called before the committee to testify at the new round of hearings it was readying.

The subpoena finally arrived in March 1951. When it was made public, Jack Warner, head of the studio where *The Crimson Pirate* was to be filmed, called Harold Hecht, Lancaster's producing partner, and ordered him to fire Salt immediately. When Hecht pleaded that Salt was still polishing the screenplay, Warner told Hecht to fire him as soon as it was finished.

The Hollywood blacklist was part of the nationwide Red Scare that cost thousands of alleged Communists, sympathizers, and innocent bystanders with liberal leanings their livelihoods and reputations. It shattered families, damaged people's health, and in some cases led to premature death and even suicides. The economic damage was devastating, as was the harm to civil liberties. Even worse in some ways was the intimate personal damage. None of those who were blacklisted expected to be shown mercy or understanding by their political enemies on the committee, or by J. Edgar Hoover's Red-hunting FBI or the Motion Picture Alliance for the Preservation of American Ideals, a right-wing pressure group formed by Hollywood anti-Communists who served as cheerleaders for HUAC and instigators of the purge. But to be shunned and betrayed by your friends and business partners was another matter—deeper, more hurtful, and more lasting.

"Hollywood was like a ghost town," Davenport recalled. "Nobody other than our own dearest friends and comrades would have anything to do with us. Nobody would speak to us. Nobody would have dinner with us. I couldn't even buy meat from the local butcher."

Salt was called to testify in Washington on the morning of April 13. The committee had a copy of his Communist Party registration card and the testimony from the previous day of Richard Collins, who had turned state's witness. Salt could have done so as well. By now the rules of the game were clear. To keep working, he needed to renounce his membership in the party, praise the committee for its courage in exposing the Red Menace, express remorse for what he'd done, and finally—to show his contrition was genuine—name the names of other alleged subversives.

It was far too much for Waldo Salt. In a written statement that he wasn't allowed to read aloud at the hearing, he declared his refusal to cooperate no matter the consequences, and he told congressional investigators that by cutting off his ability to work, they would be cutting into his soul. "This committee has attacked my whole life here, not just a part of it, not just my political opinion," the statement read. "Everything I am, everything I think, derives from my relationship to the film industry since I was twenty years old."

He didn't work again under his own name for eleven years.

Waldo and Mary picked up and left Hollywood for New York in search of work, with their two daughters, six-year-old Jennifer and three-year-old Deborah. They had hoped the blacklist's tentacles were not long enough to stretch across the country. But Waldo's personal demons were. His drinking worsened. "I was very young," Jennifer says, "but you could see it killing him. He took such pride in his work, and it was awful."

For two years they rented an upstairs apartment in Brooklyn Heights from legendary African American historian W. E. B. Du Bois and his wife, the author and playwright Shirley Graham, at 31 Grace Court, a town house owned by playwright Arthur Miller about a mile south of the Brooklyn Bridge. Through Graham, Jennifer and Deborah met other children of accused Communists, including the young sons of the condemned atomic spies Julius and Ethel Rosenberg. Later the Salts moved to the Upper West Side of Manhattan, a neighborhood with a small but cohesive community of leftist screenwriters and playwrights, many of them blacklisted.

Salt desperately tried to revive his career. He became one of twenty-three plaintiffs in the ultimately unsuccessful *Wilson v. Loew's Inc.* lawsuit alleging that the studios had illegally conspired to deny them gainful employment. With his friend the folksinger Earl Robinson, he wrote a folk opera called *Sandhog*, about the workers who built the first tunnel beneath the Hudson River. It played briefly at the Phoenix Theatre off-Broadway. "My memory of him was that he was cranky and difficult and erratic and hard to live with and obsessive," says Jennifer of her father in those early days in New York. "But when there was work involved, he never was depressed."

Waldo and Mary remained in the Communist Party until 1956, when *The New York Times* published the first account of Nikita Khrushchev's secret lecture to the Twentieth Congress of the Soviet Communist Party on the shocking crimes against humanity of Joseph Stalin. Like thousands of their comrades, the Salts were stunned and deeply disillusioned—everything they believed in and had worked for seemed to have been betrayed by Stalin and his henchmen. "It was just absolutely a devastating revelation," Mary recalled.

Most of those who had hung on in the party now left. But like plane crash survivors, many maintained close ties with each other. For one thing, they were all still blacklisted.

The main gig for Waldo and several of his screenwriting comrades was creating scripts for Hannah Weinstein, a left-wing journalist-activist who had moved to London in the early fifties and started her own independent film production company. She created *The Adventures of Robin Hood*, a hit television series on both sides of the Atlantic, and then four more shows in the adventure-swashbuckler genre. She desperately needed good scriptwriters and created a pipeline of blacklisted American talent willing to work fast, professionally, and anonymously for cut-rate wages. She wound up employing more than twenty blacklisted writers, including Salt and his good pals Ian McLellan Hunter and Ring Lardner Jr.—they called themselves "The Unholy Alliance." Admired and trusted by his comrades, Salt served as middleman and broker, negotiating pay scales and deadlines and parceling out the work to his colleagues and himself. The pay was low—at best, writers earned one thousand dollars per teleplay, far less than each of them had made in Hollywood—and the demands were intense. One letter in Salt's files from Peggy Phillips, his contact at the London office, complains about his missing a deadline and then turning in a script that was far too long and contained too many plot complexities. "I am one of your greatest fans here but am constantly on the defensive for scripts like these, so please try to understand my problem," she pleads with him.

Whatever he may have felt, Salt inevitably would reply with consummate professionalism. He signs off a typical letter to one producer: "All questions cheerfully answered. Yours in haste, but without panic, yet . . ."

They all used pseudonyms for their screen credits. Even in liberal Britain, where the blacklist was frowned upon, it was important to be discreet. Most of the big American studios had substantial investments in the British film industry and couldn't be seen to be connected even indirectly to blacklisted writers. Salt's pen name on many of his scripts was M. L. Davenport—Mary's maiden name.

"This opportunity was very important to all of us then," recalled Lardner. "We were completely cut off from the work we had been doing."

Still, tensions at home grew progressively worse. Writing was always painful for Waldo, and to work without distraction he needed a quiet environment with all of his books, notes, and papers at hand. But something always seemed to interfere. Over his desk he kept a saying from the great German novelist Thomas Mann: *A writer is someone to whom writing comes harder than to anybody else.*

At times he would simply disappear for days or even weeks. He would go on binges at his favorite bars, pick fights with other patrons and inevitably with the cops, and end up in the drunk tank until friends located him and bailed him out. By the late 1950s, while Mary and the girls remained in New York, he was mostly living back on the West Coast, scraping by on what work he could get. There were other women in his life. Waldo, whether drunk or sober, always fancied himself a ladies' man and loved being the center of attention. His sense of fun was infectious. "My dad was the kind of person who thought every day was his birthday," says Jennifer.

Occasionally he would send money home. But Mary mostly had to provide for herself and the girls through an endless series of low-paying jobs. She worked behind the counter at the Bonwit Teller department store, as a receptionist for Mount Sinai Hospital, at the Phoenix Pan-American shop, a Mexican imports store, and for the Bil and Cora Baird Marionettes. Scattered among Salt's papers at UCLA are periodic letters from Mary pleading for him to send money for the girls' medical and dental bills and private school tuitions, along with reminders of upcoming birthdays and graduations.

Mary's anguish colors every page. "It has finally become clear to me that if I go on this way I will be torn into such small pieces that I cannot possibly survive," she writes Waldo in an undated, two-page, typewritten, single-spaced letter. She pleads with him to either come back to New York and resume their marriage or break it off for good. She can no longer take the uncertainty. "If you will tell me what you want from me," she concludes, "I'll tell you whether I'm still your wife or not."

"I think my mother was just completely shattered by him," says Jennifer. "By the drinking and the leaving."

Jennifer's own relationship with her father was affectionate but complicated. "He just openly loved me, and he believed in me," she says. "But he was one of those dads who didn't know how to be Dad except by being your best friend. When I first had sex I told him, and when I had my first serious boyfriend we all did things together."

Waldo Salt's slow-building crisis came to a head in the early 1960s, just around the time the blacklist was coming to an end. The Red Scare had burned itself out. Senator Joseph McCarthy had been dead five years from alcohol-related liver disease and no demagogue of equivalent talent and brazenness had risen to take his place. The new Kennedy administration, while still locked in the Cold War nuclear arms race with the Soviet Union, sought to face forward to the New Frontier, striving to leave behind such Red Scare staples as "Who lost China?" Otto Preminger announced in January 1960 that he had hired Dalton Trumbo, one of the original Hollywood Ten, to write the screenplay for *Exodus*, his upcoming blockbuster about the birth of modern Israel. The actor Kirk Douglas announced soon after that Trumbo's name would also appear as screenwriter for *Spartacus*, Douglas's Roman slave revolt epic. A few weeks after he took office in January 1961, President Kennedy and a small entourage attended a showing of *Spartacus* at the Warner Theatre, three blocks from the White House. None of the reporters who tagged along even bothered to ask the president about the significance of his attending a movie written by a blacklisted ex-Commie.

Around this time, Waldo was able to resume writing screenplays under his own name. *Taras Bulba* (1962), *Wild and Wonderful* (1964), and *Flight from Ashiya* (1964) were "three of the worst pictures ever made," in his own frank assessment, one that was shared by many critics. "*Taras Bulba* did more to destroy my career than the blacklist ever did," he would joke, and it was true that nothing seemed to offend him more than his own bad writing.

Soon after, he reached a harrowing moment of truth. He had returned to New York after a long absence and moved into the Paris Hotel, a dormitory for international students on the Upper West Side, at 100th Street and West End Avenue, just a few blocks from where Mary and the girls lived. He had a tiny room on the top floor, with barely enough space for a bed and a narrow window seat. There was an icy draft coming through the window and he was quickly stricken with a high fever. Jennifer's sister, Deborah, who was twelve or thirteen at the time, brought him a pot of hot soup. He was half-delirious and she feared he was dying. He started talking to her about how upset and guilty he felt because he had never made enough money to properly support the family.

Deborah was shaken. Her father had always talked about how important it was to be true to yourself and do what was right. "He didn't sound like the man I knew," she recalled. "So I just said back to him everything he ever said to me."

She told him he was a great artist and a good man and he needed to get back to writing scripts he believed in. If he could do that then he would be a good father as well. "You have to stay true to yourself," she pleaded. "Don't feel bad. The most important thing you could do is to do what you most want to do."

Her words seemed to make a difference. After Waldo's health improved, he started work on a script for *Don Quixote*, the book he had long wanted to make into a movie. He never finished the screenplay—at one point it ran to some three hundred pages—but somehow working on it helped save his life. And elements of it—especially the wary partnership between two totally mismatched characters, the tall, gangly, idealistic Don Quixote full of crazy dreams, and the short, cynical, but devoted Sancho Panza grounded in prosaic practicality—would later find their way into the relationship between Joe Buck and Ratso Rizzo.

"He really did hit bottom," Jennifer recalls. "And I would say that far from being rescued, it was some kind of magical quality in him, some inner drive to be a great writer and do the best work he possibly could do that is what saved him. It certainly wasn't any of us."

"It really shocked me, it really set me back on my heels," Waldo himself recalled. "And I realized I can't blame other people for *Taras Bulba* or the two pictures that came after it, I blame myself. I allowed myself to write less than I could. And I made a vow that I was gonna—goddamn, fuck it, I was gonna write everything as well as I could, and I have deliberately developed a reputation as a slow writer because I am going to write everything as long as it takes to write it."

Then he got a break. George Litto, his loyal agent, who had loaned money to him and a handful of other blacklisted clients when things got desperate and who kept telling Waldo that he still believed in him, heard that Jerry Hellman and John Schlesinger were trying to develop a screenplay from the novel *Midnight Cowboy*. Litto took Waldo to a movie house in Westwood to see Schlesinger's *Billy Liar* and then asked, "Do you want to work with this guy?" Waldo's answer was yes.

Once Jerry Hellman got the okay from Schlesinger, he and Salt spent weeks working on a script. Waldo was a gifted sketch artist, and he would talk his way through their meetings while making odd notes and drawings. There were portraits of people, skeletal narrative bone structures, odd quotations, and other stream-of-consciousness bits and pieces. Jerry loved their wandering conversations. "Waldo seemed wise, intense, and biblical," he recalled. "His concentration was ferocious and his frame of reference broader than that of anyone I had encountered."

"He was probably the most intelligent man I've ever met."

Eventually John and Jerry signed Waldo for thirty thousand dollars. He and John embarked upon an exchange of long letters and memos, and Waldo began sending John a few pages of screenplay. When they finally met in Hollywood, just after the *Madding Crowd* debacle, John was too battered emotionally to engage in small talk.

Fingering a page from Waldo's draft, John's first words were "Why the fuck did you flash back here? This is absolutely ridiculous." Then he paused long enough to add, "Oh, I'm sorry, I like what you're doing very much."

When he first met Waldo Salt, John Schlesinger was a mess, tense, exhausted, and still licking his wounds from *Madding Crowd*. He had no desire to start work on a new project. But Jerry Hellman talked him into renting a modest beach house in Malibu with some of the advance money from United Artists. Each morning Jerry and Waldo would show up and the work would begin. John proposed they start again from page one and produce a true shooting script, which is how they spent the next four months. John would launch most of the sessions with specific ideas of what he was looking for; then, after endless discussion and debate, Waldo would be dispatched to put it all down on paper. Only he never seemed to do so until the last possible moment. Jerry would set arbitrary deadlines to try to cajole Waldo into producing actual written pages, most of which Waldo tended to ignore.

"Writing doesn't take any time at all," he would assure John and Jerry. "It's thinking about *what* to write that takes time." They failed to feel reassured.

At times he and Schlesinger fought like caged animals. "It was a very difficult relationship," John recalled. "I believe Waldo accused me of being a mean and ruthless taskmaster. His catchphrase [was] 'well, it's all in my head,' which meant of course he hadn't written a word."

Hellman found himself in the middle between two large and combustible egos. "They could quickly have come to blows," he says. "Waldo was very reflective, which would really frustrate John, who was much more technical and expected to get what he wanted when he wanted it."

Jerry doesn't remember Waldo ever taking a drink in his presence during those months in Malibu. Instead, marijuana had become Waldo's drug of choice. He would usually begin the day with a joint as fat as a small cigar. But he generally didn't smoke another until late in the afternoon. And no matter how tense things got during the day, the three men often wound down in the late afternoon by trading stories about the "assholes" at MGM, a topic that never failed to amuse and inspire John.

Waldo "always had a long-suffering smile about the way this town treated people when they were down," said John, who had never met a blacklisted writer before. "He had a way of getting angry and sometimes very angry with me, but talking about the past there was a sweetness about him."

There were two things about Waldo that John deeply admired. First was the fact that, unlike almost every other screenwriter he'd talked to, Waldo genuinely loved Jim Herlihy's novel and was happy to work with scenes and dialogue directly from its pages. It was, Waldo said, "a very strong, very powerful, and very moving book." While John and Waldo wound up eliminating most of the novel's Texas scenes, many of Joe's New York experiences remained intact, including Joe's encounters with Cass, Mr. O'Daniel, the nameless gay high school student, Shirley, and Towny, and the sad ending on the bus to Miami.

John also loved the way Waldo burrowed deep into the psyches of the characters. He rained memos on John about Joe and Ratso and their evolving friendship. Waldo was particularly concerned that their growing reliance on each other not descend into a sentimental *Odd Couple*–type relationship in which each makes lighthearted fun of the other's quirks and flaws while deeply bonding. The key to avoiding this, Salt wrote, was to emphasize the genuine conflict between the two men. "Instead of a basically idyllic companionship," he wrote in one of the memos, "there should be conflict and mistrust, held together by mutual need."

Both characters are desperate men, Waldo argued. Ratso knows he is dying and must find a way to get to Florida to stay alive, while Joe is trying to overcome his gnawing sense of despair at the failure of his New York dreams. Nonetheless, wrote Waldo, "He's not ready for a commitment to anyone or anything except self-preservation. The violence in him is real."

The dream of escaping to Florida becomes the focal point of their conflict. It represents a chance at life for Ratso—"not just survival—but a chance for everything he's ever wanted—health, wealth, security, status," wrote Waldo. But Joe resists it, "mistrusting it by instinct because Ratso is overselling it to himself and Joe."

Waldo had another creative concept that John instantly embraced. He wanted to broaden the focus of the film from Joe himself to a critique of modern pop culture. "If the focus remains narrow," he wrote in one memo, "concentrating on the subjective contradiction between the sordid reality of Joe's circumstances and the infantile naivete of his illusions, we miss the real point—that Joe's illusions are in fact the absurd reality of our time . . ."

Waldo swung for the fences with his critique. Joe Buck's world, he wrote, "is a world of king-size illusion." The memo goes on to indict "the bellicose posture of our foreign policy . . . the pripan [*sic*] symbolism of advertising . . . the witch-crushing puritanism of the Establishment's watchdogs . . . the simmering violence . . . the paranoid commercialism which judges value by price."

To capture all of this on film, Waldo wrote, everything must be processed and presented through Joe Buck's own psyche and experiences. We must watch him watch television, listen to the news on his transistor radio, react to New York's garish come-ons, using "sounds, images, random impressions, snatches of dialogue—out of the great mother television box, the whispering transistor radio, the comic strips, movies, animated cartoons, commercials, billboards, etc."

John was intrigued by Perry, the sexy, predatory dope dealer who in the novel seduces Joe and later betrays him. He saw Perry as a naturally cinematic character—a bad-boy Texan version of James Dean—and he didn't want to lose him. But Waldo insisted that Perry had to be scrapped. "The Perry story is quite unnecessary, I feel, even confusing, because it casts a peculiar doubt on the Joe-Ratso relationship," he writes. The reason? "It gives too much importance to the homosexual background . . . The Joe-Ratso relationship is not homosexual." By collaborating with Waldo, John and Jerry steered even further away from any notion that they were making a "gay movie."

Waldo argued that some of the Texas scenes could survive if they were processed directly through Joe's psyche, not as traditional flashbacks but as memories and experiences that Joe was thinking about as we watch them happen. "A flashback is only valid if it's a flash-present," he wrote, mirroring the same technique used by the makers of *Hiroshima mon amour* and *The Pawnbroker*.

Thus, when Joe Buck walks past his late grandmother Sally Buck's closed-down beauty salon near the beginning of the movie, Waldo's screenplay cuts to a brief image of the young Joe rubbing Sally's forehead to help her relax. When passing her house, Joe recalls the moment when his mother deposited him there with a perfunctory goodbye. And at several other points we catch glimpses of the passionate sexual relationship that briefly blossoms between young Joe and Anastasia Pratt and the gang rape that follows when the teenaged Rat Pack discover Joe and Annie making love in an old car outside an abandoned house.

Many viewers have found these moments, scattered throughout the arc of the movie, fragmentary and confusing, but they are meant to be as puzzling and disturbing to us as they are to Joe when he experiences them. And they are faithful to the novel because they keep us inside Joe's head. They are designed to resolve a tricky narrative dilemma while also setting and explaining Joe's mood of loneliness and despair.

The memos from Waldo kept coming: notes on the cemetery scene where Joe and Ratso visit the grave of Ratso's father; notes on a frantic woman's soliloquy at a coffee shop the two men frequent; notes on Joe's encounter with Cass, the hard-bitten woman who is his first failed sexual transaction in New York; notes on Ratso's praise of coconuts as nature's most life-sustaining food. There were eleven different screenplay drafts in all, often with different openings, as Waldo and John struggled to find the right place to begin.

Salt compared the process to a tennis match in which he and Schlesinger tried to hit impossible shots to stretch each other's game. It was frustrating but also exhilarating, and the best experience he'd had in movies since working in the 1930s with Joe Mankiewicz, his first Hollywood mentor. After all the years of pain and suffering, Waldo felt liberated and reinvigorated.

"The memos are beautiful," says Jennifer. "He wanted to dive in all the way, and John did, too. It was a completely unexpected, life-changing experience. He was such a miserable soul, and now he was just so much happier."

As painful as it was to pull actual screenplay pages out of Waldo Salt's typewriter, John and Jerry were optimistic that the process was working. Meanwhile, John found another reason to feel better about his life.

Michael Childers was a twenty-two-year-old film studies major at UCLA when he met John Schlesinger in the fall of 1967. The son of a Marine Corps colonel, Childers had attended sixteen different schools as his family moved from base to base and eventually wound up in North Carolina. When it was time for college, he chose UCLA because it had a film school and, not coincidentally, because it was the farthest possible distance from home. Once he arrived he took film courses faithfully, but photography was his true passion. He was young, gay, and strikingly handsome, with flowing blond hair, and he was keen to make the Hollywood scene. And so when the actress Kaye Ballard was looking for a date for a lonely gay filmmaker friend from London, she phoned Michael.

Childers had seen *Darling* several times, and was keen to meet the man who had made it. But he read a piece in *Time* magazine that portrayed Schlesinger as difficult and mercurial. Just to be safe, Michael invited an actor friend to come along on his date with John at the Oak Bar at the Beverly Wilshire Hotel. "Oh, shit, he's going to be a nightmare," Michael says he warned his friend. "One kick under the table and we're getting out of there."

It didn't happen. John turned out to be charming and funny, asked serious questions about Michael's life and interests, and introduced him to the actress Lee Remick, a friend of John's from London, when she walked by their table. Remick was in Hollywood to begin shooting *The Detective*, and when her costar—Frank Sinatra—came over, she introduced him as well. Michael was amazed—UCLA undergrads seldom got to meet iconic celebrities. He sent his actor friend home and agreed to go to dinner with John.

After a few more dates, John invited Michael for a weekend trip north to Big Sur and Carmel on the glorious Pacific Coast. They stayed at the Tickle Pink Inn, recommended by John's pal Natalie Wood, who said she'd spent two honeymoons there. John and Michael drank too much chardonnay, smoked a joint, and fell in love.

After that, they were inseparable. John insisted that Michael accompany him to every Hollywood party and movie premiere he was invited to. Michael loved the nightlife but felt uneasy with the way some people looked at him at these events. "They saw me as a toy boy," he recalls. John wasn't exactly in the closet, but he wasn't exactly out, either, and the sodomy laws were still on the books in California just as they were in New York and forty-seven other states. "I kept saying, 'Oh, John, you should take Lee Remick or Julie Christie to these parties.' But he said, 'No, no, I'm very proud of our relationship.'"

Michael recalls going to dinner with John one night at the lavish home of Edith Goetz, one of two daughters of Louis B. Mayer, the late MGM mogul. There was gold cutlery on the table, a white-gloved servant behind each dining room chair, and French impressionism on the walls. Rosalind Russell, Norma Shearer, and Myrna Loy were there, the aging queens of Hollywood Past. After dinner, one of the larger oil paintings was raised, revealing a movie screen. They all sat and watched the new John Huston movie, *Reflections in a Golden Eye*, starring Elizabeth Taylor and Marlon Brando. Taylor had a scene in which she was photographed naked from behind. "That's not her ass, that's a stand-in!" someone sneered. "She's got the fattest ass in Beverly Hills!" Michael and John were stunned by the vituperation.

Others in John's rapidly expanding social circle were kinder by nature. He and Michael hung out with the small British colony of gay artists—among them painter David Hockney, novelist Christopher Isherwood, and screenwriter Gavin Lambert.

John had had many romances over the years. Sometimes his heart had been broken, other times he'd been the one to do the breaking. But the relationship with Michael was different. Once it started it never really stopped, although there were many tense and painful times. They weren't always monogamous, but they were loyal. They would continue that way for the rest of John's life.

Soon after they met, John gave Michael a copy of *Midnight Cowboy*. "Is that a John Wayne western?" he asked.

"Hardly, my dear," John replied.

Michael loved the book, but he didn't believe John could find a way to make a mainstream movie out of something so raw and sexual. But he got a front-row seat for the process. John invited him to come each day to Malibu and serve as chef and babysitter for himself, Jerry, and Waldo.

As always with John, social life was an important part of the scene. Jane Fonda and her husband, the French director Roger Vadim, had a place just down the beach. So did Bob Dylan. Two doors down lived the stunningly beautiful British actress Jacqueline Bisset and her very handsome boyfriend, the French-Canadian actor Michael Sarrazin. While playing volleyball on the beach, John told Sarrazin about *Midnight Cowboy*. Sarrazin was intrigued and asked John if he could do a screen test for the part of Joe Buck. John, who thought Sarrazin's innocent open face and smoldering dark looks perfectly fit his own image of Joe, readily agreed.

When it was finally time to go to New York to begin filming, John asked Michael Childers to accompany him and serve as assistant to the director. Michael still had two academic quarters' worth of courses left to complete at UCLA. But he jumped at the chance to get real-life training in New York City. He would scout locations and take still photos of the cast and crew. He would also gather up music for John to consider for the film score. But his most important job was to keep John on an even keel. Jerry Hellman was all in favor of the idea—after *Madding Crowd*, John needed constant cheering up. "I kept him grounded," Michael recalls. "He was always a bit of a manic depressive. And the mood swings. He would go into this rage—'*Oh, my God, what have I gotten myself into?*' For such a gifted man, he had a huge lack of self-confidence, which I found extraordinary."

Hellman loved the 171-page draft screenplay that John and Waldo had developed at the beach house, but he knew there was no way it could be filmed for the $1.1 million budget they had agreed upon with United Artists. He made plans to go to New York and personally present the new script to David Picker at UA. The question of money could be brought up later. Meanwhile, he dropped off a copy to his producing partner, Arthur Jacobs, at 20th Century-Fox.

Jerry's phone rang after midnight. It was Jacobs, sounding distressed and pleading with Jerry to come by his house immediately. When Jerry got there, Jacobs told him that the screenplay was a disaster. The man who had just produced *Doctor Dolittle*, the ultimate shameless children's movie, had no desire to be attached in any possible way to something as tawdry and outrageous as *Midnight Cowboy*. The two men talked until dawn, eventually agreeing to dissolve their partnership—Jacobs surrendered his half ownership of *Midnight Cowboy* to Jerry, and Jerry in turn gave up his half of *Planet of the Apes*, Jacobs's next project.

Jerry was fine with all that. But he had to wonder: What if David Picker had the same panicky response?

10. FUN CITY

The question now is whether we can continue to survive as a city.
—John V. Lindsay

To everyone's surprise—perhaps including his own—David Picker loved the new *Midnight Cowboy* screenplay. "It was extraordinary," he recalled. "A tough, torching script; everything the Gelber script was not."

That was the good news. After which a relieved Jerry Hellman delivered the bad news: there was no way he and John Schlesinger could film this masterpiece of a script, with its many layers and visual images and multiple locations, for one million dollars. Jerry submitted a new budget totaling $2,041,560—double the original cost.

Picker was stunned. He had expected Hellman to press for more money—that's the way things worked in the movie business—but this was far beyond anything he had anticipated. "Sure, a lot of time had gone by, but to me it was still a dark little picture, just one that had a terrific script," Picker would recall. Besides, both he and Jerry knew that whatever the new amount they agreed upon, the final cost would inevitably be higher still. One item in the proposed new budget especially bugged him. Hellman was requesting that UA double to two hundred thousand dollars the fees that he and John Schlesinger would be paid. "I was irritated to say the least," Picker recalled. "I had developed *Midnight Cowboy* with him, stuck with him through another writer, had it pay off with a great script, and now he was fucking with me."

From that moment on, Picker says, he lost faith in Jerry Hellman. "You learn to trust people until you know who you can't trust, and then we don't trust them again," he says. But years of trench warfare in the movie business had also made him somewhat philosophical. "You deal with who you deal with, and if you let it make you crazy you're doing yourself a serious injustice."

In the end Picker approved Hellman's new budget, but with one significant alteration: Schlesinger and Hellman's fees remained at one hundred thousand dollars. As a show of good faith, Picker stuck to the original deal that the two men would get 60 percent of the net profits—in the unlikely event there were any.

Dropped from the original contract was the stipulation that the film be made in black and white. John had loved working with color in *Far from the Madding Crowd* and was intrigued by the chance to capture the garish heart of New York in primary colors. Plus, Jerry had come back from a dinner with the young director Francis Ford Coppola and reported that Coppola had filmed his urban comedy *You're a Big Boy Now* (1966) in color, all around the city, using natural light, even at night.

One other thing they all agreed upon: a New York City movie had to be filmed in New York City, not on some Hollywood soundstage, despite the extra costs that location shooting would inevitably incur. This decision would have a profound impact on the kind of film *Midnight Cowboy* would become.

John Schlesinger's movie did not get off to an auspicious start. A few days after he and Michael Childers arrived in New York City, in early February 1968, the Uniformed Sanitation Men's Association went on strike for seven days, leaving seventy thousand tons of garbage on the streets and sidewalks in rotting drifts and dunes. The Board of Health declared the first citywide health emergency since 1945, while fires originating in garbage rose 700 percent and fears of typhoid, dysentery, and hepatitis spread. It was if New York had been hit by a series of Old Testament afflictions—so much so that a *Time* magazine cover story later in the year would call them the New York City mayor "John Lindsay's Ten Plagues."

In truth, the city had been in a process of protracted deterioration for a decade or more, as its postwar prosperity disintegrated and factories,

manufacturing jobs, and middle-class residents fled like escaped pris-
oners, leaving behind labor unrest, swelling unemployment, and rising
crime. In the decade between 1960 and 1970, total reported crime had
tripled, robberies had risen an amazing elevenfold, and murders, rapes,
and assaults had more than doubled. Even allowing for better reporting methods, it was an extraordinary rampage. "It was a perfect storm,"
says the Columbia University urban historian Kenneth T. Jackson. "The
industries are leaving, the jobs are leaving, the city's budget goes out of
whack, and crime starts to spring up. It's not just broken windows but
abandoned cars, garbage on the sidewalks and the streets; the murder
rate soars. Suddenly, New York doesn't look like the future anymore."

Tall, patrician, and well-groomed, with matinee-idol looks and
Kennedy-esque charm, John V. Lindsay had swept into the mayor's office two years earlier on a reformist platform. He had promised to return
New York to its postwar glory days, only with less public corruption
and more racial equality. But he was greeted on his first day in office—
New Year's Day 1966—with the first citywide transit strike in New York
history. At 5:00 a.m., thirty-three thousand public transport workers
began a walkout that lasted twelve days and cost eight hundred million
dollars to businesses, grinding the city's economy to a semi-halt because
hundreds of thousands of New Yorkers couldn't get to work. The mayor
himself walked four miles that first morning from Gracie Mansion, his
official residence on the Upper East Side, to his city hall office in lower
Manhattan. He did himself no favors when, while viewing the effects
of the transit strike from a helicopter a few days later, he told the *Herald
Tribune* columnist Dick Schaap, "I still think it's a fun city."

The ensuing two years were a slow-motion nervous breakdown.
Schools, social services, air and water quality, transportation, libraries,
parks, public hospitals—all suffered steep declines. Welfare rolls increased over 40 percent. And the fragile social compact that had knitted
people and neighborhoods together and kept every group's particular
grievances in check began to crack. The city was becoming a collection
of warring tribes: whites versus Blacks, middle class versus poor, employers versus unions. Perhaps the most disheartening clash erupted between
unionized teachers and community leaders in Ocean Hill-Brownsville,

a poor, overwhelmingly Black section of Brooklyn. Prodded by Lindsay, the city's central school board had granted limited autonomy to the local school district in the name of citizen participation and accountability. The local board quickly moved to fire or transfer eighty-three allegedly underperforming teachers, all of them white and most of them Jewish, triggering a strike by the United Federation of Teachers in May 1968 that eventually spread citywide and caused one million children to miss school. Police and firefighters also staged slowdowns and threatened strikes of their own. Later that year, a walkout by fuel deliverers and oil-burner servicemen left thousands of New Yorkers without heat as winter drew near, and led the Board of Health to declare the city in "a state of imminent peril." "The ordinary New York resident," complained the *New Yorker* humorist S. J. Perelman, "is constantly on trial for something the nature of which he doesn't understand."

It was as if a large portion of New York's people had lost faith in the city and in themselves as well. Yes, it was a place where various groups fought for equal rights and an equitable share of wealth and opportunity. But it was also supposed to be a place where they could come together out of mutual experience and respect. They were, after all, New Yorkers. But the very meaning of the city had come unraveled.

Besides an epidemic of street crime, there was the specter of urban unrest and political violence. Two blocks east of Jim Herlihy's apartment on Seventh Street, in the East Village, hippies and druggies squared off against the Tactical Police Force (TPF)—New York's elite riot squad—in Tompkins Square Park in the summer of 1967. Riots broke out in East Harlem, the South Bronx, Bedford-Stuyvesant in Brooklyn, and even in midtown Manhattan following an outdoor concert featuring Smokey Robinson and the Miracles. Later that year there were week-long antiwar protests that started outside the federal draft induction center on Whitehall Street, in lower Manhattan, and spread uptown to city hall and Union Square, with face-offs between police and protestors and serious property damage.

By now the cops themselves had become another armed street gang, defending its turf and dispensing its own brand of justice and retribution against rival tribes. The overwhelmingly white police force, riddled with

nepotism, corruption, and blue-collar resentment of the liberal, pluto-
cratic mayor, lashed out against radicals, hippies, and Black- and brown-
skinned demonstrators.

The TPF was dispatched to Columbia University in the early morning
hours of April 30, 1968—the day after the *Midnight Cowboy* film
shoot began—to evict hundreds of students, faculty members, and community activists occupying four classroom buildings and the university
president's office. They were protesting the university's plans to build a
private gymnasium on public parkland in predominately Black Harlem,
as well as its participation in U.S.-government-funded defense research.
The university administration had hoped that an early morning police
action could clear the buildings without violence, but the cops themselves had other ideas. After being cooped up for several days and nights
in buses parked off the campus while awaiting orders to move in, the
police were eager to teach the long-haired, overprivileged "pukes" on
campus a lesson in working-class anger. When the orders to take up
"hats and bats" came, helmeted TPF officers and plainclothes policemen
in leather jackets waded into groups of protesters and bystanders swinging nightsticks. More than seven hundred people were arrested and 148
were injured, including twenty policemen.

Mayor Lindsay went to Washington that summer to plead for fifty
billion dollars in new federal funding for urban renewal over a ten-year
period. He came home empty-handed and angry. "This nation doesn't
give a damn about its cities," he told reporters.

Besides crime, unemployment, and political negligence, New York in
the late sixties was also experiencing an unprecedented cultural explosion of sexual expression and permissiveness in theater, music, literature,
and film. "Artists have been breaking sex taboos from the beginning of
time," wrote the cultural journalist Robert Hofler, "but probably no greater
number of those totems to repression were smashed than in the year
1968." What's more, the smashing of the taboos was extremely profitable
for many of the artists and entrepreneurs involved.

Mart Crowley's *The Boys in the Band*, which opened off-Broadway that January, treated homosexuality as a suitable subject for humor and drama without condescension or condemnation. It was an immediate hit. The musical *Hair*, a pop-rock celebration of hippies, long hair, free love, miscegenation, astrology, and pacifism that began at Joseph Papp's Public Theater in October 1967, transferred to Broadway in April 1968. It featured a rather chaste group nude scene that climaxed Act I and songs extolling the pleasures of sodomy, hashish, and other banned sexual practices and pharmaceuticals. The Broadway production sold out quickly and ran for four years, and several of its songs became hit singles. The original cast album sold nearly three million copies in just over a year.

Books written by celebrated mainstream authors and issued by long-established publishers were also crashing through boundaries of taste and sexual adventurism. Gore Vidal's *Myra Breckinridge*, released in February 1968 by Little, Brown, one of the East Coast's most respected publishing houses, became an instant bestseller. It is a spirited fantasy tale of a professor who changes his gender and goes to Hollywood, where the former he, now a she, straps on a dildo and sodomizes a young actor. The book, which the *New York Times* critic Eliot Fremont-Smith described as "a funny novel [that] requires an iron stomach," spent thirty weeks on the bestseller list. Vidal, who never missed an opportunity to settle an old score, later claimed that Myra's voice "was actually that of Anaïs Nin in all the flowing megalomania of the diaries."

One of the novels that finally nudged *Myra Breckinridge* off the bestseller list was *Couples*, John Updike's morose and coldly clinical account of lust and adultery among young married couples who trade sex partners and neuroses in Tarbox, a fictional suburb twenty miles south of Boston, published by Alfred A. Knopf. "I was sort of a crusader, in a way," Updike explained to one interviewer, "trying to make the reader read explicit sex: this is what sex is, dear reader, take it or leave it." *Portnoy's Complaint* by Philip Roth, published by Random House the following January, an ode to sexual obsession, masturbation, and parental dysfunction, was lewder, funnier, and more entertaining than Updike's buttoned-down, all-WASP affair. It outraged the American Jewish establishment, which hated to see dirty laundry exposed on the national clothesline and accused Roth of being a self-loathing anti-Semite. No matter. The book sold four hundred thousand copies its first year.

Despite the collapse of the Production Code and its replacement by a ratings system that was supposed to allow for more adult themes, mainstream commercial movies approached the borderlands of sexual expression with far more trepidation than books. One notable exception was Antonioni's *Blow-Up*. In one of their last official acts, Production Code administrators insisted on cuts in scenes involving nudity and sexual intercourse. But MGM refused, sidestepping—and mocking—the process by releasing the film through a subsidiary company. It was as if the Production Code had decided to stage its own funeral.

One of the things John Lindsay did accomplish in his first year in office was to create the Mayor's Office of Film, Theatre, and Broadcasting to encourage commercial film production in the city and ease some of the obstacles holding it back. Before the office was established, producers needed up to fifty permits to shoot on location in New York and were required to obtain separate permits for each day of work. While the Department of Commerce and Industrial Development issued the basic permit, producers also needed approvals from the police, highway, and transportation departments, as well as permission from the Department of Water Supply, Gas, and Electricity for use of wires and cables. Lindsay, in keeping with a campaign promise, authorized the Department of Commerce to issue a single all-purpose permit for shooting in city-owned locations and ordered city officials not to attempt to censor the content of films shot on public property. The new film office—which Lindsay declared the first of its kind in the United States—was tasked with helping producers negotiate cooperation from local labor unions and owners of privately owned properties, and with coordinating with a small police unit to control crowds at location sites. At a time when manufacturing jobs were fleeing the city, New York went from hosting only two feature films shot in their entirety in the city in 1965 to 366 during the eight years of the Lindsay administration.

Jerry Hellman welcomed the change. He had had a less-than-fond experience while shooting his first two films—*The World of Henry Orient* and *A Fine Madness*—in New York. During the film shoot for *Henry Orient*, he hired a production assistant whose principal job was to keep wads of cash on hand to pay off each police squad car that came by while the cast and crew were on location. "He used to sit around with his pockets bulging with cash," Jerry recalls. "It was a fucking nightmare. There was no central office and no cooperation."

This time was different. There was someone from the mayor's office whose phone number Jerry could call at any time. All kinds of permits were issued on short notice. While the cops who came by at lunchtime were still treated to a free meal in the catering facility, no money changed hands. "We really had broad and comprehensive support," Jerry says.

The early film industry had gotten its start in New York and across the Hudson River in nearby Fort Lee, New Jersey, and even after most of the studios left for the West Coast, New York stories were a major source of material for Hollywood. Films like *The Lost Weekend* (1945), *Naked City* (1948), *On the Waterfront* (1954), *The Sweet Smell of Success* (1957), *West Side Story* (1961), and *Barefoot in the Park* (1967) were generally medium-to-large-budget enterprises hampered by the high cost of hauling heavy cameras, sound trucks, lighting, and other equipment around the city. But by the late sixties the technology of moviemaking had changed. Smaller, more mobile cameras and faster film stock allowed nighttime images to be captured with far less artificial lighting. They helped open up the city to lower-budget productions and more experimental film shoots with hand-held cameras and documentary-film techniques. The slow economic collapse of many of the Hollywood studios also made New York more attractive and affordable. The home of the second-largest and -wealthiest branch of the entertainment industry after Los Angeles now boasted two generations of filmmakers, from Sidney Lumet, Paul Mazursky, Shirley Clarke, and John Cassavetes to Woody Allen, Francis Ford Coppola, Martin Scorsese, and Brian De Palma, all of whom considered New York their home turf and knew how to operate there. New York University's film program, oriented toward guerrilla-style shooting on the city's streets, sidewalks, and rooftops, came to rival the better-known and better-funded film departments at UCLA and the University of Southern California.

These filmmakers' movies were not just made *in* New York, they were increasingly *about* the city's decline. And even while they gave the city's economy a boost, they often painted a stark portrait of a troubled and decaying urban landscape.

"The city of New York has helped American movies grow up; it has also given movies a new spirit of nervous, anxious hopelessness, which is the true spirit of New York," wrote *The New Yorker*'s Pauline Kael. "The movies have captured the soul of this city in a way that goes beyond simple notions of realism. The panhandler in the movie who jostles the hero looks just like one who jostles you as you leave the movie theatre; the police sirens in the movie are screaming outside; the hookers and junkies in the freak show on the screen are indistinguishable from ones in the freak show on the streets."

City officials were well aware of the irony. After he became New York City's Police Commissioner in 1973, Donald F. Cawley complained that movies were increasingly portraying the city's cops as "insensitive, incompetent, coarse, and corrupt," and said he was disturbed because those portraits "do not reflect the type of police officer we have." But Cawley's boss was adamant. "I feel very strongly about the First Amendment," said John Lindsay. "I feel every filmmaker has the right to say what he wants."

After two years of gestation, Hellman, Schlesinger, and United Artists were keen to get the *Midnight Cowboy* film shoot started by late April so that the movie could be edited, scored, and released by the following spring. The first person Jerry hired was Kenneth Utt, a veteran associate producer, who went to work lining up New York locations, booking studio time for interior shots, putting together an overall shooting schedule not just for New York but for Florida and Texas as well, and keeping track of what it would all cost.

The other position they needed to fill quickly was a casting director.

A decade earlier this would not have been an issue. The major studios had all kept a large stable of actors on their payrolls, many of them on long-term contracts, and each studio also employed a small group of casting directors whose job was to assign the available personnel to the available roles. The studio heads, their designated producer, and sometimes, but not always, the director picked the two or three leading men and women for starring roles. Then the casting director would fill the other parts with whoever was available at the time. It often didn't much matter if the actors were a perfect fit for their roles. What mattered more was that they had a pulse and a voice, and brains enough to memorize and deliver their lines.

The collapse of the studio system meant no more in-house collections of talent and a sudden need for casting directors who actually knew something about actors and acting and could line up the right people for the roles that needed filling. Lynn Stalmaster, who cast both *Gunsmoke* and *Have Gun—Will Travel*—the two great back-to-back Saturday night television westerns on CBS—became the go-to person on the West Coast. And a tall, brown-eyed, chain-smoking woman who set up shop in a run-down Victorian-era brownstone at 153 East Thirtieth Street in Manhattan became his New York counterpart.

Marion Caroline Dougherty was born outside Hollidaysburg, Pennsylvania—gossip columnist Hedda Hopper's hometown—in February 1923. Her father owned the local hardware store until the Depression put him into bankruptcy and he was forced to become a traveling salesman. His daughter learned early on from his example what it was like to work hard yet fail. She went to Penn State on a scholarship, then to the Cleveland Playhouse to study acting, and finally—like so many others who played a crucial role in the making of *Midnight Cowboy*—she came to New York with dreams of working in show business, arriving in the mid-1940s. Her first job was designing shop windows for Bergdorf Goodman for forty-five dollars a week. She lived with three other women in a fifth-floor walk-up beneath the Fifty-ninth Street Bridge. Eventually she lucked into a job as an assistant to the casting director for

NBC's *Kraft Television Theatre*, one of the earliest and most prestigious weekly drama shows of the first golden age of television.

Dougherty's subsequent rise was based on much more than luck. From the beginning she had a feel for actors, their abilities and their insecurities, and strong convictions about which actor would work best for which role. After three years she rose to be the casting director of all Kraft productions. Her list of young hires included Paul Newman, James Dean, Jack Lemmon, Walter Matthau, Lee Remick, George C. Scott, Lee Marvin, Maureen Stapleton, Joanne Woodward, and twenty-two-year-old Warren Beatty, of whom she said, "I think I understood about every third or fourth sentence that came out of his mouth."

Early on she developed a rudimentary system of three-by-five index cards to keep track of all the young talent coming through her door. There was one card for each actor she saw, with notes scrawled in barely legible pencil. As time went on, she would add further comments in the remaining space, then flip the card over and start on the back. She minced few words. Jon Voight's card, for example, first dated May 1962, when he was twenty-three, was dubious: "Appealing, clean-cut American kid—would see as very normal high school student—maybe shy—wouldn't think he'd be good for great emotion . . . only surly."

In 1959 she took over casting *The Play of the Week*, a new anthology series, sharing duties with Marc Merson. One of her coups was to cast Robert Redford and Jason Robards Jr. for a production of Eugene O'Neill's *The Iceman Cometh*. But on the night of the program, Merson's name was the only one on the screen credit—hers had vanished. She was told it was a mistake, but soon discovered the truth: "Marc Merson had simply erased my name from the credit and written in his own instead." It was a bitter lesson in power and male privilege. Dougherty quit soon after and went to work casting *Naked City* for ABC. One of the young actors she hired was, as she described him, an "eager, gifted, prominent-nosed, pompadour-haired kid." It was Dustin Hoffman's first on-camera role.

She got Voight a role in a different *Naked City* episode in March 1963. He plays a young man whose father has been inexplicably beaten to death while parking his car in New York. The son and his mother are summoned to the scene, where they see the body of the dead man in the back of an ambulance. The mother collapses on the pavement while the son bursts into angry, bewildered tears. Voight overdoes it, hunching his shoulders, clasping his hands together, his eyes half-closed as he moans in horror, his voice cracking in grief. The performance "wasn't for real," recalled Ralph Senensky, who directed the episode. "It was forced. He was pushing. It was an actor in training." Marion Dougherty's cautionary "wouldn't think he'd be good for great emotion" proved all too accurate.

Voight himself was suitably mortified. "I thought, This is it," he recalled. "This is the end of the road, you'll never get another job. I was so bad I was physically sick. I sat down and wrote Dougherty a letter saying, 'I'm sorry, Marion, I let you down.' I must have written six letters but I ripped them up. I couldn't send them." He didn't hear from her for a while.

Dougherty could be feisty and opinionated. "Hollywood had no idea what casting was all about," she said. "They were looking for movie stars, not actors." But she also knew how to coddle the talent. "It really is like psychotherapy," she told an interviewer. "You have to appreciate people whether they're nice people or not. You meet a lot of actors who are not that likable, but you have to put that aside even if they have a huge ego and they annoy you."

Dougherty quickly developed her own set of rules for casting movies. She understood that actors were sensitive people—after all, their lives seemed governed by constant cattle calls for auditions and endless rejections. To calm them down and prepare them to do their best, she tried to provide them with as much information as possible about the role they were trying out for. "That welcoming quality was the kind of graciousness she extended to actors and directors," says Juliet Taylor, one of her original assistants, who herself went on to become one of Hollywood's most esteemed casting directors.

Actors loved her. The stories of her going to battle for performers she believed in were voluminous. Robert Redford was typical. He recalled how Dougherty persuaded the director Sidney Lumet to cast him for *The Iceman Cometh*. "Lumet didn't want me," Redford recalled almost sixty years later. "'No, he looks like a beach bum from California.' Lumet wasn't having it, and Marion sat there and said, 'Trust me.'"

Directors often wanted to see ten or twelve people per role. But Dougherty as a rule would send no more than three or four, and her selected candidates would often be very different physical types. Any of them could play the part, she insisted, and she wanted the director and producer to see the variations of what was possible. Some of the actors might present a polished performance in an audition but weren't capable of growing into a character. What you see now from this person is all you will ever get, she would warn. Whereas other actors who seemed uncertain in a tryout might well develop a more nuanced and complex performance over time. Actors like Rod Steiger, Gene Hackman, Robert Duvall, and Dustin Hoffman were famous for "searching" for their characters over the course of many rehearsals.

"No casting director can truly say, 'I knew he was gonna be a star'— because that's a bunch of baloney," Dougherty once said. "Casting is a game of gut instinct. You feel their talent and potential in the pit of your stomach. It's about guts and luck."

When it came to the entertainment business, New York was a collection of small villages. Almost all of the offices for theater people were bunched around Times Square and Broadway, while the film people were largely on Fifty-seventh Street. But Marion Dougherty Associates ventured out into the wilderness south of Forty-second Street. She rented an ancient brownstone on East Thirtieth Street between Lexington and Third Avenues, stripped the linoleum to expose hardwood floors, scraped the paint off a marble fireplace and old-fashioned plaster walls, and added Victorian-style flocked wallpaper and stuffed chairs and sofas to make the place feel homey and comfortable.

To help with the rent she sublet rooms to friends. The aspiring young screenwriter Steve Tesich (who later wrote Breaking Away and The World According to Garp) lived upstairs, while an agent named Bill Treusch occupied the basement office, near the furnace room. His clients included Diane Keaton, Sissy Spacek, Carol Kane, and Christopher Walken, all of whom seemed to be perpetually wafting up and down the stairs to harass their agent and troll for news of potential parts.

Dougherty was a proto-feminist, although Taylor says she never thought of herself as one. She hired only women to work in her office, not to make a political point, she said, but because she wasn't comfortable giving orders to men. At one point 153 East Thirtieth was nicknamed "The Brothel" because all of the people working there were women. She stayed with her abusive, alcoholic husband, who sponged off her, for more than a decade, until she finally dumped him and became involved with the director George Roy Hill, a longtime friend. And she became a major figure and mentor to younger women in a field that was often overlooked and underappreciated, despite being essential to the success of every movie.

The majority of casting directors then and now were women. "Marion would say it's because we don't get paid enough," says Taylor, who was a recent Smith College graduate when she went to work for Dougherty as a secretary-assistant in the spring of 1968. "And casting director was a new position and considered dispensable. There were certain film directors who didn't even use them. It was certainly true when I started out that most men who became good at casting usually moved on to do other things."

Jerry Hellman and George Roy Hill had both worked with Dougherty in casting television programs in the 1950s, and they hired her as casting director for their first feature film, *The World of Henry Orient* (1963), produced by Hellman and directed by Hill. Next, Hill brought her with him on location when he made the epic *Hawaii* (1966) for the Mirisch Company and United Artists. Dougherty cast a very young Bette Midler as one of the missionary children, but insisted she wear a bonnet "so you don't look too Jewish." Midler moved to New York with the money she earned and launched her singing career in the gay bathhouses of Manhattan. Meanwhile, when *Hawaii* ran so far over schedule and budget that UA decided to fire Hill, Dougherty announced she was quitting and took with her all of the files she'd compiled on local actors. The producers would have had to start from scratch to recast dozens of parts. Hill kept his job. And David Picker said he learned not to mess with Marion Dougherty.

After *Henry Orient* there was little movie work in New York until 1966, when John Lindsay opened the mayor's film office. Business soon began to pick up. "Marion's phone was ringing off the hook because everybody wanted to hire her," says Taylor.

It was a time of great creativity. Foreign filmmakers were flooding into New York and Hollywood—Roman Polanski, Louis Malle, Miloš Forman, and Tony Richardson, to name but a few. They came seeking bigger budgets, better equipment, and name-brand actors, and many who passed through town sought out Dougherty. Taylor recalls giving up her Memorial Day weekend to vacuum the floors and empty the ashtrays for the impending visit of Michelangelo Antonioni, who was looking to cast *Zabriskie Point*, his first (and last) American movie.

John Schlesinger, a former actor himself, had a sterling reputation as an actor's director. But John had never before shot a film outside the United Kingdom and he knew little if anything about American actors. Jerry Hellman understood that Marion Dougherty could be crucial to the success of *Midnight Cowboy*.

11. THE VOICE OF HIS GENERATION

Actors are a much hardier breed than any other people. We have to be as clever as rats to survive.
—Maureen Stapleton

Looking back, the pairing of Jon Voight and Dustin Hoffman to play Joe Buck and Ratso Rizzo seems blatantly obvious: the tall, blond Voight as a modern-day Don Quixote tilting at imaginary windmills on the mean streets of New York, and the short, dark-haired Hoffman as Sancho Panza. But the choice of neither actor was clearcut at the time. For one thing, in the novel Ratso is the blond and Joe the dark-haired one. In truth, John Schlesinger originally didn't want either Voight or Hoffman in his movie, and looked far and wide for alternatives.

Jerry Hellman says he first heard about Hoffman from Jack Gelber, the playwright he'd originally hired to write the *Midnight Cowboy* screenplay. In the fall of 1966, while the two men worked on the first draft, Gelber insisted on taking Hellman to the off-Broadway theater Circle in the Square to see an obscure British farce called *Eh?* Hoffman played the main character, a maniacal young Liverpool janitor pushing a broom around the boiler room in the basement of a dye factory. He was hilarious doing snappy dialogue and physical comedy—so good that the *New York Times* reviewer Eliot Fremont-Smith called him "one of the most agile and subtly controlled comedians around," and Walter Kerr, the uncrowned sovereign of New York theater critics, compared him to a young Buster Keaton.

Jerry was sold. "Everything about him struck me as being right for Ratso Rizzo," he recalls. "His shuffle, his thick neck, his whole physical appearance, which, of course, was his performance as much as his reality." The next day, Jerry called Hoffman's agent, Jane Oliver, of the Ashley-Famous talent agency, to find out more about this kid he'd never heard of.

Dustin Hoffman, it turned out, was no kid—he was twenty-nine years old and had been kicking around New York for almost a decade, trying, with painfully limited success, to make a living as an actor. Born and raised in Los Angeles, Hoffman as a teenager was short, acne-scarred, and in possession of a profoundly large nose and what one observer called "thatched-roof hair." His parents married young—neither of them finished high school—and there was never much money. They moved from place to place, and for a while during the Depression the family existed on welfare. "They were so young, so poor, and the world in which they were living was a pretty tough place," Ron Hoffman, Dustin's older brother, recalls. Dustin described it as a loveless upbringing. "I really think my brother and I grew up in a house with two people who should not have had children," he told an interviewer in 2009.

Harry Hoffman worked as a prop man at Columbia Pictures for a time, then sold furniture for a living. Lillian Hoffman named her first child after Ronald Colman, and Dustin, born six years later, had the same first name as Dustin Farnum, the silent-movie cowboy star. Lillian made Ron take tap dance lessons and gave Dustin piano lessons herself. Ron remembers Dustin sitting on the piano bench at around age five, with his mother yelling at him when he made a mistake. After three mistakes she would smack him. "Those were unpleasant moments and usually took place before dinner," Ron recalls.

From his earliest days, it was Dustin against the world. He was an indifferent student, a social outcast, and a frequent object of derision—other boys mocked his face and his height—but he was funny, strong-willed, and tougher than he looked. His grades weren't good enough for admission to a four-year college, so he wound up studying music at Santa Monica City College, a well-regarded two-year school. Even there, he was in danger of flunking out during his first year, when a friend suggested he take an acting course for an easy three credits. "It's like gym—nobody flunks," the friend told him. To his surprise, Hoffman fell in love with acting and decided to drop music and enroll at the Pasadena Playhouse, the same drama school where Jim Herlihy had studied acting and playwriting a half dozen years earlier. Dustin felt like a mole among the tall, blond Tab Hunter types—"walking surfboards," he called them—but found an acting teacher who pushed and encouraged him and helped him gain confidence. And like Herlihy had done six years earlier, Hoffman eventually made his way to New York in 1958. "I took a bus from the airport to somewhere on the East Side, and when I got out I remember seeing a guy pissing on the tire of a bus in broad daylight," he says. "New York was exciting, but it was a tough place."

Dustin was so shaken by the city, he recalls, that he spent the first three weeks holed up in the two-room apartment of his Pasadena Playhouse pal Gene Hackman and Gene's exceptionally tolerant wife, Faye. He slept on their kitchen floor. At their desperate urging, he finally moved into a sixth-floor walk-up on West 109th Street with another aspiring young actor, Robert Duvall. Hoffman recalls Duvall drying his laundry in the oven and sometimes burning his underwear. Harry and Lillian sent their son money those first few years to help him get by.

Just as New York in the fifties was a magnet for aspiring novelists and playwrights, it also attracted hundreds and hundreds of young people seeking to follow in the footsteps of Marlon Brando, Montgomery Clift, James Dean, Paul Newman, Geraldine Page, Julie Harris, Jessica Tandy, and Kim Stanley. "Any actor who was around then was driven," recalls Robert Walden, a New York–born performer who became friends with Hoffman in the early sixties. "There was a tremendous amount of hunger, appetite, and talent."

Walden met Hoffman at Lee Strasberg's Actors Studio, one of the elite training grounds for aspiring performers and home of the Method school of acting. Hoffman says he got turned down five times before he was allowed to take a class with the legendary Strasberg. Meanwhile, Hackman worked with George Morrison, another respected acting teacher, and Duvall was accepted at the Neighborhood Playhouse, which was led by the highly esteemed Sanford Meisner. Lean, hungry, and intense, Duvall was a favorite of Meisner's, who called him "the next Marlon Brando."

In the mythic version of Dustin Hoffman's early New York years, he was a hopeless ugly duckling who had no luck landing parts and no chance of ever becoming a successful actor. And it's true he was no one's idea of what a star should look like. Among other problems, he looked much too Jewish at a time when ethnic-looking actors had little or no chance at stardom—his pal Duvall said he looked like "Barbra Streisand in drag." Ron Hoffman remembers their aunt Pearl, married to their father's brother Eddie, blurting out to her nephew, "Be an actor? You're too homely."

He could be moody, demanding, and self-centered, storming out of auditions when he decided the people in charge weren't paying proper attention or taking him seriously. The first time Streisand, herself an unknown, aspiring actress, saw him, he was riding away from the Actors Studio on his motor scooter. She turned to a friend and asked, "Who's that?" The friend replied, "Oh, that's Dustin Hoffman, he's very hostile but talented."

Still, he had a raucous sense of humor—once, while working as a toy demonstrator at Macy's, he almost convinced a woman customer to buy Hackman's infant son, who was propped up on the sales counter looking like an eerily authentic doll. Hoffman and Duvall had a well-earned reputation for zany behavior and for hitting on every attractive waitress, salesgirl, and aspiring actress they met, and Hoffman, who was an excellent piano player, charmed women with his musical talent. Dustin "had more girls than Namath ever had," Duvall would recall. "He had a line standing outside his apartment even when he didn't have a name."

He struggled through an endless assortment of dead-end jobs—attendant at the New York Psychiatric Institute, coat checker at the Longacre Theater, clerk-typist at the Yellow Pages, haplessly incompetent waiter (his own assessment) at the Village Gate. Hackman, tall and strapping, moved furniture up and down six-floor walk-ups, while Duvall worked nights at the post office. Because none of them could afford theater tickets, they would "second act"—sneak in during intermission and race past the ushers to the balcony to grab vacant seats.

It took several years, but Hoffman gradually developed a reputation as an actor's actor, by hard work and steely determination. "He liked to dance around the third rail," says Walden. "He insisted on connecting to his fellow actors, and seduced them to respond in kind. And he knew how to make the whole thing *personal*." Hoffman wasn't looking for stardom or a plane ticket to Hollywood—he, Duvall, and Hackman all looked down on movie actors as beauty contest winners, not serious artists. They swore to one another to be uncompromisingly honest about their work, even if it meant living on unemployment or laboring in the typing pool. "There was dignity in being unemployed and not taking anything unless you thought it had artistic merit," Hoffman recalls. "We had no fucking idea what was in store for us. If someone had dropped from the sky at a party and said you three are gonna be movie stars, the whole place would have erupted in laughter."

Marion Dougherty loved Duvall and cast him in many television roles—"Marion got him every lead psycho part, whether it was *The Defenders* or *Naked City*," Hoffman says. Duvall, in turn, loyally talked up Hoffman to Dougherty and she became a fan—her index card on Hoffman reads: *"Bob Duvall says is very good. Very good reading for SWEET PRINCE 5/15/61 . . . use."* The show was "Sweet Prince of Delancey Street," an episode of the television police drama *Naked City* that ran in June 1961. Dougherty cast Hoffman for the part of Lester, a neighborhood wise guy who betrays his good friend Richie by carrying out a robbery in a warehouse where a security guard gets killed and making it look like Richie was responsible. Hoffman, who was twenty-three, sports a thick, somewhat Lower East Side accent, a serious pompadour, and a mouth full of chewing gum. But he handles himself well in his four scenes, and looks suitably pathetic in his big moment near the end of the show when he softly confesses his guilt to Richie's mother. What Dougherty especially admired was Hoffman's ability to hold his own in two scenes with Robert Morse, the lead guest star, an established young talent who played Richie like an emotional hand grenade.

Hoffman also impressed the playwright Murray Schisgal, who became a close friend, and the off-Broadway director Ulu Grosbard, who once told Arthur Miller that he should keep Hoffman in mind to play

Willy Loman in a future production of *Death of a Salesman*. Observing Hoffman's "awkwardness and his big nose that never seemed to get unstuffed," recalled Miller, "my estimate of Grosbard all but collapsed."

Still, by the time Jerry Hellman met him, Hoffman had put together a respectably solid and wide-ranging collection of theatrical roles, beginning in 1965 with *Harry, Noon and Night*, in which he played a hunchbacked German transvestite living with an American soldier in the ruins of postwar Berlin. The following year he won an Obie for best off-Broadway actor for his role as a fussy, forty-year-old Russian proofreader in *The Journey of the Fifth Horse*, adapted from a Turgenev novel. Which led in turn to *Eh?* in 1966 and a new level of critical acclaim.

Hellman says he wanted to sign him then and there for Ratso Rizzo, but it was too soon. John Schlesinger was off filming *Far from the Madding Crowd*, while Jack Gelber was wrestling in vain with the *Midnight Cowboy* screenplay. Then Jane Oliver got back in touch to say that the director Mike Nichols, fresh off his triumphant first movie, the film adaptation of *Who's Afraid of Virginia Woolf?*, wanted Hoffman for the lead in his next feature, a comedy to be called *The Graduate*. Hoffman was uncertain whether he wanted to do *The Graduate*—although there aren't any physical descriptions of the lead character, Benjamin Braddock, in the novel, he comes across as a tall, handsome WASP, a role that seemed tailor-made for someone like Robert Redford. According to Hellman, Hoffman said he would have turned down *The Graduate* if the timing interfered with his appearing in *Midnight Cowboy*. But Jerry made clear there was no problem—*Cowboy* would not begin filming for at least another year. So Dustin Hoffman went off to California. And when he came back the following year, he was suddenly a star.

And not just any star. *The Graduate* was a huge box office hit; shot for $3 million, it grossed $105 million in U.S. ticket sales, making it for a time the third-most-successful movie in Hollywood history. The film struck a collective nerve—droves of college students flocked to it, reading into it a cynical parable of alienation from the artificial and corrupt society they were inheriting from their parents. *The Graduate* became a cry of liberation, Simon and Garfunkel's mocking "Mrs. Robinson" (*"Jesus loves you more than you will know, whoa, whoa, whoa"*) became a counterculture anthem, and Dustin Hoffman emerged as an unlikely, inadvertent, and deeply ambivalent avatar for the generation-gap generation. His was the biggest Hollywood overnight success story since the teenaged Lana Turner was plucked from a soda fountain counter at the Top Hat Malt Shop in 1937, and the biggest pop culture phenomenon to come out of movies since James Dean. He also became a breakthrough figure as an actor—the first of his era to crash through the Maginot Line of male screen beauty, he paved the way for a talented generation of ethnic actors like Al Pacino, Robert De Niro, Richard Dreyfuss, Harvey Keitel, and Elliott Gould. "*The Graduate* was a huge breakthrough," says Walden, who was of similar stature and urban Jewish background. "Suddenly you didn't have to look like Robert Redford to get a part."

An eternally restless worrier, Hoffman very much wanted the success and the money and yet felt genuinely conflicted once they crashed unexpectedly into his life. He suddenly went from waiting on line to collect fifty-five dollars a week at the unemployment office to being hailed as the somewhat overripe Voice of His Generation. The press came racing to his door, and rather than shy away, he gave interview after interview, baring his soul, his political beliefs, and some rather creepy ruminations on subjects far and wide. He told *The New York Times* that he was seeing a psychoanalyst twice a week and that his dream role was to play Adolf Hitler; he recounted to the *Columbia Daily Spectator* how he lost his virginity at age sixteen to a twenty-year-old woman who thought she was making love to Ron Hoffman (it was dark in the room and Dustin said he imitated his older brother's voice); he told *New York* magazine he wanted to "destroy Benjamin. I know I can't beat *The Graduate* experience, but somehow I have to show I've grown, to connect, to get to them, to shake them up, to show I'm not a celluloid fluke."

It was sensory overload, but he handled it better than anyone could have expected. He even exploited it at times, using his fame to campaign for the maverick senator Eugene McCarthy's Democratic presidential primary run. "He didn't sign up for any of that," says Ron, "but his back was broad enough to carry it."

The sudden fame and fortune might have been good for Dustin Hoffman's career and bank balance, but it was bad for *Midnight Cow-*

boy, so far as John Schlesinger was concerned. He hadn't seen the gifted character actor of *Harry, Noon and Night*, *The Journey of the Fifth Horse*, or *Eh?* All he'd seen was a preview of *The Graduate*, in which he watched an awkward, clean-shaven, white-bread preppy nerd who looked to be twenty years old. John couldn't possibly imagine this fresh-faced, well-fed college kid as the scuzzy lowlife Ratso Rizzo. Plus, he didn't want to work with Mike Nichols's newly minted film star, who was almost certain to be a high-maintenance prima donna who could easily screw up his new movie. John enjoyed creating stars, not playing nanny to newly established ones.

But Hellman and Dougherty both insisted on Hoffman, who hungered for the part. He didn't much trust his success in *The Graduate*, nor did he feel he had earned it. Critics were inclined to give most of the credit to Nichols for the daring decision to cast a dark-haired ethnic schlemiel from New York in a role that had been written for a WASP-preppy–Southern California type. They were saying that "Mike Nichols had this guy who's just playing himself," Hoffman would recall. "I got so upset to prove them wrong. I was out to show that I was a character actor."

When Hoffman heard from his agent that John Schlesinger wasn't interested in him, he was flabbergasted at first. "Suddenly I'm a star and everything is being thrown at me and this English fuck suddenly doesn't think I'm right for this part?" But on second thought, he says he was impressed with the director's integrity. It made him even more determined to get the role.

But first he had to convince Schlesinger.

Horn & Hardart automats had been a New York institution since the first one opened on Broadway, between Forty-sixth and Forty-seventh Streets, in 1912. They were gleaming art deco monuments to the automation age, with a wall of small glass windows displaying hot and cold foods, along with shiny lacquered tables, cashiers in glass booths dispensing coins and tokens in return for cash, and reputedly the freshest coffee in New York. The automat was "the Maxim's of the disenfranchised," according to the playwright Neil Simon, who, like a lot of young upstarts, spent many of his early years in the entertainment business loitering inside them. Jim Herlihy was another serial frequenter—he said he wrote some of his best stuff at the automat. But like so many once-popular New York institutions, the automat was in an advanced state of decline by the mid-sixties. At one of the most prominent survivors, the H&H at East Forty-second Street and Third Avenue, much of the food was cold, stale, and tasteless, as was the once-worshipped coffee; the tables and chairs were crooked and creaky, the staff sparse and apathetic, and the patrons shifted in the evenings after five from clerical workers in business attire to the blue-collar night crews who cleaned the city's empty offices, along with junkies and people of no fixed address or occupation. It was here that John Schlesinger agreed to meet Dustin Hoffman near midnight on a chilly night in January 1968.

Hoffman showed up in the costume he had thrown together for Ratso Rizzo: dirty raincoat, battered shoes, greasy hair, and three days of chin stubble. The two men talked about Jim Herlihy's novel, the movie, and the role of Ratso, while Schlesinger—whose keen powers of observation matched Hoffman's own—took in the other patrons as they wandered inside. "He looked around and I remember him saying, 'You fit in quite well,'" says Hoffman. The two men eventually went for a stroll, taking in a billiards parlor, a bar, and other haunts that Ratso might have frequented. "Hoffman started limping along Forty-second Street," recalled Schlesinger, "and he seemed to sort of vanish into the background, which was exactly what I wanted to see—well, that's what he made me see. He was kind of auditioning—not really, but yes, really."

Well before dawn arrived, John Schlesinger officially surrendered. He told Hoffman he had the part.

A few days later they would return to the Times Square area, this time to Giordano's, a thriving Italian restaurant known for its fresh food and white tablecloths, located near the entrance to the Lincoln Tunnel a few blocks from the Port Authority Bus Terminal. When they sat down, Hoffman pointed out a middle-aged Italian maître d' who was quietly palming tips from vacated tables before the regular waiters could get there. That's who Ratso Rizzo might have become had he survived the bus ride to Florida, Hoffman told Schlesinger. He went on to talk about Ratso's survivor's instinct, his sense of dignity, and his sleazy charm.

Over dinner the two men talked frankly about life, love, and family and got a sense of each other's passionate determination to do ambitious work. There was one particularly awkward moment, when Hoffman, who didn't know that Schlesinger was gay, asked him if he thought he might get married someday. "No, no, I don't think so," John replied.

"Why not?"

"I just don't like women that much."

"What do you mean?" asked Hoffman, who was genuinely perplexed.

"The idea of waking up with a woman next to me just doesn't give me any pleasure."

A lightbulb clicked on in Hoffman's brain. "Then I understood," he recalled. "I was such a dummy."

Hoffman, who had only been able to bank three thousand dollars after his work in *The Graduate*, was ecstatic to get the part playing Ratso, but not so much that he forgot to bargain. When Jerry Hellman called Jane Oliver to offer $75,000 for his services, Hoffman told her, "See if you can get double." She did and she could. The $150,000 was nearly eight times what he'd made doing *The Graduate*.

Not everyone was overjoyed. Mike Nichols called Hoffman to mock his decision to take what was essentially a supporting role. "I made you a star, and you're going to throw it all away? You're a leading man, and now you're going to play this?"

With the deal signed, Dustin Hoffman went to work. First he reread Jim Herlihy's novel, which offered many useful clues. Later he would say the book gave him everything he needed to understand and inhabit the character. Next he returned to Times Square—"a very good film school," as he put it—to trail discreetly after its disabled denizens and observe how they navigated the crowded streets. "I remember specifically watching one guy who had a limp who lived on Forty-second Street. I'd watch him come to a corner at a stoplight with a lot of other people, and when the light turned green, he got to the other side first, before anyone else. Getting there first with a disability.

"I remember thinking, maybe that's what Herlihy was talking about. I had that image. That's who Ratso was and now I could illustrate it. Ratso overcompensated."

Hoffman worked on the limp—he took it direct from Herlihy's descriptions of a "broken grasshopper" and "a lopsided wheel"—the accent, the makeup. He added a piece of eyebrow to look like it'd been cut in a street fight. "We're always running scared—actors, writers, artists in general," he says. "The odds are you're not gonna screw in that lightbulb that's hanging from the ceiling, that it's always gonna be just out of your reach. So you do the best you can."

Next he studied photos of World War II concentration camp victims at the time of their liberation in 1945. One particular photo of defiant survivors with their hands fiercely clenched around the wire fence of their compound made him think of Ratso. "They weren't all heroes— some of them were *kapos*, [but] they were survivors," Hoffman says. "And that was my point—it was not that Ratso was a good guy or a bad guy, it was that he was a survivor . . . I thought he was dangerous if you cornered him. He'd scratch the shit out of you, like a fucking bat! He wouldn't want to, but he'd hurt you. What makes him so moving and ultimately human is that you feel that he is going to survive. Then, ultimately, he doesn't. The identification everyone has with that character is that we all like to think of ourselves as survivors, and then we die."

Hoffman added one more person to the mix—himself. He drew on his sense of isolation and resentment as a teenager, and the perpetual chip on his shoulder. "Once I figured it out, it was easy," he says. "Ratso was in my interior. That was me in high school, the outsider in me."

It was just a few days in, but Dustin Hoffman had already found the bleak core of the character he was about to create.

12. THE GOLF PRO'S SON

*All leading men and women should have something unpredictable and
dangerous about them.*
—Elia Kazan

Finding the right Joe Buck was harder.

Early on, John Schlesinger and Jerry Hellman had wisely resisted the temptation to go for a big-time star. Warren Beatty, who was dating Julie Christie and socializing with Schlesinger and Michael Childers in Hollywood, expressed interest in the role. John laughed at the idea. "He was desperate to play the part," John would recall. "He kept saying, 'Why don't you cast me?' And I said, 'Because I can't envision you failing on Forty-second Street.'" Robert Redford's agent also asked to see the screenplay, saying Redford was intrigued. There, too, the answer was thank you, he's a terrific actor, but no thank you. Even Tab Hunter, who had met Schlesinger on the gay party circuit in Hollywood, sent him a beseeching letter. John wrote back a sympathetic reply, gently pointing out that the former teen idol, now thirty-six, was a decade older than the character.

As their work on the screenplay had progressed in Malibu, Schlesinger, Hellman, and Salt had discussed Joe Buck extensively and agreed that what they needed was an actor who had a surface air of innocence yet the possibility of violence inside him. The man who immediately jumped to the top of their list was Kiel Martin, a former University of Miami drama student kicking around New York and Los Angeles as a dockworker, musician, and stand-up comic while trying out for every acting job he could find. Martin was just twenty-three—a little young for Joe—but he had an easygoing surface manner and a narrow face with piercing, wolfish eyes that hinted at danger lurking just below the waterline. John and Jerry liked him so much, they took him to Hollywood parties dressed in character and watched him charm people with his aw-shucks routine and crooked charm.

The other actor John liked a lot was Michael Sarrazin, the handsome, dark-haired, twenty-seven-year-old French-Canadian whom he'd met playing volleyball on the beach. Sarrazin was from Quebec City, and had started out in small roles in Toronto for the theater and the Canadian Broadcasting Corporation, including a live TV production playing Romeo opposite Geneviève Bujold as Juliet. He'd also studied at the Actors Studio in New York, had broken into American television, and had recently costarred with George C. Scott in *The Flim-Flam Man* (1967), playing a young army deserter who becomes the con man Scott's apprentice. John was drawn to Sarrazin's naïve wide eyes and pouty lips. He was clearly a rising star.

Another good-looking young actor was nowhere on John's list. Jon Voight, then twenty-eight, had heard from the New York casting director Marion Dougherty almost two years earlier that Schlesinger and Hellman were planning to make a film of *Midnight Cowboy*. Voight had read the novel, liked it a lot, and decided that he would be perfect for Joe Buck. He'd even sent Hellman a tape of himself in a guest appearance on *Gunsmoke*, America's most popular television drama. Jerry sent back word that he didn't think Voight was right for the part. More than a year later, Voight was in Los Angeles after spending the fall doing Shakespeare repertory theater in San Diego when he ran into Kiel Martin, whom he knew from waiting in line together at endless casting calls back in New York. Martin couldn't help sharing his good news. "I'm up for a big role," he told Voight. He mentioned John Schlesinger's name but wouldn't say more. Voight knew exactly what movie Martin was referring to. He immediately phoned his agent in New York, Jane Oliver—who also represented Dustin Hoffman, Sylvester Stallone, and several other aspiring young actors—to insist that she contact Dougherty to say he'd be coming back to the city on a red-eye flight that night and wanted to meet with her right away.

Voight showed up at the brownstone on East Thirtieth Street the next morning. Dougherty was coming out of the building as he was walking in. He spoke first, and in his ultra-sincere Boy Scout manner he apologized for having blown his big scene in the *Naked City* television episode five years earlier. She affixed her gaze on his baby-smooth face and deep blue eyes for a moment, then smiled. "Jon, that's the past," she said. "How would you like to meet John Schlesinger?"

Aspiring young actors in New York in the 1960s came in many shapes and psyches. There were angry ones and cynical ones and sincere ones and intense ones. But there weren't many joyful ones. The road was too hard and it was strewn with endless failure. "No one starts at the top in the theater," Gene Hackman once said, "and the bottom is a very ugly place."

Jon Voight was no exception. He was driven, compulsive, and uneasy. Yet he also loved his work and his fellow actors, and he was confident that if he pushed himself hard enough and got a break or two along the way he would succeed.

Voight was born and raised in Yonkers, New York, a blue-collar city a half hour's drive from Times Square, one of three brothers in a Catholic family. His mother's family was from Germany, while his father's father had come to America from Slovakia at age fifteen and worked as a coal miner in Pennsylvania before wandering east to the Hudson River Valley. His father, Elmer, was a golf pro and an avid, utterly entertaining story-teller who loved to perform. Jon and his brothers—Barry, who would grow up to become a distinguished geologist, and Wesley, who would write the pop songs "Wild Thing" and "Angel of the Morning" under the name Chip Taylor—would sit mesmerized in their beds at night while their father improvised wild tales of espionage and derring-do starring a character based on himself. Jon and his dad would watch *Your Show of Shows*, starring the great Sid Caesar, on the fuzzy black-and-white tele-vision, with Jon mimicking all of Sid's phony ethnic accents and making his father roar with laughter. But Elmer Voight also pushed his boys hard. "We could sense Dad's severe disappointment if it didn't look like we were getting to the top of the heap," Chip Taylor would later tell *The New York Times*.

Jon went off to Catholic University in Washington, D.C., with hopes of studying fine arts, including theater design. But just before his junior year someone gave him a book by the brilliant, mercurial British drama critic Kenneth Tynan, where he read for the first time about Laurence Olivier and the other great Shakespearean actors of Olivier's generation. Voight quickly caught the acting bug and decided to go to drama school once he graduated. Angst never clouded his vision. "Once I made the decision to go to New York and start school again and learn to act, I was at peace," he says. "I never had the thought that I was just testing it. I knew what I needed to do and I knew that I wouldn't give up."

Despite his soft, warm looks, Voight was a complex, moralistic person, passionate about his art and demanding of himself and others. While he never doubted his decision to become an actor, he questioned seemingly every line, scene, and gesture in every movie he acted in. Jane Fonda, Voight's costar (and fellow Oscar winner) in *Coming Home* (1978), found his approach exhausting. "With Jon everything is up for question, everything has to be tried," she said. "It makes it hard to work with him. You could never have more than one in a crowd with his level of intensity."

Waldo Salt's daughter Jennifer, who became Voight's girlfriend during the *Midnight Cowboy* film shoot, says he was deeply devoted to his craft. "He was so confident of his acting," she recalls. "Not conceited, but he just loved it and his mind worked in very imaginative ways." At the same time, he seemed to be carrying a lot of sadness. "I think he had the desire to be that angelic, perfect, flawless, and noble person," she says. "But there was a lot of darkness, demons, shame, Catholic stuff that I didn't understand, didn't see it for what it was."

Unlike Dustin Hoffman, Voight says he never had to wait tables or do odd jobs to pay for acting classes. His parents were there whenever he needed money, even though they were dubious about his prospects as an actor. And it was hard at first. Voight was a six-foot-three, apple-cheeked twenty-two-year-old with long blond hair and a sweet-looking angel face that could be mistaken for the smiling youngster on a can of Dutch Boy house paint. He looked blandly handsome but harmless, as if he harbored no interior thoughts. "I was a young-looking person," he says, looking back. "I wasn't a man yet."

Those white-bread looks helped him get a part on Broadway as Rolf, the young Austrian telegram boy turned Nazi stool pigeon, in *The Sound of Music*, but he knew that to become a real actor he needed training. His girlfriend Lauri Peters, who later became his first wife, was in the hit musical as well and helped steer him to the Neighborhood Playhouse School of the Theater, Sanford Meisner's acting school. Meisner was an avatar of the craft for aspiring young actors, an unassuming but intensely focused teacher who preached honesty, emotional credibility, and collaboration to several generations of performers, including Gregory Peck, Grace Kelly, Joanne Woodward, and Robert Duvall, Dustin Hoffman's loyal roommate. When Kelly fled from Hollywood back to New York in despair in late 1951, after feeling she had botched her performance in her first major film role, as the marshal's young bride in *High Noon*, she returned to Meisner's classes to seek solace and further training.

Voight says it took two years for Meisner to admit him to classes, but once he did, Meisner came to love his playfulness and his ability to turn his emotions on and off. "I can cry seventeen different ways for seventeen different reasons," Voight would boast. Marion Dougherty caught him in several amateur productions and created his index card for her burgeoning file. She got him his first television parts, including the disastrous *Naked City* performance. With the money he saved, he and Peters and a friend traveled to London, where he got to see his idol Olivier on the stage. One rainy day they ducked into a small cinema and watched *A Kind of Loving*, John Schlesinger's first feature. Voight says he was so touched by its humanity and humor that he wrote Schlesinger's name down in the hope of working with him someday.

He returned to New York and labored on the circuit of off-Broadway and summer theater. Most notably, he appeared in a legendary production of Arthur Miller's *A View from the Bridge* in 1965, at the Sheridan Square Playhouse in Greenwich Village, with Robert Duvall and Susan Anspach, directed by Ulu Grosbard. Voight was signed to play Rodolpho, an undocumented immigrant from Italy with romantic aspirations and a tragic nobility, and at first he didn't believe he could handle the role. But with Grosbard's encouragement he worked at it. "Maybe I was really scared, I don't know," Voight recalls, but "I was able to use all that stuff that I had been learning with Sandy, plus new things from working with Bobby [Duvall] . . . I commanded it in a certain way and it became my first insight into my real talent."

Dustin Hoffman was also involved in the production, as Grosbard's assistant director, and he watched Voight's performance evolve over time. "Voight and I saw each other every single day on *A View from the Bridge*, and he was brilliant in it," Hoffman recalls. "We sussed each other out. I think Voight said about me, 'I've never seen him act, but I think he's probably very good.'" For his part, Voight says Hoffman told him how much he admired his performance.

Still, each of them was intensely wrapped up in his own aspirations. Hoffman saw Voight, who towered over him, as something of a golden boy—certainly some of the women involved in the play's production and in the audience thought so. "My God, the girls loved him," said Hoffman. "He was tall, blond, and handsome—everything I wasn't. They'd come backstage. They wanted to marry him and mother him. He was a matinee idol off-Broadway."

Voight went on to do repertory at the Theatre Company of Boston four years after Jim Herlihy had performed there in *The Zoo Story*. He played Romeo and did a lot of other Shakespeare, several small parts in *Gunsmoke*, and a Theater World Award–winning performance on Broadway in *That Summer, That Fall*, with Irene Papas, in 1967.

Jerry Hellman's rejection of Voight's first attempt to try out for the role of Joe Buck had disappointed Jon but didn't stop him from pining for the part. What he didn't know was that Marion Dougherty disagreed with Hellman.

Dougherty thought Jerry was missing the truth about Voight—that underneath his aw-shucks, pretty-boy innocence there was a powerful actor who could do both comedy and drama and had the capacity for projecting violence that they were looking for. She wasn't the only one who thought so. Even before she met him, Jennifer Salt, herself an aspiring young actress, saw Voight in a Boston public television production of Harold Pinter's *The Dwarfs*, was impressed by his performance and his articulate commentary in a televised discussion panel afterward, and she pleaded with her father to get him a screen test for Joe Buck. Dustin Hoffman says he too lobbied for Voight with John Schlesinger: "I said, 'John, he's a brilliant actor.'"

Dougherty convinced Hellman and Schlesinger to look at Voight and several other promising young actors besides Martin and Sarrazin. According to her contemporaneous handwritten notes, Voight was one of seven performers brought in on the afternoon of Thursday, February 22, 1968, to meet with Schlesinger, Hellman, and Waldo Salt, including the up-and-coming Broadway dramatic actor Stacy Keach. Afterward, Dougherty wrote "very possible" next to Voight's name; the other six were all dismissed (she deemed Keach "not rite for cowboy"). Schlesinger, who was never immune to flattery, was charmed when Voight expressed his admiration for *A Kind of Loving*. But he didn't find Voight's smooth, kewpie-doll face terribly attractive or dramatically compelling. He told Voight that they already had four or five great candidates for the part who were slated to do a screen test the following week.

"He just didn't seem to me to be the physical image of the cowboy," Schlesinger would later explain. "I thought he was—I don't know—too butch-looking, or baby-faced, or whatever. And Jerry Hellman felt the same. Of course now I can't imagine anyone else playing the part. It's one of those ridiculous blind spots one has." Still, despite his doubts, Schlesinger gave Voight a copy of the script and told him to read it overnight and come back the next day to go over it with Waldo Salt.

Voight showed up at the Astor Hotel, near Times Square, the next morning, started talking about Joe's character, and never really stopped. "This boy is lonely, that's the essence of this film," Voight recalls telling Salt. "He's not conning anybody. He's so vulnerable and he's trying to pass himself off as a normal human being. And that's a big effort for him, which means there's comedy, a lot of comedy, but there's also this part of him that should break your heart." Salt liked what he heard, and Voight was invited back for a screen test along with front-runners Martin and Sarrazin, as well as Robert Forster, Don Stroud, and Lee Majors.

It was a three-part test. Each actor did an excerpt from a scene between Joe and Ratso, with Dustin Hoffman unselfishly volunteering to play Ratso for each candidate; then each was shot with a long lens while strolling down a busy New York street in Joe Buck's cowboy outfit to see how the actor stood out in a crowd; and finally each sat for an interview in front of a white screen, with Waldo playing the aggressive off-screen interrogator modeled after Joe Pyne, the famously belligerent television and radio talk show host of that era.

The only screen test that has survived is a partial one, just seven minutes and nine seconds of Voight under Salt's mocking interrogation. Voight is wearing a lavender western shirt embroidered with floral designs, with pearl buttons on each of the two shirt pockets, and a black kerchief around his neck, and he's carrying a black cowboy hat that he puts on about halfway through the taping. His accent sounds like it's stuck in traffic somewhere between Yonkers and Amarillo—it's clear he's never heard a real Texan talk. He's fielding a series of increasingly hostile and sarcastic questions:

> SALT: "How long's it been since you been on a horse, cowboy?"
> VOIGHT: "I told you before the show I ain't never been on a horse."
> SALT: "Don't you know it's a fag thing, this cowboy bit?"
> VOIGHT: "That's what you think!"
> SALT: "Did you ever make it with men?"
> VOIGHT: "Well, you do what you can to get by. Right?"
> SALT: "Boy, you're just one hell of a man, aren't you? What makes you think that you've got something you can sell to women?"
> VOIGHT: "'Cause I know it . . . Got something in my pants, that's all."

The screen test is a lumpy, half-baked confection of a performance, mostly hostility with a dash of vulnerability. What's missing is the sense of innocence and the good-ol'-boy charm that Joe Buck could turn on and off. Voight is all edge. It's the Neighborhood Playhouse–Angry Young Man version of Joe Buck. With the exception of the phony accent, Albert Finney could have phoned it in from London.

The next day Schlesinger, Hellman, Salt, Dougherty, and Michael Childers sat together and watched all the tapes. The first to be discarded was Kiel Martin, whose charisma seemed to have vanished once the camera was turned on (which was not the case more than a decade later on *Hill Street Blues*, the groundbreaking NBC cop show, on which an older, more weathered Martin played the recovering alcoholic J. D. LaRue with just the right mix of heedless insouciance and vulnerability). Then they crossed off Stroud, Forster, and Majors, all three of whom were deemed interesting but not quite right.

It was clear from the start that Schlesinger preferred Sarrazin to all the others, with Voight a distant second. The rest of the room quickly acquiesced to the man in charge. All except for Marion Dougherty, who kept fidgeting and shaking her head. Jerry Hellman could see she was upset and asked her what was wrong. "Nothing," she replied. "You guys are making a terrible mistake, that's all." And she stormed out of the room.

She later pulled John aside for one last try, and proceeded to commit a terrible faux pas. She told him that Sarrazin was too pretty for the part. Since the relationship between Joe Buck and Ratso Rizzo would evolve into a close and loving one, she feared the audience might come to the mistaken conclusion that the two men were gay. She'd only known John for a few days, and had no idea that he himself was gay. The quick, subtle expression that crossed his face was "just enough to tip me off." She quickly changed the subject. Ann Roth, whom Jerry Hellman had just hired to be the costume designer for the film, told John that she too preferred Voight.

No matter. Schlesinger was the director and he had the only vote that counted. He phoned Sarrazin to tell him he'd gotten the part. He even invited Sarrazin back so that Roth could take his measurements and start fitting him for costumes. It was left to Hellman to phone the others. He found it especially painful to break the news to Voight, whom he'd grown fond of over the course of the process. Voight was crushed. He was so absolutely certain he was the right person for the part that he couldn't believe that Schlesinger and the others didn't agree. "I was devastated," he recalls. "I knew I could do it. I had passion. And I knew that with Dusty we'd have something special. And I was afraid that if they didn't cast it right the movie would be a disaster."

Each of the actors had agreed before the screen test that if they were cast they'd accept a bare-minimum fee of $17,500 to play the part. Everyone had signed a paper to that effect except Sarrazin, who was under contract to Universal Pictures, which Jerry contends had agreed verbally. But when he got on the phone with a senior executive at Universal, the man said fine, now what about Michael's deal? Jerry reminded him they'd already agreed on an amount. "That was then," the man replied. "Now it's real." He threw out a round number: fifty thousand dollars, according to Jerry. Plus, he said, there were potential problems with Sarrazin's schedule. *Midnight Cowboy* might have to wait a few months.

Never exactly a model of patience, Jerry grew more and more furious as the Universal man kept talking. He put his hand over the receiver, explained to John what was happening, and said he wanted to hang up on the guy. "Do it!" John replied. Jerry slammed down the phone.

The two men began reexamining the screen tests of Sarrazin and Voight. Each time they did so, Sarrazin's looked a little worse and Voight's a little better. And Marion Dougherty kept nudging. "She said, 'Why are you going for that pretty boy Sarrazin?'" recalls Michael Childers.

They called in Hoffman, who watched the screen tests at their request but was reluctant to express a preference. When pushed, he insisted he could work with either actor. But he added a telling footnote. When he watched the scene between himself and Sarrazin, Hoffman said, "I found myself looking at me." But when he watched the same scene with Voight, "I found myself looking at Jon."

That clinched it for Schlesinger. He told Jerry to call Voight back and offer him the role. At first a wary, once-burned Voight wouldn't believe it. "Okay, is this for real," he asked Jerry, "or are you going to call me again ten minutes later and tell me I'm off?" Hellman had to reassure him several times that the offer was genuine and irrevocable. Later, when an interviewer asked John Schlesinger how he had discovered Voight, he replied, "I didn't. Marion Dougherty found him and insisted that I use him. Frankly, I didn't even want Jon Voight."

As for Sarrazin, he tore his phone off the wall when he heard he'd lost the part.

Voight's first mission was to fix his accent. He worked in New York with a Texas-born World War II veteran named J. B. Smith for a few weeks,

then headed to the Lone Star State for a week accompanied by Michael
Childers, who was scouting locations for the Texas scenes. They made
their way to Big Spring, one hundred miles east of the New Mexico
border, the kind of rawboned, fading Texas town that looked like tum-
bleweed grew on its main street. Voight hung out in bars, followed young
folks around the sidewalks, and spent a few hours serving customers in a
boot shop. He carried around a small audiocassette recorder—a new de-
vice in those days—to tape the people he met. "I didn't tell anybody I
was an actor," he recalled. "I was really trying to fit in."

A cowboy bar Voight visited one evening was particularly challenging. He sat for an hour nursing a beer and listening to the jukebox, waiting for someone to say howdy and getting nowhere. Finally, he tried to
launch a conversation with an older guy in western duds who sat down
near him at the bar. "You in cattle?" he asked.

"Oil," came the reply. Only it sounded like "*all*."

Another silent half hour went by. "The water's hard here," Voight
volunteered.

"Yeah," the cowboy allowed. "It's good for your second teeth, though."

"It was a whole night like that," Voight recalled.

Voight also participated in the selection of locals for various cam-
eos in the movie, especially the young guys who auditioned to play the
members of the Rat Pack, the gang that sexually assaults Joe Buck and
Annie Pratt. He taped each of these kids, adding them to his collection
of regional accents. Schlesinger, who had flown down for his own look
around, recalled driving back to New York with Voight, who constantly
played the tapes. "He drove us all mad by playing back the tapes inces-
santly on the way back to New York," said Schlesinger. "But he did get
his Texas drawl down perfectly in the bargain."

Listening to Voight, the director had a brilliant suggestion. "He said,
'Jon, I think you can take it up an octave,'" Voight recalls. "It was such
good advice because it put me in another dimension. It had more music
to it."

Voight had observed the politeness that young people in Texas displayed not just to their elders but to everyone they met. He incorporated
that sense of deference and respect to the strangers Joe Buck meets on

his initial bus ride to New York and to those he encounters once he gets to the city. "He's not a coarse person," says Voight. "Even though he is involved in some bizarre stuff, he's just a country boy."

He and Schlesinger started to build a friendship early on. "I couldn't have had a better pal or a wiser director," he says. "We talked about what the character was looking for in every scene and I got to understand what animated him."

Like Dustin Hoffman—and Jim Herlihy before either of them—Voight started exploring Times Square, dressed in cowboy clothes, to get a feel for the place and the kind of person he was playing. Men on the street would try to pick him up and he would play along sometimes to keep them talking. He also made a point of talking to the homeless. He had an idealistic take on their circumstances and their values—the Boy Scout in Voight again shining through. "There's an unwritten law in the Bowery," he later told Rex Reed. "Every bum has a buddy and they split everything fifty-fifty. It's very beautiful."

He even invited homeless people for dinner at his basement apartment on West Eighty-eighth Street. He said he did this for research purposes. But there were other reasons as well. "He struggled with a lot of guilt," says Jennifer Salt. "He felt like 'I don't deserve this.'"

Still, he loved the prospect of working with John Schlesinger and Dustin Hoffman, and he loved Waldo Salt's screenplay. "I believed in it so much," Voight says now, still somewhat dazzled a half century later at his good fortune.

13. THE ARMIES OF THE NIGHT

What the phuque am I doing?
—James Leo Herlihy

One person who was not overly fond of Waldo Salt's screenplay was James Leo Herlihy. He had received a copy of the final draft from John Schlesinger in early February, as did the principal members of the cast and crew. He wrote back immediately to say how much he liked the script and was "really dazzled" by Salt's narrative skills. He also endorsed the decision to omit the Perry-Juanita scenes from the novel. And he said he loved the idea of turning a loft party scene—a very small element in the novel—into a full-fledged Andy Warhol–style bacchanalia. "I think you guys have done a vast amount of brilliant work," he told Schlesinger.

Then Jim came to what he called the "misgivings department." The major one was that Joe Buck had no big moment at the end of the film that demonstrated the impact of the changes he had gone through in New York. Jim conceded that there wasn't such a moment in the novel, but insisted that the movie required it. "I believe there must be a purification, a bloody big one."

Lurking behind this, Jim wrote, was a bigger problem: throughout the screenplay Joe was simply not sympathetic enough. He needed to be "as vulnerable and humanly sensitive, basically, as Marilyn Monroe. If he's tough, or vaguely hostile, I think the picture becomes ugly and dirty." Jim added, "It's important that we (the audience) root for these guys, especially because the world they move in is so ugly."

His solution? "To put it bluntly, I think you need ME at this point" to rewrite some scenes. "A couple of weeks' work. A brush stroke here, a deletion there, a bit of re-wording."

John wrote back three weeks later to say that the casting for Joe Buck had been giving them problems but that they now had "three good Joes to choose from." As for Joe's "purification," Schlesinger insisted that the sympathy was already there in the script. But he added, it was also important to show that Joe had been toughened by his experiences in New York, so that when he faced the choice of staying in the city and tending to his career as a hustler or helping deliver Ratso to Florida to try to save his life, the stakes would be higher and the decision harder "than you actually give him in the novel."

As for Herlihy's plea to come work on the screenplay, Schlesinger simply ignored it.

The initial lack of critical response to the publication of *Midnight Cowboy* had disappointed Jim Herlihy, as did its anemic book sales. He felt tired and burned out. His life as a writer, which he'd been keen on since childhood, was losing its hold on his imagination. "I didn't like what was happening in the world," he confessed, "and it was perfectly clear my life wasn't good at that point."

For a while, he tried to fill the void by plunging into the antiwar movement. His interest was piqued while vacationing in Majorca, off the eastern coast of Spain, when he ran into a Danish tourist who showed him a copy of the *International Herald Tribune*. "Have you seen what your country is doing?" the man asked. "They're bombing Hanoi." The question startled Jim, who began reading the English-language newspaper every day and came home charged up and angry. As a World War II veteran, he had always believed the United States was a force for good in the world. "I suddenly understood that America was on the wrong side," he would recall. "We were the enemies of our own principles."

Once back in New York, Jim read the antiwar historian Howard Zinn's new paperback, *Vietnam: The Logic of Withdrawal,* and was moved to send more than one hundred copies to opinion leaders throughout the country. He joined the Writers and Editors War Tax Protest, whose initial signers included Eric Bentley, Betty Friedan, Jack Newfield, Grace Paley, Thomas Pynchon, and Gloria Steinem, all of whom pledged to withhold 23 percent of their federal income taxes, representing the proportion being spent on the war, plus any war tax surcharge Congress might enact. He also took part in antiwar protests in New York and Washington, including the groundbreaking gathering of more than one hundred thousand demonstrators at the Capitol Mall on Saturday, October 21, 1967. He joined Abbie Hoffman, Jerry Rubin, and Allen Ginsberg marching under the freak flag of the Youth International Party, or Yippies. Along with Norman Mailer, Robert Lowell, Noam Chomsky, and Dwight Macdonald, they persuaded nearly half the crowd to follow them across the Memorial Bridge into Virginia to the Pentagon. It was a wildly disparate cross section, Mailer in a three-piece suit followed by young hippies dressed like Arabian sheiks, Daniel Boone in buckskins, Martians, moonmen, Confederate generals, Batman, and a knight who clomped around in brutally hot armor. Their stated intention was to levitate the headquarters of the American war machine three hundred feet off the ground, but the 3.7-million-square-foot building, made of concrete, reinforced steel, and limestone, refused to budge. No matter. The demonstrators chanted and danced and shoved flowers into the rifle barrels of the uneasy-looking guardsmen who stood between them and the walls of the Pentagon.

Jim gave an antiwar speech on the steps of the Justice Department and later spent a night in jail after attempting to break into the White House grounds. "I like doing this," he wrote to Mary Caroline Richards, his teacher and friend from Black Mountain College. "It is my way of waging war, and it makes me feel good, or at least better."

He loved the pageantry, poetry, and utopianism, and he loved the younger generation that, as Mailer put it in his book *The Armies of the Night*, "believed in technology . . . but also believed in LSD, in witches, in tribal knowledge, in orgy, and revolution." But Herlihy was not built for the violent passions of the sixties. He was a dreamer, not a revolutionary. His kind of activism was much too civilized and sedate for bombing campaigns and "Up against the wall, motherfucker" outbursts of hatred and despair. And none of what he was doing was sufficient to conquer his own periodic sense of depression. "Yesterday I had a most difficult day, mostly spent in my studio with the shades drawn," he told Richards in a letter written the following year from Key West, "trying to regain some clear sense of what it is I'm doing here, and have been doing with my life for the last year or so. I mean, really now, what the phuque *am* I doing?"

Simon & Schuster published a slim volume of his short fiction in 1967 entitled *The Story That Ends in a Scream and Eight Other Stories*, most of which had already appeared in magazines. His attempts at new writing had virtually ground to a halt. He put them aside for a time, accepted an invitation to teach a writing course at the City College of New York—and promptly fell in love with his students. "I learned so much from that class," he later recalled. "I saw this whole new generation coming up who knew more about life, politics, the war, and values than I did. The only square in that classroom was me."

He witnessed the same thing happening outside the window of his small apartment on East Seventh Street in the East Village, near St. Marks Place and Tompkins Square Park. Jim was twenty years older than most of the hippies he saw on the street, but he loved the way they looked and the free spirit they exuded. He grew a wispy, Mennonite-style beard, let his hair grow, and started wearing long flowing shirts in solidarity.

St. Marks Place was emerging as the eastern pole of the counterculture that Jim was drawn to, just as Haight-Ashbury in San Francisco was becoming the western pole. St. Marks is a small section of East Eighth Street between Third Avenue and Avenue A, named for the nearby St. Mark's Episcopal Church in-the-Bowery. It was a neighborhood with a colorful past—Walt Whitman, Susan B. Anthony, Oscar Wilde, and Emma Goldman had all passed through St. Marks on their way to the history books, and the past half century had seen figures as disparate as Leon Trotsky, W. H. Auden, and Lenny Bruce spend time working or living there. Auden was still there when Herlihy moved into the neighborhood, living with his handsome, Brooklyn-born boyfriend, the poet Chester Kallman, in a shabby flat that was so cold in winter the plumbing froze. Auden used to walk to church in his slippers on Sunday mornings, while the Beat poet Allen Ginsberg would trudge to the Gem Spa newsstand at the corner of St. Marks and Second Avenue to buy the Sunday papers. Abbie and Anita Hoffman lived on St. Marks during the summer of 1968, and Jerry Rubin and the hippie activist Paul Krassner founded the Yippie movement in the basement of the Hoffmans' apartment building. Thelonious Monk, Charlie Parker, and Charles Mingus played the Five Spot jazz club, while the Fugs invented acid-poetry rock at the Dom, a bar that was later transformed into the Electric Circus, a happening psychedelic venue. Two blocks down Second Avenue, the rock impresario Bill Graham opened the Fillmore East, a carbon copy of his West Coast music palace, in March 1968. By then hippie boutiques had invaded the area, with exotic names like those of rock bands: the Queen of Diamonds, Something a Little Bit Different, the Owl and the Pussycat, Gussie and Becky, and Underground Uplift Unlimited, all of them on St. Marks, along with the Pas de Dieu art gallery, the Bowl and Board, and Khadeja Designs.

"The night-time was prime time on the Lower East Side," writes Joshua Furst in *Revolutionaries*, his novel based on the lives of the Hoffmans. "It was getting dark, so things were starting to hop. The sky streaked with color and the lower summer light soaking into the brick facades, making everything look like it was glowing from the inside out. Transistor radios propped on every stoop, a turf war of tunes and textures. People hanging around—on milk crates and beach chairs and the hoods of cars drinking beer out of brown paper bags. The streetlights were on and we dodged and wove around the freaks and stoners and the extended Puerto Rican families, the transvestites and punks and Ukrainian toughs, all making their parties right there on the street."

Pete Hamill, a columnist for the *New York Post* who lived a block away on East Ninth Street, recalled the teenagers who flooded into the area from the outer boroughs and the suburbs as generally sweet and naïve kids, come "to play for a while at poverty and rebellion. But too many of them found permanent trouble; I covered at least three cases of kids wrecked on acid who walked off tenement rooftops."

There were other, even more brutal ways to die young in the East Village. Linda Fitzpatrick, an eighteen-year-old high school dropout from a wealthy family in Greenwich, Connecticut, was found bludgeoned to death in October 1967 alongside James L. "Groovy" Hutchinson, her twenty-two-year-old boyfriend, on the concrete floor of the boiler room of a tenement basement on Avenue B, just a block off St. Marks. In a long, chilling front-page article published eight days later, J. Anthony Lukas of *The New York Times* captured the two vastly different worlds Linda had shuttled between. Lukas interviewed her father, Irving Fitzpatrick, a wealthy spice importer, in the thirty-room mansion a mile from the Greenwich Country Club where he and his family lived and where Linda had grown up. He told Lukas he wasn't even aware there was such a thing as the East Village ("I've heard of the Lower East Side, but the East Village?"). He and his wife had believed that their daughter, who aspired to be an artist, was making posters for an imports store and attending art classes after dropping out of the Oldfields School for girls in Glencoe, Maryland. Linda told them she was living at the Village Plaza Hotel on Washington Place with a girlfriend. In fact, Lukas found out, Linda had been staying in a run-down transient hotel with a series of boyfriends—"anybody off the street, the dirtiest bearded hippies she could find," according to the hotel clerk. Lukas contrasted the filthy hotel room, with its peeling gray dresser, "sway-backed double bed" that filled half the room, and shared bathroom down the hall, to Linda's airy bedroom at home with a white-canopied bed fit for a suburban princess.

"The Two Worlds of Linda Fitzpatrick" won Lukas a Pulitzer Prize and helped launch his distinguished journalism career. Two men were later arrested and pleaded guilty to the murders, one a twenty-seven-year-old drifter, the other a twenty-eight-year-old ex-convict and Black nationalist. They had lured Linda and Groovy to the basement with the promise of drugs, then beaten them to death for their money. Their murders were chilling evidence of the counterculture's lethal subtext—violent street crime, heroin and meth addiction, bad acid.

Although enamored of the idealistic hippie world just outside his apartment door, Jim Herlihy was well attuned to the dangers lurking around every corner. At some point he himself underwent what he described in a letter to Richards as "a violent experience, knives etc.," refusing to go into further detail. But he told an interviewer that "Manhattan today upsets me too much for me to make much sense of it."

His imagination rekindled, he began thinking about a new novel that might encompass both the love and the hate all around him.

While Jon Voight and Michael Childers were paying their visit to Big Spring in early April, Hellman, Schlesinger, Waldo Salt, Ken Utt, and others of their growing team—including their newly hired set designer, John Robert Lloyd—spread out across Texas. They had nearly two dozen possible locations to scout, from the small towns of the Panhandle to the sprawling city of El Paso, across the border from Mexico in the state's remote southwest corner, plus three more places in New Mexico. In the end, the towns they liked best were Big Spring and Stanton, located twenty miles apart off Interstate 20. "Not bad Greyhound bus terminal opposite deserted cinema," wrote John in a memo about Big Spring. "It has things that can be dressed."

When they got back to New York, Utt and his assistant production manager, Hal Schaffel, handed in their cost estimates to Jerry, who took them and added in the salaries, including twice as much money for Dustin Hoffman than they had anticipated. The total was $3.2 million—more than three times the original budget. They brought it to David Picker, who didn't get angry this time but warned them that the size of the request might well kill the project. After consulting with the senior partners at United Artists, Picker came back with a demand that they get the budget down to under $2.4 million or else UA would indeed cancel the movie. Jerry sat down with Utt and Schaffel that evening and started cutting, only he didn't alter either the screenplay or the shooting schedule.

The annals of Hollywood are full of heroic but often apocryphal tales of fake budgets and scripts that got "tightened" by simply reducing the margins of the typewritten pages. Jerry Hellman's sleight of hand with *Midnight Cowboy* was equally skillful—or devious, depending on your point of view. "We didn't take a day out of the schedule . . . We didn't eliminate a set, a costume, anything, we just erased eight hundred thousand dollars," Hellman recounted at a panel discussion for the movie's twenty-fifth anniversary, in 1994. "I went there [to David Picker's office] fully expecting that someone was going to say, 'Well, wait a minute, where is it coming from, what have you eliminated?'

"But nobody did."

14. PREPARATION

John just had that glint in his eye. He wanted to be surprised constantly.
—Dustin Hoffman

When he started out as a feature film director in Britain, John Schlesinger had been able to develop and rely on a small group of talented artists and craftsmen—among them actors Julie Christie, Alan Bates, and Peter Finch, screenwriter Frederic Raphael, film editor Jim Clark, continuity assistant Ann Skinner, and, perhaps most important of all, producer Joe Janni. But coming to the United States, and embarking on a project as unconventional as *Midnight Cowboy*, meant venturing into uncharted territory virtually alone. The shaky Hollywood studio system had proved to be of no help—no one there was interested in such a risky enterprise, and in any case the rapidly downsizing studios lacked the creative resources John needed. Like the emerging breed of independent filmmakers who became known collectively as the New Hollywood, he would have to build his own temporary company of performers and crew.

John was fortunate to have joined forces with Jerry Hellman, who had compiled twenty years of experience in the entertainment industry as a talent agent and independent movie producer. He was lucky to have United Artists, the most unconventional mainstream film company, for a partner. And he was especially lucky that his project landed him in New York at a time when the city was bursting with creative talent in virtually all of the categories he and Jerry needed: actors, screenwriter, casting director, set designer, cinematographer, and technicians, many of whom had come to the city seeking their own artistic destiny and were still in the process of establishing—or, in Waldo Salt's case, resurrecting—their careers. Jerry had come to know and work with many of these people over his own career. Now he introduced John to yet another gifted collaborator.

Ann Roth had grown up in rural Pennsylvania and studied theatrical costume and scene design at Carnegie Tech (now Carnegie Mellon) in Pittsburgh, where she arrived in 1949 just as the newly graduated Andy Warhol was setting out for New York. After graduation, in 1953, she wound up at the Bucks County Playhouse outside Philadelphia, where she fell under the spell of Irene Sharaff, one of the most elegant and revered costume designers of the era. Roth followed Sharaff to Hollywood, assisting her on five movies, and on to Broadway, where she worked on costumes for five plays under Sharaff's tutelage. Then she struck out on her own. She worked on her first Broadway play, *The Disenchanted*, written by Budd Schulberg, in 1958. Soon she was doing movies as well. She first met Jerry Hellman while working at the Cherry Lane Theatre, one of Greenwich Village's most famous off-Broadway venues, where Jerry regularly played poker with his pals backstage. He hired her to do costume design for his first feature film, *The World of Henry Orient*. And he hired her again for *Midnight Cowboy*. When she saw John Schlesinger's wicked smile, she quickly fell for him, and he for her. "It had everything to do with wit," she recalls. "John had the same sense of humor I did."

As was true with virtually every aspect of the movie business, costume design was undergoing major changes in size and scope in the 1960s. Previously, costume designers were elite members of the studio aristocracy, like Edith Head, the famed designer for Paramount, who won eight Oscars and was nominated for twenty-seven others during an illustrious fifty-eight-year career. Head's role was to dress the stars of each movie she worked on and to oversee a staff of sketch artists, wardrobe people, and seamstresses to outfit the rest of the cast. "Edith Head sat in an office and maybe designed four costumes per film, but she had an army of people under her and she worked on nine movies at a time," says costume designer Isis Mussenden, a member of the Board of Governors of the Motion Picture Academy.

Ann Roth saw her job as something very different. She started from a simple premise: costume designers don't just make outfits, they make characters. Working in New York, she created or picked out every costume for every character in *Midnight Cowboy*, and she traveled to Florida and Texas for the location shoots as well. Like Waldo Salt, she was on the set continually and was part of the core team at the heart of the moviemaking process. "I outfitted everybody, including the people who worked in the cafeteria scenes," she says proudly. "A costume designer should always be there."

Roth started work on *Midnight Cowboy* by dressing in cowboy duds all of the young actors who tried out for Joe Buck, including Jon Voight, the ultimate winner and the one she says she preferred for the part. But her real work began after Voight had been cast. Like Dustin Hoffman, John Schlesinger, and Voight himself, she headed for Forty-second Street to do research in the garish neighborhood that the film's main characters called home. She started with Ratso Rizzo. The idea was to find and obtain the clothes he would have bought from the places he would have bought them—or, in Ratso's case, the places he might have stolen them from.

One of the names that dominated New York movie marquees during the 1960s was that of the Italian film idol Marcello Mastroianni. So Roth figured that if you were a roustabout Italian kid from the Bronx like Ratso and you thought you had arrived, you wanted to look like the beautifully dressed, charismatic star of Federico Fellini's *La Dolce Vita* and *8½*. Which meant you likely wore a white suit. "I knew Dustin couldn't do the whole movie in a white suit, but that's where I started," Roth recalls. Next door to the Port Authority Bus Terminal, at West Forty-second Street and Eighth Avenue, was a shop with a sidewalk table out front piled with cheap clothes. Roth found a pair of folded white pants with a gray line of dirt along the crease of each leg. They went for twelve dollars. Next, she found a pair of shiny, high-top black shoes with pointed toes at a store up Forty-second Street toward Times Square. "They were cockroach-in-the-corner shoes," she says. "I had to have those." Then she bought a continental-cut purple suit and dyed it green. "It was mambo and the cha cha cha and all that, a short jacket and a very skinny little behind." It looked to her like some high school kid had rented it for his prom and then chucked it into a trash can after he threw up on it. And finally she bought a burgundy-red shirt from a boyfriend who had a clothing store uptown. "It said Ratso all over it."

Hoffman, fresh off the premiere of *The Graduate*, walked into Eve's Costume Company on West Forty-sixth Street, one of Roth's favorite haunts, where she had set up her wares in a small, dusty fitting room. She used the same process on him that she did on all her actors. "You and I are gonna find this character together," she told him.

"The truth is, you as a designer know what you want them to look like, but you also know that if they don't go along with it, it's not going to look good," she says of the actors she's worked with. "And so what happens is I say, 'Listen, close your eyes, close your mind, and be a dummy, let me just play.' And it ends up there are like five different pairs of shoes on the floor, here is some crappy jewelry in a dirty box, here is a box of shirts, and the pants, and you say, 'Put that on now.' I like to have the hairdresser in the room—'Do me a favor and make me a cheap pompadour here.' The actor is slightly overwhelmed if they don't know me and maybe a little annoyed. I say, 'Just let me play,' and you're playing and playing and you're trying to make the person comfortable. You're looking in the mirror and you don't see Dustin Hoffman anymore, there is someone else. I remember doing dirty fingernails on him, I didn't ask him. The pompadour was a little bit up. And I said, 'Put this shirt on, don't tuck it in all the way, just make it messy.' You look into the mirror and here's this guy who could easily sleep on a pool table. And that's what you're after."

She used the same process with Jon Voight. "Joe Buck lives with his grandmother, his pants come from Montgomery Ward, that's his best shirt, she gave it to him for Christmas. Joe's clothes were cheap, and I wanted them to look cheap. I made the suede jacket myself because I wanted it the right length. I didn't want it to be cute, I wanted it to look real and unhip so that when he stood on Park Avenue and asked, 'How do you get to the Statue of Liberty?' I wanted him to look sort of dopey. And I made his suitcase."

"Neither one of these guys was difficult," she recalls of Hoffman and

Voight. "There are actors and there are movie stars, and I don't work with movie stars. These guys were really good actors."

With *Midnight Cowboy* Roth helped created a new template for costume design. "It was an enormous influence," says Isis Mussenden. "We are responsible for each and every person on that screen, and we create the characters along with the actor and the director. Once you bring in Ann Roth, who is brazen, incredibly brilliant, and a little bit mad, it's a whole different beast."

While Roth was a well-known and much-admired artist and a friend of Jerry Hellman's, the cinematographer whom he and John Schlesinger hired that week was a virtual unknown. Adam Holender was a shy, intense twenty-nine-year-old with a thick Polish accent who had never worked on an American feature film before. But he came highly recommended by Roman Polanski, the celebrated Polish film director who grew up in Kraków, the same city where Holender was born and raised. Schlesinger and Hellman were looking for someone with an innovative visual style who could paint a film portrait of New York City that would stand out. They decided to take a chance.

Like so many of the others involved in making *Midnight Cowboy*, Holender had come to New York to create a new life for himself. He was the son of middle-class Polish Jews who had fled east from Kraków just before the German invasion on September 1, 1939, but were caught between the Nazis and the Soviets when the Red Army invaded from the other direction seventeen days later. He was three years old when he and his parents were shipped to a Siberian labor camp, where they were confined for six years, facing deprivation and a constant struggle for food, shelter, and clothing. His father, a lawyer in civilian life, labored outdoors in a logging crew; his mother made soup from weeds and wove young Adam a pair of felt boots from the cotton wicks of oil lamps, while he smuggled food in his gloves from a school outside the camp to help feed his parents. Somehow they made it through the war and returned to Kraków afterward.

Holender loved photography—his parents, who nurtured his artistic aspirations, gave him a large Kodak camera while he was in high school—and after graduation he was accepted for a position to study cinematography at the prestigious National Film School at Lodz, the same school Polanski had attended. After a rigorous five-year training course, Holender graduated into the gray, government-controlled world of Polish cinema, working on feature-length documentaries and programs for state-run television.

"Everything needed approval from the Communist Party," he recalls, "but you do learn how to dance around it." When Polanski made his breakthrough film, *Knife in the Water* (1962), says Holender, "each foot of film was screened by party ideologues." For example, there was a scene of the affluent married couple at the heart of the story driving a Mercedes. "They said there's got to be no Mercedes. So Polanski had to go back to reshoot."

After his father's death, in 1966, Holender left Poland for North America. He was required to buy a round-trip ticket on an ocean liner to Canada, even though he had no intention of ever returning home—he still has the return ticket tucked in the back of a drawer. When he got to Montreal he immediately hopped a bus to New York, arriving at the Port Authority. He hardly spoke English. He had a few names of friends who lived there but no relatives to speak of, and he wound up checking into a downscale West Side hotel. His room cost six dollars a day on a weekly basis. "I remember the price vividly," he says. "If you only have a few hundred dollars in your pocket, it matters."

His first apartment was on the corner of West Seventy-first Street and Columbus Avenue. It felt unsafe. After dark there were constant sirens. "Every other night the police cars would come from both ends of Seventy-first chasing drug dealers."

Holender's first job was to drive a station wagon loaded with camera equipment for a company that made documentary films for businesses. After a few weeks the boss came to him for help because a client was demanding an immediate reshoot and the usual cameraman wasn't available. Other projects followed, and soon he was being offered shooting jobs by other companies, including television commercials. "Suddenly I was able to feel the end of the tunnel," he says.

Howard Zieff was known in New York as the king of commercials—he created "You Don't Have to Be Jewish" for Levy's rye bread and "Mamma Mia, That's a Spicy Meatball!" for Alka-Seltzer. When Jerry Hellman approached Zieff seeking new talent for _Midnight Cowboy_, the king of commercials talked up Holender. Polanski, living in London and basking in the critical success of _Knife in the Water_, _Repulsion_, and the soon-to-be-released _Rosemary's Baby_, his American-made breakthrough, also warmly endorsed his young friend.

Wary of hiring an inexperienced newcomer, John and Jerry had Holender shoot Jon Voight's screen test to check out his professional skills. He readily passed the test. John liked him right away. He and Holender both came from documentary film backgrounds and both loved Italian neorealism. But Holender went a bit too far when he expressed effusive admiration for Lindsay Anderson's _This Sporting Life_. "John made a face," he recalls. "It turns out they hated each other."

What truly connected Schlesinger and Holender was the fact that both saw New York with the fresh eyes of recent arrivals. "It was a process of discovery," says Holender. "I came from a gray, Communist, oppressive environment, and New York was like a breath of fresh air. And it was also a special time in New York, everything was opening up. People were extraordinarily friendly and nice to me. I couldn't believe the kind of trust I got from people in such a short period of time."

Early on, Holender took Schlesinger on his first New York subway ride, from a location they were scouting on the Lower East Side back to Times Square. John was a sponge for sights and sounds. In turn, John took Adam along on the location-scouting trips to Texas and Florida.

Quiet, thoughtful, and studious, Holender insisted on shooting with a smaller reflex camera like the ones he'd used in Poland rather than the enormous Mitchell BNC, which was the Hollywood standard. His reason was simple: the viewfinder on the reflex camera gave him a truer sense of the image the camera was capturing. The veteran New York camera crew that Jerry Hellman had hired didn't approve of his choice. Nonetheless, they got him the camera he wanted. Similarly, he wanted softer, more natural lighting rather than the large, sharp klieg lights that were the New York standard. For most of the street shooting, he and Schlesinger wanted to use no artificial lighting whatsoever. "It was a constant battle," he recalls. "I was in charge, but the crew didn't like to be told to use something they thought was for still photographers or amateurs. But they were basically decent people and they did what I asked."

Holender quickly warmed to his other collaborators. He loved Waldo Salt's sense of commitment and respected Ann Roth's spirit of collaboration. Once, Schlesinger asked his opinion of a coat Roth had picked out for Ratso. Holender thought the item was the wrong style and said so, but feared Roth would take offense. To his surprise, she readily agreed with him.

"I don't think anyone could even pretend the film was going to win an Oscar," he says. "But one thing that was felt by me every single day was that I was participating in spirited work with spirited people."

While Adam Holender was coming to terms with his new crew, Marion Dougherty was lining up the rest of the cast. She signed Barnard Hughes, a fifty-two-year-old veteran of television, stage, and screen, to play Townsend P. Locke, the chatty, masochistic businessman from Chicago whom Joe picks up toward the end of the movie because he desperately needs cash to get the dying Ratso to Florida. When Towny resists, Joe brutally beats him and steals his wallet. Hughes wanted to work with John Schlesinger, but he had deep reservations about the role—he was reluctant to play a pathetic gay man and concerned about the impact seeing this violent assault on the screen might have on his two children. But his wife, the actress Helen Stenborg, told him he'd be crazy not to take the part, and he bowed to her judgment.

John McGiver, a playful, creative performer who had appeared in *Breakfast at Tiffany's* and *The Manchurian Candidate*, had no such reservations about playing O'Daniel, the religious fanatic whom Ratso fobs Joe off on after conning Joe out of twenty dollars. McGiver, an actor with wild eyes and a raffish grin, relished the seediness of the part, according to Jerry Hellman, and even got a kick from turning on and off the lit-up plastic statue of Jesus that O'Daniel keeps in the bathroom of his shabby hotel room.

Dougherty cast Bob Balaban for the part of the pimply high school kid who picks up Joe outside a movie theater on Forty-second Street and gives him a blow job in the balcony of a sleazy Times Square movie theater (the sex takes place just off camera), then admits he doesn't have the twenty-five dollars he has promised to pay Joe. It was the first movie role for Balaban, who was just twenty-two and looked five years younger, and he was thrilled to get the part. A senior at New York University in Greenwich Village, Balaban had taken a workshop in improvisational comedy with the famed improv teacher Viola Spolin at Second City in Chicago and studied acting with the equally renowned Uta Hagen at the HB Studio in the Village. Marion Dougherty had scouted him when he played Linus in the off-Broadway hit musical *You're a Good Man, Charlie Brown*, and invited him to do a screen test with Jon Voight at her office with John Schlesinger watching. "I was fairly naïve and inexperienced," Balaban recalls. "In fact, I wasn't quite sure whether *Midnight Cowboy* was a movie or a television show." He wound up doing improv with Voight of the movie theater scene for about twenty minutes and got the part. But phoning his parents afterward with the good news proved uncomfortable when he explained he would be performing oral sex on the lead character. Balaban's parents were sophisticated filmgoers—his family had been involved in the movie business for two generations and his uncle was president of Paramount Pictures for three decades. Still, he says, "I think they were fairly depressed when they saw the movie."

Another newcomer was Jennifer Salt, Waldo Salt and Mary Davenport's brainy and uninhibited twenty-three-year-old daughter, a recent graduate of Sarah Lawrence College. Encouraged by her good friend the actress Jill Clayburgh, Jennifer was pursuing a theater acting career and working in Hartford, Connecticut, where she was in the Greek chorus of a postmodern production of *Antigone*—"we wore hooded sweatshirts . . . you couldn't even see my face." Her father called to say there was a small role for her playing a hippie flower girl in the Andy Warhol party scene he had written. She took the bus to New York and met with Schlesinger, Hellman, Childers, and her dad. John was impressed by her sexy good looks and obvious intelligence, and he huddled privately with Jerry, Michael, and Waldo. He asked if they thought she might be able to play

Anastasia Pratt—"Crazy Annie," the Texas girl who falls in love with Joe and initiates him sexually. Waldo was clearly queasy about the idea of his daughter, a fledgling actress, playing a role loaded with sex, nudity, and violence. But he was also a cheerleader for her ambitions and not about to stand in her way. They sent her off to Central Park with Michael to take photographs of her and then introduced her to Jon Voight, who offered to help her with her Texas accent. Voight had already heard that she was one of those who had suggested him for the part of Joe Buck. She recalls their first meeting as more of a date than a rehearsal; soon she was sharing his modest basement apartment on the Upper West Side.

Although there were only four women's roles of any substance in the film, Dougherty believed each was pivotal and focused especially hard on casting the right performer. For Sally Buck, Joe's grandmother, she aimed high, approaching Bette Davis, Glenda Farrell, Ruth Gordon, Jo Van Fleet, and Shirley Booth, before settling on Ruth White, a lesser-known but widely respected New York theater actress. "Marion knew where the good New York actors were hidden," says Hellman.

For Shirley, the society woman whom Joe meets at the Warhol party toward the end of the film, Dougherty considered Janet Leigh, Susan Strasberg, Lois Smith, Phyllis Newman, Sally Kellerman, Carol Lawrence, and Janice Rule. Barbara Harris ruled herself out because she refused to do a nude scene. Lois Smith "gave a damn good reading for Shirley," according to Dougherty's index card on her. But in the end, Dougherty sent Schlesinger with his friends the screenwriter Garson Kanin and his actress-writer wife, Ruth Gordon, to see *How Now, Dow Jones*, a new Broadway musical, and check out a young actress named Brenda Vaccaro in what was her first starring role. John loved her dark looks and deep, sultry voice—she stood out as someone who could both snarl and laugh at herself and those around her.

Vaccaro had been born in Brooklyn but raised in Dallas, Texas, where her father and mother moved in the early 1940s to open one of the city's first Italian restaurants. Her parents paid her way back to New York as a teenager to study acting with Sanford Meisner. Members of her class included James Caan, Jessica Walter, Elizabeth Ashley, and Dabney Coleman. After her father died suddenly at age fifty-three, her mother kept the restaurant business going and continued to pay Brenda's tuition. When she graduated in 1961 she went straight into Broadway shows and managed to get regular work throughout the decade. She would be nominated for a Tony for Best Leading Actress in a Musical for *How Now, Dow Jones*. Shirley would be her first significant movie role.

But Dougherty's most unconventional choice was Sylvia Miles, for the small part of Cass, the aging call girl whom Joe picks up on his first day hustling on the streets of New York. She brings him up to her penthouse apartment, where they have a quick but lusty tryst. Afterward, when a rueful Joe reveals he's a hustler and asks her for money, she explodes in anger and tearfully relieves him of a twenty-dollar bill, purportedly for cab fare. Miles, a native New Yorker, whose age was variously listed as somewhere between thirty-four and forty-three, was another alum of Lee Strasberg's Actors Studio who had bounced around in bit parts in television and movies. During one busy time in the theater in 1960, she was simultaneously performing in the first act of Jean Genet's *The Balcony* in Greenwich Village and the second act of Tennessee Williams's *Camino Real* nearby, commuting between the two productions on a motor scooter and zipping back to *The Balcony* in time for the curtain call.

Miles first heard about *Midnight Cowboy* from a friend who loaned her the paperback and told her she was "born to play Cass Trehune." She'd even talked briefly about it with Jerry Hellman when he came to a performance of an off-Broadway play directed by Jack Gelber when Jerry and John were considering hiring him to write their screenplay. Jerry didn't seem interested in her, but a year later John Schlesinger happened to catch her on early-morning television in a horror flick called *Psychomania* (*"She was an innocent college kid . . . soon she would die!"*) and suggested her to Dougherty, who had already proposed her for Cass.

The pay for all of these fine supporting actors was minimal. McGiver got the most: five thousand dollars for a week of work; Vaccaro got twenty-five hundred dollars per week, with a two-week guarantee; Hughes only received fifteen hundred dollars.

Miles also got fifteen hundred dollars. Her contract stipulated that "Miss Miles agrees to put on weight if required and knows she will be shooting 'topless.'" Miles was willing to do whatever it took. When she auditioned for the part with Voight, he would recall, she whipped off her blouse and attacked him like a wrestler going for a takedown. "I was gonna get that part if it killed me," she said later.

When John Schlesinger walked into the ballroom of the aging Astor Hotel, on Times Square, on a Monday morning in April 1968, to begin two weeks of rehearsals for *Midnight Cowboy*, he didn't know what to expect. Waiting for him were Dustin Hoffman and Jon Voight, the two actors he had chosen, with some reluctance, to play the leads. Hoffman was thirty, Voight twenty-nine. Despite Hoffman's sudden fame after starring in *The Graduate*, neither had much movie experience. They were not exactly rivals but not really friends. Each had spent nearly a decade struggling to create a viable career in one of the most difficult and unpredictable of professions in a city that was merciless when it came to crushing the hopes of young actors. Each was supremely confident of his own gifts, but self-doubt was baked into the process of developing their characters. And each was aware that he needed the other. They were playing two vastly different men who start off as antagonists but slowly develop a partnership based on raw mutual need. Each comes to accept his dependence on the other, but the wariness between them never disappears. This was not the usual buddy movie. It was two men in an urban jungle, forced to guard each other's back while never truly trusting each other. And the relationship between the actors mirrored in many ways the volatile partnership between the characters they played.

"There was a lot of electricity in the air between us because we were young actors, vying actors," Hoffman would recall. "It's not that you don't want the other one to be good, you just don't want to look bad. On the other hand, we were kind of rooting for each other because we're all kind of the underdog."

Both men had developed a solid understanding of their characters. Voight saw the loneliness and neediness in Joe Buck, but also the humor. Hoffman understood the thwarted dignity and survivor's instinct at the heart of Ratso Rizzo. Using the description of Ratso's walk carefully laid out in Jim Herlihy's novel, Hoffman had developed a rolling gait, put stones in his shoes, and with Ann Roth's help built for himself a greasy pompadour. "It's in the book—there's nothing in that character that's created by me," insists Hoffman. "I tried to re-create what was really brilliantly written by James Leo Herlihy."

He also had acquired a set of false teeth to snap over his real ones. Dentist Arthur Poster made an acrylic shell, then painted on stains, old fillings, cracks, and shadows with what he called a "self-cure staining stick." The results, Poster reported proudly, "looked really horrible. I was pleased."

Somehow, with help from the master makeup man Dick Smith, Hoffman managed to look both seedy and yet intriguing. Voight noticed, and immediately felt anxious. "I was so jealous of Dusty's ugly teeth and that perfect limp," he recalled. "I knew I had to find the right walk for me, too."

Even before the rehearsals began, Schlesinger and Holender decided to take advantage of the frosty gray weather and leafless trees to capture with a telescopic lens the two characters walking across the Willis Avenue Bridge, which connects the Bronx and upper Manhattan. They tried to add some dialogue, but neither actor was prepared for it—Hoffman hadn't yet decided on what kind of voice he would use for Ratso. "I said, 'John, I don't even know what I sound like yet,' and he said, 'It doesn't matter, we won't even hear you, but there'll be [steam] coming out of your mouths from the cold.'"

As he limped along behind Voight's loping strides Hoffman's voice fell into a high-pitched, nasal-toned Bronx shuffle that became Ratso's voice for the entire movie. "Sometimes, when you're that scared, it's like the curtain is opening and something comes out," he recalls. "It was never done with any kind of technique, it was just a hit or miss."

Then Hoffman broke into a coughing fit so frantic that he threw up all over Voight's new cowboy boots. An alarmed Voight took Schlesinger aside and asked, "Is he gonna do that throughout the movie?"

The rehearsal sessions quickly evolved from a mere table reading of the script into a festival of improvisation between the two men, with the encouragement of Schlesinger and Waldo Salt. John had never worked with such volatile and creative performers before. He focused on the scenes between them, looking to make those moments deeper and more meaningful than what was in the script, and to capture both the fissures and the slow bonding between the characters. Salt was crucial to the process. Unlike many playwrights and screenwriters, he didn't insist that the actors stick religiously to the lines he had written for them. The screenplay, for him, was a work in progress. He was more than willing to let Hoffman and Voight develop their characters in front of him, and he helped goad them into expressing their conflicts. Waldo "wasn't a prima donna about his lines," John recalled. "And he'd very often agree that the scene hadn't gone far enough."

Schlesinger was fascinated about what the two characters might do and discuss inside the small, cold-water flat where many of their interactions took place. "I wanted to know more about what it was like for those two unlikely people to share that tiny apartment," he said. Hoffman and Voight quickly got into it, riffing on intimate matters like how they kept clean, who flushed the toilet, what they each did about body odor and masturbation. They talked about religion, reincarnation, space aliens, manhood, and their own sexuality. Waldo would trail after them around the ballroom, with a microphone attached by a long cord to a heavy Wollensak reel-to-reel tape recorder. After the sessions, he and Schlesinger would replay the tapes, and John would single out pieces for Waldo to type up and insert into the script. "We transcribed what we recorded, and there were some gems in it," John recalled.

"John just had that glint in his eye," said Hoffman. "He wanted to be surprised constantly. He craved collaboration. He didn't ever act like a bandleader, he acted like a jazz musician in a combo."

After more than thirty years in the motion picture business, Waldo Salt thought he'd seen it all. But he'd never seen anything quite like Hoffman and Voight as they got down to the business of creating and meshing their characters. "These guys were just beyond description," he would recall. Even at lunch or on breaks, neither would stop—"they just became Joe Buck and Ratso Rizzo. It's nice to feel that at least one time in your career that in a picture everything worked, and in this picture it did for me."

Schlesinger admired Hoffman's commitment to the film—his willingness, for example, to rehearse and participate in the screen tests for the half dozen finalists for Joe Buck. But he was less enamored of some of Hoffman's more creative notions. At one point Hoffman suggested adding a scene in which Ratso, eating at the counter of a cheap Times Square restaurant, leaves the joint in disgust after a Black man sits down next to him. Hoffman believed this moment would offer a key to Ratso's character: that no matter how low he felt in the social hierarchy, he considered himself superior to others. But Schlesinger dismissed the idea out of hand; he feared that adding racism to Ratso's long list of ugly character flaws would make him too unsympathetic. Hoffman had no choice but to go along.

At another point, Hoffman told Schlesinger he and Voight had agreed that "we've got to have a scene where they're in bed together." John, he recalled, turned pale. "He said, 'My God, we've barely got this thing financed and now you want to play them queer? We'll never sell this picture.'"

Voight says he admired Hoffman's constant need to push the boundaries. "He tests things, he goes that extra step to see what will happen," said Voight. "He's an adventurer, an emotional adventurer."

Jennifer Salt detected an undercurrent of sexual competition between the two actors. Hoffman, she says, "has that history of being little ugly Dustin and Jon's the big blond-haired guy. But in terms of confidence and the ability to swagger with a girl they were the exact opposite. Jon was not a cool guy, and Dustin was endlessly flirtatious and clever and with it." She says Hoffman teased her a lot about being with Voight— "'Hey, Salt, what are you doing with him?'—and I, of course, was madly flattered." Nonetheless, she adds, "When they were working together, there was a real chemistry, because Dustin is way too ambitious an actor to be less than great."

Voight insists he and Hoffman had a great relationship throughout the film shoot. "Dustin was wonderful to work with because he was always provoking and messing with things and he helped me do that as well," Voight says. "The chemistry was very good. We helped each other and we liked fooling with each other. It was very competitive and very helpful. I was grateful to be working with him."

Voight sympathized with the issues Hoffman faced as a new movie star. "The things he had to deal with off the set, all of a sudden he was the man of the hour, he was the guy."

Stardom was like a new, expensive, but ill-fitting suit that Hoffman was forced to wear. On one level he loved the attention. Suddenly he was getting good seats in restaurants and taxicabs stopped for him. He received a hundred fan letters a week. Attractive women were bountiful. A *Look* magazine article at the time recounts a moment when Hoffman, in an air-conditioned limousine with his manager and the *Look* reporter, spots a blond model on the sidewalk whom he had admired in a drugstore a few minutes earlier. Hoffman rolls down his window. "Quick—get in! We'll give you a ride. We saw you in the drugstore!" Dazed, she climbs onto a jump seat and they exchange phone numbers. After they drop her off, he wonders aloud if she will call him. He knows he won't call her. Then he hears himself and stops short. "I just have to get over this period," he tells the reporter, "that never in my life have I been so in love with myself."

At times it was all too much for him. "You know how I knew I'm a star?" he later told interviewer Larry King. "I'm walking down Fifth Avenue and a girl wearing a T-shirt who was—to quote W. C. Fields— bountifully endowed by the Creator, recognizes me. She lifted up her T-shirt, she doesn't have a bra on. She says, 'Would you sign me?'"

As a newcomer to the States, John Schlesinger was fascinated by the brazen atmosphere and the strange sights America always seemed to offer. While living in Los Angeles, he had wandered up and down Hollywood Boulevard, which had the same sleazy feel as Times Square, soaking it in and making mental notes. One night at Canter's deli, an all-night coffee shop on Fairfax Avenue, he saw a strung-out woman sitting at a table with her young son. She was playing with a toy mouse, running it up and down her arms and over the boy's head and face.

"That's a wonderful image," John recalled. "I don't think I could have dreamed that up, it was something completely from life." He described the scene to Waldo, who incorporated it into the screenplay.

On another evening he was watching *The Joe Pyne Show* on television when Pyne brought on a doggie wigmaker from Phoenix who dressed his poodle in sexy outfits and sprayed mouthwash into the dog's mouth for bad breath. "I remember sitting in [the] rented house in Malibu on a purple bedspread with pink wallpaper and a television on the wall and a remote control, which I'd never seen before," John recounted years later. He immediately grabbed the phone and called Waldo to tell him to turn on the TV. "You've got to see this!" he said. Later they had a researcher track down the wigmaker to his home in Phoenix and reshot the scene, which appears on the TV set while Joe Buck is taking a bath in his cheap hotel room and pondering his string of utter failures as a paid stud. "Every talk show which I tuned into, every radio thing, every commercial, everything was grist for the mill," Schlesinger would recall.

When he got to New York, John's antenna remained constantly engaged. He and Waldo would wander the city on foot, talking about the movie and hunting for more bits. One day near Times Square he saw a man sprawled on a crowded sidewalk. Passersby just stepped carefully around the body and kept going. Another day a woman barged into a coffee shop and started talking loudly and animatedly about a confrontation she'd just had with a policeman outside. Both moments found their way into the script.

"It's the most extraordinary city in the world," John said of New York. "You can stand on any street corner, and something infinitely worse than you could ever imagine or more extreme, more extraordinary, is going on just out of vision. It's the one city in the world where I've been and seen things that leave me feeling that I cannot believe my eyes and ears." John even hired a cross-dressing male prostitute—"something of a madam," he would recall—to advise him on the authenticity of the Times Square scenes.

New York was generously offering him much more than he could ever use. "I tried to breathe into the film the mixture of desperation and humor which I found all along Forty-second Street."

15. STOLEN SHOTS: THE NEW YORK FILM SHOOT

What if my mother sees my tits before she sees my face?
—Brenda Vaccaro

Monday, April 29, 1968, was a crowded and noisy day in New York City's perpetual street opera of culture, politics, and violence. The city issued new statistics that morning showing major crimes had jumped nearly 25 percent during the month of March, with the murder rate rising 39 percent. A *Look* magazine editorial pronounced the Vietnam War a mistake and urged U.S. military withdrawal as quickly as possible. An ad on the *New York Times* daily book review page celebrated the climb of *Myra Breckenridge*, Gore Vidal's acerbic transsexual satire, to the top of the fiction bestseller list. *Hair*, the immensely popular counterculture musical, opened on Broadway that evening at the Biltmore Theatre. And a few hours later, nearly one thousand helmeted police officers emerged with clubs and blackjacks from blacked-out vans and buses and stormed the Columbia University campus to put a violent end to a weeklong sit-in by protesters there.

Amid all the drama, few New Yorkers even noticed that a movie company had started filming on the streets of Manhattan.

The one thing practically everyone involved remembers about the filming of *Midnight Cowboy* is that the man in charge didn't seem to enjoy it very much. John Schlesinger had always been a notorious mass of insecurities and raw nerve endings during film shoots, repeating almost daily his pained mantra of moaning about how bad the rushes looked and how could they ever have believed anyone would pay money to see such a ridiculous piece of shit. But this time it was worse. He was starting off with two lead actors whom he hadn't originally wanted and didn't really know. He was in a strange city that was in the midst of its own prolonged political, social, and economic trauma. And he had a crew that he didn't trust or feel comfortable with.

Some of the questions quickly resolved themselves. With the camera turned on, Dustin Hoffman and Jon Voight continued to impress Schlesinger with their creativity and commitment. For the very first scene they shot that morning—the poignant moment in the pawnshop where Joe Buck parts with his beloved portable Zenith transistor radio for a mere five dollars because winter is coming and he and his sick companion Ratso Rizzo are penniless and starving—Hoffman improvised a little light tapping of a child's xylophone on a table during the transaction. John recognized immediately that Ratso was in good hands. Hoffman was also letter-perfect in capturing Ratso's incessant practice of larceny, whether pickpocketing tomatoes from a sidewalk fruit and vegetable stand near the Port Authority Bus Terminal or purloining a fedora from a hat cleaner's shop. His performance had just the right blend of humor and desperation.

John was equally pleased with Voight. His height, his striking blond looks, and his faux cowboy outfit made him a unique sight, easy to spot on even the most crowded New York street. "Jon is a tall fellow," says Adam Holender, the cinematographer. "All you had to do is put him on Fifth Avenue and put a fifty-millimeter lens three blocks away and he always stood out above the crowd."

Much of the first few weeks of the film shoot were spent leapfrogging around Manhattan shooting outdoor scenes. They started on Park Avenue near East Seventieth Street, where Joe Buck fails to pick up an attractive older woman who falls for his plaintive request for directions to the Statue of Liberty and then realizes what he's really after; they then proceeded to the sidewalk in front of Tiffany's, at Fifth Avenue and Fifty-seventh Street, where Joe encounters a well-dressed man lying passed out on the pavement as pedestrians walk on by unperturbed; and then on to the Plaza Hotel, at Fifth Avenue and Central Park South, where Ratso leads Joe toward the seedy hotel where Mr. O'Daniel, the phony evangelist, holds court.

Schlesinger occasionally lost patience with the seemingly endless

thought process of his two brilliant young actors. While he was filming Joe Buck's procession around town, he received a note from Voight
asking every actor's quintessential existential question: "What's my motivation?" Schlesinger said he fired back a sarcastic (but accurate) reply:
"a good fuck for which you'll get handsomely paid."

Most of these scenes were what was known in the movie business as
"stolen shots"—filmed without the knowledge or consent of bystanders.
Because of the low budget they were operating under and the imprac-
ticality of disrupting traffic-choked Manhattan streets and sidewalks
in the middle of the workday, Schlesinger, Holender, and their crew
couldn't afford to rope off an area and hire a small army of extras to walk
up and down the street for take after take. Instead, they would set up
their camera in a van with one-way glass or in a tall wooden crate where
no one could peer inside, and they would film the principals with a long-
range telephoto lens. Professionals were used for shots of Voight trailing
after specific women in search of customers, but otherwise most of those
in the street scenes were unwitting volunteers. Because Hoffman was
dressed and heavily made up in the character of Ratso and Voight was
a virtual unknown, the two actors could walk the streets without being
recognized or disturbed. Even Voight's cowboy outfit didn't draw many
stares from blasé New Yorkers.

One of the most memorable stolen shots—indeed, what would become one of the most memorable moments in modern cinema—took
place at the corner of Sixth Avenue and West Fifty-eighth Street, when
a taxi barreled into the crosswalk where Joe in his western duds and
Ratso in Ann Roth's prized white suit were trying to cross. "*I'm walkin'
here! I'm walkin' here!*" yells an enraged Ratso, slamming his hand down
twice on the hood of the cab. Hoffman has always claimed that the scene
was strictly an improvisation on his part when a rogue taxicab that was
not connected to the film company burst into the crosswalk trying to
beat a red light. Hoffman was furious, he says, because he and Voight
had timed the scene over and over so that they would make it into the
crosswalk just as the light turned green. "This cabdriver tried to beat
the signal and he almost hit us, and I yelled out," Hoffman recalls. "Not
only was I pissed, my brain was gonna say, 'Hey, we're makin' a movie

here!' and I knew I couldn't say that, so in a flash I changed it to 'I'm walkin' here!'" Hoffman says Schlesinger came racing out of the van asking "What happened? What happened?" When Hoffman explained, Schlesinger said "I want that" for the movie. So, Hoffman says, "we set it up and we did a few more takes" using a crew member as the cabdriver. They also added on the spot Ratso's subsequent lines: "Up yours, you son of a bitch! You don't talk to me that way. Get outa here!"

The problem with Hoffman's account is that the scene actually appears in Waldo Salt's screenplay, beginning with a draft dated November 24, 1967, six months before it was shot. Both Schlesinger and Hellman have long insisted that the original cabdriver was a member of the crew, assigned to drive through the intersection at that precise moment. The draft script calls for Ratso to slam the fender of the taxi, pretending to be struck and falling back into Joe's arms. He then recovers, strolls casually in front of the cab, and bites his thumb at the driver in silent contempt. Hoffman improvised the words that give the scene its indelible punch line and provide a key to Ratso's character. "It was the very essence of what I wanted to convey about Ratso—his dignity," said Hoffman. "We may see him as a lowlife, but he asserts himself. And I think people recognized the truth of it."

The cast and crew next headed downtown to the Lower East Side, at the corner of Suffolk and Broome Streets, one of lower Manhattan's most dilapidated outposts, where the associate producer, Ken Utt, had found for them a site of utter desolation among a row of deserted turn-of-the-century tenements that were about to fall under the wrecker's ball. Utt and the film company had no idea, of course, that they had stumbled across a prime example of the blight, negligence, and broken promises that characterized New York's steep decline in the late sixties.

The area had once been the heart of the old ghetto that Jewish immigrants just off the boat from eastern Europe—presumably including Jerry Hellman's and Dustin Hoffman's grandparents—had flocked to in the late nineteenth and early twentieth centuries. Most of the Jews had long since fled, leaving the immediate area and its crumbling slum housing to working-class Puerto Ricans and African Americans. In 1965 the city announced plans to purchase twenty acres along the southern side of Delancey Street, level the slums, and build stores, offices, and modern housing. Heralding "the rebirth of the Lower East Side," officials promised that the eighteen hundred families displaced by the project would have first crack at returning to new low- and moderate-income apartments.

It never happened. The buildings came down but the land would remain vacant, according to *The New York Times*, "a fallow stretch of weed- and rat-ridden parking lots" for the next fifty years, due to lack of public funds and the maneuverings of state and local politicians who quietly conspired to keep poor residents from returning.

The wrecking balls and demolition crews had started the teardown in 1967 and were still going at it when the *Midnight Cowboy* production crew arrived the following spring. The crew filmed Voight and Hoffman walking the cracked, deserted sidewalks—Voight striding like a young John Wayne while Hoffman ratcheted himself forward in a frenzy of arms and legs—and then took the iconic still photograph of the two men in a doorway at 63–65 Suffolk Street that became the movie's main poster and most enduring image.

The original thought was to use as Ratso's squat one of the ruined apartments in the condemned building across the street at 64–66 Suffolk. The apartment was known in the novel as the X-flat because of the large *X*'s taped across its windows to mark the rooms as abandoned and prevent the glass from shattering due to the heavy vibrations from nearby demolitions. But the work crews were moving so quickly that Schlesinger and Hellman realized they could not hope to secure the area for the duration of the filming. There were also many genuine squatters and drug addicts camped out in the building; Utt feared he and the film crew might show up for work one morning and find the location stripped of its furnishings. The set designer John Robert Lloyd, a St. Louis native with two decades of experience creating sets for plays, movies, and television in New York, insisted he could re-create the interior of the X-flat on a soundstage at Filmways, the studio warehouse up on East 127th Street in East Harlem, which Jerry had rented to shoot interior scenes. John was deeply skeptical but gave Lloyd the okay to try.

Taking full advantage of the Mayor's Office of Film, Theater, and Broadcasting's one-stop permit-shopping service, Lloyd got permission from the city for a construction crew to tear out an entire two-room condemned flat, including kitchen and bedroom, makeshift plumbing, walls, and windows, and transport it to Filmways for reconstruction. The Filmways building was a former city transit garage that had been converted in the late fifties into a movie studio with offices and makeup and wardrobe rooms. It was located in an edgy part of town and had all the charm of a dank, gray moving van warehouse. But it had one cavernous, multistory space large enough for a movie set, and that's where Lloyd had the pieces of his slum apartment deposited. He insisted that John and Jerry stay away until his work was completed—he had already experienced John's anxieties often enough to know he didn't want the director barking orders over his shoulder during the set's reconstruction. When John and Jerry finally got their first look a few weeks later, they were stunned. The Filmways X-flat was an exact replica of the original, right down to the broken furniture and the smell of urine. The only thing missing was the rats. "The absolute necessity to be authentically grungy was not to be found in scenery made in a shop," says Lloyd Burlingame, a celebrated Broadway set designer who was friends with Jim Herlihy and discussed with John Robert Lloyd how he had re-created the X-flat. "It was a brilliant and brave solution and totally true to what Jamie wrote in both style and content."

Schlesinger, boiling over with anxiety at the start of the film shoot, was less happy with other members of his team. The first to stumble was a young assistant director who couldn't cope with John's demands for quick solutions to problems in framing and shooting a scene on location in the crowded, seedy Times Square bar where Joe first meets Ratso. "The more the pressure increased, the more our young AD came unglued and chewed his fingernails to the cuticle," Jerry Hellman recalled. Ken Utt fired him the next day and proposed they replace him with Burtt Harris, a vastly more experienced assistant director who had worked with the cream of New York filmmakers, including Elia Kazan, Sidney Lumet, and Robert Rossen. Harris had originally been Utt's first choice but had turned down the offer because he was committed to

"His gaze was intense."
James Leo Herlihy in New York
in the 1950s (University of Delaware)

"I've met someone here."
Dick Duane's 1950s publicity
still. He was smart and witty,
and had a three-octave range
as a singer.
(Courtesy of Dick Duane)

"There was an aura about her."
Anaïs Nin, Herlihy's mentor
and intimate friend, in 1959
(Photograph by Deigh-Navin,
NY World-Telegram & Sun /
Library of Congress)

Tennessee Williams and literary friends— Thomas McGuane, Truman Capote, and James Kirkwood—in Key West (Key West Art and Historical Society)

Self-portrait of the artist as a young man: Jim Herlihy in 1965 (University of Delaware)

"A very lively place." A double-feature promise of thrills and kicks on Forty-second Street in 1967
(United Press International / Library of Congress)

Growth of Overt Homosexuality In City Provokes Wide Concern

By ROBERT C. DOTY

The problem of homosexuality in New York became the focus yesterday of increased attention by the State Liquor Authority and the Police Department.

The liquor authority announced the revocation of the liquor licenses of two more homosexual haunts that had been repeatedly raided by the police. The places were the Fawn, at 795 Washington Street near Jane Street, and the Heights Supper Club at 80 Montague Street, Brooklyn.

The city's most sensitive open secret—the presence of what is probably the greatest homosexual population in the world and its increasing openness—has become the subject of growing concern of psychiatrists, religious leaders and the police.

One division of the organized crime syndicate controls bars and restaurants that cater to the homosexual trade. Commenting yesterday on the situation, Police Commissioner Michael J. Murphy said:

"Homosexuality is another one of the many problems confronting law enforcement in this city. However, the underlying factors in homosexuality are not criminal but rather medical and sociological in nature.

"The police jurisdiction in this area is limited. But when persons of this type become a source of public scandal, or violate the laws, or place themselves in a position where they become the victims of crime they do come within our jurisdiction.

"This matter is of constant concern to us in our efforts to

Continued on Page 33, Column 1

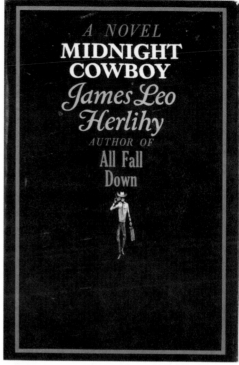

A *New York Times* front-page headline in December 1963 reflecting the conventional wisdom of its era

The original Simon & Schuster hardcover book jacket for *Midnight Cowboy*. Herlihy's mother told him the novel was pornographic.

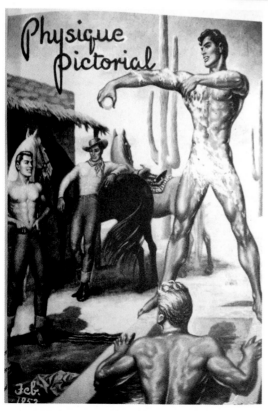

All the young cowboys coming out clean on the cover of *Physique Pictorial*, February 1953 (Library of Congress)

"I understood . . . that silly girl." Julie Christie with Dirk Bogarde in *Darling*, 1965
(*Look* / Library of Congress)

Jerome Hellman and John Schlesinger at the Malibu beach house where they worked on the *Midnight Cowboy* screenplay, fall 1967
(Courtesy of Michael Childers / Jerome Hellman)

The screenwriter Waldo Salt and Schlesinger working on the screenplay
(Courtesy of Michael Childers)

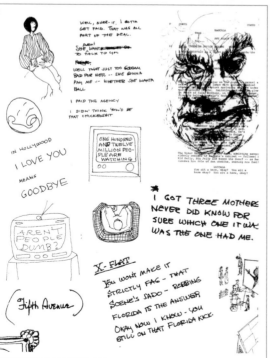

A page from Salt's diary of notes and sketches for *Midnight Cowboy*
(*Scenario* / Courtesy of Jennifer Salt)

Salt in San Antonio on the Texas location hunt, spring 1968 (Courtesy of Michael Childers)

Schlesinger in Big Spring, Texas, a pumpjack on the horizon over his right shoulder (Courtesy of Michael Childers)

"A surface air of innocence yet the possibility of violence." Kiel Martin, an early favorite for the role of Joe Buck (Courtesy of Michael Childers)

Casting director Marion Dougherty in the mid-1950s in a sea of publicity shots of aspiring actors (*Sunday Mirror* / Margaret Herrick Library)

Dougherty's casting card for Dustin Hoffman. "Bob Duval [*sic*] says is v.g.," she noted in pencil. (Marion Dougherty Foundation / Margaret Herrick Library)

Dougherty was more wary of Jon Voight: "Appealing clean cut Am. kid," she wrote. "Wouldn't think he'd be good for great emotion." (Marion Dougherty Foundation / Margaret Herrick Library)

"Welcome to Fun City." Mayor John V. Lindsay and staff inspect the garbage-strewn streets of New York during the 1968 sanitation workers' strike. (Associated Press)

The roundtable screenplay reading in the ballroom of the Astor Hotel near Times Square. It was here the improvisations began. Clockwise from left: Schlesinger, Hoffman, Barnard Hughes, Brenda Vaccaro, Voight, and Sylvia Miles
(Courtesy of Michael Childers)

Voight reading Joe Buck's lines. "There's comedy . . . but there's also this part of him that should break your heart."
(Courtesy of Michael Childers)

"I'm walkin' here!" Hoffman's classic improvisation when a cabbie ran a red light. But the scene, though not the dialogue, was in the script. (United Artists / Shutterstock)

Trying not to disrupt traffic near the Plaza Hotel. Voight and Hoffman are facing Schlesinger in the foreground. (United Artists / Photofest)

The hustler gets out-hustled by his first female customer. "I was gonna get that part if it killed me," Sylvia Miles recalled.

(United Artists / Photofest)

Schlesinger and Brenda Vaccaro. "What if my mother sees my tits?" she asked him.

(Courtesy of Michael Childers)

Voight and Jennifer Salt in Rome after the *Midnight Cowboy* shoot ended. His sudden fame was just around the corner.

(Courtesy of Jennifer Salt)

Hoffman as Ratso. "I thought he was dangerous if you cornered him." (Gotfryd Collection / Library of Congress)

Joe Buck cruises a Times Square arcade shooting gallery for customers. He was learning "what to say, what not to say, when to close the deal," wrote Herlihy. (Courtesy of Michael Childers)

Fake snowflakes on a hot June night as Joe and Ratso head to the Warhol-style loft party
(Courtesy of Michael Childers)

Warhol superstars Viva and Joe Dallesandro with Michael Childers between them prepping for the party scene
(Courtesy of Michael Childers)

Adam Holender, the Polish-born director of photography, on the set of his first American feature film. "I was participating in spirited work with spirited people." (Courtesy of Michael Childers)

Harry Nilsson prepares for a late-night take of "Everybody's Talkin'" at New York's famed Studio IA (Courtesy of Michael Childers)

Musical director John Barry and a weary Schlesinger that same evening (Courtesy of Michael Childers)

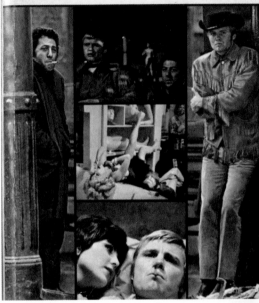

DELL
5611
75¢
NOW AN EXPLOSIVE MOVIE STARRING
DUSTIN HOFFMAN AND JON VOIGHT

MIDNIGHT COWBOY

James Leo Herlihy

The Dell paperback, with movie stills on its cover, whose sales helped make Jamie Herlihy a wealthy man

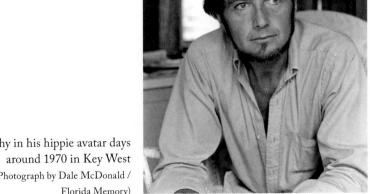

Herlihy in his hippie avatar days around 1970 in Key West
(Photograph by Dale McDonald /
Florida Memory)

Dustin Hoffman outside his burning Greenwich Village apartment in March 1970, after a Weather Underground bombmaker accidentally set off fifty pounds of TNT next door (Associated Press)

Jon Voight accepts the Best Director Oscar for John Schlesinger, who was too anxious and pessimistic to attend. (Margaret Herrick Library)

Michael Childers and John Schlesinger on vacation in Bodrum, Turkey, in 1988
(Photograph by Pat York / Copyright © Pat York)

Ratso and Joe hovering on the corner of Broome and Suffolk Streets in a 1968 publicity shot
(United Artists / Photofest)

The same site, now Essex Crossing, in March 2019, with luxury apartments under construction, ranging from $1.7 to $7.3 million
(Courtesy of the author)

help supervise the filming of Kazan's semiautobiographical novel *The Arrangement*, set to star Marlon Brando. But Brando backed out at the last minute and Kazan suspended the film shoot (he later replaced Brando with Kirk Douglas), freeing up Harris for *Midnight Cowboy*.

Harris was a supremely self-confident hipster who lived on Greenwich Avenue in the Village, wore love beads and wooden clogs on the set, smoked dope with Dustin Hoffman, and generally calmed everyone's nerves. He and John got along with a minimum of anxiety. At the end of each scene the anxious director would turn to Harris and ask, "Burtt, will it work?" to the point where Harris began addressing John as *WIW*.

Harris was also one of the few people whom John allowed to tease him about being gay. The assistant director's job includes getting the set ready as per the director's instructions. When all was prepared, Harris would announce, "We are ready for you, my queen." At which point, Schlesinger would smile, nod, and promise Harris he would soon be needing a new job. "Your day is coming," John warned.

"Burtt was winging it," says Adam Holender, "but with charm."

Still, despite Harris's best efforts, tensions often ran high. The crew was an experienced, hard-core set of New York technicians, proud members of local crafts unions. Schlesinger was worried that they would hate both the movie's subject matter and the director's homosexuality. "John had expressed to me all his fears," recalls Jerry Hellman. "What will happen when I come on the set, a gay man? Will people call me faggot? He was honest with me and he was also very frightened." Hellman says he pledged to Schlesinger that if anyone stepped out of line they would immediately be fired.

Whatever their negative feelings toward John, the crew kept them mostly to themselves. But Michael Childers was another matter. Some crew members were openly hostile to the young man they tagged as the boss's toy boy. "I was their big scapegoat and they made my life miserable," Michael recalls. "Oh, it's the director's boyfriend!" They invoked union rules to prevent him from taking still photographs on the set. Some of them barked at him whenever he came near. "I'd go home and cry every night," Michael recalls. "It was rough. And John was enraged."

Schlesinger himself later said, "It wasn't a very happy film. I hated a lot of the technicians on the New York crew."

Holender, who was by Schlesinger's side every day of the film shoot and sometimes bore the brunt of his frustrations, says the conflicts with the crew were essentially cultural. "John wasn't comfortable with them," he recalls. "They were a very good crew of superb technicians, the best New York had to offer at that time, but they all came from a certain background—mostly Irish Catholics—and John's flamboyance wasn't much to their liking."

Schlesinger also clashed at times with Holender and his camera crew. Adam had done an excellent job of coordinating the lighting of the stairway outside the X-flat, which was shot at the original tenement building, with the lighting of the X-flat itself after it was re-created at Filmways, allaying John's fears that the flat's interior would look like an artificial stage set rather than the real thing. But although he admired Holender's work, John complained that many of the sets were too elaborately lit, costing the production time and money. At one point, on a hot day, while shooting a dream sequence at a vacant, disused subway station in Brooklyn, he grabbed a broom and smashed a series of lights. Jerry Hellman went off with John and Michael that weekend to the cottage John was renting on Fire Island, the heart of the gay summer scene, where they discussed firing both Holender and his gaffer, the man in charge of lighting. They decided to keep Adam but let the gaffer go, and they replaced him with a classic New Yorker named Willie Meyerhoff, a compact bundle of energy who promised he could "shoot this sucker with a couple of flashlights." The schedule began to speed up, and John grew more and more pleased with Holender's work, which he felt became edgier and more powerful as the film shoot progressed.

As cinematographer, Holender had a front-row seat to the various conflicts taking place behind the scenes. He quickly sensed there was a budget crisis hovering over the film shoot. While John himself always insisted on the best-quality work regardless of cost, Holender says, "Suddenly the production manager would come to me and say, 'We cannot afford to have two dollies on this scene, we have a budget problem and it takes too long.'" Things would quiet down for a while and then the manager would be back with more complaints. "The pressure was to do things faster. You sensed people wishing you would stop caring as much and just get it done." Holender recalls a moment near the end of the shooting on New York streets when there was no appropriate-sized dolly available to roll a very large camera down a Sixth Avenue sidewalk. "Somebody on the equipment truck had one of those little things on four wheels and I asked him to bring it and a piece of plywood and put the camera on that, and it was done," he says.

Schlesinger found his American actors more playful and freewheeling than their British counterparts. Sylvia Miles was fiercely determined to play Cass, the quintessential tough-as-nails New Yorker, without compromise or any effort to make her appear sympathetic. Cass had learned to take care of herself—she didn't harbor any illusions or expect anyone's sympathy. Bob Balaban played the mewling high school student at the run-down movie house with the same uncompromising honesty. John personally identified with the kid, whom he described as a gay bar mitzvah boy.

Balaban was on-screen for less than three and a half minutes but says they shot his scenes in reverse chronological order and over several months—an indication of how fragmented and difficult it was to line up locations in New York, even with the help of the mayor's office. First they did the men's room scene, which was shot in the bathroom of a cheap hotel near Times Square sometime in May. Then, in June, they shot the balcony scene at the Fillmore East, on Second Avenue in the East Village. And they finished with a brief shot of Balaban's character eyeing Joe Buck, outside a cheap second-run grindhouse on Forty-second Street, in September, after the film company had returned from Florida and Texas. Despite the fragmented nature of the shoot, Jerry Hellman was moved by Balaban's performance. It was "one of the most profoundly affecting and believable scenes in the movie," he says.

Overcoming his misgivings over playing the part of Townsend Locke, the sadomasochistic gay businessman from Chicago, Barnard Hughes was fully committed once the cameras started rolling. When John had difficulty figuring out how to make Joe Buck's brutal assault on Towny with a telephone receiver appear realistic, Hughes took John aside and told him he was wearing false teeth and could spit them out without using his hands. He did so on camera just before Joe jams the receiver into Towny's gaping mouth. The effect was shocking. Schlesinger was delighted and amazed at Hughes's lack of vanity.

Hoffman and Voight were a constant revelation. They never let up, discussing their characters every day at lunch and continuing their improv exercises well into the film shoot. "It was a pleasure to see two actors not only cooperating but feeding off each other," says Holender. "It improved the quality of the work tremendously."

There were times toward the end of a long workday when one man would help pull the other through one last take with gentle encouragement and other times when one would goad the other to do better or face having the scene cut to emphasize the other character. "We really did like each other, and at the same time we were very competitive," Hoffman recalls.

A key moment occurred when the two men arrive at the drab entrance hall of a loft building where they've been invited to a psychedelic "Witches' Sabbath" party. The scene was filmed on a sweltering June night in lower Manhattan; Schlesinger recalled the temperature hitting ninety-eight degrees, but perhaps he was measuring his own feverish state—weather records for that month showed no days where the thermometer exceeded ninety. In any case, the crew revved up a machine that poured fake snowflakes made of corn starch on Voight and Hoffman as Joe dragged Ratso down the sidewalk and then up the front steps to the drab foyer inside the building. Ratso was struggling to catch his breath, his face streaked with perspiration, his lips a pale blue. The script calls for Joe to pull out his shirttail and wipe Ratso's head dry. But Voight and Hoffman took it further. As Joe wipes Ratso's head, Ratso rests his face against Joe's bare abdomen and places his left arm around Joe's back. It's a tender moment, done quickly and silently, yet it suggests both the depths of Ratso's illness and the growing intimacy between the two men. Schlesinger adored it. "That was something they did, not something I suggested," he said, "and it's a very very beautiful moment that I've always thanked the actors for." Hoffman was proud of it, too—he felt it captured the growing bond between Joe and Ratso that they themselves could never acknowledge. "The audience knows they're seeing something that the characters aren't consciously aware of," he said.

Schlesinger appreciated Hoffman's willingness to try anything and his sharp, perverse sense of humor, which was often directed at himself. On the days when they broke for a long lunch during the shoot, John would insist on eating at one of the nicer midtown restaurants. Hoffman would arrive late, and always in costume and character, limping to the table and making the maître d' and the waiters uncomfortable. John, himself a born mischief-maker, loved the performance.

Dozens of women would gather outside police barricades at the locations where the movie was shooting—not just teenyboppers cutting high school classes but middle-aged women who came to watch the Jewish Cary Grant. Jerry Hellman had to hire four private security guards to protect Hoffman from his ardent army of fans. "Please let me see him, please!" pleaded one teenaged girl with glasses. One day an older woman standing just behind the barrier where the public was herded got upset when Hoffman, who was busy going over a scene in the screenplay with Voight, didn't respond to her demand for an autograph. She kept trying to get his attention without success. When the two men left their seats to do the scene, she cried out, *"Mr. Hoffman, I paid for you!"*

Few of the onlookers knew who Voight was, and his anonymity gave him a degree of protection from the rancorous hero worship they aimed at Hoffman like a loaded pistol. But Voight caught the eye of one elderly bystander, who flirted with him one afternoon across a narrow sidewalk police barricade. "Well, you're pretty, I'll say that, you *are* pretty," she told him, evoking his shy Joe Buck–type smile. "So don't be bewildered, darling. Anything you want to know, you just ask me."

Brenda Vaccaro was excited to be appearing in her first major movie, and she and Schlesinger generally got along fine—John loved teasing young actors, especially women, and she teased him right back. But she was also strong-willed and assertive and felt she deserved to be taken seriously. She enjoyed working with Jon Voight because he always seemed game to try anything a fellow actor wanted to do. At one point she suggested that the morning after Shirley and Joe have their tryst, the scene should show Shirley paying him the twenty dollars for his sexual services she had agreed to. Voight was all for trying it, but Schlesinger rather haughtily dismissed the idea as a waste of time and film. Vaccaro wouldn't back down. "I didn't like his fucking attitude—he could be so bitchy sometimes," she recalls. She pleaded that he at least film the scene both ways. "It was my instinct," she says. "What was I going to do, just walk away?"

John reluctantly caved. But after watching the two versions, he conceded. "Actually, darling, you're right," he told Vaccaro. "We'll do it your way."

A bigger problem arose over how to film the big sex scene from the night before. At first, when Joe and Shirley get to her apartment and jump into bed, he fails to achieve an erection. After some mocking double entendres on her part, he rises to the occasion and they engage in a snarling test of strength that climaxes with mutual orgasms. Vaccaro had reluctantly agreed to do the scene nude but insisted her nipples be covered by pasties. Schlesinger had faced a similar problem with Julie Christie while making *Darling*, and he had bullied her into allowing him to shoot her nipples. But Vaccaro wouldn't budge. She had insisted on a clause in her contract that prohibited her nipples being shown in the released film and now she was invoking it. "It's my screen debut," she told Schlesinger. "What if my mother sees my tits before she sees my face? Do you know what you're doing to my life?"

Still, she recalls, "The pasties were driving me crazy. They were sticky, they were itchy, it was awful. He said to get rid of them."

It was the ever-resourceful Ann Roth who came up with a solution. She had met a shady guy who loaned money to longshoremen from a parking lot next to her apartment building. As she walked home one evening she saw a red fox-fur coat in the back seat of his car that she couldn't resist. He said she could have it for two hundred dollars. She thought it might make a great coat for Shirley, the affluent socialite. "I figured if she doesn't wear it I'll wear it," Roth recalls. After pondering the nipples dilemma, she took the coat to Schlesinger and drew him a picture. "Look, John," she told him, "her loft is cold, she's gonna be naked. She needs to wear this to stay warm." John, she says, "loved the idea."

Roth announced it to Vaccaro and Voight. "I think she should be fucked in fox."

"Fox?" asked Vaccaro.

"Yes, nothing but fox," Roth replied.

Thanks to the fur and some skillful editing, there are plenty of naked backs and thighs and lots of heavy breathing in the scene, but just one brief flash cut of a woman's nipple.

Like Ann Roth with her resourceful bag of tricks, Waldo Salt was constantly on call for writerly emergencies. He sat in on all the rehearsals, produced rewrites on demand, and even supplied the voice over the phone of Maury, the irritable sugar daddy who pimps for Cass, Sylvia Miles's character, while paying the rent for her penthouse apartment. Salt was available whenever a scene didn't play the way John thought it should. As late as May 30—more than a month into the film shoot—Waldo was still producing new pages for the Cass scene and the cemetery scene, where Ratso and Joe visit the grave of Ratso's father, as well as a new five-page opening scene for the movie that was quickly scrapped, just like a half dozen predecessors, by the chronically uneasy Schlesinger. His most crucial house call came toward the end of the New York shoot, when he got a panicked call from Schlesinger at eleven in the morning. "Your scene isn't fucking working," he told Waldo. "Get down here."

It was the pivotal moment when Joe returns to the X-flat from his night of paid sex with Shirley. He's carrying a small grocery bag with warm socks, mentholatum, cough syrup, and aspirin for Ratso that he's bought with Shirley's money, only to find Ratso in a rapidly deteriorating physical state and panicking. He had fallen down a flight of stairs after the psychedelic party the previous evening and now he's shivering, sweating, and frightened because he can no longer walk. Joe says he'll go for a doctor, but Ratso stops him—he wants no cops, no doctors. He's afraid they'll stick him in Bellevue, the city hospital for the indigent. "Once they get their hooks in you you're dead."

This suddenly becomes a critical moment for Joe, who must decide whether his loyalty lies with his newly promising male hustler career or with his dying friend who's desperate to get to Florida for a chance to stay alive. But Schlesinger and the two actors could sense that the scene wasn't jelling—it was coming across as too cloying and sentimental.

Salt showed up at Filmways around noon looking like he'd just fallen out of bed. "His hair was all over the place, he was baggy-eyed and bloodshot," recalls Voight.

"What's this scene about?" Schlesinger demanded, and Waldo took a minute to read through the script before starting to break it down. Waldo told them that Joe is sympathetic to Ratso's plight, but he's also angry at Ratso because he's finally succeeded in scoring with a woman for money and is hoping to entice many more, and now Ratso's illness is standing in the way. Waldo told them that the gifts Joe has brought home to the X-flat are his way of telling Ratso goodbye, it's been nice to know you, but I'm on my way and you're on your own. "Joe's selfish," Waldo told Voight. "He's looking at Ratso as an inconvenience in his life from getting what he's always wanted." Waldo pointed out an accusation Joe throws at Ratso: "Just when everything's going my way, you gotta pull a stunt like this."

"Whoa," recalls Voight, "that made the whole scene work for me. Waldo was the one that saved the day."

"That's very good, thank you, Waldo," said Schlesinger. And Waldo Salt went home.

For Salt, the moment epitomized the sublime beauty of working with Schlesinger and two superb actors. "My dad had never had people who adored him and respected him and wanted him to collaborate like that," says Jennifer Salt. "He'd always lived in fear of producers, the bad guys. But these were his colleagues. They were his brothers."

In Jim Herlihy's novel, the big party scene is a hipster-style affair out of the late 1950s, with marijuana, brown capsules of uncertain substance called "bombers," two guys holding hands on the dance floor, and live music from a jazz trio consisting of bongo drums, recorder, and jug. It is hosted by Hansel and Gretel MacAlbertson, identically dressed twins living off Broadway in an East Village loft. They see Joe having coffee at the Eighth Street Nedick's in Greenwich Village and hand him a flyer inviting him to attend. But by the time of the film shoot, that kind of party felt at least ten years out of date. Michael Childers, who served as *Midnight Cowboy*'s unofficial envoy to the increasingly bizarre world of New York's pop culture scene, suggested that John and Jerry transform the party into an Andy Warhol–style pop art happening. Waldo Salt, who himself had been to more than a few of these events in his informal role as cool, stoned Hollywood screenplay writer, bought into the idea. Michael recruited Paul Morrissey, a filmmaker who was working at Andy Warhol's Factory creating avant-garde movies, to help them figure out how to organize and film the scene.

Like Jon Voight, Morrissey had been raised in Yonkers. A tall, austere man with a constant scowl on his face, Morrissey was a walking contradiction by comparison with the young, stoned-out, hippie acolytes who worshipped Warhol and competed for his favor. He loved classic Hollywood movies, didn't smoke or drink, and despised the sex-and-drugs culture Warhol was presiding over at the Factory. According to Ultra Violet, one of Warhol's troupe of "superstars," Morrissey had the soul of a social worker and the politics of a conservative Republican. He was already nursing a deep well of resentment and jealousy about Warhol, who took credit for creating the films that Morrissey felt were his own artistic product.

Michael took John for dinner one evening at Max's Kansas City on Park Avenue South, just across Union Square from the Factory. It was one of Warhol's favorite haunts—he had his own table, where he presided over his entourage of superstars, including Ultra Violet (whose real name was Isabelle Collin Dufresne), Viva, Holly Woodlawn, Taylor Mead, and Joe Dallesandro, their photogenic young superstud. Michael and John also met Salvador Dalí, Robert Rauschenberg, Paloma Picasso, and Yves Saint Laurent at Max's. "Teeny boppers and sculptors, rock stars and poets from St. Mark's Place, Hollywood actors checking out what the underground actors were all about, boutique owners and models, modern dancers and go-go dancers—everyone went to Max's and everything got homogenized there," Warhol would recall in *POPism*, his 1980 memoir.

Schlesinger was intrigued by these exotic creatures. "John thought they were rather extraordinary freaks," says Michael, "all these drag queens shooting up in the bathroom and Andy being vacuous." John was fond of staging party scenes in his films—the tawdry Paris sex show in *Darling*, the barn dance in *Far from the Madding Crowd*, and further down the road, the bar mitzvah reception in *Sunday Bloody Sunday* all revealed small but important truths about the worlds he was depicting. His nephew Ian Buruma speculates that John wanted to use the party scene in *Midnight Cowboy* to show the vastly different layers of society that coexisted uneasily in late-sixties Manhattan.

By inviting them to appear in the scene, Schlesinger and Childers were tickling Warhol and his gang on their most tender spot. Parties were not just their obsession but their reason for being. "There was always a party somewhere," Warhol would write. "If there wasn't a party in the cellar, there was one on the roof; if there wasn't a party in a subway, there was one on a bus; if there wasn't one on a boat, there was one in the Statue of Liberty."

Warhol was at the height of his pop art celebrityhood and his own self-cult. He saw himself as part visionary, part entrepreneur. "We were seeing the future and we knew it for sure," he boasted in *POPism*, adding, "We weren't just *at* the art exhibit—we *were* the art exhibit, we were the art incarnate."

Others didn't buy Warhol's vision. "Fame was the name of the game," said Truman Capote, who knew more than a little about that particular subject. "Not really talent. Not Art." Money, of course, was part of it, too, as was Warhol's genius at recognizing new waves of innovation in art and printing and employing them on his ride to fame. "Warhol's art is about currency, in every sense of the word," writes Adam D. Weinberg, director of the Whitney Museum, in the preface to the catalog for the Whitney's 2018 Warhol retrospective.

Warhol fawned over major celebrities like Capote, John Lennon, Mick Jagger, Bob Dylan, and Susan Sontag, while setting minor ones against each other. "He'd just lick his chops and sit back and watch these people have at each other and pretend he didn't know anything about it," said Danny Fields, a former music industry executive, journalist, and keen observer of the scene. "He would let them crawl all over each other's egos and bodies and reputations to get closer to him. Quite a collection."

Amphetamines, barbiturates, amyl nitrate, heroin, and LSD were among the drugs of choice in Warhol's magic kingdom. It was hard not to notice that many members of his crowd died premature deaths from drug abuse that he claimed to know nothing about, including his most glamorous superstar, the charismatic but drug-addled socialite Edie Sedgwick. The French-born Ultra Violet would later brand Warhol "a brilliant con artist" and "the spiritual father of AIDS, casual gay sex and equally casual needle-sharing having been the ritual daily fare at the Factory." Yet he moved the art world, and certainly the art business, into a new era of big money and celebrity worship, a place where fifteen minutes of fame could seem like an eternity.

Warhol, Morrissey, and their followers were fascinated by Hollywood and hungry for the riches and fame that its star-making machinery could still bestow. By the mid-sixties Warhol had announced his retirement from painting and spent most of his creative time making films. Some were excruciating avant-garde exercises like *Sleep* (1963)—six and one-half hours of a man sleeping—and *Empire* (1964), an eight-hour static portrait of the Empire State Building. Others, like *My Hustler* (1965) and *Chelsea Girls* (1966), packed occasional moments of humor or drama in what otherwise came across as badly lit, out-of-focus, tedious home movies about sex, drugs, voyeurism, and boredom. "Warhol's films get people in the audience to stare at a face and a moment," says film historian Ronald Gregg. "He filmed in real time and then slowed it down to silent-movie speed to force us to stare even harder. It's a bit like looking at a piece of art. He was a tease, and the joke is overdone until it's not really funny anymore." Still, Gregg, along with other critics, credits Warhol with expanding the boundaries of what movies could be. He finds, for example, artistry and pathos in *Chelsea Girls*. "It still speaks to me."

Chelsea Girls, a three-hour series of long vignettes on a split screen, was filmed over four days on a three-thousand-dollar budget. It was a breakthrough commercially—the first Warhol movie to be shown at mainstream aboveground movie houses in New York and the first to make a substantial profit. The *Newsweek* film critic Jack Kroll called it "The *Iliad* of the Underground." Hollywood also paid attention. While the film techniques were less than rudimentary, the fact that *Chelsea Girls* played uptown suggested the old taboos were collapsing. "What may be a provocative theme today, may seem quite ordinary three or four years from now," David Picker told Vincent Canby of *The New York Times*.

John and Michael asked Warhol to play an underground filmmaker in their *Midnight Cowboy* party scene, but he was uneasy about publicly exposing himself in a setting he couldn't control. Instead, he suggested Viva, the most stylish, photogenic, and funny of the superstars, a woman with a sharp acidic tongue, a taste for outrage, and few inhibitions. She and Morrissey helped the movie crew round up a handful of other Warhol regulars and some forty extras for the party shoot. Some of the superstars, including Viva, whose real name was Janet Susan Mary Hoffmann, came out one weekend to John and Michael's cottage on Fire Island. John got seriously stoned on marijuana, something he'd seldom done before.

At first the superstars were excited to be in a Hollywood movie. But they soon realized that most of them were only going to appear in a black-and-white eight-millimeter film within a film, to be directed by Morrissey and Childers, or else as extras. Only Viva and a six-foot-five-inch, strikingly handsome nineteen-year-old actor named Gastone Rossilli would have brief speaking parts, playing the spaced-out MacAlbertson twins, Hansel and Gretel, the party's wealthy socialite hosts. "We were bitter at first," recalled Ultra Violet. "Don't they trust us? Don't they think we have enough talent to appear with the Hollywood people?" Still, the Factory people were happy to get paid—those with speaking parts got $125 a day, while extras were paid $25 plus lunch. For his own films, Warhol had paid most of them exactly nothing.

Rossilli was not a Warhol person but an aspiring actor who had studied with Sanford Meisner and appeared off-Broadway in the Circle in the Square production of *Iphigenia in Aulis*, starring Irene Papas. The keen-eyed Marion Dougherty had admired his performance as Achilles—Rossilli, with his helmet of perfectly coiffed curly locks, looked like the ideal Greek warrior—and summoned him to her town-house office, where he auditioned for Schlesinger. "I was young and very naïve and very serious about my work," Rossilli recalls. "It was a very exciting time and a kind of innocent time as well. People were breaking all sorts of rules and regulations and thinking, Wow, this is terrific."

Viva, who possessed both the talent and the prominent cheekbones to have a shot at becoming a genuine movie star, was thrilled for even a small role in a mainstream film. On the afternoon of June 3 she called Warhol to tell him that she and Rossilli were uptown at Mr. Kenneth's renowned hair salon, on East Fifty-fourth Street, trying out hairstyles and matching colors for their roles. As they were talking, she heard several loud pops across the phone line—at first she thought it was someone cracking a whip, but then she realized she was hearing gunshots from inside the Factory. The shooter was Valerie Solanas, an angry, thwarted, and deeply disturbed woman—author of the manifesto for her self-created Society for Cutting Up Men (SCUM), of which she was the sole member. Solanas was furious with Warhol for refusing to produce her play, *Up Your Ass*, which she considered a brilliant treatise on male domination and female liberation. Warhol owed her money, she kept insisting, as well as respect. She had arrived at the Factory seeking retribution and packing a .32-caliber handgun.

Solanas shot Warhol twice at close range; the two bullets passed through his stomach, liver, spleen, esophagus, and both lungs. He was in surgery for five hours and almost died on the operating table. Still, as soon as he was out of intensive care, he phoned a writer at *Life* magazine who had been working on a major piece about him to ask about press coverage of the shooting. Warhol was crushed to learn that the assassination of Robert F. Kennedy, shot dead in Los Angeles three days after Warhol was attacked, had pushed him off the front pages and dropped him out of *Life* altogether. RFK's death also meant Schlesinger and his crew had to suspend outdoor shooting for a day because the line of mourners outside St. Patrick's Cathedral, on Fifth Avenue, where the coffin was on display, stretched for twenty-five blocks.

It seemed sadly fitting that the shooting of a pop artist who worshipped celebrity had been superseded by the shooting of an even larger celebrity. To cheer Warhol up, Viva went around the *Midnight Cowboy* film set with a portable tape recorder asking the cast and crew to send him messages. Ann Skinner, John's loyal aide, who had arrived from London to visit the film set, felt like she had landed in some exotic land. "Get well, Andy," she spoke into the machine.

Warhol's recovery was slow and painful, and the *Midnight Cowboy* party went on without him. First John and Adam Holender filmed the coffee shop scene where Hansel and Gretel spot Joe Buck, take his photo, and hand him a flyer inviting him to their party. They were dressed by Ann Roth in identical leather trench coats, black kilts, and boots. For the party scene itself, John Robert Lloyd once again put together a superb set in the cavernous studio at Filmways that convincingly played the role of a Lower East Side loft, the perfect spot for a psychedelic happening. On June 28, a chartered bus pulled up outside Max's Kansas City at seven in the morning to pick up fifty Warhol recruits and ferry them to East 127th Street, where Roth oversaw the dressing of their self-chosen outfits. Viva, who knew how to command a crowd, took charge, ordering everyone to listen to instructions and do what they were told. She charmed many of the important film people, including Waldo Salt and Burtt Harris, each of whom decided she was in love with him. "It was six days of wonderful mayhem and controlled chaos," Harris recalls.

The professional actors at times were overwhelmed by the spectacle. "The party scene got a little bit crazy," says Brenda Vaccaro. "There was no discipline, no security. I walked into my dressing room, and two people were on my bed fucking. Most of them were just high on dope."

The Warhol people weren't the only ones who were smoking marijuana while the cameras rolled. Schlesinger, who had growing increasingly fond of grass during his weekends at Fire Island, suggested that Jon Voight and Brenda Vaccaro smoke a joint in a photographic darkroom where they adjourn for some impassioned necking after their characters meet. Michael Childers supplied the equipment—red lights and trays of film developing chemicals—from his own darkroom. Bathed in a warm red light that enhances the eroticism of the moment, they entwine their fingers around each other's hands while they make out.

The party went on continuously into the evening after the actual film shoot had wrapped for the day. The free love and drugs on offer offended the straighter members of the crew, for whom alcohol was the only acceptable substance for recreational abuse. Willy Meyerhoff, the gaffer who had stepped in to help light the film shoot, told Jerry Hellman that as a staunch Catholic he couldn't abide the pot smoking. He agreed to stay on until the party sequence was in the can, but quit the crew immediately afterward.

The party scene takes up less than eight minutes of the final cut of the movie. Nonetheless, says Gastone Rossilli (who later changed his first name to Paul), it captured a basic truth about New York's pop culture world in the sixties. "There was this incredible mix of high society and low society, and everybody would go," he recalls. "And so a society woman like Brenda Vaccaro's character, a successful young professional, of course she would be there. And a young, attractive hustler like Joe Buck, they saw him, he looked interesting, they took a picture and said, 'C'mon, of course, you're coming, too.' This is what the city had to offer in those days. It fit perfectly into the film."

Andy Warhol, recovering slowly from his wounds, grew jealous that John Schlesinger was making a movie about a male hustler in Times Square—Andy's subject and turf. "They're moving into our territory," he complained to Paul Morrissey. With Warhol's blessing, Morrissey went ahead to make his own hustler movie, *Flesh*, starring Joe Dallesandro, about a male prostitute who sets out to raise two hundred dollars to pay for an abortion for his wife's girlfriend. Shot over four days for four thousand dollars, it came out in the fall of 1968, more than a half year before *Midnight Cowboy*. It contained full-frontal nudity, one erection, voyeurism, and fetishism—all of the pornographic eroticism that *Midnight Cowboy* carefully tiptoed around. It ran for seven months at the Garrick Theatre on Bleecker Street, then moved uptown for several more weeks.

Still, Warhol always saw the *Midnight Cowboy* film shoot as a missed opportunity for himself and his superstars. He understood that if both Hollywood and the underground were making movies about male hustlers, people would inevitably go see the Hollywood version because it was less threatening and it *looked* better. John Schlesinger should have given him a budget and the autonomy to make a true film within the film. "I was so jealous," Warhol would later recall. "I thought, 'Why didn't they give *us* the money to do, say, *Midnight Cowboy*?' We could have done it so *real* for them."

Of all people, Andy Warhol, who existed and trafficked in the twilight zone between reality and imagination, should have understood that John and Jerry didn't want a movie about real male hustlers or a real psychedelic happening, just the *appearance* of each. And thanks in part to Warhol's people, that's exactly what they got.

16. NOSE CONES AND RATTLESNAKES: THE FLORIDA AND TEXAS FILM SHOOTS

Do you really think anyone's going to pay money to see a movie about a dumb Texan who takes a bus to New York to seek his fortune screwing rich old women?

—John Schlesinger

The New York film shoot wrapped up on July 9, several days after they finished shooting the Warhol party scenes. After a week of postproduction work, John Schlesinger and the film crew took off for Florida. It was as if the film company had entered some kind of time loop. Having shot the dominant center part of the film, which takes place in Manhattan, they would now move forward in time and film the ending, then go on to Texas and shoot the very beginning of Joe Buck's life and the circumstances that led to his journey to New York. It had been a grimy and humid summer in the city—Manhattan had felt to John like an oven with the dial turned all the way to broil. He should have been happy to escape. But Florida promised to be even hotter.

As usual, Waldo Salt came along for script revisions on the fly. The first sequence to be shot in Florida was Ratso's fantasy about his new life, a daydream he engages in one evening while waiting across the street from the Fifth Avenue hotel where Joe has gone to meet a "date," a young woman whose name and address Ratso has purloined from a male escort service.

Even though he'd finally fled the pressure cooker of New York, John was still a very anxious director. When they arrived at the Diplomat Beach Resort in Hollywood, Florida, just north of Miami Beach, he took one long stroll around the pool and the nearby beach and came back demanding a rewrite of all the fantasy scenes—Ratso, without his limp, overtaking Joe in a foot race down the beach; Ratso getting his shoes shined while Joe receives a manicure poolside; Ratso shooting craps by the pool with five elderly matrons in bathing suits and furs; Ratso wearing a cream-colored sports coat with an RR crest on the jacket pocket and a black cowboy hat that he doffs to acknowledge the women calling his name from the hotel balcony; and finally Ratso in a chef's hat putting finishing touches on a poolside buffet and reading off bingo numbers before a sun-tanned platoon of older women. They filmed the foot race with every possible ending: Joe winning easily, the two men tied, and Ratso pulling ahead triumphantly. John became enchanted by the intense brightness of the Florida sun, the garish colors, the feeling of decadence, even the hideous white paper cones that the women wore over their noses to prevent sunburn—"I loved the nose cones, so I went mad and put them on everybody," said John.

He still wanted more humor and energy in the fantasy scenes. He huddled that evening with Jerry Hellman, Dustin Hoffman, Jon Voight, and Waldo Salt, after which Waldo went back to work. For once, he finished the rewrite on time, and John was very satisfied with the results.

Waldo also excelled in his usual capacity as cynical wise man. Adam Holender recalls spending a long day driving around Miami with John and Waldo searching for suitable locations. Adam and John spent considerable time complaining about United Artists' rejection of their request to rent an expensive crane for a long shot of a bus for the climactic shot following Ratso's death, and Waldo grew annoyed. "Look, you guys don't understand," he told them. "Studios have a little pile of money. They want to have a bigger pile of money. The business they're in is film-making, and that's where you come in. You spend the money; they hate you." It was, says Holender, "a lesson about capitalism from Waldo Salt."

The process of reviewing each day's work was unwieldy: the exposed film had to be flown to New York every evening by courier, processed by a lab, and then flown back to Miami the next day. Jerry's staff would pick it up and deliver it to a local screening room, where John, Jerry, Adam, and other members of the crew would view the results. Fortunately, the rushes looked great. The fantasy scenes, with their loose-limbed physical comedy, would provide a fresh ocean breeze of a respite from the bleakness of the New York sections and allow Dustin Hoffman a chance to briefly step out from the city's dark shadows and play Ratso as an entertainer/con man in the glaring spotlight of the harsh Florida sun.

Hoffman's nerves, like John's, seemed on edge. He tensed up when a busload of female admirers showed up unexpectedly outside the hotel on the first day of filming. To make matters worse, Jerry Hellman had neglected to arrange a car to pick him up and take him to see the dailies of the fantasy scenes. John summoned Jerry to his suite, where he dressed him down in front of Hoffman. Jerry understood that John was doing this to impress Dustin and calm him down, and Jerry claims it didn't bother him. But he couldn't help comparing Hoffman's high-maintenance attitude to Jon Voight's quiet, no-drama approach and the close ties he forged with the crew.

Ratso's death scene on the bus was shot starting on a causeway, with the camera and its operator harnessed to a platform built on the outside of the vehicle and peering through the window so that it captured not only the two actors sitting inside but also reflections of the palm trees and hotels as the bus passed by. It was terribly hot and the bus's air-conditioning was going full blast. Hoffman had so much trouble keeping his eyes open without blinking after Ratso expired that Hellman brought in a doctor to anesthetize his eyes with special drops.

Jerry was worried about expenses, which already had exceeded the total budget by several hundred thousand dollars. Even the fact that the dailies were looking terrific was of little comfort. Throughout his career Jerry was used to hearing talk about how great the dailies were on a given film only to discover that the actual movie turned out to be terrible. He believed that the writing, acting, camerawork, and directing on *Midnight Cowboy* were superb, but so much depended on editing choices, sound, and music, all of which had yet to happen. He was also anticipating a grim reality in his personal life lurking just over the horizon—that once the film was finished, he would be totally on his own. His business partnership with Arthur Jacobs was over; he had no new movie lined up to start work on. He wasn't even sure whether he wanted to go back to Los Angeles by himself or remain in New York, where his two children were living with his now ex-wife. His bank account was low and his meager advance money from the movie was already drained. He didn't have his own apartment there. And private school fees for his two kids would be due again soon. Despite all his hard work on _Midnight Cowboy_, Jerry's self-confidence was shot. In early September he would turn forty, a landmark moment he did not anticipate with joy. "I felt I existed in the center of a big empty hole," he recalled, "and when I was alone with myself I feared that it was going to swallow me without a trace."

Big Spring, population thirty thousand, is located in the heart of West Texas, at the geological meeting place of the arid Staked Plains and the vast Edwards Plateau. For ten generations the area had served as a strategic watering hole for Comanche warriors on their way south to Mexico every spring to raid for horses, cattle, and slaves. An invasion of white settlers, Texas Rangers, and U.S. Army cavalrymen over forty years vanquished the Comanches in the longest war ever fought on American soil. Buffalo hunters followed, laying waste with ruthless efficiency to vast herds, leaving behind a prairie so covered with bleached bones that one rancher could recall trekking the length of his property without his feet ever touching dirt. The most recent invaders were oilmen whose machines sucked hundreds of thousands of barrels of petroleum out of the ground.

The old cattle ranches were shriveling, but Big Spring remained a traditional Texas town, dominated by frontier culture, cars, alcohol, and church life, "isolated by its geography, shielded by its sand and wind and locals bent on keeping the status quo," writes the author Bryan Mealer, whose great-grandfather had come to Big Spring from Georgia in 1892.

No one in the town had ever seen anything quite like the invasion of the _Midnight Cowboy_ film company, with its exotic collection of actors and crew and an armada of trucks, catering vehicles, and special air-conditioning equipment designed to cool the location shoots in the blistering summer heat.

The God-fearing residents of Big Spring were thrilled at the chance to participate in a real live Hollywood movie. Word spread far and wide that the movie folks were looking to hire authentic locals—an ad in the *Big Spring Herald* listed "rodeo-type performers, gospel singers, a 45–50 year old Negro male musician, boys 19–24 years old, and a blond man, six foot one or two." Wealthy oilmen and ranchers from all over Texas were intrigued—a handful flew in on their private jets to audition for even the smallest of parts. "In the end none of the heavy hitters made the cut," Jerry Hellman recalled.

Few if any of the residents knew what *Midnight Cowboy* was really about. The *Herald* had demurely described the movie as "a late western" in which a young man sets out for New York from his small Texas town "in search of love and success." They had no idea that Joe Buck was dreaming of becoming a male prostitute and that *Midnight Cowboy* was replete with sexual content, straight and gay. When they found out later, "people in town were scandalized and felt betrayed," writes Mealer, whose grandmother Opal had been one of the singers in the baptism scene. "It would take years for Opal to live down her role."

One morning soon after the film company arrived, they took some forty locals out to Moss Creek, east of town, to film the scene in which a young Joe Buck, played by ten-year-old Gary Owens, a blond-haired Big Spring boy, is baptized in the creek while the extras sing hymns on shore accompanied by guitar and accordion. John Schlesinger, dressed in a straw cowboy hat, plaid shorts, and cowboy boots, had first rehearsed his makeshift choir in the coffee shop of the local Ramada Inn, before busing them out to the site. He urged them to add more emphatic "amens" and "hallelujahs" as the baptism ceremony took place. The preacher was played by Truman Friday, a former traveling evangelist and boot shop proprietor, now serving as a pastor of Temple Baptist Church and Midland County deputy sheriff. John left nothing to chance—he even had an underwater camera flown in from Los Angeles for a shot from young Joe's perspective as he goes under the surface. More dollar signs and red ink flashed before Jerry's anxious eyes.

Later in the day, young Owens spent more than an hour hurling jars and bottles at a mirror in a long-vacant store dressed as Sally Buck's vintage 1950s beauty parlor. A *Dallas Morning News* reporter at the scene captured the moment, and John's relentless perfectionism. "Too fast," the director said. "Let's try again." The crew brought in a new mirror. "Three takes later, he was happy," the *Morning News* reported.

Jon Voight had left Florida and arrived in Big Spring a day or two ahead of the rest of the film company, to reacquaint himself with the locals and re-create a reasonably authentic version of the accent and gait of the young men of the area. By the time the filmmakers arrived, Jerry recalled, Voight seemed to blend in effortlessly with the teenagers recruited to play members of the Rat Pack, the oversexed and under-educated teenaged boys who gang-rape both Joe and Annie in the night-marish scene that Joe replays in his head on the bus to New York.

Joel Mick, a retired real estate salesman from nearby Odessa who studied drama and speech at the University of Texas at Austin, says Voight did a great job of capturing the authentic accent and sensibility of Big Spring. "I remember seeing *Giant* as a kid, and you could tell when Rock Hudson was trying to be a cowboy, and I don't think he ever got there," says Mick. "But *Midnight Cowboy* was different. It looked and sounded like Big Spring." As for the accent, Mick says, the key is to drop the last syllable of each word, so that "a lot of three-syllable words become two-syllable words, and a lot of two-syllable words become one syllable." *Isn't* became *ain't* and *going* became *gone*, as in *I'm gone out now, be back later*. "Voight did a marvelous job," was Mick's verdict. "Joe Buck sounded like a classic West Texas character."

Not all of the Rat Pack were local boys. Randall Carver, twenty-two, had recently graduated with a degree in theater, speech, and broadcasting from West Texas State University (now West Texas A&M) in the Pan-handle town of Canyon, when he read in *Weekly Variety* that *Midnight Cowboy* was being filmed in Big Spring. Carver had had some acting experience playing in amateur productions and in *Texas!*, an open-air, pioneer historical pageant staged each summer in Palo Duro Canyon. He hopped in his car and drove nearly four hours to meet with the assis-tant casting director Vic Ramos at the Ramada Inn. Carver wore a straw cowboy hat and a faded denim jacket he'd bought for fifty cents from a roadside stand on his way to his audition with John and Jerry. "I knew what they wanted," he recalls. "I did my small-town punk attitude—I said *yep* and *nope*. I think they saw some creative awareness on my part." He not only got hired, he got the only Rat Pack part with a line in the movie.

Carver's big moment took place inside a movie house in nearby Midland where he and his Rat Park buddies sit behind Joe Buck and Annie and mock her for her promiscuity and Joe for kissing her. "Kissing Crazy Annie, you better drink a whole goddamn drugstore, man," is his one line, as he and his pals follow her down the aisle. The next flash cut shows Carver lying on top of her in the back of the theater. "They kept pulling my pants down further," he says of the movie people, "and I kept pulling them up."

He and Jennifer Salt never spoke to each other. "She was a professional and she was in her own realm with that character," he recalls. "That girl was in her head, she had her own handle on that, and she came across very sympathetic."

As hot as Miami had been, Big Spring was worse—over one hundred degrees by early afternoon on most days. The film company remained there and in nearby Midland for close to three weeks, shooting most of the opening sequences of the movie, part of Joe Buck's journey to New York, his memories of growing up alone after being abandoned by his mother and neglected by his grandmother, and the night scenes of the Rat Pack's gang rape. John and Jerry and their assistants searched for days for suitable places to stage each scene.

They found the perfect spot for the rape scene on the outskirts of the little town of Stanton, located on a slight rise halfway between Big Spring and Midland, on Interstate 20. The Milhollon House was a turn-of-the-century mansion, built by a wealthy cattle rancher and his wife, that had fallen into disrepair from decades of neglect. It had a haunted, decaying look—broken windows, peeling paint, missing or ill-fitting doors—just the kind of place where young people might gather to drink, shout, and screw without fear of interference from parents or the local authorities. It came to be known to the cast and crew as the Ghost House. The first sequence to be shot there was a night scene where a naked Joe and Annie would be caught making love in an old car parked outside the house and chased by young guys with flashlights. Hellman and Holender brought the crew and their heavy equipment to the abandoned house in the morning to get things ready.

But the house wasn't quite as empty as it looked. One of the workers heard a suspicious rattle, and all work suddenly stopped while the locals went hunting. They came back with a dead rattlesnake and the unwelcome news that dozens more had established a colony under the floorboards. Texas houses generally don't have basements, but there was good shade and plenty of room for snakes to crawl in the gap between the floor and the ground at the Ghost House. Jerry dispatched one of the locals to town; he returned with a rattlesnake posse consisting of a half dozen men armed with rifles, handguns, ropes, lanterns, and thick gloves. Everyone else fled the site and the hunters went to work. Like an armchair general, Jerry fielded periodic reports back at his hotel command center. By the time the sun began to set, fifty-one rattlers had been captured and killed. The men couldn't guarantee there weren't more lurking somewhere, so Jerry hired them to patrol the film set full-time. He and John also agreed that this was information they did not need to share with Jon Voight and Jennifer Salt, who only found out about it after the film shoot was finished.

Waldo Salt had been a constant and helpful presence on the film set from New York to Miami to Big Spring. But when they got to the Stanton scene, he decided he didn't need to watch his twenty-three-year-old daughter be gang-raped on film, even if it was just make-believe. He left for Mexico, where, on August 26, he finally filed for divorce from Jennifer's mother, citing "the incompatibility of temperament existing between the parties." He and Mary had been estranged for a decade, living apart much of that time. Three months after the divorce became final, he married Gladys Schwartz, an art teacher and painter he had met in New York.

Voight and Jennifer were left by themselves to deal with the trauma of the forthcoming rape scene. Jon was particularly anxious about Jennifer. She would be chased around the outside porch of the house by the Rat Pack members as they tore off her flimsy dress. Then one of the gang would climb on top of her and she would scream repeatedly as he pretended to sexually assault her. Voight spent a long time talking to the young man, a local with no prior acting experience. Voight even took Jennifer and the guy to dinner, and afterward they all played miniature golf together. The idea was to bond with the guy so that he would see Jennifer as a real person and be careful in the way he treated her during the filming of the scene.

Voight decided not to be present on the set the night of the film shoot for fear that he would be too upset and protective of Jennifer. "I think everybody felt it would be best if he wasn't there," Jennifer recalls.

She doesn't remember what John Schlesinger was doing at the location that evening. Instead, it was Burtt Harris, the assistant director, who supervised on the set. He made sure that a wardrobe woman was waiting with a robe just off camera to immediately cover Jennifer's naked body any time the shooting stopped.

The rape scene, although raw and frightening, occupies only a few seconds of screen time. Still, it took several hours to shoot, and Jennifer recalls the evening as an unsettling ordeal for her. "It's important to say that when it was shot nobody gave a shit about that. Nobody was particularly sensitive to how it was to be the female in that situation. I kind of had to leave my body to get through it because it was so unpleasant."

The wardrobe crew had given Jennifer a nude-colored body suit to wear, but the night was so brutally hot and sticky that she quickly stripped it off. "I felt that the most horrible thing in the world was that people were seeing my bare ass, and that was so humiliating I could not even discuss it. And this kid was just on top of me and all over me and it hurt and no one gave a fuck and it was supposed to look like I was being raped. And I was screaming, screaming, and it was traumatic in some way that couldn't be acknowledged. It would be acknowledged now, but it wasn't acknowledged then. So I buried my being upset."

She got back to the hotel room long after midnight to find Voight still awake and worried about her. His concern only angered her more. "I got mad at him for interfering in my little moment," she recalls.

One of the results of the death of the Production Code and the rise of the New Hollywood in the late sixties was more female nudity and more graphic depictions of sex and sexual assault of women in American movies. *Billy Jack*, *A Clockwork Orange*, and *Straw Dogs*, all of them released in 1971, would feature brutal rape scenes. In many instances the actresses involved weren't informed ahead of time about the intensity of the scenes or allowed to rehearse them in advance, for the sake of so-called realism. The director Sam Peckinpah said he wanted "the greatest rape scene ever" in *Straw Dogs*, and actress Susan George said she wasn't allowed to read the script before the filming began. Maria Schneider said she had no idea that her director, Bernardo Bertolucci, and her co-star, Marlon Brando, decided that Brando would dip his fingers in a stick of butter and pretend to anally penetrate her during the filming of *Last Tango in Paris* (1972). "I felt a little raped," she would recall three decades later.

Many years later, after her father's death and her decision to quit working as actor and turn to screenwriting, Jennifer Salt described the Texas rape scene in a piece for a writing workshop. Her teacher was appalled. "She said that I needed to know that I had in fact been raped and I had to treat it as such and let it sink in as such and admit that I was traumatized."

Looking back fifty years later, Jennifer agrees. Today's film contracts often spell out strict limits on nudity and require a choreographer for sex and rape scenes and an intimacy coordinator to monitor the impact of these scenes on actors and crew. But in 1968 Jennifer was expected to deal with it all by herself. "What I think is that those were the days when that's what was done. You don't know that you're being violated. You were not cool if you were not willing to take off your clothes. Things had changed in the movies and things were opening up and people were being naked all the time. And after I did that part and was going to auditions, I can't tell you how many times I had to agree to undress for people. It was the beginning of that era."

Because she was sexy, funny, and seemingly uninhibited, Jennifer became known as one of the more free-spirited young women of the New Hollywood. The reality, she says, was very different. "I was always a peer pressure person. I didn't like smoking pot, but I smoked it all the time. I didn't like taking acid, but I took it. I didn't like anything about that lifestyle. One of the big things was being fearless about being naked. It was considered the cool way to be. So I just never for a second thought it was anybody else's problem but mine."

Thanks to Jim Herlihy's well-plotted novel, John, Jerry, and Waldo had always known how their movie would end. But they had a terrible time agreeing on the opening, and had kicked around a dozen or more ideas, none of which quite worked for John. Then Michael Childers made a suggestion. On the ride into Big Spring he had driven past the old Sahara drive-in movie theater, just off Interstate 20. The place looked sad and deserted, and Michael thought it could be a perfect metaphor for young Joe Buck's sense of abandonment. They changed the name to the Big Tex Drive-in, put a little boy on a wheezing metal rocking horse in front of the big outdoor screen, and had a gift-wrapped visual metaphor for their opening image.

By now John was completely fed up with his rebellious film crew, whom he felt had continued to dig in their heels and undermine him at every turn. The last straw came at the hotel one evening when they had refused John's invitation to come watch the dailies without being paid overtime, in accordance with New York union rules. "They didn't want to come down from drinking their tins of Coors beer down the flight of stairs to see it," John would recall. "They were bored creatures." John exploded. He told Burtt Harris to "get rid of them all, send them all back to New York, they're dreadful." He only relented after Harris calmly explained that firing the crew at this late stage would trigger a major delay and add another bloated expense line to their ever-expanding budget deficit.

The actors generally were spared John's wrath. He and Voight had grown particularly close over the four months of shooting. A former actor himself, John was impressed by how hard Voight worked, how much he understood about Joe Buck's character, and how he had managed to build that character from the inside out over the course of the shoot. But Voight could see that John was slowly losing his composure. At the end of a long day when temperatures had climbed upward of one hundred degrees, Voight sought some shade behind a trailer and came upon

John standing alone. "He was red-faced and sweating and shaking, and I thought he might be having a stroke," Voight recalls. But Schlesinger's distress was more emotional than physical. He looked at Voight and asked, "Do you really think anyone's going to pay money to see a movie about a dumb Texan who takes a bus to New York to seek his fortune screwing rich old women? Why would anyone care?"

Voight, a consummate performer, stood there for a moment, and then delivered a perfect, heartfelt reply: "John, we will live the rest of our artistic lives in the shadow of this great masterpiece."

Schlesinger smiled and began to calm down. He invited Voight to watch the rushes together, something he had seldom done before. But before he ran the film, John stood in front of the projector as if he were on a stage. Raising his arms before an imaginary audience, he announced, "I've given you Alan Bates and Julie Christie and now, ladies and gentlemen, I present to you Jon Voight!"

17. IMAGES AND MUSIC

Everybody's talkin' at me,
Can't hear a word they're sayin'
—Fred Neil

J ohn Schlesinger and Jerry Hellman came back to New York in early September and spent ten days with reshoots, various inserts, and supplemental interior shots. Then John went off to London with Michael Childers for a well-earned holiday. He came back at the end of the month to discover there were serious problems with the early editing of the film. Patience was never one of John's virtues, and he quickly lost any he might have had in dealing with the man he and Jerry had chosen as editor.

Hugh A. Robertson had been recommended by the director Arthur Penn, who had hired him as the associate editor of Penn's Oscar-winning *The Miracle Worker* in 1962. Robertson had also worked on *12 Angry Men* (1957), *The Fugitive Kind* (1959), *Lilith* (1964), and *Mickey One* (1965). Born in Brooklyn of Jamaican parents, Robertson studied at the New Trade Institute for Motion Pictures in New York and the Sorbonne in Paris. He wanted to be a director and saw film editing as the clearest path to get there. But it took him eleven years to be admitted to the Motion Picture Editors Union of IATSE, the International Alliance of Theatrical Stage Employees, the coalition of crafts unions that dominated movie production. He was the union's first African American member. Both John and Jerry felt they were striking a blow for racial equality by hiring him for *Midnight Cowboy*.

Proud and sometimes prickly, Robertson "was a wonderful, talented editor, a charming man," recalls Irene Bowers, who worked as an apprentice film editor on *Midnight Cowboy*. "But he also had a kind of self-sabotaging streak. . . . It wasn't an aggressive attitude, but more like 'you're not going to make me do anything I don't want to do.'"

Robertson and his crew had been viewing and editing rushes at his private editing lab, located in the Brill Building, on Broadway and West Forty-ninth Street, known as the buzzing center of New York's commercial pop music industry. But when John showed up after returning from London, he was deeply unsettled by what he saw. The editing was not only way behind schedule but seemed flat and uninspired. John quickly decided that Robertson lacked the sophistication to shape into coherence the vast and intricate collection of scenes and images that he and Adam Holender had filmed. Robertson had even started farming out portions of the edit to outsiders without consulting John or Jerry. "Hugh Robertson was a catastrophe," says Jerry.

For his part, Robertson felt that John had done a ham-handed job of filming. He was particularly scornful of John's corrosive vision of New York City, calling it ignorant and superficial. It was, Robertson complained, "an Englishman's view, not the real New York." He later told the syndicated columnist Marilyn Beck that the entire film shoot had been a disaster. He claimed that Jon Voight had relied on Dustin Hoffman for direction throughout the filming and that "the only part we didn't edit drastically were the scenes Dustin was in alone"—although the final product has no such scenes except for a brief moment when Ratso scavenges for free food at the Warhol party. Robertson added that the production was in constant disarray and that the Warhol party scene in particular had been "conceived in turmoil and executed in what became a near-orgy atmosphere." Most of the original party footage had to be drastically trimmed or burned.

"It was almost like a comedy routine between John Schlesinger and the editor," says Adam Holender, who visited Robertson's cutting room often that fall. "They would abuse each other with a sense of humor, but under the humor was a deep disconnect between the two men." Hellman says the relationship quickly turned toxic. "The more deeply John became involved, the more frustrated and angry he became."

Besides wielding a deft scissors, the film editor's job can be a delicate psychological balancing act. "You're putting yourself between the director's vision of the movie he hoped to make and what he actually shot," says Alan Heim, an Oscar-winning film editor who knew Robertson well. "It's an education process, and if you're going to confront everybody or be defensive about what you've done you don't get hired again."

Schlesinger decided he needed his own man at the editing table, and the man he wanted was Jim Clark, the veteran British film editor of *Darling* and *Far from the Madding Crowd*. Clark was known back in England as the "Dream Repairman" for his ability to rescue celluloid lost causes. Clark, an irrepressible truth-teller who shared both John's moral outrage and his sardonic sense of humor, thought "Mortician" was a better label. "I was forever touching up the corpses of the films that were wheeled in to me," he recalled.

Clark had served an apprenticeship in the early fifties at the renowned Ealing Studios in West London, home of some of the finest British comedies of the postwar era. In those days, he would recall, the people who snipped and pasted together reels of film were known as "cutters"—wielders of blunt scissors and pots of glue. Many of them got their jobs through nepotism and had little or no interest in the films they edited—few of them even went to the movies during off-hours. But Clark believed film was an art form and deserved to be edited with creativity and care. After leaving Ealing, he edited puppet films for Disney, then moved on to documentaries. His big break came as an assistant editor on *The Prince and the Showgirl* (1957), a romantic comedy starring Marilyn Monroe and Laurence Olivier. After that he found himself in demand.

Clark had fixed some of Schlesinger's cinematic problems before, most notably on *Darling*, where he had rescued a terribly flat and lifeless scene of Diana Scott's wedding to her wealthy Italian prince. Clark had helped John turn it into a newsreel-style spectacle, with energetic jump cuts and a seriocomic narrator that got across the glamour and excess the event was meant to epitomize.

In truth, by the time reels of film reach the editing table, it's often too late to "save" a movie or turn a bad film into a good one. What Clark gave Schlesinger was a professionalism and trust that the skittish, insecure director knew he could count on. Clark would listen to John carefully and, like a fast-acting tranquilizer, calm his nerves. He wound up editing eight of John's feature films over a fifteen-year period. Bryan Oates, who worked in the editing room with the two men on several of these pictures, said some of John's rages were so volcanic, he should have been arrested. Bursting with anxiety and anger after seeing one set of rushes, John would lash out at all involved.

"Well, what are we going to do about this?" he would cry. "This is terrible! It's not going to work!"

Jim would reply, "John, it *will* work, just give me a minute and I'll show you." And usually he succeeded.

Clark wasn't a member of the American film editor's union, nor did he have a green card allowing him to work in the United States. But John and Jerry decided they could slip him in by calling him a "creative consultant" and keeping Hugh Robertson and his editing crew on the payroll. When Robertson realized he wasn't being fired, he was surprisingly amenable to having Clark involved. Robertson assumed Clark was one of John's boyfriends (not true) and that having him around might humor the short-tempered director (absolutely true).

Clark looked at the existing reels that Robertson had worked on and concluded that most of them were fine: the writing, direction, and acting were all extraordinary, and he felt the editing was adequate. But he believed the film was far too long and the opening sequences were a mess. Waldo Salt's screenplay had combined moments from Joe Buck's bus ride to Manhattan with flashbacks of his life in Texas and "flash-presents" that depicted Joe's state of mind as the journey began. Clark quickly decided he would have to start over by taking the first two reels, directed by John and shot inside the bus in thirty-two millimeter, back to the original rushes and reediting every shot. It took him three weeks to do so. "Little by little," he later wrote, "we found a way of integrating the flashbacks and using sound and somehow making the sequence have a flow which it hadn't had before."

Setting up shop at Robertson's lab, Clark quickly came to realize it was a study in organized chaos. During the course of the day the two assistants Robertson lent him would disappear into the men's room together for long stretches. Clark soon figured out they were smoking dope in there—a lot of it. "These guys were high from morning til night and nobody cared," Clark would recall. Reels of developed but unedited film were piled in boxes under benches and in cupboards. The most crucial find was forty minutes of sixteen-millimeter footage that a second unit had shot outside the bus, of sights that Joe saw through his bus window. "Nobody had bothered to look at it," Clark said.

While Clark was working to integrate and shape all of this material, Schlesinger and Robertson worked in an adjoining room cutting other parts of the movie. It wasn't going well. Clark could hear Schlesinger's voice rising in volume as he lost patience. He would come storming into Clark's room red-faced, his bald head gleaming with sweat. "You've got to get that scene away from that fucking Black Panther!" he would tell Clark, who later remarked, "Clearly the white liberal period was over." Robertson, a tall, powerful-looking man who towered over Schlesinger, would mock the director after he left the building. "Momma sure had the rag on today!" he would say, pointing his omnipresent cigar at Clark. "He thinks he's made a great movie, but it's really a tourist's view of New York."

John himself was never sure. After long days in the editing room, Clark would often walk him back to his luxury apartment on the East Side and John would pepper him with doubts. "Will it work? Will anyone want to see it? What do you really think?" No matter how many times Clark would reply, "It's great. It will be a big hit," John could not be convinced. "But are you really sure? How do you know?"

With John looking over his shoulder, Clark reedited the Warhol party scene to make it more coherent, although neither man was ever fully satisfied with the result. Despite drastic cuts, they still felt it dragged. The two men also worked their way through the Texas flashbacks with Joe Buck and Crazy Annie. Schlesinger had originally conceived of those scenes as a continuous, chronological narrative, but now he and Clark concluded they *were* far too long and disrupted the flow of the main story of Joe Buck's adventures in New York. Clark cut them deeply. Like the innovative film editors of *Hiroshima mon amour*, *The Pawnbroker*, and *Blow-Up*, he used flash cuts and jumbled the chronology, fixing these moments and images into Joe Buck's memory and creating a state of dreamlike trance. Some audiences found the scattered snippets mystifying, but they successfully reflected Jim Herlihy's focus on Joe's dreams in the novel without veering too far from the central narrative.

In the end, said John Schlesinger, Jim Clark saved his movie. Clark himself demurred. "Not true, of course," he would recall. "The film was already great when I first saw the rough cut. Let's just say I helped to improve the goods and enjoyed myself thoroughly, knowing I was working on something very special. But I didn't save the film because it didn't need saving."

Michael Childers was an overlooked and underestimated player in the creative team that produced *Midnight Cowboy*. John had pushed to hire Michael as his assistant because he was in love with his handsome twenty-two-year-old boyfriend and couldn't bear to leave him behind in California. Jerry Hellman had embraced the idea because he hoped Michael would help keep John grounded and functional. Neither man anticipated the valuable contributions Michael would make to the movie—serving as John's envoy to the exploding New York art, sex, and drug scene, helping to create the movie's Warholian bacchanal, and suggesting the evocative opening moment at the drive-in theater. But perhaps his most important contribution was the song that not only launched the film but embodied its defiantly enigmatic spirit.

One of Michael's assignments was to provide John with a steady supply of record albums to help him come up with appropriate songs to use while creating the director's cut of the film. Like many directors, John liked to edit his scenes to music, changing images to the rhythm of the songs he chose. "I will not see a first cut of a film without a temporary score added to the picture, because watching a film silently, in places where you know music is going to play some part, is extremely misleading and depressing," he once explained.

In the pile of new albums Michael brought him was *Aerial Ballet*, a deceptively ambitious collection of twelve songs by an obscure L.A. singer-songwriter named Harry Nilsson that had come out in July. Most of the cuts were Paul McCartney–style pop confections—they were tuneful, inventive, and, at first encounter, relentlessly lightweight. But the more John heard them, the more captivated he became. And one song in particular grabbed his attention and wouldn't let loose.

"Everybody's Talkin'" was a two-minute, forty-one-second burst of infectious energy. It was the simplest of tunes—two verses and a bridge, an instrumental break and a repeat of the bridge and the first verse, followed by a long fade behind Nilsson's scat singing that soared up and down the scale like a high-flying bird. John loved the sweetness of the melody and the wistful, rebellious spirit of the lyrics, and he decided to use it as the temporary track to guide and pace his edits. Its rhythm seemed to align perfectly with his images. And he gradually came to realize that the emotional spirit of the lyrics was perfectly aligned with Joe Buck's character.

"Everybody's Talkin'" was the only cut on the album that hadn't been written by Nilsson. Its author was Fred Neil, an equally obscure New York singer-songwriter who was a fixture of the folk music scene in Greenwich Village in the mid-sixties. Neil had come to New York from his home in south Florida a decade earlier and worked as a songwriter and occasional session man at the Brill Building. He wrote (with Beverly Ross) "Candy Man," the B-side to "Crying," a smash hit single by Roy Orbison, and "Come Back, Baby," recorded by Buddy Holly. But Neil had no patience for pop songwriting in the heavily commercialized Brill Building style, and he quickly drifted forty blocks south to the Green-wich Village coffeehouse scene. He sang with a deep, bluesy voice while strumming a Cuban-designed, industrial-sized twelve-string guitar—together the two instruments, man and machine, could overpower any music venue in the Village.

In his memoir *Chronicles: Volume One*, Bob Dylan recalls meeting Neil at the Cafe Wha?, a basement club that Dylan wandered into soon after arriving from Minnesota in the bitterly cold winter of 1961. Neil ran the daytime show, and was himself the main attraction.

"Fred had the flow," Dylan writes, "dressed conservatively, sullen and brooding, with an enigmatical gaze, peach-like complexion, hair splashed with curls and an angry and powerful baritone voice that struck blue notes and blasted them to the rafters with or without a mike. He was the emperor of the place, even had his own harem, his devotees. You couldn't touch him. Everything revolved around him. He played a big dreadnought guitar, a lot of percussion in his playing, piercing driving rhythm—a one-man band, a kick in the head singing voice. He did fierce versions of hybrid chain gang songs and whomped the audience into a frenzy."

One of Neil's most loyal friends and followers was John Sebastian, a classical musician's son who grew up in the Village and became a master blues harmonica player and then the lead singer and songwriter of the Lovin' Spoonful, one of the great mid-sixties American pop bands. He remembers Fred Neil as "an incredible swinging genius and also the flakiest guy I ever met. He had already had experience of brushes with fame and he really didn't like it. He was very happy as a kind of undiscovered quantity there on MacDougal Street."

Neil had recorded two highly regarded folk albums for Elektra Records, and had written some classic songs, including "The Other Side of This Life," "A Little Bit of Rain," and "Blues on the Ceiling," with simple melodies and laconic, evocative lyrics. "Fred could make a lyric sound like it had just fallen out of his mouth," says Sebastian, who played harmonica on both albums. "It doesn't call attention to itself, but it was faultless." But Neil's work ethic was spotty and his passions unstable. Friends say he loved women, booze, and dope, including, eventually, heroin. "Freddie would go to the club fucked up, he was always fucked up," said Paul Rothchild, who produced Neil's two Elektra albums and admired his talent but loathed his unreliability.

In the mid-sixties record labels were signing and acquiring folk music performers by the barrel, searching for the next Bob Dylan, Peter, Paul and Mary, Joan Baez, or Judy Collins. Capitol Records signed Neil in 1966 and brought him out to Los Angeles to record. The resulting album, like the two Elektra records, was an instant cult classic but sold few copies. Originally entitled *Fred Neil*, it was released in December 1966. Herb Cohen, Neil's then-manager, told *The New York Times* that "Everybody's Talkin'" was the last song recorded for the album. Neil was worn out and anxious to get back to Florida, but Cohen pleaded with him to come up with one more song. Fred retreated to the bathroom and came back a few minutes later with a modest, concise ballad that summed up his longing to go home. He recorded it in one take, packed up his guitar, and headed back to Miami.

With its plainspoken lyric and minimalist melody, "Everybody's Talkin'" captured the essence of Fred Neil. "It has that Fred quality of uncertainty, his wanderlust, his willingness to ignore what others said or did," says Sebastian.

Neil's version was slow, deep, and soulful. "The way he sings that bridge just puts me away," says Sebastian. "Because I know how badly he wanted to get back to that world, get out on his sailboat where people couldn't reach him."

> I'm going where the sun keeps shining
> Through the pouring rain . . .
> Skippin' over the ocean like a stone

"Everybody's Talkin'" came to Harry Nilsson's attention in the fall of 1967, when Rick Jarrard, Nilsson's recording producer at RCA headquarters in Los Angeles, heard it on his car radio while driving to the studio one morning. "I could hear there was something special there, so I called the station to find out who it was," Jarrard recalls. He quickly got a copy of the album and took it to Harry. Nilsson at first was reluctant to record the song—all the other cuts on *Aerial Ballet* had been written by him, and he had no particular interest in adding someone else's work to the mix. But Jarrard was insistent. "I said, 'Harry, you gotta do this song,'" he recalls. "Harry didn't even like the song. He did it as a favor for me."

Brooklyn-born Harry Nilsson had been kicking around the L.A. music scene for nearly five years. He was writing songs that only rarely succeeded in getting recorded; his one small success was a song that sat near the bottom of a New Christy Minstrels album in 1963. He was still working nights as an operations manager at a local bank when Jarrard signed him to a modest recording contract in January

1967. Harry was a small guy with a lopsided grin, blond cowlick, and serious drinking problem that he likely inherited from his alcoholic mother and that conspired later in life, along with a voracious cocaine addiction, to ravage his heart and lead to his premature death at age fifty-two. He also had a three-and-one-half-octave vocal range that his amazingly sweet and resonant voice could climb up and down like a stepladder. Critics labeled him the best pure American male singer of the rock 'n' roll era.

Jarrard rounded up the ace session men who had played on the album's other tracks: Larry Knechtel on bass and piano, Jim Gordon on drums, and Al Casey on acoustic guitar. He told them he wanted a faster, livelier tempo than the Fred Neil original, and he had Casey launch it with the sparkling, rhythmic fingerpicking that drove the song forward. Harry added a rough temporary vocal. Then Jarrard turned to George Tipton, Nilsson's arranger, and asked him to write a string arrangement to anchor the melody and the vocal. The first one Tipton came up with was too busy for Jarrard's taste. He took Tipton aside and asked for what he described as a simple high suspended note for the strings—"the holdout of the high note over the chords," says Jarrard—as the song winds along. Tipton added a deep cello line under Nilsson's wordless staccato vocalisms at the bridge. The song then reprises the spare, dreamy lyrics. "It was beautiful," Jarrard says.

Nilsson came back to the studio and rerecorded his vocal, complete with its falsetto scat-singing climax. The finished product was a perfect marriage between Nilsson's wistful, insistent singing and the sweeping blend of guitars and violins. Jarrard, who earlier in the year had produced *Surrealistic Pillow*, Jefferson Airplane's breakthrough album, with the Top Ten singles "Somebody to Love" and "White Rabbit," was sure he had another hit. But "Everybody's Talkin'" went nowhere that summer, peaking at Number 113 on the Billboard Hot 100 chart. It sold well in Southern California, but the self-styled omniscient music executives at RCA showed no interest in promoting it nationally.

Lots of more famous artists had songs they were eager for John Schlesinger and Jerry Hellman to use for the film's theme song. Joni Mitchell wrote "Midnight Cowboy" especially for the movie, but

John found it too literal. Leonard Cohen called Jerry's apartment and sang him "Bird on a Wire" over the phone. Again, no go. Jerry talked to the Scottish folksinger Donovan about writing a complete score for the film, but nothing came of the conversation. Even Bob Dylan showed up at Jerry's apartment one afternoon with a guitar case strapped to his back. He took out an acoustic guitar and strummed a song that Jerry can no longer recall. Most likely it was "Lay Lady Lay," which Dylan had written specifically for the film but had delivered far too late for consideration. When Jerry explained that they had already settled on "Everybody's Talkin'," Dylan nodded, silently packed up the guitar, and left. "I never, ever saw him again," Jerry says.

Schlesinger was happy with his decision, but United Artists was not. Its contract with Hellman and Schlesinger stipulated that UA would own all music rights to the movie, including any profits from music publishing and a soundtrack album. The music executive at UA, which had scored a huge success four years earlier with the soundtrack for *A Hard Day's Night*, wanted an original theme song for *Midnight Cowboy* that UA could copyright and own. After first hearing "Everybody's Talkin'," the A&R (artists and repertoire) man said it was such a basic tune that "anybody can write a song like that."

"Like who?" an incredulous Schlesinger asked.

Nilsson was also keen to have one of his own original songs featured in the movie. At UA's urging, Schlesinger invited Harry to the production office in New York and showed him four reels of the unfinished film. Then he introduced Nilsson to John Barry, the British composer and record producer who had recently been hired as musical supervisor for the movie. The two men went off together and worked on two or three new songs, including Nilsson's "I Guess the Lord Must Be in New York City," a lively tune with a catchy lyric, written by Harry in the same bouncy tempo as "Everybody's Talkin'." Schlesinger wouldn't bite—he felt it was a pale imitation of Fred Neil's song. And Barry said he agreed. "It was just impossible" to top "Everybody's Talkin'," he recalled, "because when something works that well you can't argue with it."

From the beginning John Schlesinger was looking for a musical score that was pop-flavored but diverse, with songs that were, in his words, "rhythmically pretty hip and could embrace the various aspects of the New York scene." One year earlier Mike Nichols had broken new ground with *The Graduate* by using Paul Simon's evocative folk songs—none of which had been written for the movie except the catchy, exuberant "Mrs. Robinson"—to reflect and comment on the protagonist's state of mind throughout the film. The soundtrack album, featuring six Simon and Garfunkel songs, rose to the top of the *Billboard* charts.

John had never used this sustained pop music approach in his own films before, but he was eager to try. And John Barry was the right conductor-songwriter-musician to try it with.

Barry, who was thirty-four, came from the northern English city of York. Tall, thin, and thoughtful, Barry had a long face, dark curly hair, and the self-confident manner of someone who had been involved in popular entertainment virtually all his life. His father was a wealthy show business entrepreneur who owned eight cinemas and theaters in the Yorkshire region. Barry was involved in the family business from an early age. "I ran movies," he would recall. "I sold ice cream. I sold orange juice. I passed out programs. I swept the floor. When I was fifteen years old I could go up into the projection booth and run the whole thing."

When it came to movies, Barry knew what was good, what was bad, and what was boring. And he knew what he liked. He loved *The Treasure of the Sierra Madre*, which he reckoned he watched twenty times in one week. "I think I know every line."

He started piano lessons at age eight, took up the trumpet at fifteen, and studied classical harmony and counterpoint. He played in military bands while doing his army service, then formed his own pop instrumental music group, the John Barry Seven, which straddled the rapidly shifting ground between jazz, pop, and rock in the immediate pre-Beatles years. He produced ten hit records for the British pop singer Adam Faith, then started composing and arranging musical scores for movies, starting with *Dr. No* (1962), the first James Bond film. Barry didn't write the Bond theme, but he arranged it, memorably combining two genres from two generations: the trademark electric guitar twang of rock and the brass-heavy exclamation points of big-band-style jazz. He wrote and arranged the soundtrack for *Goldfinger* (1964), including the music for the title track, which featured Shirley Bassey's saucy, booming vocal backed by a muted, sensual wah-wah trumpet, which became a big hit on both sides of the Atlantic. "It's vulgar, it's wonderful!" exclaimed Robert Brownjohn, who designed the movie title sequences to match the rhythm of the song.

"*Goldfinger* was John's big breakthrough as a movie music composer," says Jon Burlingame, who teaches film music composing at the University of Southern California. He got to know Barry personally, and admired the man and his work. "That's where everything comes together for him. It's the first time he writes an entire score, and *Goldfinger* just kicks ass.

"A movie composer not only connects the audience to the music, he also has to connect both to the image on the screen and the vision of the director. With *Goldfinger* John is reinventing the movie score—it's partly pop, partly jazz, and partly orchestral—and he knows how to apply music to image."

By the time Barry went to work for Jerry Hellman and John Schlesinger, he had won three Oscars for best original movie songs or overall scores, for *Born Free* (1966) and *The Lion in Winter* (1968). He had left Swinging London, where he had shared a flat with the actor Michael Caine and conducted a zealous social life, and relocated to New York to try to launch a musical version of *The Great Gatsby* on Broadway.

John Schlesinger had clung tenaciously to "Everybody's Talkin'" as the main theme and introduction to the film. But he wanted something even more wistful to accompany a melancholy scene of Joe Buck's lonesome ramble around the streets of Times Square. John had edited the scene using Bob Dylan's "Sad-Eyed Lady of the Lowlands," an achingly poignant ballad from his *Blonde on Blonde* album that runs eleven minutes and twenty-two seconds, and Barry came up with a fitting counterpoint using the same rolling rhythm. Barry's "Midnight Cowboy" theme is an instrumental anchored by a yearning chromatic harmonica played by the great Belgian jazz musician Jean-Baptiste "Toots" Thielemans. The song sounded like it came straight from a lonesome prairie but was even more deeply evocative when played in the background of a solitary walk through the cold, impersonal urban setting. "You see these guys walking around, and there's this terrific sadness in the air," said Barry to his biographer, Eddi Fiegel. "That's what life is like there, and it's not going any place. That harmonica theme was the soul of that character in New York."

Barry, who possessed the supreme self-confidence that John Schlesinger often lacked, claimed he wrote the whole thing in twenty minutes in an apartment on Fifth Avenue. "That's how it's done. You think about it a lot, clear your mind—and then that's it."

He wrote four more songs for *Midnight Cowboy*, including "Florida Fantasy," an Austin Powers–flavored light romp for Ratso's dream of beach resort life in the Sunshine State; and "Fun City," a breezy, jazz-inflected piano instrumental that echoes the old *Route 66* television show theme. He also commissioned two songs from Elephant's Memory, a six-piece New York art rock band mostly remembered for having backed former Beatle John Lennon in his brief New York radical prophet incarnation, and "He Quit Me," a kick-ass soul song written by newcomer Warren Zevon. Barry would later call John Schlesinger the most musically knowledgeable director he'd ever worked with, and he was proud of the score they put together.

To record the songs, Barry took the artists and his own handpicked orchestra to one of New York's great music production cathedrals, Studio IA, located on the top floor of a seven-story building at the corner of Seventh Avenue and West Fifty-second Street. The site of CBS Radio's first broadcast studio in the early 1930s, the space had been revamped into a resonant but quirky recording venue. Phil Ramone, one of the studio's owners, who would become one of the most celebrated record producers of the era, recalled IA as "essentially an A frame with a domed ceiling. Its walls were covered with soft fiberglass and fabric—midrange sounds passed through the fabric and were absorbed by the fiberglass, while high-frequency sounds would bounce off the walls and rebound into the room." The room was huge—two thousand square feet altogether. The floor was made of oak. "Once the sound left an instrument it was reflected off the floor because the walls were so far away."

Ramone, in his 2007 memoir, said he and Barry scored *Midnight*

Cowboy "to picture"—the musicians sat in the studio and played each cue as the film was projected on a screen. Barry's scoring and orchestration were precise; he took just three to four days to record the entire score. He recorded with Nilsson several new versions of "Everybody's Talkin'" to use at various moments of the film, including a short version that incorporates a brief but resonant harmonica run by Thielemans. "When I heard the elongated string sound on the *Midnight Cowboy* theme I was blown away," recalled Ramone.

As for United Artists' keen desire for an original song it could own, the matter was finally resolved several months later, when Jerry Hellman and John Schlesinger showed the nearly finished film to the UA music executive who had originally objected to "Everybody's Talkin'." This time, hearing it as an integral part of the movie and seeing how it fit the story line and images, the man had a much different reaction, according to Schlesinger. "My God! Where'd you get that music from?" the UA man asked him. "The number's just perfect!"

18. THE X RATING

Whatever you hear about Midnight Cowboy *is true!*
—United Artists ad campaign

David Picker at United Artists had lived up to his promise to leave John Schlesinger alone to make the movie John wanted to make. Picker had only visited the set once, at Jerry Hellman's invitation, to hang out one evening on the sidewalk outside the Gotham Hotel, at Fifth Avenue and Fifty-fifth Street, subbing for the fictional Berkley Hotel for Women, where Picker watched Jon Voight as Joe Buck (with help from a stuntman) get thrown down the front steps by a doorman after he comes on to a shocked female resident. Picker didn't go to Florida, he didn't go to Texas. Unlike his colleagues at other studios, he didn't watch the daily rushes of the work in progress. "We never saw a foot of dailies *ever*," he says proudly. Picker even kept his lip buttoned as the budget—supposedly set in stone at $2.2 million—started to creep up to and over $3 million as Hellman hired John Barry, one of the world's most high-priced movie music men, to create and oversee the soundtrack, and Schlesinger and Adam Holender kept filming more and more images and inserts that John and Jim Clark sprinkled throughout the movie.

At Clark's urging, Schlesinger and Hellman also hired Pablo Ferro, renowned in both Hollywood and Madison Avenue as a brilliant and flamboyant image designer, to do the opening screen credits. The Cuban-born Ferro was already famous for the skinny, hand-drawn credits he had designed for Stanley Kubrick's *Dr. Strangelove, or How I Learned to Stop Worrying and Love the Bomb* (1964) and the cool-breeze, split-screen multiplying images he created for *The Thomas Crown Affair* (1968). Ferro planned to keep things simple for the *Midnight Cowboy* credits—just somber white letters atop images of Joe Buck in his new cowboy outfit and cowhide suitcase leaving his cheap motel in Big Spring and making his way to the diner where he plans to quit his job as busboy and dishwasher. But Ferro needed more shots of Joe moving purposely up the sidewalk to the rhythm of "Everybody's Talkin'" to create a bouncy, breezy effect. So he and Holender took Voight and a makeshift camera crew in a station wagon across the Hudson River to New Jersey one morning.

It was a tight fit done without budgetary approval. Among other problems, Holender recalls being short an assistant cameraman and needing to find a way without one to keep his long 600-millimeter lens in focus. His solution was to tie a rope around Voight's waist and keep it taut so that the distance between the actor and the camera never varied. First he filmed Voight's head and upper body with the rope tied around the actor's waist, then he moved the rope higher and did the same shot with Voight's lower body. Ferro was able to mix the two so that the rope was never visible. "We had zero money to do this, but we knew what we were after," Holender recalls.

Ferro also created the montage of images for the television set that changes channels to the thrusts and grunts while Joe and Cass are having sex while lying atop the remote control.

Finally, after months of tinkering with sounds and images, Jerry Hellman sent word to UA: the movie was ready for viewing. The screening was scheduled for a weekday morning at the company's movie lab on West Fifty-fourth Street. Picker himself didn't much care for the venue. The walls were a soft green and the curtain didn't rise or divide but slid creakily the entire length of the screen. Usually, Picker says, he would see a new movie alone, or perhaps with the UA triumvirate of Arthur Krim, Robert Benjamin, and Arnold Picker, David's uncle. But this time, for reasons he cannot totally recall, Picker decided to invite the house—not just the top execs, but the sales and distribution people, even the secretaries. It was like rolling the dice on an all-or-nothing bet.

John and Jerry had arrived in a state of mutual high anxiety, each reinforcing the other's deepest fears. The two men were largely silent on the way to the venue. But as their taxi pulled up to the site, John gripped

Jerry's arm tightly and asked his usual self-loathing question: "Really, Jerry, do you think anyone in their right mind will pay good money to see this rubbish?"

Hellman, for once, said nothing.

Inside the screening room, John took the seat directly behind Arnold Picker, and David took the seat directly behind John. No one could see anyone else's face. After 113 minutes, amid the final plaintive wails of Toots Thielemans's harmonica, the curtain awkwardly slid back into place. The room was silent. Then Arnold, whom David considered the toughest critic among UA's ownership trio, turned around to John and announced, "It's a masterpiece." The room burst into applause.

"Let's all go to lunch," said David.

Not everyone was quite so happy with the final product. Marion Dougherty loved the performances. She took special pride in the brilliant work of Jon Voight, the actor she had so passionately advocated for. She thought Dustin Hoffman was equally wonderful and was pleased with each of the main supporting actors—Sylvia Miles, Ruth White, John McGiver, Jennifer Salt, Bob Balaban, Brenda Vaccaro, and Barnard Hughes—who had been handpicked by her and John Schlesinger.

But there was one infuriating problem that obliterated her enjoyment. On-screen credits are keenly valued and jealously guarded in the movie business; it's the only time the mostly anonymous artisans and film crew get any public recognition. And a single-card credit—one name alone on the screen—is the most valued recognition of all. But casting directors, most of whom were women, were generally subjected to low wages and relative obscurity, their names stacked among three or four others on a card. Lynn Stalmaster, who was a man, had broken through this long-standing practice in June 1968 and gotten a single-card credit for *The Thomas Crown Affair*, and Dougherty believed she deserved the same level of recognition for *Midnight Cowboy*. When the credits rolled at the beginning of the film, however, the card with her name had three others on it as well, with hers at the bottom.

Dougherty went up to Jerry Hellman immediately after the screening and complained. She claims he told her that the movie was finished and nothing could be done. "He came up with the lame excuse that it was 'too expensive' to change," Dougherty would recall in her memoir, published in 2015. "Too expensive! This hurt me more than anything else in my fifty-year career."

She issued an ultimatum to Hellman: either put my name on a single card or take it off altogether. Jerry, to her surprise, chose the latter. "She said to me, 'Take it or leave it, this is what I want,'" he recalls. "'Fine,' I said, 'I'll leave it,' and I took it out completely."

Hellman, in his own defense, says he was certain that Dougherty would cool off after a day or two, come back to him, and work something out. But she didn't. And he says he's sorry in retrospect that he didn't give her what she was asking for. "Looking back now on the success of *Midnight Cowboy*, I regret not having done it at that time," he says. In a 2013 documentary film on Dougherty's life and work, his contrition went even further. "I must say it was clear that if ever a casting director earned a single-card credit, she had on *Midnight Cowboy*," he said, "and I've regretted for forty-five years that I hadn't given it to her."

Dougherty, who died in 2011, never forgave him. "She talked about it for years," recalls Juliet Taylor, her friend and former assistant. "It just stuck in her craw for the rest of her life. I'm not kidding. It made her so mad." It angered her friend David Picker as well. "I thought that was absolutely offensive," says Picker, "and there's nothing Hellman could ever have done to correct that feeling of mine."

Dougherty said John Schlesinger was also angry about the way she was treated and apologized to her, but he didn't intervene. "I am honored to say that John became a good friend of mine," she wrote. "I loved his honesty, his wonderful eye for the actor's talent, and his humor about himself and others."

Marion Dougherty got her first single-card credit in 1972, for *Slaughterhouse-Five*, directed by George Roy Hill, her longtime collaborator and companion. Three years later she cast *The Day of the Locust* for Schlesinger and Hellman. Even for that film she didn't get her own single card, but shared one with Dianne Crittenden, who was credited with "additional casting."

Dustin Hoffman was also less than pleased with what he saw at the screenings he attended. His problem wasn't with the credits—under his contract he got star billing for the film, with his name appearing before Jon Voight's. But it was impossible not to notice that Voight was in every scene in the movie, while Hoffman's character didn't appear until the twenty-fifth minute. It was as if he finally had come to understand that the name of the movie was *Midnight Cowboy*, not *Midnight Ratso*. Hoffman had signed on because he wanted to demonstrate his skills as a character actor, without quite realizing that this meant he wouldn't be the movie's main focus. He was especially unhappy that Schlesinger had cut some of the improvisational Chaplin-esque physical comedy he'd done in the Warhol party scenes. "I'm not a perfect person, and I was very upset," Hoffman says. He recalls asking Schlesinger, "Why'd you cut my best stuff out?" John's response, according to Hoffman, was that "it had to be Jon's story, or words to that effect. And when I watched it [again], I said, Oh, I get it, he's right. It all came back to Voight."

By now Hoffman had cut ties with Jane Oliver, the talent agent who had represented him during some of his hardscrabble New York theater years, and hired Walter Hyman, a Broadway producer who was recommended to him by his fellow actor Elliott Gould. Hyman exuded confidence and competence in managing Hoffman's business affairs, and he charmed Hoffman and his entire family and quickly became one of his closest friends. "He had a big black Cadillac and a driver named Joe," recalls Ron Hoffman, Dustin's older brother. "And he was good at his job. He knew his way around town and he knew his way around people. He was a real showbiz guy."

Schlesinger and Hellman held a screening for the entire cast and crew on a Sunday afternoon in February, to be followed by a forty-third-birthday celebration for John. Hoffman came to the screening with his new manager. Michael Childers recalls Hyman looking at his watch during the screening and asking Hoffman loudly enough for Schlesinger to hear, "Dustin, when do you come into this movie?" Hoffman said little afterward and didn't come to the party. Instead he sent Hyman, with a book for a present. When John asked what Dustin had thought of the movie, Hyman replied, "Well, I think you'd better talk to him personally about that."

After the party ended, Schlesinger and Voight went to Hoffman's apartment together to see what was going on. Hoffman insisted that he thought the movie was very good. But he didn't convince Schlesinger. "He clearly was upset by something," said John thirty years later, "and I've never really to this day been able to put my finger on it. I have a feeling that he felt Jon Voight had run away with the film. I just don't know what had got into him, but something had."

Hoffman himself says he doesn't recall having any serious issues with the film—"I thought it was a terrific movie and John had done a great job." But he remembers attending a preview at the Brill Building screening room where "people walked out in droves" during the scene where Bob Balaban's pimply high school kid performs oral sex on Joe Buck. "We thought this could end everybody's career," Hoffman told Larry King in a 1994 television interview. Hoffman said he feared that the movie, despite being excellent, was too raw for audiences. "People would get up at that point and just walk out of the theater," he told King. "And we said, 'We've got big problems.' I liked the movie. We felt it was a great movie. We felt it was a movie that was not going to be accepted."

Not every preview audience agreed. An anonymous reviewer from *New York* magazine reported that on the night he attended a screening, "the most veteran of audiences wound up in tears and, after a wrenching moment of silence, that Big Movie applause." Jerry Hellman recalls audiences bursting into laughter at quintessential New York moments like Cass's tantrum and Ratso's cursing of the errant taxi driver.

Still, Hoffman became so concerned that *Midnight Cowboy* would damage his career that he immediately signed on to do *John and Mary*, a bland romantic comedy costarring Mia Farrow about a one-night stand that blossoms into romance. The idea, said Dustin, was for him to "look like a respectable person" and wash away the possible stain of Ratso Rizzo. But mostly he threw himself into *Jimmy Shine*, a Broadway comedy written by his good friend Murray Schisgal, with music by Paul Simon. Critics generally panned the play but praised Hoffman's deft comic performance, and the production ran for six months. Lots of people wanted to see the Jewish Cary Grant onstage. And afterward as well: girls lined up every night outside his dressing room after the show waiting to catch a glimpse of the star labeled "the fifth Beatle" by *Time* magazine. "Oh my God, it's him . . ." *Time* recorded the chatter among these fans. "What a groove, look at that nose . . . It's so beautiful. Did you dig those muscles? . . . Did you touch him? Yes. Oh my God."

Meanwhile, there was more seemingly bad news about *Midnight Cowboy*: the newly established Code and Rating Board of the Motion Picture Association of America had given the movie an X rating, potentially a kiss of death at the box office.

Only it hadn't. And it wasn't.

The enduring myth is that a prudish rating board, repelled by *Midnight Cowboy*'s scenes of fellatio, sodomy, homosexuality, and sadomasochism, and fearful of the wrath of local community leaders and vigilante-style censors, slapped an X on the film. The X meant that no one under seventeen was allowed in the theater, and it suggested to some mainstream moviegoers that the rating board had effectively judged the movie to be pornographic. Later on, when *Midnight Cowboy* became the only X-rated film to win the Academy Award for Best Picture, an embarrassed rating board supposedly pleaded with the producers to resubmit the movie. The board asked Schlesinger and Hellman to eliminate just a few seconds of dialogue, anything at all, so that board members could claim the movie had been toned down and therefore had earned an R. But after the filmmakers defiantly refused to cut even one frame, the board sheepishly gave the movie an R rating anyway. John and Jerry told versions of this story for many years and others have repeated it, at times with their own creative embellishments.

The truth is very different.

When United Artists submitted the movie to the MPAA's rating board early in 1969, the board came back with an R rating, noting the movie's graphic portrayal of male hustling but acknowledging its worth as a serious drama. R stood for "Restricted"; it meant that children under sixteen (changed to seventeen in 1970) would not be admitted unless accompanied by a parent or adult guardian. But the rating was rejected—not by the Motion Picture Association but by the cochairman of United Artists, Arthur Krim.

Soft-spoken and serious, with an industry-wide reputation for being smart, tough, and fair-minded, Krim was a classic Hollywood power broker. He was so powerful he didn't even feel the need to live in Hollywood, much preferring New York. He wore a gray suit to the office every day of his working life and was considered to be both the brains and moral conscience of the UA operation. "His mind was like a bear trap," recalled David Picker. "Once something got into his head, it never got out." Krim was the kind of businessman for whom the phrase "pillar of the community" was invented; he engaged in politics, the arts, and charitable causes, and he was a major fundraiser for the Democratic Party and a close friend of President John F. Kennedy. After JFK's assassination, he quickly became one of Lyndon Johnson's closest advisers; he even had his own room at the White House for his weekly overnight trips. "No one had won LBJ's trust and admiration more than Arthur Krim," wrote Jack Valenti, one of the president's former aides, who now was the head of the MPAA and the father of the new ratings system.

Krim was uneasy about *Midnight Cowboy*, worried that an R rating meant children could be exposed to the movie if their parents weren't vigilant. He decided to consult an expert who happened to be a neighbor of UA cochairman Robert Benjamin out in Great Neck, Long Island. Aaron Stern was a psychiatrist and a member of the faculty at Columbia University's prestigious medical school. Stern was personable, self-assured, sophisticated, and smooth-talking—so much so that he made one writer for the *Los Angeles Times* swoon: he described Stern as "an urbanely packaged man, with gray, contoured hair, sharp but pleasing features, the sure moves of an athlete, and the alertness of a fighter-pilot." Like Krim, Stern styled himself a liberal in heart and soul. But like many of his fellow shrinks, he clung to the conventional wisdom that homosexuality was a deviant lifestyle choice that children needed to be protected from at all times. Homosexuals, he argued, were narcissists who chose to be gay because they could only love people exactly like themselves. "Theirs is a choice born of fear," he would later write. "They withdraw from the frightening demands of a relationship with someone of the opposite sex and move into relationships with others who mirror themselves." None of these sweeping generalizations were verified by actual research. They were merely Aaron Stern's deeply cherished, fact-free opinions.

It was *Midnight Cowboy*'s "homosexual frame of reference," Stern would explain in a 1971 radio interview, that caused him the most concern. "That's no problem for an adult. If you choose the homosexual life, that's fine. But before you make that choice, you should understand what homosexuality stands for. If you're a thirteen- or fourteen-year-old, and you've never had intercourse with a woman that is gentle, tender, communicative, sensitive, and if the way in which it's depicted by John Schlesinger in the film is your only criterion for evaluating intercourse— and if you recall the scene with Brenda Vaccaro, they get into a power struggle over who's on top, and the next day she then says, 'You're one of the greatest I've ever had, and I'm telling my girlfriend about you.' To a kid in the audience who's never known more meaningful interaction, he could completely distort this and be stripped away of his opportunity for meaningful choice."

Stripped of its convoluted language, Stern's message was that *Midnight Cowboy* might cause young men to become gay. His fears mirrored and affirmed those of Krim, who decided after consulting with Stern to reject the board's R rating and self-rate the movie with an X. Since Krim's maneuver was done behind the scenes, most people assumed the rating board was responsible. The X rating damaged the film's commercial prospects—newspapers and TV stations in many cities refused to accept advertising for an X-rated film, and half the country's theaters even refused to book an X-rated movie. One state legislator in Texas proposed adding a fifty-cent tax on the ticket price of every X-rated film and singled out *Midnight Cowboy* as one of the reasons why (the measure never came to a vote). After the movie won Best Picture, United Artists returned to the board and asked for an R. The board members, who'd been publicly mocked as prudes for the X rating, were somewhat puzzled but complied with the request—after all, they had rated it R in the first place and saw no reason not to do so again. "There was no issue about it," recalls Stephen Farber, who was a student member on the rating board and later became a prominent film critic and film studies professor at UCLA. "We watched the movie again and then everybody voted R. It was not controversial."

Farber found the notion that a movie might have the power to change a teenager's sexual orientation "bizarrely paranoid . . . but I think [Stern] was definitely reflecting the views of the time about homosexuality within the psychiatric profession."

Jack Valenti, who was desperate to extricate himself and the Motion Picture Association of America from the endless culture wars over movie censorship, was so impressed with Stern's self-assurance and eloquence that he hired him as a consultant to the rating board and later appointed him administrator of the code. Stern went on to dominate the board, issuing arbitrary rulings based on his own psychological theories and sensibility, and intimidating movie producers into making twice the number of editing changes to their films than had been requested under the previous Production Code. When Farber and another former board member, Estelle Changas, wrote an op-ed piece in *The New York Times* criticizing Stern's reign, the ratings czar enlisted three prominent directors and producers—Ernest Lehman, Sam Peckinpah, and Don Siegel—to write letters to the *Times* supporting him (the fact that all three filmmakers had movies in production that would soon be up for rating by Stern's board went unremarked upon). After Stern resigned from the board, two years later, a remorseful Valenti told the *Times*, "I once made the mistake of putting a psychiatrist in charge, Aaron Stern."

When Valenti had instituted the ratings system, with the support of Hollywood's most influential wise men, the year before *Midnight Cowboy* was up for review, X was meant to be seen as a respectable rating for a legitimate adult-themed film. It was, in the words of the *Los Angeles Times* film critic Kenneth Turan, "a moment before the rating became a moral football . . . when it seemed that Hollywood could deliver thoughtful adult entertainment without the world coming to an end." Among the quality films given X ratings were Lindsay Anderson's *If. . .* (1968), Robert Aldrich's *The Killing of Sister George* (1968), Luchino Visconti's *The Damned* (1969), and Haskell Wexler's *Medium Cool* (1969). But X quickly became a scarlet letter—a mark of shame and a tacit accusation of pornography. There was even concern that ABC might refuse to run clips from an X-rated Oscar nominee on the annual Academy Awards television broadcast. Still, Dustin Hoffman's fears—that the X rating would damage *Midnight Cowboy*'s chances of finding an audience and being recognized for its artistry—proved to be unfounded.

The National Catholic Office for Motion Pictures, successor to the dreaded Legion of Decency, took an entirely different approach. The office's official organ, the *Catholic Film Newsletter*, gave a relatively lenient A-IV rating to the film, calling it "a strong and at all times masterful story of the imperceptible growth of friendship between two outcasts who, in being reduced to one another, find a rich and poignant relationship that, however unlikely, has the ring of humanity at its purest."

United Artists not only took the X rating in stride—it was their idea, after all—but found a way to capitalize on it. *"Whatever you hear about* Midnight Cowboy *is true!"* boasted one of the first ads. Gabe Sumner, UA's veteran chief of advertising and promotion, understood that the younger, more engaged moviegoers who were *Midnight Cowboy*'s target audience would be attracted rather than repulsed by the X rating. "The quality was there, no question—I was sure Hoffman and Voight would be Academy Award nominees," he recalls. "The question was how to make the movie more potentially exciting to the general public. I felt the controversy over the X rating would give it an extra dimension. The movie needed to get out of the art house and into the public square."

Sumner, with the support of David Picker and the UA brass, devised a marketing campaign that centered around opening the film slowly, first in one theater each in New York and Los Angeles in May, then expanding it in July to ten major cities around the country. "I saw *Midnight Cowboy* as something that had to be nurtured—slow openings, careful screenings—let it percolate, let people hear about it," he says. Nineteen days before it officially opened, UA held a special screening for critics. It was a risky strategy to show it so early—the critics could have sunk the film before it was officially released. Instead, many of them heaped praise upon it. Sumner's next set of ads quoted *Look* magazine calling the movie "a reeking masterpiece. It will kick you all over town," and

Rex Reed labeling it "infuriating, lacerating. A nasty but unforgettable screen experience." By the time the movie opened, audiences were
primed and ready.

Midnight Cowboy premiered on Sunday, May 25, 1969, at the Coronet
Theatre, on Third Avenue between East Fifty-ninth and Sixtieth Streets.
In keeping with New York City's prolonged labor strife in that era, the
invitees had to cross a picket line manned by striking members of the staff
of Walter Reade, the company that owned the movie house. The viewing
was followed by a party at Wednesday's, a swank uptown discotheque
where Jim Herlihy, who had been flown up from Key West for the premiere, met Waldo Salt for the first time. "They embraced like a pair of
collaborationists in a humanist revolution," wrote the counterculture
journalist Paul Krassner, who was looking on. "I liked him immediately," Jim said of Waldo.

Herlihy's expectations for the movie had been low, and he was pleas-
antly surprised at how much he enjoyed it. He found himself laughing out loud at Ratso's *I'm walkin' here!* moment—which was not in the
novel. "I thought, Wow, I'm involved in this thing, this is interesting,"
he recalled. "And it turned out to be a really nice picture."

Jim was less kind to John Schlesinger. He didn't like the scene where
Joe Buck brutally beats up Towny—even though it was taken almost
word for word from the novel. "I wanted it out of the picture because
I thought it was just too much," Herlihy said. He was even more upset
with the sexual encounter between Joe Buck and Bob Balaban's pimply
high school student—although it too is taken directly from the novel
except for the location, which was changed from a rancid tenement roof-
top to the balcony of a sleazy movie grindhouse. "It was hard to watch
and totally unnecessary," Jim complained. "I'm afraid I bummed up
Schlesinger's party by harassing him about it."

If so, John didn't seem to notice. He and Jerry Hellman were basking
in the good feeling about that first public screening. At some point in the
evening, the *New York Times* film critic Vincent Canby's review arrived.
Although not a total rave, it was more than good enough. While "not a

movie for the ages," Canby wrote, "as long as the focus is on this world of cafeterias and abandoned tenements, of desperate conjunctions in movie balconies and doorways, of ketchup and beans and canned heat, *Midnight Cowboy* is so rough and vivid it's almost unbearable." And Canby loved the performances. Dustin Hoffman's Ratso "is something found under an old door in a vacant lot . . . Hoffman looks like a sly, defeated rat and talks with a voice that might have been created by Mel Blanc for a despondent Bugs Bunny. Jon Voight is equally fine."

Archer Winsten's *New York Post* review, which arrived the next day, pronounced the movie "so extraordinarily good, and surprising, in so many ways that it's hard to give it adequate praise." A good part of the genius lay in the casting, wrote Winsten, who said Voight's "characterization is complete and wonderful." Hoffman, he added, "is a talent of astounding power and versatility."

Time magazine's anonymous critic didn't care for John's direction, commenting that he "sometimes seems less interested in Buck and Rizzo than in himself, covering his film in stylistic tics and baroque decorations." But the reviewer loved Voight and Hoffman's performances. "Hoffman has progressed by stepping backward to a supporting part. It is an act of rare skill and rarer generosity. No matter how well Ratso is performed, *Midnight Cowboy* is, after all, the tale of Joe Buck. It is a mark of Voight's intelligence that he works against his role's melodramatic tendencies and toward a central human truth. In the process he and Hoffman bring to life one of the least likely and most melancholy love stories in the history of American film."

Not everyone loved the movie, of course. Pauline Kael of the *New Yorker* loathed its social commentary and accused John Schlesinger of indulging his own excesses. "The satire is offensively inaccurate—it cheapens the story and gives it a veneer of almost hysterical cleverness." The "spray of venom is just about overpowering," she added, "but the two actors save the picture." Roger Ebert of the *Chicago Sun-Times* labeled it "an offensively trendy, gimmick-ridden, tarted-up, vulgar exercise," while *Life* magazine's Richard Schickel rejected the relationship of Joe Buck and Ratso Rizzo, which was both figuratively and literally the heart of the film. "One could accept mutually exploitative, explicitly stated faggery," wrote Schickel, whose homophobia leaked out onto the page. "To what, though, can we attribute the pretty impulse that overtakes them, converting them from a pair of dreary louts into tender comrades? Only as a fake, I fear. Or the act of desperate movie makers copping a plea."

But Stanley Kauffmann, who had stirred so much anger in the gay arts community with his takedown of homosexual playwrights in *The New York Times* in 1966, was enthusiastic—so much so that it was almost as if he were seeking to make amends for that earlier piece. "Herlihy's compassionate but relatively unsentimental American-Candide style made the book bloom like a flower in the gutter," wrote Kauffmann. "Schlesinger has understood the book; with intelligence, flourish, and extraordinary skill, he has made an unusually moving film."

In retrospect, some critics saw *Midnight Cowboy* as blazing a trail during the brief golden era of the New Hollywood. With its frank, adult treatment of sexuality, the movie crashed through the gates that *The Graduate* and *Bonnie and Clyde* had tried to storm two years before. But whereas those two groundbreaking movies had gotten tepid critical responses, *Midnight Cowboy* received a relatively warm reception. "It was a rare moment," the British film critic Gwilym Mumford wrote many years later, "when Hollywood saw the coming changes in cinema and, rather than ignore them and hope they went away, rolled out the red carpet."

The truly enthralling verdict came the day after the opening, when Michael Childers fielded a phone call from Judy Smith, John's secretary, who told him the line for tickets at the 598-seat Coronet stretched all the way to the Fifty-ninth Street Bridge. "You've got to come down and see this," she said. John and Michael hailed a taxi and drove around the block several times staring at the crowd. They got out at Bloomingdale's, across Third Avenue from the Coronet, and made their way upstairs to watch from the window of the men's clothing department. The people waiting, who were mostly members of what *The New York Times* called "the under-thirty brigade," set a new one-day record for attendance at the theater, and long lines continued all summer and into the fall. The movie played a record thirty-seven straight weeks at the Coronet, grossing more than $1.4 million at just that one theater.

Although John and Jerry may have been fed up with Dustin Hoffman's reluctance to publicly embrace and promote the movie, they had to concede that his star power played a major role in its soaring success. Nineteen sixty-nine was the year he vaulted from nonexistent to fourth on the Quigley Top Ten Money Makers poll, behind Paul Newman, John Wayne, and Steve McQueen. He would remain in the top ten for three more years straight and in the top twenty-five for fourteen of the next sixteen years. If anything, his status as a counterculture icon solidified after *Midnight Cowboy* because he proved he was not just a movie star but a gifted character actor as well. His audacious decision to take the role—a decision he had quietly come to regret—validated not only his own extraordinary ability as an actor but the values of the young fans who admired him.

A few weeks after the movie opened, Hoffman shared the cover of *Life* magazine with Wayne under the headline "Dusty and the Duke: A Choice of Heroes." Inside the ten-page photo spread—all the Wayne images were in color, all of Hoffman's in black and white—contrasted Hoffman's "restless, introverted city dweller" with Wayne's "solid, conservative outdoorsman." The piece concluded that while "Duke and Dusty have huge and loyal followings, split largely by generation . . . many a moviegoer, whatever his age, still finds himself cheering for both."

By early August *Midnight Cowboy* had pulled in more than a million dollars even though it was only playing in eleven cities. Young people dressed in bell-bottoms, see-through blouses, and what the *New York Times* reporter Marilyn Bender called "an abundance of hair" waited on line outside the Coronet anywhere from thirty minutes to two hours to see the film, with regular tickets priced at three dollars each. It was earning money at twice the rate of *Tom Jones* five years earlier, which had been a smash hit. Gabe Sumner's marketing strategy had succeeded.

"Sure the price is ridiculous," Ellen Henschel, a waitress and aspiring actress seated on the pavement, told Bender. "But lots of good things cost money," added John Borden, a musician.

19. THE MOVIE

I can see by your outfit that you are a cowboy.
—"Streets of Laredo"

Midnight Cowboy, the movie, begins with a blank white screen
and a young boy's fantasy—the sound of cowboys and Indi-
ans, gunfire and war whoops from an old western—and then
we see the boy himself, all alone, riding a rocking horse in the kiddie
playground below the Big Tex drive-in movie screen to the creaking of
rusted springs and a ghostly prairie breeze and somebody singing "Get
Along Little Doggie" as if it were an act of defiance.

It's Joe Buck, singing in the shower of his cheap motel room, then
toweling off and dressing himself in new cowboy duds—pearl-buttoned
western shirt, fringe leather jacket, black hat, and narrow-toed boots,
plus cowhide suitcase—checking himself out in the mirror and pleased
with what he sees: a tall, round-cheeked, blond-haired stud who looks
ready to take on the world. He's soon out the door, marching past the
abandoned El Rio movie theater with the marquee still announcing John
Wayne's *The Alamo* like the engraving on a tombstone, while the glisten-
ing, jingle-jangle fingerpicking of a guitar on the soundtrack kicks into
gear the wistful, enigmatic theme song, "Everybody's Talkin'."

Joe quits his job as a dishwasher at Miller's Restaurant, explaining
to a bemused coworker his plan to move to New York City and become
a hustler servicing bored and frustrated married women who are desperate for sexual adventure and willing to pay for it. He boards a bus
that will take him from small-town Texas to the country's most exciting
and dangerous city. Joe is looking not just to find his future but also to
burst out of the shell of isolation in which he has been confined since

childhood. Images of that isolation flash quickly across the screen—Joe as a little boy being abandoned by his young mother; Joe left alone in his grandmother's house while she pursues the men passing through her life; teenaged Joe being torn away from Crazy Annie, his first and only love.

Over the long bus ride, he is polite, friendly, wide-eyed, and honest, but not overly bright—"I only get carsick on boats," he confides to a fellow passenger. The billboards passing by his bus window offer aspirational advice—IF YOU DON'T HAVE AN OIL WELL . . . GET ONE!, one sign demands. JESUS SAVES, promises another, perched atop a dilapidated Texas shack that the Savior must have overlooked. Joe's ear is constantly pressed against his white transistor radio, hearing pitches for God and money while he fantasizes about all those wonderful New York women, their sexual and emotional needs, and their pocketbooks.

At first Joe in cowboy garb wanders the streets of Manhattan in dumb amazement. The city announces itself with a series of classic New York moments: Joe floating above an anonymous sea of people on a crowded Fifth Avenue sidewalk; checking out a well-dressed man lying unconscious on the pavement outside Tiffany's as fellow pedestrians step carefully around the body; trailing after attractive women who seem adept at ignoring him; watching in dumb amazement as a new acquaintance confronts a taxicab that has invaded his space inside a crosswalk. It is, as filmmaker and architect James Sanders writes, "a city of action, a place where things *happen*."

But New York's hardened predators soon take advantage of Joe's naïveté and goodwill, beginning with Cass Trehune, who teaches Joe his first hard lesson in how to hustle a sucker out of twenty bucks. Sylvia Miles's torrid six minutes and seventeen seconds set the definitive pattern. She's a real New York chick—tough, manipulative, angry, and remorseless. She's followed, in turn, by O'Daniel, the semi-deranged preacher played by John McGiver, who seems to be recruiting Joe for both religious and sexual purposes. Bob Balaban is utterly convincing as the pimply "bar mitzvah boy" who uses Joe for sexual gratification and then whines his way out of paying for it. Brenda Vaccaro's Shirley is an alluring but vindictive society woman. Having paid for Joe's services, she feels she has also bought the right to demean him when he fails to deliver in bed, balancing an ashtray on his chest and challenging him to a game of Scrabble, an opportunity to mock his painful semi-literacy. Barnard Hughes conveys the desperate longing and self-hatred at the core of Towny, the masochistic paper salesman from Chicago who seeks Joe's company in Times Square and then invites a savage beating for money.

Jon Voight is in every scene with every supporting actor, usually playing mouse to their cat. "Each of us had our own little play to be in," recalls Balaban. "Everybody had something great to do and they were all stupendous."

These hardened New Yorkers strip Joe of everything he owns: his money, his precious cowhide suitcase, his transistor radio, his cherished illusions, his fragile self-respect.

The climax of the first third of the movie takes place on Forty-second Street, with a slowly starving Joe roaming the sidewalks desperate to make a buck. He passes a half dozen other young male hustlers, each dressed like himself in cowboy garb, smoking cigarettes, striking poses, seeking to lure someone into a quick, transactional bout of sex. Each of these men is hoping to accumulate enough cash to get off the mean streets before winter sets in. As night turns to day and back to night again, Joe wanders aimlessly, his plastic Zenith whispering aspirational rhetoric into his ear. *Why worry about your future?* a woman's voice asks over the airwaves. *What do you want more than anything in the world?* In the background Toots Thielemans's harmonica launches into a plaintive tune reflecting Joe's longing and solitude.

Over the next few minutes, Joe locks eyes through the plate-glass window of a coffee shop with a haunted-looking man scraping food from dirty plates who could pass for his doppelgänger; stares with bemused disbelief as a junkie feverishly runs a toy mouse up and down the arms and face of her young son at a diner; and spills ketchup on his only pair of pants while trying to forge a surreptitious meal out of condiments and a packet of saltines.

Ratso Rizzo turns out to be Joe's unlikely savior. Ratso has started out as just another parasite taking a bite out of Joe's rapidly dwindling wallet. But after conning Joe out of twenty dollars and leaving him in the hands of O'Daniel, the crazed evangelical, Ratso runs into Joe again and invites him to stay in the abandoned slum apartment where Ratso has been squatting. This isn't from kindness or pity; Ratso desperately needs someone to look after him as winter closes in and his consumptive lung disease worsens.

The X-flat is New York's brutal essence: cold, harsh, barely livable. It becomes the setting for the most intimate, poignant, and hopeless moments of the movie. It reflects both Ratso's low-life day-to-day reality and his resourcefulness. There are two mismatched easy chairs for sitting, a greasy army cot and battered floor cushion for sleeping, a stained, circa-1930 gas stove next to a filthy sink, a decrepit wooden kitchen table with a torn linoleum top, and a collection of tin dishes, bent utensils, paper napkin holder, sugar dispenser, saltshaker and mismatched coffee mugs, all seemingly purloined from various diners and coffee shops. But Ratso's dreams also reside in this dreary cave; hanging from the dingy walls are a collection of posters for Florida orange juice, and a larger poster near the cot with a photo of a smiling family of four admiring a grove of orange trees.

The tall blond Texan and the dark, feral con man from the Bronx are opposites in almost every way. Each is demanding and highly critical of the other, and each man's bank account of trust has run down to nothing. Each makes clear he would prefer to rely on anyone else. But there is no one else. Ratso makes wicked fun of Joe's naïveté, of his failures as a male hustler, of his cowboy outfit and his body odor. "Frankly, you're beginning to smell," scolds Ratso, "and for a stud in New York that's a handicap." Joe, the country mouse, is less agile verbally but just as critical. He mocks Ratso's sexuality—"When's the last time you scored, boy?"—and falls back on threats of violence. But Joe's assertions do not impress Ratso. "I get it—you're a killer," he says with a smirk.

Then Ratso plays the gay card. "In New York no rich lady buys that dumb cowboy crap anymore," Ratso tells Joe. "They're laughin' at you on the street . . . That's faggot stuff. You wanna call it by its name: that's for fags."

"John Wayne," Joe replies. "You wanna tell me he's a fag?"

Still, Ratso's jibes penetrate Joe's shell and disturb the core of what little self-esteem he has left. Standing passively in the doorway, he pleads. "I like the way I look. Makes me feel good. And women like me, goddammit."

Despite their hostility, the men share moments of mutual dependence and occasional admiration. Joe, after first making fun of Ratso's home-cooked meals as disgusting, soon digs in, wielding a bent spoon with his arms raised above his shoulders, country boy style. Ratso carefully cuts Joe's hair and likes what he sees. "Not bad, for a cowboy," he opines. Their domesticity comes to resemble a marriage—minus the sex—with Joe playing the husband and Ratso the wife.

Winter is coming—the water dripping from the faucets of the sink turns to ice. The two men hop around to keep warm while the transistor radio plays a cruelly mindless ditty, taunting them that "orange juice on ice is nice!"

Moments later Joe is seen pawning his precious Zenith for five dollars. Soon after, he sells a pint of his blood for ten more.

John Schlesinger had directed many fine actors, and would work with many more over his four-decade career. But he said he never directed a better pair than Dustin Hoffman and Jon Voight. Indeed, fifty years later it is hard to name two male stars who achieved more in a mainstream feature film than these two. Their performances are a matched set— it's impossible to separate Hoffman's from Voight's. They complement each other physically, emotionally, and intellectually. Through constant discussion and improvisation they helped shape and rewrite their own roles, and they did it together. It is one of the cinema's greatest dramatic achievements.

Hoffman's is the showier piece of acting. Ratso Rizzo is the perfect character actor's role. The bad teeth, the greasy, combed-back pompadour, bristling like a rooster's, the frantic limp that resembles a crippled bird, the scratchy voice that rises and falls—Hoffman uses all of these physical features and mannerisms to construct a character who demands to be treated with dignity even as he wallows in squalor and despair. Still, for all its naturalism and honesty, Hoffman's performance never lets you forget you're watching an actor at work. He uses his deft physicality and sense of timing to evoke laughter from the most unlikely of situations—like when he manages to stuff Joe's laundry into a pregnant woman's coin-operated washing machine for a free cleaning or helps Joe get back his dry-cleaned hat without paying.

"Dustin's a great comedian," Voight recalled. "I think a picture like this could be very depressing, disturbing, but with that element [of humor] we can take that walk with these guys . . . and not get weighted with despair."

But ultimately, this is Joe Buck's story and therefore Jon Voight's movie. He finds all of the loneliness inside Joe, all of the feigned bravado, the anger, and the desperation, and all of the comedy. Joe Buck is a fish out of water not just in New York but everywhere he goes. Voight's Joe is kind to small children and other vulnerable humans—those who are most like himself—yet also capable of stunning brutality, as he finally demonstrates with his attack on Towny in the film's final New York moment.

The Towny scene, in which Joe's desperation leads him to an unspeakable act of violence, is the movie's most powerful and uncompromising. John Schlesinger and Waldo Salt—working directly from Jim Herlihy's novel—insisted on presenting it in all its raw brutality, even though it presents a dark, ugly side of Joe that he has warned about but never actually displayed before. Some of the cast and crew had deep reservations—including Michael Childers, who argued it could easily turn viewers against Joe. Preview audiences seemed to confirm Michael's fears. But John insisted that the scene remain. He felt it demonstrated Joe's commitment to saving Ratso's life at all costs, and also illustrated how much New York City's iron code—survival of the fittest—has finally worn away Joe's gentle nature. The beating, abhorrent and inexcusable, casts a grim shadow over the rest of the movie. But without it, *Midnight Cowboy* would be too pat and redemptive.

Joe has changed in other ways as well. The lonely Texan who tried to conquer New York and its jaded denizens with his goodwill and phony sexual bravado has come to understand that the only way he can connect with other people is to embrace his own vulnerability. He jettisons his cowboy gear at a brief stopover after the bus reaches Florida; it's a symbolic act of self-renewal. Joe is finished with illusions of sexual conquest and is longing for an honest life and human relationships based on real feelings, not bombast. He wants to become a whole person. But his savage beating of Towny undermines his search for salvation. When Ratso dies, Joe looks frightened and almost ready to cry. He's lost his only friend and compass. He doesn't know his fate, and neither do we. This is not the storybook ending we wanted for Joe, but something much more ambiguous and authentic.

Jon Voight's performance is transcendent. From the opening scene, when he steps out of the shower, until the conclusion, when he cradles Ratso's dead body in his arms, Voight squeezes all of the pathos and humor out of Joe's character without a whiff of sentimentality. But it's Voight's quietest, most restrained moments that reveal his true mastery. That scene in a cheap cafeteria where he takes a seat across the table from a meth junkie and her young son is one of his finest. He says nothing but watches in stunned fascination, his eyes widening in disbelief. When he spills the ketchup on his pants, the look on his face is one of hopeless surrender; this is what rock bottom looks like. Voight's certainty with the character is eloquent. As he would later tell an interviewer, "It's almost more comfortable for me to be Joe Buck than it is for me to be me."

Watching the movie some fifty years later, Hoffman recalls the essence of his collaborator at work. "One thing I saw about Voight was the joy that he had doing it and the joy he had being an actor. I mean he was born to be an actor. He was gloriously happy, you could see it, the confidence. This was the greatest experience of his life so far."

John Schlesinger was keenly aware that a movie is more than just performances. He gave Ann Roth full license to exercise her fertile imagination in dressing these characters, and she responded with memorable costumes for both men and for Brenda Vaccaro as well. He clung tenaciously to Nilsson's recording of "Everybody's Talkin'" because he understood that the music needed to evoke Joe Buck's emotions and dreams rather than parrot back the narrative; and he commissioned John Barry to create a wordless, lyrical ballad to balance the boisterous energy of "Everybody's Talkin'" with something quieter and sadder.

John was often derided by critics as a flamboyant showman without subtlety or dignity. But *Midnight Cowboy* makes a strong case for his artistry. The first thirty-five minutes—from Joe's departure from Texas to the moment when Ratso deposits him at Mr. O'Daniel's hotel room door—is a masterful study in smart, economical cinematic narrative. The same is true of the segments of Joe's slow descent into poverty and despair before he meets Ratso again and of all of the X-flat scenes that follow. Still, there are a handful frenzied moments in *Midnight Cowboy* that try our patience: the O'Daniel scene itself is hyperbolic and puzzling, although John McGiver's over-the-top performance is crazily entertaining. The problematic Warhol party scene, eight minutes in which nothing much happens, never captures our imagination, but its documentary-like presentation of a certain kind of oblivious hedonism that flourished in the drug-and-sex-heavy psychedelic era feels uncannily accurate.

The film critic Rex Reed called *Midnight Cowboy* "probably the most savage indictment against the City of New York ever captured on film." Everywhere he goes, Joe comes across victims of New York's casual cruelty and indifference. Schlesinger uses these moments as both subtext and context, constantly evoking the wider world surrounding Joe and Ratso.

Even the city's billboards serve as commentary and counterpoint. When Ratso and Joe limp home across the Willis Street Bridge to Manhattan after visiting the grave of Ratso's father, they hobble past a Northeast Airlines billboard advertising flights to Florida (Ratso's dream of paradise) and promising STEAK FOR EVERYBODY AT LUNCH AND DINNER. The sign atop the Mutual of New York office building, across from Joe's hotel, reads MONY, and the half-literate Joe assumes that's how the word is spelled.

Schlesinger isn't always subtle about images, but Adam Holender is. His cinematography is deep and precise. Holender films Joe consistently looking at mirrors and windowpanes—the motel room mirror at the film's beginning, the gum machine mirror in the subway station. When Joe needs to gather his strength, he looks at himself and pledges to move forward. The most haunting image is the coffee shop window through which he watches a glum young man lifelessly wrestling with garbage pails and a large tub of dirty dishes, just as Joe once did in Texas. From Joe's expression, it's clear he's seeing himself in the man's hollow eyes. Holender and his gaffers constantly position their lights behind Joe to highlight his innocence and naïveté. The city itself seems naturally lit and increasingly dingy as winter creeps in, while the Florida scenes are bright and saturated with color. Ratso is shot in lengthening shadows in the X-flat as his life and health slowly seep away. The editing at the X-flat constantly shifts between Joe and Ratso, then pulls back to show us the two men together. Sometimes the images move jerkily to the rhythm of the music, while at other times the camera slows down to watch as the two protagonists test and goad each other, thrusting and parrying, each trying to get used to having another person in his life whose feelings and well-being he is responsible for.

While the basic narrative is bleak, there is much humor in *Midnight Cowboy*. From the immovable bellhop who refuses to leave Joe's cheap hotel room without a tip, to the sly way Cass maneuvers twenty dollars out of Joe's wallet, to Ratso's deft physicality in checking every pay phone for loose change and smoking every cigarette butt down to his fingertips, the movie bristles with bitter comedy.

Ultimately, however, it's *Midnight Cowboy*'s compassion that makes it memorable. "John most admired humanist filmmakers like Truffaut and Satyajit Ray," says his nephew, Ian Buruma. "What interested him was not politics but human behavior. And what I find most impressive about *Midnight Cowboy* is that he took two down-and-outers who are not prepossessing in any way and made them so human and so understandable that in the end your heart goes out to them without being sentimental, and that was a real achievement."

As the Canadian writer Lex Corbett points out, it's Voight and Hoffman who embody and deliver Schlesinger's humanistic vision. "These two actors—at the beginning of their respective careers—bring a level of sustained anguish that leaves the viewer with the distinct impression of real people whittled down by the trials of life," she writes. "Even as we understand Joe and Ratso as symbols of American decay, they are people first. That is where *Midnight Cowboy* succeeds the most and why it is still so watchable. The universal humanity displayed in this film keeps it from feeling dated."

"Who's he?" Shirley queries Joe Buck about Ratso Rizzo at the psyche-delic party where she meets this very odd pair of street people. "Oh, God, don't tell me you two are a couple."

Whenever they were asked, John Schlesinger and Jerry Hellman in-sisted that *Midnight Cowboy* was not a "gay movie," just as Jim Herlihy had insisted it was not a "gay novel." What they meant was that Joe and Ratso don't have sex with each other. The two men don't even hud-dle in bed together for warmth in the increasingly chilly X-flat. What John and Jerry feared, of course, was that the film would be shunned if mainstream audiences decided it was beyond the pale. Yet Shirley was onto something. The story, which was written by a gay novelist, and the film, which was made by a gay director, both depict several homosexual encounters and a deep, intimate friendship between two lonely men. Still, as film historian Mark Harris points out, the movie isn't a story of lib-eration, pride, or self-esteem, but of loneliness and survival in daunting circumstances.

The movie at times emits a noxious homophobia. Joe and Ratso peri-odically declare their contempt for "faggots" and "faggot behavior," their views seemingly justified by the pathetic actions of the "real" homosex-uals in the film, including Bob Balaban's sniveling high school student and Barnard Hughes's masochistic businessman. "I deserve this," moans Towny as Joe Buck beats and robs him. "I brought this about myself, I know I did!" he exclaims. "Oh! How I loathe life!"

Still, it's possible to see Joe and Ratso's angry declarations as a flimsy cover for their own sexual ambivalence. Both men clearly were taught in childhood to embrace the widely accepted condemnation of homosexu-ality. Yet their growing regard for each other sends a different message. The bus ride to Florida helps strengthen their bond, but Ratso's death breaks it before Joe can determine what it ultimately means.

Some gay viewers criticized the film for the weak, seamy characters played by Balaban and Hughes. Yet for others the movie, no matter how raw, served as welcome recognition that gay life existed. "Gay themes come without the slightest whiff of sensationalism," writes Matthew Kennedy in *The Bay Area Reporter*. "Homophobia is in service to plot and character, and is absent the 1960s cinematic expectation that any glint of same-sex desire requires subsequent torture and death." Kennedy, who teaches anthropology and film history, sees *Midnight Cowboy* as "part of Schlesinger's quiet revolution in homosexuality on the screen," along with *Darling* and *Sunday Bloody Sunday*, the film that follows *Midnight Cowboy* in Schlesinger's oeuvre.

Vito Russo, in *The Celluloid Closet*, his landmark 1981 book on homosexuality in the movies, dismisses *Midnight Cowboy* as a homoerotic buddy movie, one of several at that time where the ambiguous sexual attraction between two men is exploited but never consummated or even acknowledged. Chief among these films was George Roy Hill's *Butch Cassidy and the Sundance Kid* (1969) with Paul Newman and Robert Redford. Russo cites a humorous remark by Joanne Woodward, Newman's actress wife, that "Bob and Paul really do have a chemistry. Someday they'll run off together and I'll be left behind with Lola Redford."

But Russo also detects a welcome subversive element in *Midnight Cowboy* when Ratso criticizes Joe's cowboy outfit as "faggot stuff," raising doubts about the authenticity of this American masculine ideal. "This defines the fear," Russo writes. "If there is no real difference between the cowboy hero and the faggot on Forty-second Street, then what remains of American masculinity? This scene comes closest to saying that the costume is only an image, as much a lie as all the other ways in which we force the movies to serve our dreams of an America that never really existed."

The core of *Midnight Cowboy* is about two men struggling to survive and define themselves. "The film brought issues of male sexuality, male intimacy, male trauma, and male damage to the fore in ways that had never been examined in Hollywood with such explicitness and sympathy," writes Gary Needham, a film studies professor at the University of Liverpool. He calls it "a new type of liberated Hollywood film," freed by the demise of the Production Code to explore masculinity in an entirely new and more frank manner.

The movie is not kind to women. Joe's mother and grandmother are prostitutes who abandon him emotionally and physically and help launch his cruel isolation. Cass and Shirley, the two New York women he meets and beds, are predators—Cass, the aging call girl, gets an excellent orgasm and twenty bucks from Joe, while Shirley gives him money but mocks his faltering literacy and his flaccid penis. Later, after they have engaged in wild, uninhibited sex, Shirley tries to make amends by recommending Joe's services to her unhappily married female friends. She even seems a tad wistful, as if she has begun to suspect there may be more to this faux cowboy than just an erection. But it's too late for them; Joe must leave her and go to Ratso's rescue whether he wants to or not. While _Midnight Cowboy_ lacks the poisonous misogyny that reeks through the pores of New Hollywood movies like _The Wild Bunch_, _MASH_, and _Straw Dogs_, it simply is not very interested in women. This places it in the same category with dozens of other male-oriented films of its era, including _Butch Cassidy_, _Easy Rider_, _The French Connection_, _Wild Rovers_, _The Godfather_, and _Scarecrow_. The protagonists of these movies, writes the film critic Caroline Madden, "may not necessarily have a sexual desire for one another, but certainly a romantic one."

The truth is that, with the exception of the brief flashbacks of passion between Joe and Crazy Annie, there is no romantic sex in _Midnight Cowboy_, either straight or gay. John Schlesinger uses the new freedom of the cinema to depict sexual expression in a cold, almost clinical, antierotic way. The sex we see is about money or power or obsession or lust; the one thing it is never about is love.

Schlesinger could not have been oblivious to the fact that Joe Buck's outfit, heterosexuality, and aspirations to become a stud amount to a classic gay male sex fantasy. But he insisted that anyone believing that this was "queer coding"—signaling to the initiated that Joe was gay—was engaged in wishful thinking. "I'm not concerned about gay lore or anything else," John told an interviewer for _The Village Voice_ in 1975. "I was simply concerned with making a film that seemed to me true to the character."

Maybe so. But many gay viewers knew better. After the film was released, the cover image of the next issue of _The Advocate_, the monthly tabloid based in Los Angeles that called itself the "Newspaper of America's Homophile Community," was a still photograph from _Midnight Cowboy_ of a naked Jon Voight from the scene in Shirley's bedroom.

Schlesinger himself always defended his depiction of the predatory sexual acts in *Midnight Cowboy*—both heterosexual and homosexual—as reflecting the brutal reality of life in New York City for those like Joe Buck living on the rough edge of society. But the movie's surprising success enabled him to embark on yet another project he'd long contemplated, one that explored an entirely different social milieu and sexual behavior.

Sunday Bloody Sunday focuses on a love triangle whose apex is Bob, a bisexual young artist. He is having affairs simultaneously with Daniel, a prosperous, middle-aged London physician, and Alex, a female management personnel recruiter and divorcée. Both Daniel and Alex are in love with Bob, who is fond of each of them but committed only to himself and his artistic aspirations. There are no secrets here—each of Bob's lovers knows of the other's existence—but there is much unrequited longing. Alex is especially restless and unhappy and yearns for more than Bob can ever give her. She engages in a one-afternoon stand with a male client in an effort to make Bob jealous (he isn't). She has a row with her mother over the fact that her parents still have occasional dinners with her ex-husband who wants her back, and she criticizes Mom for suffering Dad's infidelities and generally boorish behavior. "Why do you put up with it?" she demands.

Her mother replies by astutely nailing Alex's impossible expectations of life and love. "You keep throwing your hand in because you haven't got the whole thing," she tells Alex. "There is no *whole thing*." As for her own marriage, her mother says, "You think it's nothing, but it's not."

The screenplay, written by the novelist and film critic Penelope Gilliatt, was loosely based on John Schlesinger's own two-year, on-again, off-again affair with John Steiner, a handsome young British actor who was involved with John at the same time Steiner was having an affair with a woman. The doctor in the movie, played with sharply observed dignity, humor, and compassion by Peter Finch, is Jewish and has a strong commitment to family and tradition, but has not revealed his homosexuality to his parents nor any of his relatives. His sensibility reflects that of Schlesinger himself (although John's parents knew he was gay). Glenda Jackson is equally brilliant as the sharp-edged, restless, and dissatisfied Alex.

The film is in many ways a comedy of manners about upper-middle-class, trendy Londoners and their families—their politics, their sexual habits, their discontents. Two moments in particular stand out. Early on in the story, during a weekend when Bob is supposed to be helping Alex look after her sister's four children in Hampstead—the affluent north London neighborhood where Schlesinger was born and raised—he slips out to Daniel's house for a break. The two men embrace and share a long, passionate kiss—the first ever depicted between two men in a mainstream feature film. "Gay characters in the movies had to that point almost always been depicted as deviants—criminals, tormented drunks, or limp-wristed, lisping creatures—allowing straight audiences to feel superior or comfortably amused," Ian Buruma writes. "An upper-middle-class doctor and his boyfriend kissing on the lips, casually, affectionately, no different from any straight couple, was a much greater challenge."

Film historian Vito Russo pointed to the movie's remarkable sensitivity and frankness. "It was a film in which alternative sexuality was taken for granted, something that gay activists had been asking for all along," he writes.

The second moment comes at the end, after Bob has gone off to America to seek his artistic fortune. Daniel speaks directly to the camera about why he has been willing to settle for an imperfect relationship with his narcissistic and unreliable young lover. "People say what's half a loaf, you're well shot of him," says Daniel, "and I say I know that. I miss him, that's all. They say he never made you happy and I say, but I *am* happy, apart from missing him."

There was great tension with the crew on the film set during the kissing scene. David Harcourt, the cameraman, leaned back and asked Schlesinger, "Is this really necessary?" John assured him it was. Murray Head, the twenty-four-year-old straight actor who played Bob, was less troubled. "I just thought it was a kiss and a very pleasant thing, but the whole crew was uncomfortable," he recalled. The resolutely heterosexual Peter Finch, an Australian with a keen sense of humor and no apparent inhibitions when it came to acting out the scene as written, handled it with aplomb. "I just closed my eyes and thought of England," he told interviewers.

Just as David Picker had done with *Midnight Cowboy*, United Artists held its first preview screening of *Sunday Bloody Sunday* for a wide range of executives and staffers, including secretaries and assistants. Only this time it didn't go so well. "There was a lot of lighting up of cigarettes and wobbling of knee joints, and they were obviously embarrassed," Schlesinger would recall. "The publicity department, which had seen us right through *Midnight Cowboy* with huge enthusiasm, met me after the screening and said, 'Well, you've given us a hard one, John.'"

The film got respectful reviews and did reasonable box office in large urban centers like London and New York. Everywhere else, however, it died a quick death. Some theaters refused to book it because of its treatment of homosexuality. London newspapers quoted the singer Shirley Bassey, a friend of Finch's, who complained that the kiss had made her sick to her stomach and sent her racing out of the theater. Nonetheless, the movie swept the BAFTAs—Britain's equivalent of the Oscars—for Best Picture, Best Director, Best Actor and Actress, and Best Editing.

John declared himself more than satisfied, calling *Sunday Bloody Sunday* "probably the best thing I've ever done. It's also the most personal." Still, he had learned a hard lesson. If he wanted to be a big-time successful director in Hollywood—and he most definitely did—he would need to deliver more mainstream projects.

Midnight Cowboy and *Sunday Bloody Sunday* are very different films, with different paces, styles, and concerns. Yet each is set in a major city on the brink of disorder. *Cowboy*'s New York is a predatory jungle for the homeless and the forgotten, while *Bloody Sunday*'s London is undergoing governmental crisis and labor unrest. Taken together, the two movies are almost documentary-like in capturing the political and sexual anxieties of their era. Glenda Jackson sees the parallel. "*Midnight Cowboy* was the sort of film that really captured the energy of America and its character in that era," she says, "just like *Sunday Bloody Sunday* captured the character of Britain at that time."

While John Schlesinger was still officially in the closet—he did not publicly disclose his sexuality until the early nineties—*Sunday Bloody Sunday* was his cinematic declaration. It was welcomed and celebrated in the gay community in ways that *Midnight Cowboy* never would be.

"*Sunday Bloody Sunday* saved my life," said the Pulitzer Prize–winning novelist Michael Cunningham. Growing up in Pasadena in the sixties, "all I could imagine for myself was a life of furtive sorrow which involved, to my young mind, skulking around with a lapdog in my arms looking for love in the men's room of the Greyhound station, with guys who would probably beat me up afterward. Then I saw Peter Finch play a complicated, honorable gay man, simply and fully human. It was revelatory. I began to believe, after seeing that movie, that I could have a future as neither more nor less than myself, and that being myself was more than enough to be."

John always insisted that "this film is not about the sexuality of these people." The movie's true concerns are the characters' longing to connect with the people they love and hope will love them in return, and what happens when those characters are forced to settle for less than they long for. These are among John's most profound and enduring themes.

"The official East Coast line on John Schlesinger's *Sunday Bloody Sunday* was that it is civilized," wrote the critic Roger Ebert in a wise and astute review. "My notion, all the same, is that *Sunday Bloody Sunday* is about people who suffer from psychic amputation, not civility, and that this film is not an affirmation but a tragedy. I think *Sunday Bloody Sunday* is a masterpiece, but I don't think it's about what everybody else seems to think it's about. This is not a movie about the loss of love, but about its absence."

20. EXPLOSIONS

You don't need a weatherman to know which way the wind blows.
—Bob Dylan, "Subterranean Homesick Blues"

One month and two days after *Midnight Cowboy* opened at the Coronet, a different kind of revolution took place across from Christopher Park, a narrow triangle of open space presided over by a bronze statue of the bantam Civil War general Philip Sheridan, in the heart of Greenwich Village. At one twenty on a Saturday morning, a half dozen uniformed officers from the First Division Public Morals Squad stormed the Stonewall Inn, at 53 Christopher Street, a squat, unyieldingly utilitarian, Mafia-owned gay bar known for its watered-down drinks and uninhibited clientele. There were some two hundred people crammed inside its two dark rooms, dancing, drinking, and looking for companionship at the start of a hot, muggy weekend. They were ordered to leave the premises, while workers at the bar, which didn't have a liquor license, were arrested, along with a handful of drag queens.

Police raids were a standard occurrence of gay life in New York and everyone inside the Stonewall knew the drill. Patrons might seethe over the humiliating treatment they faced in supposedly permissive New York, but they generally didn't resist. This time was different. Jolted by the rough treatment uniformed officers used in subduing one trans-dressing lesbian, the crowd gathered outside the bar burst into cries of "Police brutality!" and "Pigs!" and some threw rocks and bottles at the cops. Someone dropped a large concrete block on a police car; someone else hurled a bag of wet garbage into the open window of another cop car, drenching a senior officer in soggy coffee grounds and rotten eggshells. The Tactical

Police Force—the same elite squad that had staged their own middle-of-the-night police riot at Columbia University a year earlier—broke ranks and pummeled the mob with nightsticks and shields, chasing rioters and onlookers down the narrow nineteenth-century streets and alleyways. Thirteen people were arrested and dozens more were injured, including four police officers. Confrontations continued throughout the weekend.

The Stonewall riots were hardly the first street fight between cops and homosexuals over gay rights, and perhaps not even the largest. But they came at a pivotal moment in the history of gay liberation. And the new dividing lines were not just between gays and cops, but between younger, more assertive gays who demanded their freedom and flaunted their sexuality, and their elders, generally more conservative in politics and dress, who worried that the movement would spin off its axis and lose all hope of gaining respectability and acceptance. Less than two weeks after Stonewall, the Gay Liberation Front was born at a meeting at Freedom House, on Fortieth Street, muscling aside the older, more politically moderate and culturally conservative Mattachine Society and Daughters of Bilitis as the new face of the gay rights movement. "Do You Think Homosexuals Are Revolting?" asked a flyer for a protest meeting a few weeks later. "You Bet Your Sweet Ass We Are!"

It was no accident that this was taking place in late 1960s New York, cradle of so many raucous social and political movements. Gays had participated in and learned from the protests and street brawls of civil rights and women's liberation activists, antiwar protesters, and student demonstrators. These battles had helped affirm certain principles and strategies—that freedom in America could no longer be confined to one race, gender, or sexual orientation, and that an effective strategic approach had to include street demonstrations as well as lawsuits and political pressure. Women's liberation had provided another key element—by uncoupling sex from reproduction, the movement not only succeeded in helping liberate women but offered a pathway to equality for gays as well. If sex was also about pleasure and emotional fulfillment, then *any* sexual activity between consenting adults—straight, gay, bisexual, polymorphous—deserved equal protection. Still, if anyone harbored the illusion that the sexual revolution had vaporized homophobia in New

York, all they had to do was observe the police bust at the Stonewall and the headline of the New York *Daily News*'s gleefully mocking article: "Homo Nest Raided, Queen Bees Are Stinging Mad."

To everyone's surprise, including virtually all of the people involved in making it, *Midnight Cowboy* became the third-highest-grossing film of 1969, eventually pulling in $44.8 million and making John Schlesinger and Jerry Hellman multimillionaires. Waldo Salt, whom John and Jerry had rewarded by doubling his share of their profits from 2.5 to 5 percent, made close to a million dollars, as did James Leo Herlihy, who had the same share. But perhaps the most surprised beneficiary was John's friend Kaffe Fassett, the American artist who had first alerted him to the novel. John summoned Fassett to his London office and gave him a check for five thousand British pounds as a finder's fee. "This was a vast fortune for me," recalled Fassett, "as I was living on less than one hundred pounds a month." He used it to help buy a flat.

United Artists also did well. And behaved well. The movie had gone nearly a million dollars over budget, and UA's executives could have clawed back that money from the profits they paid to Schlesinger and Hellman. At a meeting of the top brass, David Picker asked, "Does anyone feel we should take back points from John and Jerry?" No one raised their hand. They knew their partners had delivered a movie that was both excellent and profitable. "You go to an art gallery and you instantly know when you're looking at a work from an artist that says something that other people can't," says Picker. "John was able to make a movie that other filmmakers couldn't do."

Midnight Cowboy was just one of several cutting-edge films that surprised and shook the cultural arbiters of 1969. *Easy Rider* stunned studio executives by its success, although critics had widely varying assessments of its quality. It was made by two bastard children of the studio system—the director Dennis Hopper, thirty-three, who, as a young buck in the James Dean mode, had worked as a character actor in mainstream studio films for more than a decade; and the producer Peter Fonda, twenty-nine, son of Henry and brother of Jane, the rebellious offspring of Hollywood royalty. *Easy Rider* is a road picture that dispatches the two rebels on souped-up Harleys into the troubled heart of an angry and violent America. The movie has lyrical cinematography by László Kovács, a powerful musical soundtrack that sets a new standard for the use of rock music in films, and a sly, charming performance by a little-known B-movie actor named Jack Nicholson. It is also saturated with soggy counterculture clichés about sex, drugs, and rock 'n' roll—"doing your own thing in your own time," as Fonda's Captain America puts it. He and Hopper's Billy the Kid are cinematic archetypes—the tall, stoical Fonda and the comically chatty space cadet Hopper. The long-haired, self-righteous hippie martyrs lose the battle, but win the heart and mind of the movie.

In truth, *Easy Rider* hasn't aged well, except as an artifact of classic American naïveté and self-destruction. Still, it has the facile Euro-cine sensibility of the late-sixties works of Jean-Luc Godard and Michelangelo Antonioni. The *New Yorker* critic Pauline Kael astutely identified it as a "cult film," something that young counterculture audiences found irresistible because it conveys "a whole complex of shared signals and attitudes that rings true to the audience's vision." As for the studio execs, they found it hard not to notice that *Easy Rider* cost only four hundred thousand dollars to make and ultimately earned more than one hundred times as much in ticket sales. As Joan Didion noted, "every studio in town was narcotized by *Easy Rider*'s grosses."

The bolder and more innovative film released that same year was *Medium Cool*, the cinematographer Haskell Wexler's jagged blending of fictional narrative and documentary centered around real news events of 1968. Wexler depicts the fictional relationship between a television news cameraman (Robert Forster) and an Appalachian widow (Verna Bloom) whom he meets and falls in love with in Chicago during the 1968 Democratic National Convention. Wexler inserts his characters into actual events, including the streets of downtown Chicago during the convention riots and police crackdown. Embedded into the story is a scathing critique of establishment news media ethics, its voyeurism and lack of a moral code. Wexler and his cast and crew are caught up in the rioting. Someone on the soundtrack calls out, "Look out, Haskell, it's real!" as a tear gas canister fired by riot police detonates near the spot where the director is shooting. The movie concludes with a preciously existential Godardian car crash.

The final moment has Wexler turning and pointing his movie camera directly at the audience, evoking the dangers and mysteries of the media age. *Medium Cool* sometimes uses a sledgehammer to pound home its points, but it is prophetic about where our national obsession with cynically prepackaged and manipulated television news would lead us. The *New York Times* critic Vincent Canby called the film "awkward and even pretentious" yet marveled at Wexler's skill in producing "a kind of cinematic Guernica—a picture of America in the process of exploding into fragmented bits of hostility, suspicion, fear, and violence."

Midnight Cowboy also launched a decade of dark, gritty New York films—including *Klute* (1971), *The Panic in Needle Park* (1971), *The French Connection* (1972), *The Godfather* (1972), *Mean Streets* (1973), *Serpico* (1973), *The Taking of Pelham One Two Three* (1974), and *Dog Day Afternoon* (1975); *Shaft* (1971), *Superfly* (1972), and *Across 110th Street* (1972) used Harlem in particular as their backdrop for brutal stories of crime, drugs, and urban violence. But *Midnight Cowboy*'s truest fraternal twin is Martin Scorsese's *Taxi Driver* (1976). Both films are about military veterans who come to New York to act out their fantasies. Both characters run afoul of the city's malign culture. But Joe Buck eventually finds someone to share and cushion the misery, while Travis Bickle will always remain alone. Joe is limited by his intellect and his isolation, but he is sane; Travis is deeply disturbed. His one-room apartment is just as dreary as Ratso's X-flat, but with no possibility of escape. He subsists on junk food, pops pills, obsessively watches porn, and talks to himself in the mirror as he practices his quick draw. He deepens his own solitude, rejecting the few people who try to get close to him. He can't sleep. He talks of an apocalyptic storm like the one that Noah confronted in the Book of Genesis: "Someday a real rain will come and wash all the scum off the street." The cab is his ark for the coming flood, the space capsule that he maneuvers around a hostile planet. "Loneliness has followed me my whole life, everywhere," he narrates. "There's no escape. I'm God's lonely man."

Eventually, and inevitably, Travis drives himself into a frenzy, and stages a bloodbath to act out his holy wrath. While Joe's moment of violence against Towny is a sudden lashing out that shows his commitment to Ratso, Travis's is a premeditated act of rage. Joe is searching for redemption, Travis for vengeance. Joe's fate at the end of *Midnight Cowboy* is uncertain, while Travis's seems preordained. Unless he is stopped, we can see a direct path to political murder—indeed, John Hinckley Jr. became so closely identified with the character of Travis and with the actress Jodie Foster, who plays a young prostitute whom Travis seeks to rescue, that Hinckley sought to assassinate President Ronald Reagan to get her attention and win her love. A defense expert at Hinckley's trial said the defendant had "absorbed the identity of Travis Bickle" to the point of wearing the same army fatigue jacket and boots and developing an obsession with guns.

Travis is correct; for him there is no way out. The worst dangers do not reside in the city but within himself. *Midnight Cowboy* may be bleak, but *Taxi Driver* is a gothic horror story. In the seven years between the two films, New York's slow decline and fall had accelerated into an avalanche. The city that had been America's greatest, richest, biggest, and most glorified had turned into America's pariah—"a crime-ridden, fiscally profligate, graffiti-festooned moral cesspool," in the words of the film critic J. Hoberman. Travis hates New York with a vengeful fury; he's not just a prophet of doom but an instrument of destruction. That he survives and will presumably strike again is the measure of director Scorsese and screenwriter Paul Schrader's abiding pessimism about the city and its future. The media's celebration of this twisted killer's massacre is an eerie harbinger of the morally coarsened and unhinged world we now inhabit.

With its tawdry depiction of sex and sleaze, *Midnight Cowboy* crashed through many cultural barriers, but *Taxi Driver* angrily obliterated them. When it was first released, its unrelenting power overshadowed *Midnight Cowboy*, just as Scorsese's standing as a great director overtook John Schlesinger's. But over the years, the quieter pleasures of *Midnight Cowboy*, including the brilliant collaboration between Dustin Hoffman and Jon Voight, have reasserted its stature as a movie of equivalent quality.

Curiously enough, neither actor reaped extra financial benefits from *Midnight Cowboy*'s box-office success. Hoffman's new business manager,

Walter Hyman, met with Jerry Hellman in August 1969 to plead for a small percentage of John and Jerry's profits. Hyman cited Dustin's "enormous contribution" to the film—not just his superb performance as Ratso Rizzo, but the time he had spent helping vet the actors who auditioned for the part of Joe Buck, and the many weeks of inspired improv, both formal and informal, with Jon Voight once they had both been cast. Hyman also said his client had been poorly represented by Jane Oliver when the original deal was struck. None of these arguments moved Jerry. He and John were still annoyed that Hoffman had been a no-show at promotional events for the movie. "I told Walter, quite frankly, that my own reaction to that suggestion was entirely negative," Jerry wrote in a note to John. "I can see no reason personally or professionally for doing anything at all for Dustin Hoffman." John's written response has not survived. In any case, Hoffman got no points.

No one apparently considered being generous to Voight. He was just as crucial to the movie's success as Hoffman, and he had made only $17,500 for a picture that had taken up nearly six months of his life. But *Midnight Cowboy* drastically changed his career. Suddenly, he was a star. Rex Reed profiled him in *The New York Times* the week the movie opened and accurately predicted what would happen next. "This may be the last time Jon Voight ever walks The Street without being mobbed," Reed wrote. "After *Midnight Cowboy*, he'll be like Paul Newman—a movie star for whom anonymity is only a nostalgic memory."

Voight recalls walking into a small gift shop in Manhattan to buy presents for his nieces a few weeks after the movie opened and being followed inside by more than a dozen people who trailed behind him like he was their spiritual leader as he picked out items and took them to the cash register. He also recalls coming home for lunch one day to the basement apartment he shared with Jennifer Salt, on the Upper West Side, to a constantly ringing telephone. Voight's phone number was still listed, and Jennifer was upset because the phone had been ringing all morning. It rang again as they were talking. Voight picked it up. It was a stranger requesting his presence at an event. Voight said he couldn't make it, hung up the phone, and it immediately rang again. Another stranger with another request. After two or three more rapid-fire calls, Voight yanked the wire from the wall. He lay down on their bed—the mattress was on the cement floor—and stared at the ceiling while Jennifer's dog Ruby licked his face. "My life had changed," he recalls. "It wasn't an unpleasant thing. It just took over. I was a different person now."

Offers started pouring in. He signed up to play Milo Minderbinder in *Catch-22* (1970), the new multistar film project by Mike Nichols. The film sputtered—it was overshadowed by Robert Altman's crazed, anarchic antiwar movie *MASH*, released that same year—but Voight's performance was widely judged one of the best things in it. He also did *The Revolutionary* (1970), an intensely observant film about the gradual radicalization of a university student in a repressive society. Here, too, Voight, who was in every scene, gave an accomplished and convincing performance, alongside Robert Duvall and Seymour Cassel, two superb supporting actors. Jennifer also had a small role. The movie got a few excellent reviews—Roger Ebert called it one of the year's best films and said it astutely captured the rise of the radical left. But it got little attention and sank without a trace. Still, the message of *The Revolutionary* was powerful and clear—that radicalism is the response of idealistic people, some of them thoughtful, others governed by their emotions and egos, to the slow-building accumulation of legitimate grievances that are either ignored or repressed by those in power.

Voight was reluctant to embrace the demands of sudden stardom. "He was looking for another challenging part that had redeeming social value and he just couldn't find it," says Salt. One of the roles he discussed was the male lead in *Love Story*. Voight read the novel and the screenplay and says he turned down the role. He told the producer, "I'll spoil this. I'll do too much with it. I'll find a way to make it complex. It's better if you find somebody who can just do this character as he is." Ryan O'Neal, says Voight, was a much better choice. Robert Evans, head of production at Paramount at the time, estimated Voight could have made eight million dollars in salary and share of the box office. Later Voight would turn down one of the lead roles in *Jaws*, the 1975 Steven Spielberg blockbuster.

"Everybody made their own choices," Voight says. "If it was the old Hollywood, Dusty and I would have had two films a year. They would have written into our contracts: go do this." Instead both actors, now officially considered movie stars, were on their own, looking for something as good as *Midnight Cowboy*. Voight's little speech to John Schlesinger in Texas about how they would spend the rest of their careers in its shadow proved sadly prophetic. As he himself said at the time, "I just think I'm never gonna catch Joe Buck again."

His politics remained far to the left. He befriended the New Left activist Abbie Hoffman and took Jennifer to Chicago to watch Hoffman on trial with his Chicago Eight comrades on charges of conspiracy, inciting to riot, and other alleged crimes related to the protests at the 1968 Democratic National Convention. Voight went partly to express solidarity and partly to get into the mindset for his role in *The Revolutionary*. It was a frightening experience for both him and Jennifer. The federal courthouse was an armed camp. They were frisked for weapons and drugs before being allowed to enter the courtroom. "The marshals were walking up and down the aisles with their arms crossed, looking at us as if we were outlaws," Voight recalled. "There was a tremendous amount of paranoia." When Voight laughed out loud at something the defense lawyer William Kunstler said in court, the marshal threatened to evict him. And when the defendant David Dellinger's teenaged daughter started to cry while listening to testimony, the marshal grabbed her arm and yanked her from the courtroom. "What I saw in Chicago really shook me up so I don't know what to believe anymore," Voight said at the time.

Meanwhile, Jennifer was having problems of her own. Being with a boyfriend who suddenly had become a major movie star was annoying at best, especially when she was trying to establish her own acting career. "I wasn't prepared to be a good partner to someone who was going through what he was going through," she says. The adulation he was receiving irritated her; the fans who stopped them on the street were often demanding and bothersome. Always the Boy Scout, Voight tried to be accommodating—he'd been brought up to be polite. But she was Waldo Salt's uninhibited daughter, taught by her father's unvarnished example to be bluntly honest even if it meant being rude. She felt herself being suffocated and outshined. "We had very different sensibilities," she recalls. "We saw what was going on through such a different lens, and I gave him very little support and very little kindness. I drove him crazy." By the beginning of Oscar season, in early 1970, "he was so done with me, and I think we were really done with each other."

Dustin Hoffman had a far more frightening brush with radical politics. He was at his office on West Fifty-fifth Street just before noon on a Friday in early March of 1970 when he got a phone call telling him there had been an explosion in the town house next door to his new apartment at 16 West Eleventh Street in the Village. He rushed home to find fire trucks, ambulances, police cars, and howling sirens on the edge of a raging tower of smoke and flame, and his wife, Anne—they had been married the previous May—in a state of shock as she pulled possessions from their burning apartment. Hoffman rushed in to help while a crowd gathered outside to watch and news photographers took shots of the now famous movie star carrying an oil painting by a friend out his front door.

The original assumption by police was that the explosion was the result of a gas leak. But investigators soon discovered the truth. The blasts—there turned out to be three in all—were caused by dynamite in the process of being packed into two pipes that were to be used as bombs by members of the Weather Underground, the radical leftist faction that had split off over the past year from Students for a Democratic Society. Many of those involved had participated in the SDS-led protests at Columbia University in the spring of 1968. The pipe bombs, which were also packed with nails, were meant to be used that evening to blow up a dance hall outside Fort Dix, New Jersey, where dozens of off-duty soldiers and their dates would be gathering. It was planned as an act of terror to kill as many soldiers and civilians as possible, part of a new campaign to wage war against the American state and its purported lackeys.

The Weathermen may have been far off the deep left end of American politics, but they were steeped in popular culture. Their very name came from the lyrics of Bob Dylan's "Subterranean Homesick Blues," and their multipartner sex practices were straight out of the sexual revolution handbook. Terry Robbins, the leader of the West Eleventh Street cell and self-taught bombmaker, had a fixation with *Butch Cassidy and the Sundance Kid*, telling his comrades that even if the attack on Fort Dix didn't succeed, at least they would go out in a blaze of glory—just like Butch and Sundance in the movie.

The town house was owned by James Wilkerson, a wealthy former ad executive, whose twenty-four-year-old daughter Cathy had borrowed it while her parents were vacationing in the Caribbean; the parents were due home that evening. Unknown to them, Cathy was a member of the Weather Underground and had turned the house into a bomb factory for Robbins and three other comrades. Another comrade had purchased two fifty-pound cases of dynamite for less than sixty dollars from an explosives company in New Hampshire and driven them down to New York. Robbins was working at a table in the sub-basement wiring the pipe bomb to a timer when he inadvertently set it off. The two bombs exploded, as did at least one of the dynamite cases, instantly killing Robbins and two others. A stunned Wilkerson was upstairs taking a shower when the explosions rocked the building. She pulled her friend Kathy Boudin out of a burning pit and the two women vanished before investigators arrived.

One of those killed was Ted Gold, a twenty-two-year-old recent Columbia graduate who had been one of the more thoughtful and articulate of the campus radicals during the protests of 1968. Somehow, over the two years since then, Gold had been transformed from an idealistic student activist into a committed terrorist ready and willing to engage in the mass murder of young men and women in the name of a revolution that would never happen. His crushed body was found beneath the basement's concrete staircase. Later, someone put up a handmade sign in a shop window on nearby Eighth Street. It read TED GOLD DIED FOR YOUR SINS.

The third and final explosion blew a massive hole in the wall of the adjoining building, which housed Dustin and Anne's second-floor apartment. His recently purchased antique desk fell into the hole. Anne was described as shaken as she came out of the building, "biting her lip and looking glassy-eyed after she rushed back into her home to rescue her dog." As Anne and Dustin ran in and out of the building carrying their possessions, the crowd outside grew, waving to him and his wife and shouting encouragement.

Hoffman was appalled. Already bruised and jaded by the constant public attention he'd been subjected to since *The Graduate*, he was convinced the smiling onlookers were enjoying his and Anne's desperation. They were "really knocked out," he said later, "because they were getting their two favorites—a disaster and a celebrity—at the same time."

The Greenwich Village explosions were the deadliest of some 370 bombings that the city's bomb squad reported between January 1969 and September 1970. Most of them did minor damage, but the constant threat, exacerbated by regular street demonstrations against the Vietnam War, rubbed raw the city's frayed nerve endings. One of the most extraordinary confrontations occurred two months after the bombing, when two hundred construction workers in hard hats, swinging clubs and crowbars, rampaged through a peaceful antiwar demonstration on Wall Street, injuring seventy people. The mob then invaded city hall, forcing officials to raise to full staff the American flag that had been flying at half-mast to mark the killing by Ohio National Guardsmen of four student protestors at Kent State University earlier in the week. Witnesses said police made no effort to stop the assault. The hard hats even tried to storm Trinity Church, where medical workers had set up a first-aid station to treat injured demonstrators. The reporter who wrote the story for *The New York Times* was Homer Bigart, sixty-two, a legendary war correspondent who had covered World War II, Korea, and Vietnam and won two Pulitzer Prizes. Bigart had bad eyesight, a stammer, a prominent beer belly, and a pugnacious manner, and he was beloved by his colleagues. His byline was one more eerie signal that the war in Southeast Asia had come all the way home.

21. THE OSCARS

Hollywood lives at a considerable remove from the rest of the society, lives and thrives entirely on its myths.
—John Gregory Dunne

Ever since the first Academy Awards presentation, on May 16, 1929, at the Hotel Roosevelt in Hollywood, the annual ceremony has been a ritual of self-esteem and self-congratulation performed by people who are far wealthier and more glamorous than the rest of the world. But the forty-second Academy Awards, on April 7, 1970, had more than wealth and glamour on its mind. An invisible cloud of anxiety hung over the event, which was watched on television by some 60 million Americans and 250 million international viewers in forty countries via a live-feed satellite or videotape. No bombs went off, but in keeping with the times the limousines of the three thousand begowned and dinner-jacketed guests had to navigate around some fifty protesters denouncing Hollywood stereotypes of Mexican Americans with placards pledging "Power to the Chicanos."

After welcoming everyone to "the most star-studded and surprise-packed Academy show of all," Gregory Peck, the tall, distinguished, leading-man-handsome president of the Motion Picture Academy of Arts and Sciences, got straight to the point. "Most of us these days are asking ourselves these questions," he intoned. "What is the meaning of the new freedom of the screen? Is it something to be feared? Should the screen be censored?" What did audiences want? How far was too far?

There followed a six-minute-and-twenty-second documentary film offering answers from a pantheon of nine of the world's most respected directors, all men, including Ingmar Bergman, Federico Fellini, Akira

Kurosawa, David Lean, Mike Nichols, and Billy Wilder. In interviews edited down to two or three sentences each, they offered heartfelt banalities about censorship, nudity, liberty, and culture. Kurosawa warned that "with total freedom without any restraint the world will be chaos," while Wilder lived up to his reputation as Hollywood's most sardonic wordsmith by arguing for "more nudies . . . what we should have is saturation bombing until we're good and sick of it." Then came John Schlesinger, a relative newcomer, with a much different message. He used his brief moment to beseech young people coming into the movie business to insist on artistic freedom. "It's terribly important for them that they fight with all the energy they have and never, ever take no for an answer," he declared.

Schlesinger was included because *Midnight Cowboy* had been nominated for seven Academy Awards, including Best Picture, the first (and last) X-rated film ever to be so honored, and Best Director, plus three awards for acting (Jon Voight and Dustin Hoffman for Best Actor and Sylvia Miles for Best Supporting Actress), as well as Best Adapted Screenplay (Waldo Salt) and Best Editing (Hugh A. Robertson). Few had high expectations that an X-rated movie about an aspiring male prostitute made in New York by a predominately East Coast crew of artists and craftsmen would do well at the Hollywood-centric Oscars. Still, in the conversation about liberty, license, and moral standards, John had captured a seat at the table.

He himself was in London the day of the ceremony, shooting *Sunday Bloody Sunday*. David Picker at UA, sensing a possible upset, had pleaded with him to suspend the film shoot for a few days to fly to L.A. along with Michael Childers, at UA's expense. But John, still the emperor of anxiety, refused to make the trip. "He was so pessimistic about our chances," Michael recalls. "He couldn't bear the embarrassment of coming all that way and then losing."

Jerry Hellman was at the Oscars, wearing a tight-fitting tuxedo and slightly askew bow tie, his curly brown locks pouring over his ears like a British rock star. In the lobby before the event began, Hellman ran into his old friend George Roy Hill, director of *Butch Cassidy and the Sundance Kid*, the year's most entertaining movie, which also had seven nominations and was considered the odds-on favorite for Best Picture. Hill certainly seemed to think so. He told Hellman, "Jerry, I just want you to know that *Midnight Cowboy* is a wonderful picture, too."

Hellman didn't try to argue. "I really didn't think that we had a chance," he recalled. "We were outsiders, we were a non-establishment film, we had an X rating, we hadn't made the picture in Hollywood. We had everything going against us."

Onstage, things turned from sanctimonious to sneering after Peck ceded the podium to comedian Bob Hope, who launched his annual monologue with a shot of homophobic disdain. "This is the night the Oscars separate the men from *The Boys in the Band*," he told the audience, referring to Mart Crowley's groundbreaking gay comedy-drama, which had been playing off-Broadway in New York for two years. The film version directed by William Friedkin had opened two months earlier. "It's been quite a year for movies," Hope went on. Alluding to Richard Burton's Oscar-nominated performance as Henry VIII in *Anne of the Thousand Days* and as a gay hairdresser in *Staircase*, Hope asked, "Did you ever think you'd see Richard Burton play both a king and a queen?"

Hope was just getting started. "This will go down in history as the cinema season which proved that crime doesn't pay but there's a fortune in adultery, incest, and homosexuality," he declared. "That's what we're honoring tonight . . . a sadistic king, a consumptive drifter, a male hustler, a school teacher dropout, and a one-eyed sheriff. This is not an Academy Awards, it's a freak-out, ladies and gentlemen."

The camera panned the audience, which laughed uneasily.

On paper, the leading candidates to win big on Oscar night 1970 were *Anne of the Thousand Days*, which led the field with ten nominations, and *They Shoot Horses, Don't They?*, which had nine. *Anne* was a worthy but lumbering Henry VIII Tudor epic—"one of those almost unbearably classic movies, like *A Man for All Seasons* and *Becket*," wrote Vincent Canby in *The New York Times*, who knew he was supposed to like those kinds of films but couldn't quite manage it. The large number of nominations *Anne* received was mostly a tribute to Hal B. Wallis, the venerable seventy-one-year-old Hollywood producer who put together the project, and to the superb performances of Richard Burton, Geneviève Bujold, and Anthony Quayle, all of whom were nominated for acting awards. *They Shoot Horses*, a Depression-era melodrama, was livelier and grittier, and made more money, but its utterly glum subject matter—the desperate attempts of poor couples to win a marathon dance contest with a prize of fifteen hundred gold dollars—limited its popularity among Academy members. A likely tip-off of how the Academy truly felt was that *Horses* wasn't nominated for best picture.

Butch Cassidy and the Sundance Kid, by contrast, was lively, cheeky, and fun, thanks to a sparkling original screenplay by William Goldman, for which he had reportedly been paid a record four hundred thousand dollars, and deftly comedic performances by Paul Newman and Robert Redford in the lead roles, although neither man was nominated for Best Actor. In any case, most observers were certain that this particular award was in the bag for John Wayne, officially for his performance as the one-eyed marshal Rooster Cogburn in *True Grit* but in reality in honor of many fine performances over a forty-year film career spent mostly in the saddle. But when it came to Best Picture, *Butch Cassidy* and *Midnight Cowboy* were the quality candidates. Both movies were archetypal buddy pictures. But *Butch Cassidy* was a contemporary romantic comedy masquerading as a western—what it lacked in authenticity it made up for in charm, craft, and charisma—whereas *Midnight Cowboy* was a weighty drama with a lot more on its mind and two lead performances that more than matched Newman's and Redford's. *Butch Cassidy* was the big box office winner of the year, eventually grossing $102 million, while *Midnight Cowboy* was a distant second. Still, *Butch Cassidy* had its detractors. Roger Ebert found it slow and bloated, while Pauline Kael condemned it as "a glorified vacuum . . . it's all so archly empty." A comparison of their theme songs showed the contrast between the two films: "Raindrops Keep Fallin' on My Head," from *Butch Cassidy*, was a slick piece of late-sixties pop music ear candy that had nothing whatsoever to do with the movie's characters or theme, whereas "Everybody's Talkin'" captured Joe Buck's heart and soul and the movie's restless spirit.

John Schlesinger had lost for Best Director for *Darling* in 1965, but three of the last seven Oscars had gone to British directors. Hollywood loved a British accent—it connoted class and seriousness, two qualities that the motion picture business always seemed a bit short of.

Gabe Sumner at United Artists and his West Coast publicist, Lloyd Leipzig, had a minuscule budget for Oscar promotion—no money for the lavish events that Universal and 20th Century-Fox hosted for Academy members for *Anne of a Thousand Days* and *Hello Dolly* (which also received seven nominations). Universal, which hadn't won an Oscar in any major category in the seven years since the studio had been bought by MCA, had served up a dinner of three-inch-thick prime rib, beef stroganoff, and imported champagne before a special screening of *Anne* even before the nominations were announced. "We were really hurting and we decided that this was going to be our year," an unnamed employee told *The New York Times*. Still, Sumner and Leipzig came up with a modest but effective ad campaign for *Midnight Cowboy* that featured striking sepia-toned stills from the movie. "We used a different image with every full-page ad," Sumner recalls. "If it didn't catch your eye on Wednesday, maybe it did on Thursday. It was a terrific movie. We didn't need anyone to stand up and give a speech. We knew what we had."

Unlike the bloated Oscars shows of modern times, the 1970 program ran a svelte two hours and twenty-five minutes. *Butch Cassidy* won the most awards—four altogether, two of them for its songs and score, the work of Burt Bacharach and Hal David, the most successful American pop songwriting team of that era. But it was *Midnight Cowboy* that captured the most attention, beginning with Schlesinger's surprise inclusion in the brief documentary at the beginning of the show. Soon after, Voight and actress Katharine Ross announced Waldo Salt as winner for Best Adapted Screenplay. Salt looked more like an electrified elf than an aged wise man as he vaulted up to the stage in a dark tuxedo, round sunglasses, crooked grin, and pixieish bangs curling like question marks over his forehead and supersized ears. There was so much he could have said about the Hollywood blacklist, the betrayals by employers and friends, and the grim years of struggle and despair that had followed. But his brief speech didn't go near any of those subjects. Instead, after exchanging an affectionate hug with Voight, he took the enigmatic high road. "It's very exciting," he declared. "I want to thank all of the beautiful people who helped to make *Midnight Cowboy*. Most of all, I want to thank all the people who are going to see it. May their number increase."

"He was very careful about choosing his words," says his daughter Jennifer, who was sitting in the audience that evening with a smile of delight on her face. The caution wasn't because her father was afraid or didn't want to rock the boat, she says, but because he didn't want to be seen as some kind of political victim. "He was bigger than that."

As expected, John Wayne beat out both Voight and Hoffman, who didn't attend the ceremonies, for Best Male Actor in a Leading Role. In an interview the following year with *Playboy* magazine—notorious because he attacked African Americans and Native Americans as inferior to white people—Wayne called *Midnight Cowboy* "perverted . . . a story about two fags." Still, he expressed a grudging respect for the two leads. "Damn, Hoffman and Voight were good," he told friends after watching the film. "Both of them. More than good—great. That is acting."

Sylvia Miles lost to Goldie Hawn in *Cactus Flower*, while Hugh A. Robertson, the rebellious and outspoken film editor, lost to Françoise Bonnot, editor of the political thriller *Z*.

Some of the most creative collaborators on *Midnight Cowboy* got no recognition whatsoever. Ann Roth, the brilliant clothes designer whose costumes for *Midnight Cowboy* broke new ground for flamboyant realism, was not nominated. It would be fourteen more years until she got her first nomination, for *Places in the Heart* (1984), and twelve more before she won, for *The English Patient* (1996). The casting director, Marion Dougherty, the other woman who played a critical role in *Midnight Cowboy*'s artistic success, was overlooked because there was not in 1970, nor is there today, an Oscar category for Best Casting. "Everybody's Talkin'" was not nominated for Best Song because it was not originally written or performed for the movie, although Harry Nilsson later won a Grammy for Best Contemporary Male Vocal Performance. John Barry's work as musical supervisor was also ignored by the Motion Picture Academy, but he too won a Grammy for Best Instrumental Theme for the *Midnight Cowboy* song featuring Toots Thielemans's lonesome harmonica.

Adam Holender, the deeply talented cinematographer, also failed to get a nomination.

John Schlesinger's Oscar for Best Director was perhaps the evening's biggest surprise. He was up against three of America's most respected mainstream directors—George Roy Hill for *Butch Cassidy*, Arthur Penn for *Alice's Restaurant*, and Sydney Pollack for *They Shoot Horses*. The fifth nominee, Costa-Gavras for *Z*, was considered to have no chance. But the British magic held. Voight, who was sitting next to Jennifer Salt, went up again, this time to collect for the director he so deeply admired. Voight explained that John was in London shooting his next picture—*Bloody Sunday*, as Voight mistakenly called it, leaving the audience to imagine it was a British crime thriller.

Voight's brief acceptance speech included a small grace note that John Schlesinger had insisted upon—one that acknowledged the importance of the novelist who had invented the characters and the story and the vivid scenes and dialogue that John and Waldo and the actors had brought to life on the screen. Speaking for Schlesinger, Voight said, "For him I'd like to say he'd like to thank James Leo Herlihy for his novel and all his American friends who made him feel so at home and worked so hard for something he cared so very much for."

After that, the big prize for Best Picture was no real surprise. The presenter was Elizabeth Taylor, who had been poured into a low-cut blue gown, her perfect pearl-shaped face wreathed in floating dark curls and a $1.5 million diamond necklace that sparkled every time she moved her lips. Her eyes opened wide as she announced the winner. "It was certainly a shock to Elizabeth Taylor," Jerry Hellman later recalled. "I felt she didn't know what it was, or who I was, or how we got there."

When *Midnight Cowboy* was announced, Jerry looked more stunned than Liz, but he was a model of brevity onstage. "I'd like to thank you all very much on behalf of everyone connected with the making of the film," he said, "with a particular thank-you to David Picker and United Artists, who made it all possible." And off he went, clutching the Oscar like a cat burglar who had just pulled off an incredible caper and was hoping to make his escape before anyone noticed.

Bob Hope sprang back up for some closing remarks. This time he discarded the homophobia but overplayed the self-celebration. Reading glassily from cue cards, with all the sincerity of a carnival barker, America's greatest comedian solemnly declared that "Hollywood peddles not only dreams but truths. The figures on the screen are not just shadows but living, breathing people who try to solve their problems as their conscience dictates. Never again will Hollywood be accused of showing a lollipop world.

"More and more films have explored the broad spectrum of human experience," Hope went on. "They have fearlessly and, for the most part, with excellent taste examined behavior long considered taboo. The worldwide popularity of American movies proves that Hollywood speaks a universal language, and the neighborhood movie house is in a sense a meeting place of all the people."

To demonstrate Hollywood's new social consciousness, Hope noted that two weeks earlier, one thousand American movie theaters had shown a tribute film about the late Dr. Martin Luther King and donated all the proceeds to a fund in King's name "to help solve America's racial problems in a nonviolent way, the Martin Luther King way." This was, Hope said, "evidence of our industry's eagerness to participate in the struggle to solve one of the nation's pressing problems."

But whatever else might have been demonstrated that evening, it was obvious that Hollywood was incapable of leading a deeply divided and rancorous America anywhere at all. Actress Shirley MacLaine, who was watching the show at an Oscars party with a collection of fellow Hollywood liberals—including Lee Marvin, Jack Cassidy, and Shirley Jones—at the home of the writer Gwen Davis and her husband, the producer Don Mitchell, got the last word, yelling at the TV screen, "Oh, shut up, Bob Hope."

22. FROM JIM TO JAMIE

The fact is this: the lonely man, who is also the tragic man, is invariably the man who loves his life dearly.
—Thomas Wolfe

Whatever his true feelings about the movie of *Midnight Cowboy*, Jim Herlihy was delighted and deeply moved that John Schlesinger thanked him by name in the Oscar acceptance remarks conveyed to the audience by Jon Voight. "You're so sweet and generous to have shared your lovely moment of super-success last night," he wrote in a letter to John the following day. "I was genuinely happy to hear your thanks for the book at such a moment. It was totally unexpected, uncalled for, and thoroughly appreciated."

But Jim had another matter to discuss. He'd recently finished a draft of *The Season of the Witch*, a new novel about the adventures of a seventeen-year-old hippie girl who runs away from her home in Michigan and ends up in the East Village, ground zero of the counterculture revolution. He told John he felt it was the best writing he'd ever done—and the most cinematic—and once he had refined the draft he wanted John to read it. While he realized John was likely booked with film projects for the foreseeable future, he believed this new novel might appeal to him. Jim still harbored a deep hunger for success and fame and a growing fascination with movies as a visionary technology that could free humankind from the chains of government oppression and conventional thinking, and he was keen to sign John up quickly. "Ideally, the book and the film should appear as close together in time as possible," he wrote dreamily. John wrote back eight days later to say that while he did have some projects he was committed to, he would love to read the novel as soon as it was ready. Nothing ever came of it—indeed, it would have been hard for anyone but Jim to imagine that Schlesinger would have been interested in revisiting the mean streets of New York so soon after *Midnight Cowboy*.

Jim's life wasn't as glowing as his letter to Schlesinger suggested. The five years since the original publication of *Midnight Cowboy* had become a protracted, marijuana/hashish/LSD-enhanced roller coaster ride, with steep climbs to an almost giddy sense of self-enlightenment punctuated by sudden plunges into despair. Along the way he had begun to retreat from the life he had led previously. Feeling increasingly suffocated by the hard work of churning out prose, he was writing less and less. He picked up stakes once more, abandoning New York, the city where he had come of age as a writer, playwright, and actor, and spending almost all his time in his beloved Key West, where he had sought to build a refuge and play the role of New Age hippie guru. He even abandoned "Jim," the name he had gone by all his adult life, and returned to "Jamie," his nickname from childhood. As he told Mary Caroline Richards, his dear friend and mentor from Black Mountain College days, who had always known him as Jim and had difficulty making the adjustment, "The name my soul hears no matter what I'm called is JAMIE."

The unexpected commercial success of *Midnight Cowboy* was a huge windfall for the man now known as Jamie. Besides his 5 percent share of the 60 percent of the movie's profits that Jerry Hellman and John Schlesinger received from United Artists, he also reaped royalties from the reissued paperback of the novel, with a cover featuring an iconic movie still of Dustin Hoffman and Jon Voight, which sold in the hundreds of thousands of copies. Jamie was cagey about divulging the amounts involved, telling one interviewer he had only cleared two hundred thousand dollars after taxes. His real take was at least double that amount.

His expressed attitude about the money was one of supreme ambivalence, bordering on annoyance. "When they dumped all this money on me it turned me into a bookkeeper," he told an interviewer for the *New York Post*. "I would like to do without money altogether. I feel sort of nagged all the time by people to give it away." Still, he insisted *Midnight Cowboy* had had little impact on his life. "I was old and tough and I had had other successes," Jamie claimed. "I've had enough money since I was thirty, so it didn't change my life at all."

This was, of course, a barefaced fantasy. Jamie Herlihy had never before had and never again would have a success to remotely rival *Midnight Cowboy*, and the money made a huge impact on his life, although not necessarily a positive one. "*Midnight Cowboy* has made me too well known for my comfort and has put some things off balance," he confessed to Mary Caroline. "People whose names I don't know call me collect from distant places and tell me of their need for money. There were three such calls today. My mail contains an average of one a day of similar tales and pleas. Certain people I've known for a long time look at me sideways, and laugh hard when I'm not really very funny. I feel called upon to respond to things that I don't want to have to respond to at all."

Still, the money gave him the freedom to do as he pleased. He used some of it to renovate the cottage at 709 Bakers Lane that was his principal residence in Key West and to build a studio out back of the main house. The handmade peace sign symbols and the mandalas he painted and mounted on the crossbeams below the living room's ceilings are still visible. He also bought his mother a comfortable two-bedroom cottage in town, where she lived until her death in 1976.

Now that he had escaped New York, he took the three thousand dollars bequeathed to him by his friend Tallulah Bankhead, who had died in 1968, at age sixty-six, of double pneumonia, hastened by emphysema, alcoholism, and drug abuse, and bought a Mercury Cougar convertible. He recruited his good friend Evan H. Rhodes, a handsome young playwright, novelist, and sculptor, and took to the road. They spent roughly six months and logged thirty-five thousand miles roaming the western United States, visiting communes and other hippie-style communities, mostly in rural areas, smoking dope, dropping LSD, and enjoying the many varieties of free love whenever it appeared. "I was in and out of communes," he would recall. "I just really sat and listened for a long time and got my little ole life charged."

He sounded thrilled when discussing the new generation of hippie commune members with an interviewer for the *Chicago Tribune*. "It's a damned necessity people learn to live together harmoniously because of economic circumstances," he said. "*The New York Times* says there are two thousand communes in the county. There must be more they don't know about. The whole culture is being affected by the consciousness of those few. Man is a great survivor. He does what he has to; his faculty for love might grow. When in history has there been that many people involved in this pursuit?"

He came home to Key West with full notebooks and hundreds of photographs. At first he thought about publishing a journal of his travels or a series of journalistic reports about the New America. But he inevitably began turning his impressions into fiction, taking the hippies he had met on his travels and reimagining them in New York. It took him a year to write fifteen hundred pages. Rhodes helped him begin the long process of boiling it down to novel size. But finishing the manuscript was an ordeal. Jamie turned to Dick Duane, no longer a lover but still the person he most trusted to oversee his tortuous writing process. Duane was forging a new career as an agent for writers and performers, and he had a new partner in business and love, Bob Thixton, a navy veteran he'd met in Key West. Still, Dick set to work on Jamie's behalf, renting a set of cottages on Fire Island for two months during the summer of 1969 for Jamie, Rhodes, Jamie's agent and close friend Jay Garon, Dick himself, and a secretary to take dictation and type up drafts. Not only was Jamie coping with writer's block but also with the regular arrival of drug dealers who were summoned to Fire Island. Dick recalls one dealer who stashed a bag of grass in a washing machine to hide it from the maid. She came in unsuspecting, did the laundry, and the dope was washed away with the soap suds. The dealer was asked to return with more product.

"Jamie was smoking too much, the very strong, expensive stuff—grass and hash—and I couldn't keep him focused," Duane recalls. "It would just take away his consciousness. What he began to do was fight that natural grotesque thing he wrote about so brilliantly. He was trying to free himself of it." He and Dick also fought over cutting sections of the book that Dick felt amounted to soapbox speeches that stopped the narrative dead in its tracks.

"I was resisting and I couldn't honestly go on," says Dick. "Jamie said, 'If you want it out you'll have to cut it yourself, but you realize it will be like cutting my wrists.' And then he said, 'I will never write again.' I think he was looking for an out. You could feel it."

Somehow they got the novel done and delivered to Simon & Schuster in time for publication in April 1971.

Like a refugee from a totalitarian regime, seventeen-year-old high school dropout Gloria Random runs away from her home in Belle Woods, Michigan—"this dainty quilted prison," as Gloria calls it—and joins up with a gentle, gay draft-dodger friend, nineteen-year-old John McFadden. They head for New York on a Greyhound bus, similar to the one Joe Buck had taken from Texas to Manhattan in *Midnight Cowboy*. Gloria is seeking her estranged father, who's working as a history professor somewhere in the city, while John is seeking a place to hide from the law. As a friend tells her, New York is "the only place in the country where a person could get really lost."

High on Dexedrine, marijuana, and hashish, they have imagined New York to be the Emerald City of their inchoate hippie dreams. What they discover is something very different: "New York hell. Insanity commonplace. Dog turds everywhere. Constant noise. Air filthy, causes nose and skin to itch. Traffic thick. More horns than cars."

The novel consists of a series of Gloria's diary entries from early September through mid-November 1969. Jamie's writing does an eerily dead-on imitation of a wide-eyed, spiritually incoherent seventeen-year-old who is both wise and heedless, self-aware and naïve, empathetic and clueless. It's a dangerous narrative strategy, if only because Gloria's exploding New Age consciousness—she takes on the pseudonym Witch Gliz and becomes an acolyte at the altar of sex, drugs, and astrology—is too large burden for a reader to bear over the course of 384 pages.

The narrative spine of the novel is Gloria's search for her father, whom she eventually tracks down. Hank Gliss is a man of old-fashioned left-wing views, deep skepticism about the sanity and sincerity of the new generation of hippies, and even deeper loneliness. When Gloria finally finds him, she conceals the fact that she's his daughter. A sad comedy of errors ensues, with each feeling sexual longing for the other. But nothing physical happens between them.

The narrative takes many detours along the way and occasionally grinds to a halt for several pages at a time. There are long riffs about spirituality, reincarnation, the purpose of life, the meaning of world peace, the efficacy of communism, and the golden age that the young hippies are meant to embody. In the end Gloria returns home to Mom and Michigan in time for Thanksgiving. But she is preparing to leave again as soon as the holiday is over. Her search for Wonderland has only just begun.

"*The Season of the Witch* is to other novels what Woodstock is to a chamber music concert," boasted the book jacket. "By bringing to it the full impact of his exceptional storytelling powers, Herlihy has produced what may well be regarded as the first major work of fiction of the Aquarian Age." The ever-faithful Tennessee Williams provided an enthusiastic blurb: "The writing of James Leo Herlihy, especially in this latest and, I believe, his best work, is rooted in the new youth and their revolution. He knows their special, almost cabalistic language and uses it brilliantly. He knows their hang-ups, their loves, their faiths." The book was the Literary Guild selection for May 1971.

Some reviewers loved the novel, treating it as if it were the literary equivalent of Margaret Mead's anthropological dispatches from Samoa. The novel "crosses the generation gap and provides the view from there," wrote L. E. Sissman in *The New Yorker*. After seven years of journeying through youth culture (it's hard to know exactly where Sisman got that number), Jamie Herlihy had "brought us back one of the first full—perhaps too full; my only major complaint with the book is its unnecessary length—and reliable renderings of the new consciousness. It should be required reading for anyone too old to be a part of it."

Others were considerably less captivated. "Story of a 'now' child pure drivel" was the headline of a brutal review in the *Philadelphia Express News*. Christopher Lehmann-Haupt, in *The New York Times*, poked fun at the book and its author. "I suppose it's just a matter of where your head is at," his review began. If you're a new head, "the kind that jets into the ionosphere on love zaps and letting it all hang out, you're going to go with Gloria Random all the way." Others, Lehmann-Haupt concluded, may have more difficulty. He complimented Jamie on his "touch for reading souls and seeing the world their way. And he dreams up some funny scenes and groovy dialogue." But the reviewer was skeptical of "the collective-soul sessions, ghosts that talk the we-are-God trips, and the power of love that Herlihy lays down.

"I didn't know quite how to take it all," Lehmann-Haupt concluded, "except not too seriously."

Jamie was deeply disappointed with the critical response to *The Season of the Witch*. He attributed it to bourgeois politics and conventional thinking, arguing that reviewers felt threatened by hippie culture and criticism of the establishment. "Most of the reviewers were terrified of the hippies and suspect I might agree with them," he told an interviewer.

Still, he took to the road to help promote the book. He told an interviewer from *Variety* that *Witch* had already sold four times as many copies as *Midnight Cowboy* during a similar period. "I made absolutely sure there was a film in it," he said. "A wonderful, big film. And it will attract a really gifted director." He said George Roy Hill had expressed great interest but had to pass because his schedule was booked for the next two years. But Jamie claimed another director was interested, although he wouldn't name him (perhaps he was referring to John Schlesinger's tepid letter?). Then he added, contradicting himself, "There's really no big clamor for the book. I think everybody's scared of it." As for future books, Jamie confessed, "Well, I don't have anything in mind to write. In fact, I think I'm finally going to be able to break that habit."

It was a telling interview—a mixture of enthusiasm, wariness, self-involvement, and fantasy, with all of the tangents and internal contradictions that increasingly marked Jamie's meandering thought process.

In other interviews he said he was tired of locking himself in a room to write, as opposed to living life to the fullest. Writing flowed from "one's sense of the past and hopes for the future," he told one interviewer. "And I'm more interested in my daily life now than I was when I was a fiction writer." Painters had colors and living forms to draw them out of their souls and into life itself. "The poor writer usually just has his little glass of alcohol and his cubicle. I guess I don't like the life of the writer anymore."

The last piece of sustained prose James Leo Herlihy wrote for publication was the lead essay for a collection of arguments about modern sexual mores entitled *Sexual Latitude: For and Against*, also published in 1971. In ten sweeping pages he makes an impassioned plea for sexual license. Nude beaches in California, sex scenes in mainstream movies, the movement to end priestly celibacy, homosexuals asserting their right to make love to one another—he celebrates all of these phenomena as welcome signs of liberation. And he paints an apocalyptic portrait of a world on the brink of self-destruction from widening starvation, smog-choked cities, and political unrest. Sizing up these challenges, he offers the sexual revolution as a heroic and humanistic response.

"Sex, in a word, is having a heyday," he writes. "Perhaps we could consider the possibility that there resides in our sexual nature a wisdom far deeper than that for which it is usually accredited. Perhaps, that is, there is something in us that knows what it is doing. . . .

"The time has come," he concludes, "to fill the White House, the seats of Congress, and the governors' mansions across this land and all the world with the greatest lovers we can find among us." There is nothing in his prose to suggest that he's anything but serious.

Six psychologists or psychotherapists were also tapped for pieces for the book, none of whom were buying Jamie's vision of peace, love, and understanding, especially when it came to homosexuality. Alexander Lowen, the executive director of the Institute for Bioenergetic Analysis in New York, agrees that homosexuality should be decriminalized, but still condemns it as a "moral offense . . . against the dignity of man." The renowned psychologist Bruno Bettelheim calls homosexuality "a perversion" that causes "severe psychological damage." Fred Brown, a professor of psychiatry at the Mount Sinai School of Medicine, says gay men "whose psychopathology prevents them from enjoying the richness of a meaningful heterosexual relationship . . . are fated to find their satisfactions in what is essentially a caricature of the normal male-female relationship." None of these distinguished shrinks want to lock up gay people; they just want to cure them of their "disorder."

It was, after all, 1971. Two years after the Stonewall riots and the visible emergence of the gay liberation movement, the apostles of the psychiatric establishment were still unwilling to consider gays and lesbians as in any sense "normal." It would take two more years and much lobbying before the American Psychiatric Association would awaken from its self-inflicted nightmare and remove homosexuality from the *Diagnostic and Statistical Manual of Mental Disorders.*

The only writers in the anthology who squarely confront the moral blindness of the establishment's views are Del Martin and Phyllis Lyon, two founders of the Daughters of Bilitis, a lesbian organization started in San Francisco in 1955. After describing in charming, unadorned prose their own love affair and their commitment to gay liberation, the two women undermine their opponents' arguments with one elegantly simple sentence: "The cult of psychoanalysis has created sickness where there is no sickness, so it can effect a cure where there is nothing to cure."

Jamie's essay, in comparison to Martin and Lyon's, sounds borderline satirical in its naïve and grandiose declarations, although Jamie surely believed every word. What's missing is even a single reference to his own sexuality. Unlike his lesbian allies, the public James Leo Herlihy remained firmly in the closet.

Despite his ambivalence over its success, *Midnight Cowboy* became an unavoidable reference point in Jamie's life. "Everybody would knock on the door at Bakers Lane and ask for the guy who wrote *Midnight Cowboy*," says Bob Thixton. "His life became so busy in a way that he never wanted."

At first he welcomed with warmth and generosity the young hippies, drifters, runaways, and draft dodgers who showed up at the cottage. He offered up his home and yard as a place for love-ins, be-ins, and weddings in the garden. "I suppose what made me so happy with those beautiful creatures was the sense they gave me that the marginal people to whom I'd been drawn all through my life were suddenly having a heyday," he said. Larry Claypool, a frequent guest in those days, re-membered a pillar inside the main cottage that people could climb to a platform with a mattress and high-quality stereo speakers. "You could lay tripping on acid for hours digging the stars through an open skylight and listening to music."

The novelist and screenwriter Thomas McGuane, who lived in Key West and partook of the sex, drugs, and rock 'n' roll that always seemed on offer, recalls Jamie as "a great fellow, much too generous to us hip-pies and sorta-hippies who hung around his house abusing his patience." Subject to blue moods, Jamie "seemed to use his own amiability as cam-ouflage for an elusive nature and ever-pending disappearance."

But it all eventually soured. "All the dopers would come on the bus," recalls Thixton. "[Jamie] would have notes—'Shut the Drawer,' 'Knives Go in Here'—because they would disrupt whatever ordered life he had."

Thixton recalls Jamie inviting him and Dick Duane to dinner at Bakers Lane one evening. "I'll never forget that he was so happy we were coming. And they had spread out something like a Persian tent all over the floor inside and we were sitting out there drinking wine and Jamie had been smoking, obviously, and some kid named Yellowtail was cook-ing the dinner who had never cooked before. After much delay, Jamie goes, 'Yellowtail, where's the food? It's time for dinner,' and suddenly we smell smoke coming out from the kitchen. Yellowtail had decided he would cook the fish in pine needles, and it was the worst godawful meal you'd ever had, and there was a *why-do-I-try?* look on Jamie's face. We ended up going out."

When he finally decided he couldn't handle the constant flow of people and gawkers, Jamie bought a farm property in Hops Bottom, in a remote part of Susquehanna County, in northeastern Pennsylvania, between Scranton and Binghamton, New York. There were thirty-nine acres altogether, including three inhabitable houses, a nine-acre lake called Jeffers Pond, and six acres of virgin hemlock forest. "I have nine canoes," he boasted. The rest was meadows suitable for crops. He invited Mary Caroline Richards to move there and set up a communal struc-ture. Although she was past fifty, Mary Caroline was still a back-to-the-land hippie at heart, a poet, potter, and painter whose affection for Jamie never wavered even when her patience waned. They quickly fell out over the new farm. Mary Caroline had expected Jamie to live there at least part of the year, but he generally stayed away and was disappointed when the place failed to blossom into a full-fledged commune like the ones he and Evan Rhodes had visited out west.

Despite the tensions between them, Jamie continued to confide in Mary Caroline about things he couldn't or wouldn't discuss with anyone else. "I guess what I've been trying to say all along about me is that I'm a manic depressive and the swings are so wild they scare me," he confessed to her in a two-page, densely handwritten note in March 1972. "So far I have been able to go with the lows okay and ride the highs without making too much of a fool of myself. But I am very worried about this and find myself trying to achieve a reasonable and accurate view of what's happening to me."

His most revealing letter, perhaps because it sounds the most desperate, came later that same year, a handwritten, six-page cry for help in capital letters, underlined words, boxes, and sentences that climb up one side of the page and down the other. "I am swinging!" he exclaims. "Life simply does not INTEREST me enough to support it unless I can feel my usefulness to its flow."

He concludes with a confession and a plea. "I am none too sure of myself these days. I have been behaving like a manic-depressive all winter. Maybe I am not getting across what I mean to get across. Maybe I am not writing the letters I think I am writing. Please help me in this."

Jamie's mania had been trailing him all his life, periodically storming his defenses. While he left no psychiatric records, his letters suggest its impact on his fragile sense of well-being. "I was never so much concerned with what life might do to me," he once wrote, "as with what I might do to myself."

It is reasonable to suggest—and impossible to prove—that Jamie's homosexuality might have played a role in his struggle with depression. Andrew Solomon, author of *The Noonday Demon*, a masterwork on depression that won the National Book Award in 2001, cites studies showing elevated rates of depression, panic disorder, and suicidal impulses among gay men and women. Solomon, whose book is based on extensive research, interviews, and his own experiences as a gay man who has battled depression, writes that the intense homophobia and social stigma directed at gay people by their families and society at large lead many to hide their sexuality or risk shame and rejection and cause "a terrible loneliness that afflicts much of the gay population."

Loneliness is the overarching subject and theme of all of Jamie's fiction and his plays. Surely he knew it intimately.

He started winding down friendships with people in Key West, including his long rapport with Tennessee Williams. "I had dinner with Tennessee one night," recalls Tom McGuane, "and Jamie's then current blue mood came up. Tennessee said to me, 'Tom, you know why Jamie's depressed? Because his writing is not very good.' I didn't, and still don't, know what to make of this. Maybe a mentor's envy of his student's popular success."

Dotson Rader, Williams's friend and companion, has a different view of the playwright's alienation from Jamie. Rader says Jamie was "running, like, a flophouse in Key West. He had a lot of hustlers, street boys, and it was really druggy, a lot of booze. He was out of control. You'd go to a party at his place and the backyard would be full of kids. They were sweet and dear, but you knew they were paying to crash in his pad with sex or drugs. And Tennessee at that point was really kind of turned off by him."

In the end, Jamie himself was turned off by Key West and all it had come to represent. He sold the house on Bakers Lane in 1973, around the same time he left for Los Angeles. Many friends were surprised. "I would expect that all of us who knew Jamie in Key West in those days are sorry that he went out of our lives," says McGuane. "He was regarded with great affection by anyone who knew him."

When Jamie first got to Los Angeles, he went under the name "Jamie Hathaway." None of his old acquaintances could find him. It was as if he had created his own personal witness protection program. "I'm trying not to repeat the errors of Key West," he told Lyle Bongé, his old friend from Black Mountain College days, "where I had finally become such a public entity there wasn't much for me to chew on."

EPILOGUE

An era can be said to end when its basic illusions are exhausted.
—Arthur Miller

With the money he earned from *Midnight Cowboy*, both the royalties from the novel and his share of the profits from the movie, James Leo Herlihy started a new and quieter chapter of his life in Los Angeles. He bought a two-story hillside house on Landa Street in Silver Lake, five miles northwest of downtown, with a backyard view of the iconic HOLLYWOOD sign. Known as the "Swish Alps," Silver Lake was one of L.A.'s liveliest gay neighborhoods. The Black Cat Tavern on Sunset Boulevard had been the scene of protests against police raids more than two years before the Stonewall riots in New York.

Jamie taught courses in writing at the University of Southern California and as a visiting professor at Colorado College and the University of Arkansas, traveled frequently to Europe and North Africa, and gave acting lessons at workshops run by his friend Milton Katselas. He gardened, he cooked, he painted, and he drew. He spent more time with old friends like Jimmy Kirkwood and Mary Caroline Richards and mentored young writers who came to his door seeking advice from the noted author of *Midnight Cowboy*. One of them was twenty-four-year-old Jeffrey Bailey, who interviewed Jamie for *The Advocate* and wrote a glowing essay about his work, launching an intimate correspondence that continued until his death. There were occasional dinners with the distinguished film director George Cukor and a yearlong affair with the actor Rock Hudson. "Did I mention," he wrote Bailey, "that after knowing Rock intimately for a year, I was present when someone told him I'd written

Midnight Cowboy, and his entire response was 'oh, I didn't know it was a novel.' Isn't that endearing?"

By his own account, Jamie's sex life was uninhibited. "I have a lot with a lot of different people," he told Bailey. "But I don't view it as The Numbers Game. And I don't believe any longer that I'm a floozie because of it. I'm in love with all of 'em."

Meanwhile, he and Anaïs Nin renewed their deep but combustible friendship. By now she was living with Rupert Pole, one of her two "husbands," in a glass house on Hidalgo Avenue, on the other side of Silver Lake. It had been built for them by Pole's half brother Eric Lloyd Wright, grandson of Frank Lloyd Wright. She called it her "house of mirrors." The main space was a Japanese-style studio with a superb view of the lake.

The fame and veneration she had hungered for had come late in her life, with the publication of the first of seven volumes of her diaries, beginning in 1966, when she was sixty-three. The diaries offered a self-portrait of a sensitive, strong-willed woman struggling for self-discovery and independence, and refusing to bend to the men seeking to dominate her professionally, emotionally, and sexually. These books were followed and punctuated by various works of sexual awakening that became bestsellers, including *Delta of Venus* (1977), *Little Birds* (1979), and *Henry and June* (1986). The books helped cement her reputation as, in the words of one *New Yorker* writer, "the fairy godmother of the new literary domain of women's erotica." But the acclaim was all too short-lived. In 1974 she was diagnosed with the uterine cancer that would kill her three years later. When she died, the *New York Times* obituary listed "Hugh Parker Guiler, also known as Ian Hugo," as her husband, while the *Los Angeles Times* listed Rupert William Pole.

There are only a handful of mentions of Jamie in her last volume of diary entries. In one she writes of her encouraging him to publish his own journals, which he had kept at her insistence. "A strange case, so rare, of justice," she writes in the winter of 1973–74. "[Jamie] Herlihy sustained my writing by his articulate appreciation. Now, I interested [my publisher] in his diary, and it may be published." Her last reference comes a few weeks later, when she notes that Jamie "is moving into a new house across the lake from me with a gentle, sweet, radiant hippie called Rainbow."

Jamie helped nurse her during those final years, took it upon himself to answer the mail that came pouring in "in cartons and cartons" from her newfound fans, and was deeply shaken by her death. He had, after all, loved her dearly even though he was well aware of her affects, defects, and suffocating charm. "She could have run for president and been elected," he told Noël Riley Fitch, one of her biographers. "Everyone who knew her liked her. How [could] you not like someone who loved you that much and was that open to you?"

Jamie's own writing career had ground to a halt. His profound ambivalence, tinged with depression, hardened into paralysis. At times, he confessed, he felt helpless and lost. "It seems to me time that I had work to do," he confessed to Mary Caroline in an undated letter from the late seventies. "I can't stop worrying about it, make every decision in terms of it. I am still a child, alas and alack, but I haven't a child's innocence or vitality—only the helplessness. If you know any renewal prayers, pass 'em on, honey."

Jeff Bailey encouraged him to undertake a memoir, but it came to nothing. "Truth to tell," he wrote to Bailey, "I haven't got a clue what to write anymore."

Part of the process of shutting down was to scale back his ties with friends from his writing days. His friendship with his former lover Dick Duane faded after the excruciating experience of churning out *The Season of the Witch*. He later discovered that Dick had read portions of his journals without permission. This infuriated Jamie, and in retaliation he destroyed the journals altogether. Jamie being Jamie, he rationalized what he had done in a most convoluted way. "I realized that my diaries were no longer performing a useful function for me," he told Bailey in the *Advocate* interview. "I had needed a concrete way of externalizing the changes that were going on inside me, but when they stopped helping my individuation process, I decided to stop keeping them and I tore them to shreds. It was an act of release, I suppose, release from my past."

Destroying the journals was, in effect, a declaration of independence from both Anaïs and Dick, who had once been the two most important people in his life.

While he would denigrate *Midnight Cowboy* at times, referring to it as *Midcow Nightboy* or *Midcow Night-tits*, at other times he would concede its significance. "My best work as an actor was playing a quasi-hustler in *Zoo Story*," he wrote in a rare journal entry toward the end of his life. "My best work as a writer was in *Midnight Cowboy*, creating Joe Buck. Both Jerry in *Zoo*, and Joe in *Midcow* (as well as Ratso Rizzo, his sidekick) are outsiders, marginal figures who do not fit in the center of society. I wonder if I have not been escaping the pain of the outsider in the past fifteen years."

Although he hadn't acted onstage or in a movie in seventeen years, Herlihy agreed to appear in a supporting role in a feature film at the behest of the director Arthur Penn, a friend from Black Mountain College days. *Four Friends* (1981), Penn's earnest epic of 1960s radicals, got good reviews but bombed at the box office. Jamie was chillingly effective as Mr. Carnahan, a wealthy Long Island businessman who suddenly turns the wedding reception of his daughter into a nightmare of deranged carnage.

For a while he worked as a masseur, claiming to see it as the direct opposite of writing. "I like the wordlessness of the work," he wrote Richards. "The needs of my clients to have their bodies touched is tremendously moving to me. Sometimes their strongest need seems to be for sexual release, and that's cool, but mostly I feel I am administering to a profound physical loneliness that goes back to the cradle, and fulfilling it fulfills something in me."

Herlihy's regard for Tennessee Williams, which had frayed toward the end of his time in Key West, was restored in the mid-seventies, when Grace Herlihy, Jamie's mother, was dying of breast cancer. Williams pitched in with great sympathy. "Tennessee was in Key West during much of that time and he was enormously considerate," Herlihy wrote to novelist Paul Bowles in Morocco. "Sent flowers, messages. Cooked for her. Even showed up at the funeral mass, volunteering to act as pallbearer. I was impressed and moved by it all."

Williams died suddenly in February 1983, in the Hotel Elysée in New York, one of his favorite haunts. Groggy from two Seconals, one of the many varieties of pills on his bedside nightstand, he had awoken in the middle of the night and reached for another, only to mistakenly pick up a plastic cap from a bottle of eyedrops. The cap got stuck in his throat and choked him to death. Jamie expressed deep sadness, but saw the cruel irony. "Somehow, the whole thing had been acceptable, barely but acceptable, when I thought he'd croaked au naturel, stroke or whatever," he told Bailey. "But choking on a Murine bottle cap in Tallulah's old hotel? I don't understand that kind o' poetry."

Soon there would be many more deaths, from an epidemic that arrived unannounced and unexpected starting in mid-1981 in New York, San Francisco, and Los Angeles. Men developed flulike symptoms that would come to be diagnosed as Human Immunodeficiency Virus, or HIV, leading over the course of a few months or years to full-blown Acquired Immunodeficiency Syndrome, or AIDS. The first of Jamie's friends to be stricken was Bill Lord, a handsome young man who had moved into Jamie's bed and then into his home in 1977 and never left. They were no longer lovers by 1982, when Lord started displaying HIV symptoms, including chronic diarrhea, night sweats, fever, and weight loss. He underwent a slow, steady decline, climaxing with his death in March 1986. Jamie nursed him throughout every stage of the ordeal.

Bill's death hit him hard. "I do not have the faintest notion of what to do with my life," he would write five months after. "Odd when you consider how I yearned to be free of Bill."

Other deaths would soon follow. "My closest friend here told me last night that he will be dying in the next couple of weeks," he wrote to Mary Caroline in August 1987. "I love him dearly and am feeling greater strain and distress than with any of my other pals who have died recently."

The loss that hit Jamie hardest was that of Jimmy Kirkwood. They had been dear friends, writing partners, and occasional lovers for more than three decades. Kirkwood had written five novels and a half dozen plays, but his most famous work was as cowriter of the book for *A Chorus Line*, which won him a Tony Award and a Pulitzer Prize in 1976. As the

New York Times theater critic Frank Rich noted, it was the first Broadway musical "to deal matter-of-factly with homosexuality, and from an inside point-of-view that makes its gay men seem far more accessible than the martyrs and oddballs that typified stage homosexuals in mainstream American dramas of the post–*Boys in the Band*, pre-AIDS era."

Kirkwood had a warmth and generosity of spirit that matched Jamie's own, and his illness depressed Jamie deeply. He flew to New York in March 1989 to say goodbye. One month later, Jimmy was dead.

In January 1992 Jamie embarked on a five-week car trip east that wound up in Key West, where Evan Rhodes, his old traveling companion, organized several dinners with old friends. Still, AIDS seemed to stalk Jamie even in Key West. "The changes are profound and astonishing," he wrote to Bailey. "AIDS has taken a huge swipe at the place, and it is no longer a 'gay resort' . . . Ten years ago ninety percent of the couples strolling Duval Street would have been gay. Now it's more like ten percent."

Six months later Jamie began noticing his own symptoms. By Labor Day test results confirmed what he already sensed. "I have joined the ranks of the HIV-positive and the virus has really kicked the shit out of me," he told Jeff. "I'm weak & short of breath and don't expect to be around long. I'm not at all drawn to the idea of 'fighting this thing,' as the younger men quite appropriately do. To me, at sixty-five, it would be like fighting a gift from God: I have never had the faintest interest in living beyond the time of life I'm now arrived at and there seems to me a fabulous poetry in having found my death in doing what has always been my favorite activity—making love."

He went a step further with Mary Caroline Richards, telling her he welcomed the news and knew what he would do about it. "I hope you won't be distressed—I'm not," he wrote. "When things get too sticky I intend to gobble a mouthful of pills and see what the other side of paradise is all about."

The year that followed was a constant struggle. "My body has aged something like four years in one," he told Bailey. "My hands often but not always shake quite a bit. My hearing is more and more of a joke. I feel also the withdrawal of Eros and only the palest scraps of sadness about it."

Just as he had nursed many friends during their final days, so his friends cared for him: Joe Frazier, an Episcopalian priest and former member of the Chad Mitchell Trio, who rented the upstairs of the Landa Street house after a weakened Jamie was confined to the ground floor; architect Leonardo Chalupowicz from Argentina, who was likely his last regular lover; poet and filmmaker James Broughton.

Jamie had discussed suicide with Anaïs Nin the first time he met her at Black Mountain College, when he was twenty years old, and he had raised the subject occasionally throughout his life. But there is no evidence that he had ever actually attempted it. Now it was as if the disease were giving him permission.

As the clock neared midnight on October 20, 1993, he ground up a vial of sleeping pills and dissolved the powder in liquid. Then he carved into a small notebook his last sliver of prose in a graceful, looping calligraphic scrawl:

> The cup is before me, if anybody asks, how was he before he took his cup, and as he picked it up and as he tossed it back . . . Well, I'm writing this in the quiet eye of what's happening, sending this communique from the moment at which the cup is lifted.
>
> I feel great, like: This is the Life! And This is the death! And WHOOPIE! The milkie liquid will not be delicious, but it won't be bad, I've tasted a spoonful. I can handle it easy. And now—words are getting in the way.
>
> Love, Jamie

After their stunning success with *Midnight Cowboy*, Jerome Hellman and John Schlesinger attempted two ambitious collaborations during the seventies. *The Day of the Locust* (1975), based on the apocalyptic, satirical 1939 Hollywood novel by Nathanael West, juxtaposed the moral corruption of the studio system with the growing unrest of the ordinary folks who flocked to L.A. seeking their share of the American dream. Lavishly financed by Paramount and beautifully filmed, it brought together many of the artisans from *Midnight Cowboy*, including Waldo Salt, Jim Clark, John Barry, John Robert Lloyd, Marion Dougherty, Ann Roth, and Michael Childers. But this time the magic was missing. Schlesinger tended to blame the two leads, Karen Black and William Atherton, who he felt were overwhelmed by their roles. But many of the scenes were slow, strange, and dyspeptic, reflecting in part the contempt both John and Waldo harbored toward the hucksterism and self-delusion at the heart of American popular culture. In short, the movie was a downer. "Even the people who liked it very much said it left them stunned and depressed," says Hellman.

He and John tried again with *Coming Home* (1978), which explored with pathos, sensitivity, and a dash of melodrama the problems of damaged Vietnam War veterans and those who loved them. The actress Jane Fonda was the driving creative force behind the film, and she recruited Jerry and Waldo Salt respectively to produce and help write it, and Jon Voight to play the male lead. At first Schlesinger, who was eager to work with all of these artists, signed on as director. But after watching them gather dozens of real-life stories from paraplegic vets, spouses, and caregivers, he decided he was the wrong person for the job. "He said to me, 'Listen, Jerry, the last thing in the world you need on this film is a baroque English faggot. I have no way of listening to these men,'" Hellman recalls. "I knew he was right." The American director Hal Ashby took it over.

The following year, Jerry produced and directed *Promises in the Dark*, a melodrama starring Marsha Mason that fell short critically and financially. His last film production was *The Mosquito Coast* (1986), starring Harrison Ford. The seven films he produced in his career achieved seventeen Oscar nominations and won six. In 2001 he married Elizabeth Empleton, who worked for nonprofit organizations promoting film events. She is, he says, his ideal partner: calm, well-organized, and patient.

For Marion Dougherty's sixtieth birthday, in 1983, her loyal companion George Roy Hill threw her a surprise party at Chatfield's, one of Manhattan's finest restaurants and Dougherty's favorite—she had devised the recipe for the club's renowned caviar pie. Among the celebrated guests were Dustin Hoffman, Warren Beatty, Hume Cronyn, and Jessica Tandy.

Some ten years later, a campaign by these influential friends to get Dougherty Oscar recognition for her groundbreaking work as a casting director failed, despite support from Clint Eastwood, Robert De Niro, Glenn Close, and Woody Allen. Still, many successful female casting directors, starting with Juliet Taylor, took every opportunity to acknowledge Dougherty's impact on their careers and celebrate her pioneering role. Over the next decade casting directors organized to form their own union, affiliated with the Teamsters, and negotiated their first collective contract. In 2016, five years after her death, Dougherty's West Coast counterpart, Lynn Stalmaster, became the first casting director to receive an Honorary Oscar. Still, the ultimate goal of having casting directors receive their own annual Oscar category has yet to happen.

Midnight Cowboy launched Adam Holender's distinguished career as a cinematographer of feature films, noted especially for his skill in capturing New York's gritty visual poetry. Working with directors like Jerry Schatzberg, Paul Newman, and Wayne Wang, he shot *The Panic in Needle Park* (1971), *The Effect of Gamma Rays on Man-in-the-Moon Marigolds* (1972), and the Brooklyn-based *Smoke* and *Blue in the Face* (both in 1994). A large Andy Warhol print of Marilyn Monroe has hung in his East Side apartment living room for more than fifty years, a memento of his experiences in meeting Warhol and filming the artist's people for the party scene in *Midnight Cowboy*.

Ann Roth has worked as costume designer on more than a hundred feature films and Broadway plays, and has been nominated for four Oscars and eleven Tonys, winning one of each. In the spring of 2018, at the age of eighty-six, she had three blockbuster productions on Broadway at the same time—*Carousel, Three Tall Women,* and *The Iceman Cometh.* The following year she had five: *To Kill a Mockingbird, King Lear, The Waverly Gallery, The Prom,* and *Gary: A Sequel to Titus Andronicus.*

Midnight Cowboy jump-started Waldo Salt's screenwriting career in dramatic fashion. He went on to write or cowrite screenplays for *The Gang That Couldn't Shoot Straight* (1971), *Serpico* (1973), *The Day of the Locust* (1975), and *Coming Home* (1978), for which he won his second Oscar. *Serpico,* which told the story of a noted maverick New York City patrolman who testified against corrupt fellow officers, explored issues of loyalty and betrayal that had haunted Salt ever since his best friend, fellow screenwriter Richard Collins, named him as a Communist in 1951 before the House Committee on Un-American Activities.

Salt became a writer-in-residence at Robert Redford's Sundance Institute, teaching workshops and helping young writers develop their skills. It was the perfect role for him—talking about his favorite subject to a crowd of eager young acolytes with whom he shared large quantities of marijuana. When Salt died in 1987 at age seventy-two, Redford praised him at his memorial service for his dedication and intellectual honesty. The Sundance Film Festival's annual screenwriting award is given in his name.

Jennifer Salt pursued an acting career in movies and television throughout the 1970s and '80s, including a starring role in Brian De Palma's *Sisters* (1972), with her good friend Margot Kidder. She and Kidder rented a lopsided A-frame on Nicholas Beach, north of Malibu, that became a clubhouse for some of the best-known filmmakers and actors of the New Hollywood era, including De Palma, Martin Scorsese, Steven Spielberg, and Richard Dreyfuss. Jennifer was reputedly the group's best cook and most pungent wit. She appeared in small but memorable roles in Robert Altman's *Brewster McCloud* (1970) and the Woody Allen comedy *Play It Again, Sam* (1972), as well as a four-year stint on *Soap,* a prime-time television comic soap opera. But she grew tired of the Hollywood rat race and the profound lack of meaningful parts for women in their forties and beyond. After her father's death, she started writing film scripts and teleplays, and became a writer and executive producer on two of Ryan Murphy's hit television shows, *Nip/Tuck* and *American Horror Story*. She also cowrote with Murphy the screenplay for the hit movie *Eat Pray Love* (2010), starring Julia Roberts. She is well aware she has followed in her father's large footsteps. "I feel like he knew I was waiting to discover myself as a writer," she said.

Soon after the enormous success of "Everybody's Talkin'," Harry Nilsson fired Rick Jarrard and George Tipton, his devoted record producer and music arranger. He then joined forces with Richard Perry, perhaps the hottest producer of the era. Together, they made *Nilsson Schmilsson*, released in 1971, which reached number three in the U.S. album charts, led by "Without You," a soaring pop aria that topped both the U.S. and U.K. singles charts and won for Nilsson his second Grammy for Best Male Vocal Performance. Restless as ever and in the grip of an ever-intensifying addiction to alcohol, cocaine, and all-night partying, Nilsson soon parted ways with Perry. He hooked up with John Lennon in 1973 in what became known as the "Lost Weekend," the eighteen months when the former Beatle, separated from his wife, Yoko Ono, drank and drugged his way toward self-destruction on the West Coast in the company of the ever-available Harry. Lennon eventually overcame his demons and returned home to New York, but Nilsson did permanent damage to his vocal cords, his soft, sweet four-octave voice reduced to a passionate but painful growl. Lennon tried to make amends by producing Nilsson's next album, *Pussy Cats*, a lumbering collection that sold tepidly and revealed just how wasted his voice had become. His career started a long slide to oblivion that included filing for bankruptcy after his financial manager stole hundreds of thousands of dollars from him. It ended with his death from a heart attack in Los Angeles, in January 1994, at age fifty-two. It was a tragic finish to the man whom Richard Perry had once called "the finest white male singer on the planet."

Dustin Hoffman might not have had a road map for navigating stardom, but he managed to deftly find his way. After the weak tea of *John and Mary* (1969), he embarked on a series of challenging and memorable roles, from Arthur Penn's *Little Big Man* (1970), to Sam Peckinpah's ultra-violent *Straw Dogs* (1971), Franklin J. Schaffner's *Papillon* (1973), in which he costarred with Steve McQueen, Bob Fosse's *Lenny* (1974), Alan J. Pakula's *All the President's Men* (1976), costarring Robert Redford, and John Schlesinger's *Marathon Man* (1976). He won his first Academy Award for Best Actor in Robert Benton's *Kramer vs. Kramer* (1979), and another for playing Raymond, the autistic older brother in Barry Levinson's *Rain Man* (1988), which costarred Tom Cruise. In between came perhaps his most iconic role, in *Tootsie* (1982), directed by Sydney Pollack. Hoffman played Michael Dorsey, a hard-luck middle-aged actor who pretends to be a woman in order to land an unlikely starring role in a television soap opera. The screenplay, cowritten by Larry Gelbart and Hoffman's close friend Murray Schisgal, with contributions from Elaine May and Barry Levinson, echoed Hoffman's lonely decade of struggle to become a successful actor in New York in Dorsey's frustrated aspirations and obnoxious perfectionism. It was, said one critic, the "role Hoffman had been studying for all his life."

In his cumulative body of work, Hoffman obliterated the artificial boundary between character actor and leading man. Whatever the role, whether comic or tragic or both, he was utterly convincing. At the same time, audiences always knew he was Dustin Hoffman, with charm, intensity, and a modern sensibility. The same was true of his acclaimed Broadway stage performances in *Death of Salesman* (1984)—the playwright Arthur Miller cheerfully admitted he had vastly underestimated Hoffman's talent when they had first met two decades earlier—and *The Merchant of Venice* (1989).

Still, no matter how high he climbed, Hoffman never seemed to escape the feeling of being an outsider, one man against the world, wielding his devotion to craft and his subversive sense of humor as defensive weapons. There were periods of serious marijuana use and what he himself once described as an addiction to sex. In his acceptance speech for *Kramer vs. Kramer*, he played the naughty provocateur, noting that the

Oscar statuette had no genitals and thanking his parents for not using birth control. But then he launched into an impassioned tribute to the thousands of actors who struggle in vain for recognition yet remain dedicated to their profession. "When you're a broke actor, you can't write, you can't paint, you have to practice accents while you're driving a taxi cab," he told the audience, adding that he proudly shared his Oscar with those overlooked members of his "artistic family." The speech brought down the house.

Having just turned eighty, he was still working regularly as an actor when media reports in the fall of 2017 cited eight women who accused him of sexual misconduct, dating back to the 1970s and '80s. Hoffman apologized publicly to one of the women, the writer Anna Graham Hunter, who said he had sexually harassed her when she was a seventeen-year-old production assistant on the 1985 TV movie of *Death of a Salesman*. The allegations, Hoffman stated, were "not reflective of who I am." He later said he had no memory of the incident and didn't believe he'd done anything wrong. His lawyer fired off a letter to *Variety*, which had published the accounts of three of the women, calling the accusations "defamatory falsehoods." But the allegations had a chilling effect on his acting career, and he struggled to find work in a world he had taken by storm a half century earlier.

After his triumphant performance as Joe Buck, Jon Voight's acting career waxed and waned. He took starring roles in a range of movies, and returned to the stage in 1973 to play Stanley Kowalski to Faye Dunaway's Blanche DuBois in a Los Angeles production of *A Streetcar Named Desire*, all the while turning down major film parts he either didn't believe in or felt he was wrong for. He finally won an Oscar as Best Actor for *Coming Home*. Originally offered the part of the cuckolded husband (ultimately played by Bruce Dern), he lobbied intensively to play the lead role of Luke, the paraplegic Vietnam War veteran. His performance captured all of the anger, frustration, courage, and soulfulness of a spirited man physically confined to a wheelchair. The scene in which he gently guides Jane Fonda's character, a frustrated housewife searching for her own autonomy, through the process of having sex with a paraplegic, is one of the most poignant moments in modern cinema. He was nominated again for an Oscar for Best Actor in 1985, for *Runaway Train*, an adrenaline-laced thriller in which he and Eric Roberts played escaped convicts.

By the nineties Voight began appearing in memorable supporting roles, such as Nate the Fence in Michael Mann's crime thriller *Heat* (1996), the rogue agent Jim Phelps in *Mission: Impossible* (1996), Franklin D. Roosevelt in *Pearl Harbor* (2001), and sportscaster Howard Cosell in *Ali* (2001), for which he was nominated for Best Supporting Actor for a role in which he deployed the remnants of his native Yonkers accent. Even as the parts grew smaller and the movies weaker—see *Anaconda* (1997)—Voight garnered praise for his rich performances. He also won a Golden Globe Award for best supporting actor for his work in the long-running Showtime television series *Ray Donovan*.

As fine as his acting was, it was often overshadowed by his personal and political life. Gossip tabloids and websites focused on his rocky relationship with his daughter, the film star Angelina Jolie, while the news pages reported his sharp turn to the right beginning in the 1980s. He rediscovered his Catholic faith and conservative roots, and denounced "Marxists" and "Communist-based stuff" for hijacking the antiwar movement he had once championed. He held the left responsible for the slaughter of Vietnamese civilians and the Cambodian holocaust after American forces pulled out of Southeast Asia, and said he was "quite ashamed" of his own former beliefs. He even denounced his participation in *Coming Home*. After vocally supporting the losing presidential campaigns of the Republicans John McCain in 2008 and Mitt Romney in 2012, Voight veered further right to become a passionate acolyte of Donald Trump, whom he called "our greatest president since Abraham Lincoln."

Still, he never spoke with anything less than awe and admiration about the making of *Midnight Cowboy*. In panel sessions and interviews over the years he endlessly praised Dustin Hoffman, Waldo Salt, Adam Holender, and the various supporting actors, and expressed deep gratitude to Marion Dougherty and Jerry Hellman for helping him get the role of Joe Buck. But most of all he talked about how he had worshipped John Schlesinger, who had challenged and supported and helped him conquer this first and most rewarding movie role.

"It was such a well-made film," says Voight. "It was gritty in a way no one had ever seen before, but it was so full of life. These were American characters that you'd never seen on screen before, with questions raised that you'd never seen raised before. I just loved being part of it."

WORK, LIVE, SHOP, PLAY, HERE, invited the billboard outside Essex Crossing, an ambitious 1.65-million-square-foot complex of office and retail space and luxury housing rising on Manhattan's Lower East Side in 2019. Its website exhorted potential buyers to "own the dream," with prices for homes ranging from $1.7 million to $7.3 million. More than half of the 1,079 apartments were said to be reserved for low- and middle-income tenants.

Nothing could have better illustrated the trajectory, both downward and upward, of New York City since *Midnight Cowboy* was made fifty years earlier. Essex Crossing sits on the exact site where John Schlesinger filmed Jon Voight and Dustin Hoffman walking the shabby, crime-infested streets to Ratso Rizzo's ruined X-flat. During the filming, the cast and crew could hear the jackhammering and resounding boom of the wrecker's ball from the demolition going on all around them. But the flattened lots remained vacant for nearly five decades because of a lack of money, competence, and political will.

All over New York, things got worse before they got better. The city teetered toward bankruptcy throughout the 1970s, a decade of its worst economic decline since the thirties. The city lost more than six hundred thousand jobs, unemployment rose to 11 percent, and one in seven New Yorkers were on welfare. The population fell by eight hundred thousand—more than the combined populations of Alaska and Wyoming. The Lower East Side and the Bronx became "wastelands of drugs, abandoned buildings, muggings, robberies, and arson," wrote the *New Yorker* essayist Louis Menand. "Signs of blight were everywhere, a kind of urban eczema." Brochures distributed at airports by New York's police union, angered at cutbacks to the force, warned visitors: WELCOME TO FEAR CITY.

Slowly and painfully, in fits and starts, things began to improve. One striking change was a dramatic decline in the crime rate in the 1990s. The city's murder rate, which peaked at 2,245 in 1990, began to fall precipitously. Demographic changes, the financial market boom, and modern policing practices all played a role, as did a general economic improvement nationwide, although crafty politicians like mayors Rudolph Giuliani and Michael Bloomberg rushed to seize the credit.

Some of the biggest changes took place along Forty-second Street. The seventies had been an era of further deterioration—more porn shops, massage parlors, live sex shows, and increased crime and drug use, overseen by organized crime and sanctioned by a corrupt and incompetent police department. The crack cocaine epidemic of the eighties only exacerbated the problem. One study concluded that Forty-second Street between Broadway and Eighth Avenue was the most crime-ridden block per square foot in the city.

There were many elements in the area's recovery. Besides the plummeting crime rate, the rise of the home video industry demolished the economic foundation of the street's porn empire—customers could now rent porn from their neighborhood video store and watch it from the comfort and safety of their own homes. The crack cocaine epidemic eventually burned out due to tougher policing and the soaring mortality rate among high-intensity users. The "upzoning" of the area, first initiated by the Lindsay administration, gave city government new tools to evict or restrict sleazy businesses. Many historic jewels were lost in the process of demolition and rehabilitation, including the venerable Helen Hayes and Morosco theaters. Local neighborhood groups bemoaned the corporatization and gentrification of the area, but in the end they cut deals for their communities and themselves, and bowed to the inevitable.

The future of Forty-second Street lay in returning it to its roots as a mainstream entertainment center. Local business leaders persuaded the Disney Studio head Michael Eisner to invest in renovating the New Amsterdam Theatre, a crumbling century-old dowager with a beaux-arts façade and art nouveau interior. By the year 2000, Forty-second Street was on its way back—rendered loud, bland, Disneyfied, and harmless, but safe and profitable. Not unlike Hollywood itself.

Midnight Cowboy cast a large shadow over the rest of John Schlesinger's film career. He was always looking for another big hit, both for the money to fund the lavish lifestyle he adored but also to assert his artistic significance. Having reached the pinnacle of success with *Midnight Cowboy*, he refused to believe he couldn't do it again. He never quite got there.

Following *The Day of the Locust*, Schlesinger's next film was a major success, although one that few critics took seriously. *Marathon Man* (1976) was an international thriller that he turned into a quasi-horror movie. The cast—including Dustin Hoffman, Laurence Olivier, Roy Scheider, William Devane, and Marthe Keller—seemed oddly mismatched. When Hoffman showed up on the set one morning bleary-eyed and exhausted from preparing for a scene by staying out all night, Lord Olivier famously asked Schlesinger, "Oh, why doesn't he just *act*?"

Every time the narrative started to flag, John killed off another major character or, in one memorable scene, subjected Hoffman's character to the most cringe-inducing bout of dental torture in cinematic history. New York looked suitably grungy and claustrophobic. The nightmarish script, written by William Goldman and based on his novel, threw in the Holocaust, the McCarthy-era Red Scare, and Cold War–style paranoia. The plot was only semi-coherent, but on a visceral level it worked. *Marathon Man* was John's last big commercial hit.

After bailing on *Coming Home*, John went back to England to make his own film on the impact of war on private lives, uniting with his old collaborator, the producer Joe Janni. *Yanks* (1979) was the story of two American airmen and their love affairs with two English women during World War II. Beautifully acted by Vanessa Redgrave, William Devane, and Richard Gere, it was tender, restrained, and slow-moving, and it failed to inspire critical or box-office success. John's next picture, *Honky Tonk Freeway* (1981), was a twenty-four-million-dollar misbegotten flop.

He would go on to make a handful of smaller but critically acclaimed movies, including *The Falcon and the Snowman* (1985), *Madame Sousatzka*

(1988), and *Cold Comfort Farm* (1995), and two exquisitely written and acted short films for BBC television, *An Englishman Abroad* (1983) and *A Question of Attribution* (1991). He also directed operas and plays in Europe and America. But the movies he later made were largely second-hand and second rate, assignments he took on rather than projects he himself created.

"John was a wonderful artist, with tremendous intellectual curiosity," says Peter Bart, a senior executive at Paramount Pictures who later became the editor of *Variety*. Of all the British filmmakers who came to America in the sixties and early seventies, Bart believes Schlesinger was the most gifted. But Hollywood had moved far away from his type of distinctively original and personal movies and into an era of big-budget blockbusters and superhero epics. Two of the New Hollywood icons, Steven Spielberg and George Lucas, helped create the new template with *Jaws*, the *Star Wars* trilogy, and the *Indiana Jones* action series. A few canny survivors, like Martin Scorsese and Robert Altman, managed to carve out niches and breathing space for their unique artistic signatures. But others, like Francis Ford Coppola, Peter Bogdanovich, William Friedkin, and Sam Peckinpah, despite occasional flashes of brilliance, faded. "Hollywood had changed," recalls Michael Childers. "The writing was on the wall."

Michael's own career took off after *Midnight Cowboy*. He created the mixed-media work for the long-running erotic revue *Oh! Calcutta!*, was a founding photographer for Andy Warhol's *Interview* and *After Dark* magazines, and photographed more than two hundred covers for magazines, including *GQ*, *Esquire*, *New York*, *Elle*, *Paris Match*, and British and Italian *Vogue*. His photos are in the collections of some two dozen art museums and libraries, including the National Portrait Gallery, the Victoria and Albert Museum, the British Film Institute Library, and the Margaret Herrick Library of the Academy of Motion Picture Arts and Sciences in Beverly Hills.

Michael remained a constant in John's life. The two men threw lavish parties in their house on Rising Glen Road, one of the hidden enclaves of the Hollywood Hills. Bette Midler sang; Elton John and Dustin Hoffman played piano; Mick Jagger, Paul and Linda McCartney, Natalie

Wood and Robert Wagner, Bob Fosse, Christopher Isherwood, and Gore Vidal all came to see and be seen. The gossip columnist Liz Smith reported that "the fit and the fashionable always seem to find their way to Schlesinger's."

Despite the openness of his relationship with Michael, John still refused for many years to publicly discuss his sexuality. He took a small step forward in a 1988 interview in *The Advocate* with the author Boze Hadleigh, declaring that "almost all of my films have gay characters" and expressing his desire to make an AIDS-themed film. But his official emergence did not come until 1991, when he joined seventeen other distinguished British gay and lesbian artists and filmmakers in signing a public letter in support of his friend the actor Ian McKellen, who was under fire from left-wing activists for accepting a knighthood from the Conservative government. The letter, which openly identified the signers as gay, called the knighthood "a significant landmark in the history of the British Gay Movement."

John and Michael were planning to move back to England when he decided instead to plunge into one more Hollywood project. *The Next Best Thing* (2000), starring Rupert Everett and Madonna, was a comedy-melodrama about two devoted friends, a gay man and a straight woman, who decide to have a baby together. It turned out to be an excruciating disaster to make—the egos and temper tantrums of the stars were beyond the director's fading control—and equally hard to watch. The critic Roger Ebert called it "a garage sale of gay issues, harnessed to a plot as exhausted as a junkman's horse."

Still, the film could not tarnish John's earlier achievements in making uniquely astute films about men and women and their aspirations and illusions. As he grew older, he was especially proud of the honesty of his treatment of openly gay characters and themes in *Darling*, *Midnight Cowboy*, and *Sunday Bloody Sunday* and regretted not doing more. "John made homosexual love look perfectly natural, and by doing so struck a bigger blow for emancipation than most demonstrations could ever achieve," wrote his nephew Ian Buruma.

On New Year's Day 2001, while sitting on the terrace outside his home in Palm Springs, John suffered a debilitating stroke that left him paralyzed on one side and made speech increasingly difficult. His energy and spirit steadily waned. Friends who came to see him, including his dear Julie Christie, couldn't help but note the decline. With Michael Childers by his side, he died on July 25, 2003.

Nine years earlier he had prowled the streets of Times Square with the *New Yorker* writer Tad Friend for the twenty-fifth anniversary of *Midnight Cowboy*. He was dressed like an aging Midnight Cowboy himself that day, in a rich blue leather jacket, black felt cowboy hat, crimson scarf, black trousers, and periwinkle socks. What was left of his hair was white as snow, as was his closely trimmed beard.

Forty-second Street was still seedy, but the omnipresent porn shops, hustlers, drug dealers, and junkies were nearing the end of their reign. Many of the old theaters and coffee shops were boarded up, awaiting the arrival of the wrecking ball that would soon begin the process of transforming the area into a G-rated playground. John reminisced about making the movie and how much things had changed in the years since. Not just Forty-second Street, but the massive changes in the movie business that would have rendered *Midnight Cowboy* all but impossible to make in the new blockbuster era.

He recalled how he hadn't wanted to cast either Voight or Hoffman for the movie, how sweltering the New York summer had been, and how some gay critics had condemned what they saw as the film's demeaning portrayal of homosexuals. He was proud that he had not played it safe. "We were lucky that it all worked," he told Friend.

He sounded both humble and defiant.

"I was recently at dinner with a top studio executive," he recounted, "and I said, 'If I brought you a story about this dishwasher from Texas who goes to New York dressed as a cowboy to fulfill his fantasy of living off rich women, doesn't, is desperate, meets a crippled consumptive who later pisses his pants and dies on a bus, would you—'

"And he said 'I'd show you the door.'"

SOURCES AND ACKNOWLEDGMENTS

"Sometimes I hear these stories and I don't know if they're real or not," said Jon Voight, reminiscing at a twenty-fifth-anniversary celebration in 1994 about the making of *Midnight Cowboy*. "They're always good stories, though."

It hasn't always been easy to separate reality from myth in writing about the making of *Midnight Cowboy* and the turbulent era it reflects. James Leo Herlihy was often less than candid about the origins of his gritty seriocomic novel and his feelings about the movie that was made from it. Certain tall tales have taken hold about the casting of the lead actors, the improvisation of the famous "I'm walkin' here" scene, and the original decision to rate the movie X and, after it won the Best Picture Oscar in April 1970, to re-rate it R. Memories grow unreliable, stories get more polished with constant retelling, some of the edges get sharper while others are smoothed beyond recognition.

Fortunately, I've had tremendous help over the past four years from participants, archivists, film scholars, and journalists, as well as access to archival materials, books, newspapers and magazines, film journals, documentaries, and feature films. With the financial support of an Academy Film Scholars research grant from the Academy of Motion Picture Arts and Sciences, I've visited libraries and conducted interviews in Austin, Boston, Hanover (Pennsylvania), Key West, Los Angeles, New York, Newark (Delaware), Rancho Mirage (California), South Egremont (Massachusetts), and Washington, D.C., as well as London and Paris. My thanks to Shawn Guthrie at the academy.

I am deeply grateful to Jeffrey Bailey, Dick Duane, and Bob Thixton for sharing memories of James Leo Herlihy; Jeffrey, who is Herlihy's literary heir and faithful guardian of his legacy, has granted me permission to quote from the author's published novels, plays, and letters. Lloyd Burlingame, Tony Falcone, Alicia Bay Laurel, and Thomas McGuane recounted their own memories of Herlihy, and Robert Ward, author of *Understanding James Leo Herlihy*, the only book devoted to his work, was generous with his time and insights. Robert Gottlieb cordially fielded my inquiry about Herlihy, whom he edited at Simon & Schuster. I interviewed Christopher Bram, Mart Crowley, Samuel R. Delany, Robert Hofler, Kenneth T. Jackson, Charles Kaiser, Paul Krassner, and Dotson Rader about New York in the sixties. Marc Aronson of Rutgers University's Department of Library and Information Science drew up a helpful list of books about Times Square. A special thanks to Billy Nemec, who took me and my wife on a bespoke and carefully researched tour of Forty-second Street and Times Square that re-created many of the area's sites and spirit from a half century ago. It helped jog my own memories of New York in the late 1960s, when I was a struggling student at Columbia University but an avid filmgoer who probably spent more time in the Upper West Side's classic repertory movie houses and the cheap grindhouses of Times Square than in the classroom.

On the movie side, Michael Childers, Ian Buruma, and Ann Skinner were essential guides to the life and art of John Schlesinger. Michael was generous not only with his time and memories but also with access to his evocative photographs. Jerome and Elizabeth Hellman graciously permitted me to read and quote from portions of Jerry's unpublished memoir, an invaluable guide to the making of *Midnight Cowboy*. Jennifer Salt shared her frank and pungent memories of her parents and of her experiences during the film shoot and afterward, and Adam Holender recalled with insight and charm the making of his first American feature film. I also interviewed or exchanged letters and emails with Bob Balaban, Peter Bart, Irene Bowers, Kevin Brownlow, Randall Carver, Julie Christie, Stephen Farber, Burtt Harris, Murray Head, Alan Heim, Dustin Hoffman, Glenda Jackson, Kate Lardner, Andria Litto, Joel Mick, Isis Mussenden, David Picker, Paul Rossilli, Ann Roth, Gabe Sumner, Juliet Taylor, Brenda Vaccaro, Jon Voight, and Catherine Wyler. Jon Burlingame, Rick Jarrard, John Sebastian, and Richie Unterberger recounted the musical achievements of John Barry, Fred Neil, and Harry Nilsson. Robert Walden gave a firsthand account of breaking into the New York theater scene with his friend and fellow actor Dustin Hoffman. Erin Bockman, Ronald Hoffman, and Ellen McCarthy helped connect me to Dustin, and Ron and Ellen shared their memories of his rise to success; Randy Erickson, Kyle Otto, and Liz Rodriguez aided me in reaching Jon Voight. The film editors Ed Landler, Tom Fleischman, and Lisa Dosch helped me track down Alan Heim and Irene Bowers. The journalists and film scholars who guided me along the way include Peter Biskind, Ronald Gregg, J. Hoberman, Ann Hornaday, Noah Isenberg, Leonard Maltin, Geoffrey O'Brien, Rebecca Prime, and Paul Stekler. My friends Sharon Waxman, the founder and editor in chief of *The Wrap*, and Karen Stetler of the Criterion Collection were knowledgeable and encouraging, as always.

In Key West I was welcomed by Arlo Haskell and Katie Leigh, my friendly hosts at the Key West Literary Seminar; Mark Hedden of the Friends of the Key West Library; Brian Antoni, owner and guardian of 709 Bakers Lane; the poet and artist Kirby Congdon; Lynn Mitsuko Kaufelt, whose *Key West Writers and Their Houses* is a literary gem; the writers and filmmakers Carey and Jane Winfrey; the archivists Tom Hambright and Breana Sowers at the Monroe County Public Library; and the curator and historian Cori Convertito at the Key West Art & Historical Society.

Bob Egan of PopSpots NYC, who is a dedicated pop culture gumshoe, pinpointed many of the elusive New York locations where *Midnight Cowboy* was shot, as did the Bowery Boys history website of Tom Meyers and Greg Young, and the producer-director Edwin Samuelson, another astute New York film buff.

Librarians and archivists are, in my experience, unfailingly generous, well-informed, and sympathetic when know-next-to-nothings like myself stumble into their temples of knowledge. Among those whom I most relied upon this time around are Timothy Murray, head of special collections, and the library assistant Valerie Stenner at the University of Delaware Library; Jason Baumann and Meredith Mann at the New York Public Library's Manuscripts and Archives Division; Cassie Blake at the Motion Picture Academy Film Archives; Matt Severson, director, and Louise Hilton, Jenny Romero, and Val Almandarez at the Academy's Margaret Herrick Library; Ned Comstock and Dino Everett at the University of Southern California's Cinematic Arts Library; Jonny Davis and Victoria Bennett at the British Film Institute; Heather South at the North Carolina State Archives; Zoran Sinobad and the staff at the Library of Congress Motion Pictures Reading Room; Emily Wittenberg at American Film Institute's Louis B. Mayer Library; Cristina Favretto and Nicola Hellman-McFarland at the University of Miami; and Hilary Swett at the Writers Guild Foundation. Special thanks to John Calhoun, chief reference librarian of the New York Public Library for the Performing Arts, who has been my wise and supportive guide to all things NYPL; and to the film historian Barbara Hall, who has recently compiled and edited with Rocky Lang her own classic movie book, the critically acclaimed *Letters from Hollywood: Inside the Private World of Classic American Moviemaking*. I am also grateful to the staff of the Central Library in my hometown of Arlington, Virginia, and to the many staff members who serviced my requests at the majestic Main Reading Room, Performing Arts Reading Room, and Microfilm & Electronic Resources Center at the Library of Congress.

Among the books listed in my bibliography, George Chauncey's *Gay New York* and Marc Eliot's *Down 42nd Street* are deeply researched accounts of the history and anthropology of the Times Square area, and Daniel Hurwitz's *Stepping Out* is a fun and highly informative walking guide to Manhattan's gay and lesbian past. Ada Calhoun's *St. Marks Is Dead* is a charming historical portrait of a neighborhood. Charles Kaiser's monumental *The Gay Metropolis* and Lillian Faderman's *The Gay Revolution* are essential histories of their era. Martin Duberman's *Cures* and Edmund White's *City Boy* are lively and compelling memoirs. Christopher Bram's wonderfully readable *Eminent Outlaws* is a thoughtful introduction to the lives and works of Gore Vidal, James Baldwin, Truman Capote, and other postwar gay writers. Dotson Rader's *Tennessee Williams* is an intimate and irresistible memoir of the great playwright. Robert Hofler's *Sexplosion* covers with appropriate gusto the five pivotal years between 1967 and 1972 when New York's pop culture scene burst open. *POPism* explores the same cultural storm through the eyes of one of its principal fomenters, Andy Warhol. James

Sanders's *Celluloid Skyline* is a vastly entertaining guide to New York and the movies. Vito Russo's *The Celluloid Closet* and Alexander Walker's *Hollywood England* are required film histories. Ian Buruma's two affectionate and illuminating memoirs of his family and his gifted uncle, *Their Promised Land* and *Conversations with John Schlesinger*, and William J. Mann's authorized and authoritative biography, *Edge of Midnight: The Life of John Schlesinger*, are prerequisites for anyone seeking to understand the filmmaker and the man.

The New York Times, as always, was the most definitive source of news both political and cultural of the era I write about. And while I did not spare the *Times* from scorn for reflecting the homophobic biases of the pre-Stonewall era, I must also point out that it broke ground in publishing Merle Miller's powerful "What It Means to Be a Homosexual," in *The New York Times Magazine* in January 1971, and his "Afterword" four months later, at a time when publications like *Harper's*, *Time*, and *The New York Review of Books* were still depicting gay people as diseased and depraved.

I benefited from the research assistance of Elizabeth Crowley Weber and Beth Corzo-Duchardt, as well as from the calm expertise of Alice Crites, my friend and former *Washington Post* colleague, who received long-overdue recognition as a cowinner of the 2018 Pulitzer Prize for investigative reporting.

Gail Ross of the Ross Yoon Literary Agency in Washington, D.C., has been my devoted and indefatigable representative over the course of four books. Thanks also to Howard Yoon and Jennifer Manguera at the agency. And to Johanna Ramos-Boyer at JRB Communications in Fairfax Station, Virginia, for helping to create an excellent broadcast and social media campaign.

Colin Dickerman of Farrar, Straus and Giroux edited this book with skill and care, asking compelling questions, offering encouragement, and focusing his death ray on my awkward similes and metaphors. Ian Van Wye was knowledgeable, supportive, and faster than the speed of light in responding to my email queries, while Greg Villepique performed an eagle-eyed and rigorous copyedit. Thank you as well to Alexander Star, Alex Merto, Frieda Duggan, Janine Barlow, Stephen Weil, and the entire team at FSG.

My longtime comrades David E. Hoffman, David Maraniss, Richard McCann, Liza Mundy, and David Rowell hashed out ideas with me and commiserated over the various obstacles I faced; their reward was to be conscripted into reading the manuscript. A new friend, Christopher Bram, also joined the reader corps. Collectively they caught many mistakes and offered useful suggestions. Any factual errors in this book are strictly my responsibility.

Other friends who contributed sympathy and advice include Margaret Edds, Tom Frail, Blaine Harden, Jim Hoagland, Susannah Jacob, Steve Luxenberg, Steve Mufson, Jocelyn Noveck, Jack Shafer, and Agnes Tabah. Among those who offered hospitality during this long journey were Rick Levine and Janet Gold in New York,

Arnold and Lorel Zar-Kessler in Boston, and Larry Ceplair and Christine Holmgren in Santa Monica, California.

Betsyellen Yeager and I first saw *Midnight Cowboy* together in 1970 at a run-down movie house in Hadera, Israel, with Hebrew, Arabic, and French subtitles that cluttered the screen and a boisterous audience of sunflower-seed-chewing Israelis. Neither of us could have anticipated all the adventures that lay before us, but I am forever grateful that we've shared them together. I am thankful for our three children and their spouses, who have provided their mother and me with a new generation of radiant grandchildren to love and cherish.

This book is dedicated to the memory of three dear friends. Alan Finder, who died of COVID-19 on March 24, 2020, was a superb journalist at *The Bergen Record*, *Newsday*, and *The New York Times*. He and his wife, the graphic designer Elaine Isaacson, have been a cherished part of our lives for more than forty years.

Greg Katz was a dedicated and resourceful journalist whom I first met in 2002 when we were both based in London. He and his wife, the architect Bea Sennewald, loaned us their house in Chiswick for five consecutive Augusts while I worked on book projects at the British Film Institute. Greg died of COVID-19 on June 23, 2020.

Nick Redman was an Oscar-nominated documentary filmmaker, movie soundtrack producer, and cofounder of Twilight Time, the Blu-ray vintage movie label. He and his wife, the writer-producer Julie Kirgo, have been sources of expertise and support ever since I launched my unexpected expedition into movie-book writing a decade ago. Nick died on January 17, 2019.

Their warm conversations, generosity, and love inspired this book and its author.

Arlington, Virginia
October 2020

NOTES

LIST OF ABBREVIATIONS

AFI: American Film Institute, Los Angeles

BFI: John R. Schlesinger Papers, British Film Institute, London

BU: James Leo Herlihy Papers, Howard Gotlieb Archival Research Center, Boston University

DEL: James Leo Herlihy Papers, Special Collections, University of Delaware, Newark, Del.

GETTY: Mary Caroline Richards Papers, Getty Research Institute, Los Angeles

HELM: Jerome Hellman Papers, Private Collection

JLH: James Leo Herlihy

JRS: John R. Schlesinger

LAT: *Los Angeles Times*

MCR: Mary Caroline Richards

MHL: Margaret Herrick Library of the Motion Picture Academy of Arts and Sciences, Beverly Hills

NIN: Anaïs Nin Papers, Charles E. Young Research Library, UCLA

NYRB: *The New York Review of Books*

NYU: Jack Gelber Papers, Fales Library and Special Collections, New York University

NYT: *The New York Times*

SALT: Waldo Salt Papers, UCLA

USC: Cinematic Arts Library, University of Southern California

EPIGRAPHS

vii   *"for the filmmakers I came to love and respect"*: "Martin Scorsese: I Said Marvel Movies Aren't Cinema. Let Me Explain," *NYT*, Nov. 4, 2019.

vii   *"No one should come to New York"*: E. B. White, *Here Is New York* (New York: Harper & Brothers, 1949), p. 10.

INTRODUCTION

3 *"I like the surprise of the curtain going up"*: Ian Buruma, *Conversations with Schlesinger* (New York: Random House, 2006), p. 6.

4 *the studio flew three hundred journalists to London*: *Dallas Morning News*, Sept. 22, 1967.

4 *"sluggish, indecisive, and banal"*: Bosley Crowther, "Magnificence Is No Longer Enough," *NYT*, Nov. 5, 1967.

4 *"It was frightfully slow"*: Buruma, *Conversations with Schlesinger*, p. 96.

5 *"Be very careful what you do next"*: Ibid., p. 97.

6 *"all of a nation's impulses"*: Charles Kaiser, *1968 in America: Music, Politics, Chaos, Counterculture, and the Shaping of a Generation* (New York: Grove Press, 2018 [thirtieth-anniversary ed.]), p. xix.

7 *"The city arouses us"*: Alfred Kazin, "The Writer and the City," *Harper's*, Dec. 1968.

7 *"the city's true mythic counterpart"*: James Sanders, *Celluloid Skyline: New York and the Movies* (New York: Knopf, 2001), p. 21.

7 *a vast film school*: for the examples cited, including Sarris, Scorsese, Ochs, and Lopate, see Marc Eliot, *Down 42nd Street: Sex, Money, Culture, and Politics at the Crossroads of the World* (New York: Warner Books, 2001), pp. 98–101, and Bob Dylan, *Chronicles: Volume One* (New York: Simon & Schuster, 2004), pp. 265–66.

8 *"Each art breeds its fanatics"*: Susan Sontag, "The Decay of Cinema," *NYT*, Feb. 25, 1996.

9 *"so rough and vivid"*: Vincent Canby, "Midnight Cowboy," *NYT*, May 26, 1969.

I. THE WRITER

11 *"None of us feels . . . entirely normal"*: Kay Bonetti, "Interview with James Leo Herlihy," April 1982 (Columbia, MO: American Audio Prose Library audio-cassette), accessed at the Library of Congress.

11 *"There was an aura about her"*: Anatole Broyard, *Kafka Was the Rage: A Greenwich Village Memoir* (New York: Vintage, 1997), p. 34.

11 *"waifs, psychic and intellectual orphans"*: Alfred Kazin, *New York Jew* (New York: Knopf, 1978), p. 104.

12 *"He had laughing Irish eyes"*: Anaïs Nin, *The Diary of Anaïs Nin: Volume Five, 1947–1955* (New York: Harcourt Brace Jovanovich, 1974), p. 23.

12 *"He said it smiling, defiantly"*: Ibid.

12 *"She had her face beautifully painted"*: Mary Harris, "Interview with JLH," Nov. 1972, North Carolina Museum of Art, Raleigh, p. 41.

12 *"Picture, if you will, youngsters who were just developing"*: Deirdre Bair, *Anaïs Nin: A Biography* (New York: G. P. Putnam, 1995), p. 330.

13 *"a life-long double-mindedness"*: JLH, "The Art of Being a Person," *Anaïs: An International Journal*, July 1983.

13 *"She gave me all the attention"*: Harris, "Interview with JLH," pp. 36 and 39.

13 *"nine of the ten nuns that I studied under"*: Bonetti, "Interview with JLH."

14 *"I knew I wanted to write"*: Ibid.

14 *"I never really believed sex was bad"*: John Mitzel, "Interview with JLH," *Gay Weekly*, Sept. 25, 1976.

14 *"School paralyzed me"*: JLH letter to Mrabet, Jan. 7, 1974, DEL.

14 *an ensign named John Lyons*: Harris, "Interview with JLH," p. 1.

15 *"if there was something you wanted to learn"*: Ibid., p. 28.

15 *her "warmth and vulnerability"*: Martin Duberman, *Black Mountain College: An Exploration in Community* (New York: Anchor, 1973), p. 293.

16 *"They had me in mind"*: Jeffrey Bailey, "Interview with JLH," *The Advocate*, Aug. 25, 1976.

16 *"The drawings all began to look alike"*: Harris, "Interview with JLH," pp. 15–16.

16 *"he was doing me this great colossal favor"*: Ibid., p. 13.

16 *"This training affects practically every muscle"*: Pasadena Playhouse Association, "School of the Theatre," 1944 brochure, p. 2.

17 *"He had these beautiful shoulders"*: Author's interview with Jeffrey Bailey.

17 *"'Gee, Mr. Jones'"*: Mary Daniels, "A Grown Up Midnight Cowboy," *Chicago Tribune*, April 26, 1971.

17 *"I'm going to Detroit tomorrow"*: JLH to MCR, Aug. 23, 1949, GETTY.

18 *"I write a lot these days"*: JLH to Nin, undated 1951 letter, NIN.

18 *"I wonder if you know"*: JLH to Nin, Aug. 13, 1951, NIN.

18 *"Come to New York"*: Nin, *Diary: Volume Five*, p. 78.

19 New York *"can destroy an individual"*: E. B. White, *Here Is New York* (New York: Harper & Brothers, 1949), pp. 9–10.

19 *"moment of grace"*: Jan Morris, *Manhattan '45* (New York: Oxford University Press, 1987), p. 12.

19 *"the capital of the Twentieth Century"*: David Reid, *The Brazen Age: New York City and the American Empire: Politics, Art, and Bohemia* (New York: Pantheon, 2016), p. 58.

19 *"New York had never been so attractive"*: Broyard, *Kafka Was the Rage*, p. 7.

20 *"homosexuals had converged"*: Gore Vidal, *The City and the Pillar* (New York: Vintage, 2003 [paperback ed.]), pp. 163–64.

20 *"You can imagine how long I lasted"*: JHL to Mitchell, April 21, 1952, DEL.

21 *"It's up in Central Park taking a leak"*: Paul Krassner, "Flicks and Kicks: *Midnight Cowboy*," *Cavalier*, p. 5, n.d.

21 *"New York is impossible"*: Ibid.

21 *Duane was a nightclub singer*: Author's interview with Dick Duane.

22 *"gay desire was illegal"*: Edmund White, *City Boy: My Life in New York During the 1960s and '70s* (New York: Bloomsbury, 2009), p. 25.

22 *"His gaze was intense"*: Lyle Bongé, "Obituary of James Leo Herlihy," *Independent*, Oct. 29, 1993.

23 *"I've met someone here, Ed"*: JLH to Mitchell, Aug. 28, 1952, DEL.

23 *"Jamie was so charming"*: Author's interview with Duane.

23 *"You had to be a real cuckoo"*: Ibid.

2. THE LAZIEST BOY

24 *"I don't trust success"*: "Interview with John Schlesinger," *American Film*, Nov. 1987, p. 17.

24 *"I hope you've gotten over Alan Cooke"*: Author's interview with Ian Buruma.

25 *"I knew I didn't fit in"*: Ian Buruma, *Conversations with John Schlesinger* (New York: Random House, 2006), p. 9.

25 *"We were always directed by John"*: William Mann, *Edge of Midnight: The Life of John Schlesinger* (New York: Billboard Books, 2005), p. 45.

25 *"the laziest, most selfish & feckless boy"*: Ian Buruma, *Their Promised Land: My Grandparents in Love and War* (New York: Penguin, 2016), p. 176.

25 *"spinelessness & inertia"*: Ibid., p. 204

26 *saved the lives of twelve German Jewish children*: Ibid., pp. 137–48.

27 *"I think that's my affair"*: "Films for the Madding Crowd," JRS interview by Len Richmond, BBC Radio, March 8, 1977, transcript, p. 7, BFI.

27 *"like a whore's drawers"*: Ibid., p. 5.

27 *"We are making a piece of shit"*: Author's interview with Ann Skinner.

27 *"He was a drama queen"*: Author's interview with Buruma.

28 *films, fucks, and food*: Buruma, *Conversations with John Schlesinger*, p. xxvi.

28 *"I often get angry"*: "Films for the Madding Crowd," p. 5.

29 *"It afforded me the chance to fail"*: JRS interview, Aug. 4, 1970, BBC Transcription Service, p. 2.

30 *"We got the boy to cry"*: Alexander Walker, *Hollywood England: The British Film Industry in the Sixties* (London: Michael Joseph, 1974), p. 49.

30 *"if one of these ever gets on my desk"*: "The Profits and the Loss," *Sunday Times*, Feb. 3, 1963.

31 *"He was well-dressed and blustery"*: Author's interview with Skinner.

32 *"There didn't seem any point in going on"*: Brian McFarlane, *An Autobiography of British Cinema* (London: Methuen, 1997), p. 476. For the most thorough ac-

counts of the rise of "Free Cinema" and kitchen-sink films, see McFarlane and Walker's books.

33 *"Implicit in our attitudes . . . is a belief in freedom"*: Walker, *Hollywood England*, p. 28.

33 *"they can't direct movies"*: Pauline Kael, "Muddling Through," *The New Yorker*, Nov. 23, 1968.

34 *The film "peeled away a lot of layers"*: McFarlane, *An Autobiography of British Cinema*, p. 578.

34 *"could have a great future"*: Walker, *Hollywood England*, p. 64.

34 *"Courtenay wouldn't have carried a spear"*: McFarlane, *An Autobiography of British Cinema*, p. 191.

34 *"The nature of actors has changed"*: *London Daily Express*, Nov. 16, 1961.

35 *"hedonistic, abrasive, volatile"*: David Kynaston, *Modernity Britain: Book Two, A Shake of the Dice* (London: Bloomsbury, 2014), p. 108.

36 *"The way I see it is this"*: Stan Barstow, *A Kind of Loving* (London: Michael Joseph, 1960; London: Corgi, 1978), p. 272.

36 *"I would like to discover you"*: "Interview with John Schlesinger," *American Film*, p. 13.

3. TWISTED APPLES

37 *"Writing is so lonely"*: Cleveland Amory, "Tradewinds," *Saturday Review*, May 20, 1971.

37 *"lavish rejection letters"*: JLH to Mitchell, Aug. 10, 1952.

38 *he had held forty-three different odd jobs*: Kay Bonetti, "Interview with James Leo Herlihy," April 1982 (Columbia, MO: American Audio Prose Library audiocassette).

38 *"The entire island seemed to have been submerged"*: JLH, *The Sleep of Baby Filbertson and Other Stories* (New York: Dutton, 1959; reprinted as *Crazy October* [New York: Lancer, 1970]), p. 12.

38 *"His bed was like a slab"*: Ibid., p. 25.

39 *"a kind of mania of vision"*: Christian Kiefer, "Groggy from Stolen Phenobarbs: An Appreciation of JLH," *The Paris Review*, March 17, 2017, https://www.theparisreview.org/blog/2017/03/14/groggy-from-stolen-phenobarbs/.

39 *"It was nice to be the center of attraction"*: JLH to Nin, 1954, NIN.

39 *his true literary father was Sherwood Anderson*: Bonetti, "Interview with James Leo Herlihy."

40 *"an odd and interesting drama"*: Brooks Atkinson, "At the Theatre," *NYT*, Oct. 28, 1953.

40 *"It didn't bore me"*: *New York Post*, Oct. 28, 1953.

41 *"I have everything I can rationally expect"*: JLH to Nin, 1955, NIN.

41 *"My cavities were so numerous"*: JLH to Bailey, 1986–87, DEL.

41 *"a queasy feeling in my belly"*: JLH journal, 1986–87, DEL.

41 *"He wanted to live that wilder life"*: Author's interview with Dick Duane.

41 *"I do love him more"*: JLH to Nin, 1952, NIN.

42 *"The boy is a little too pretty"*: Nin to Rupert Pole, 1952, NIN.

42 *"He could go from being that wonderful loving man"*: Author's interview with Duane.

42 *"a Campbell's Soup and Kraft Cheese neighborhood"*: JLH to Nin, Aug. 31, 1956, NIN.

42 *"I felt cleansed"*: JLH to Nin, n.d., 1953, NIN.

43 *"You got tired of those New York winters"*: Author's interview with Kirby Congdon.

43 *"The place is a paradise"*: *Letters of Wallace Stevens*, p. 224.

44 *"we're free to be children here"*: "KWLS Founder David A. Kaufelt turns 70," n.d., https://www.kwls.org/key-wests-life-of-letters/kwls_founder_david_kaufelt _is/. The words are inscribed on a plaque outside the Monroe County Public Library, Key West.

44 *admired with "total awe"*: Lynn Mitsuko Kaufelt, *Key West Writers and Their Houses* (Englewood, FL: Pineapple Press, 1986), p. 73.

45 *"It was inexpressibly comforting"*: Ibid.

45 *"There were times when it was loving"*: Author's interview with Duane.

45 *"The town excited me too much"*: Kaufelt, *Key West Writers and Their Houses*, p. 70.

46 *"I hope you enjoyed yourself"*: William McKeen, *Mile Marker Zero: The Moveable Feast of Key West* (New York: Crown, 2011), pp. 49–50.

46 *"The subject of abortion is taboo"*: Patricia Bosworth, *The Men in My Life: A Memoir of Love and Art in 1950s Manhattan* (New York: HarperCollins, 2017), p. 158.

47 *"a tall shambling man"*: Ibid., p. 160.

47 *"original [and] overwhelmingly dramatic"*: Brooks Atkinson, "Theatre: 'Blue Denim,'" *NYT*, Feb. 28, 1958.

48 *"I've never heard so many laughs"*: *New York Post*, Oct. 19, 1958.

48 *"a gothic and grotesque experience"*: Bonetti, "Interview with JLH."

49 *"robust, humorous, and original"*: "Strange Fruit," *Time*, Jan. 12, 1959.

49 *"Herlihy writes with an edge of iron"*: Nelson Algren, "The Sad Amphibia," *The Nation*, Jan. 31, 1959.

49 *"we're talking about the Dark Ages"*: JLH *Advocate* interview, Aug. 25, 1976.

50 Berry-berry *"was like some drug"*: JLH, *All Fall Down* (New York: Avon, 1977), p. 157. Subsequent quotations are from pp. 137, 148, and 34.

51 *"Don't tell a writer what they're doing badly"*: Author's interview with Duane.

51 *"a deft and superior novel"*: Quoted in "The Critics Applaud *All Fall Down*, The Brilliant First Novel by James Leo Herlihy," " E. P. Dutton press release, 1960. It includes excerpts from the *NYT, New York Herald Tribune Book Review*, and *Time*.

52 *"Beatty played him contemptuously"*: Marjory Adams, "You Can See Jim Herlihy Act or Read His Works," *Boston Globe*, Aug. 29, 1965.

52 *"Everyone likes him"*: Nin, *Diary: Volume Five, 1947–1955* (New York: Harcourt Brace Jovanovich, 1974), pp. 78–79.

52 *"Jim is the only one who is alive"*: 1956 journal entry, pp. 109–110, NIN.

52 *"It has thrown me into a panic"*: JLH to Nin, Sept. 28, 1953, NIN.

53 *"[Jim's] enthusiasm sustains me"*: Nin, *Diary: Volume Five*, p. 96.

53 *"Relationship with Jim Herlihy endangered"*: Ibid., p. 135.

53 *"it wouldn't be worth much if I'd lost you"*: JLH to Nin, 1959, NIN.

53 *"I behaved very badly"*: Nin, *Diary: Volume Five*, p. 150.

53 *"your faith in your voice"*: JLH to Nin, summer 1957, Anaïs Nin, *The Diary of Anaïs Nin: Volume Six, 1955–1966* (New York: Harcourt Brace Jovanovich, 1976), p. 95.

53 *"the secret of your seduction"*: Ibid., p. 91.

54 *"I cannot lie to you"*: Ibid., p. 218.

54 *"He went into total depression"*: Author's interview with Duane.

54 *"My work lost a lot"*: JLH letter to Bailey, July 15, 1977, DEL.

54 *"I could not choose Anaïs over my career"*: Noël Riley Fitch interview with JLH, Nov. 27, 1990, Fitch Papers, Harry Ransom Center.

54 *Stig Dagerman, who had killed himself*: JLH to Nin, April 2, 1962, NIN.

4. DARLING

56 *"Bastard, bastard, bastard"*: Julie Christie, letter to author re: JRS, June 27, 2017.

56 *"let's go back to the hotel"*: Ian Buruma, *Conversations with John Schlesinger* (New York: Random House, 2006), p. 65.

56 *"Come on, you must be quicker"*: Ibid., p. 66.

57 *"if this were a real wedding"*: "The Man with the Candid Camera," *Manchester Evening News*, May 11, 1962.

57 *"You ridiculous faggot!"*: William J. Mann, *Edge of Midnight: The Life of John Schlesinger* (New York: Billboard Books, 2005), p. 178.

57 *"They were always fighting, Joe and John"*: Author's interview with Ann Skinner.

58 *"All you have to do"*: Mann, *Edge of Midnight*, p. 359.

58 *"There was an inclusiveness"*: Author's interview with Skinner.

58 *"It was absolutely life as it was lived"*: Brian McFarlane, *An Autobiography of British Cinema* (London: Methuen, 1997), p. 59.

58 *John, of course, couldn't have cared less*: Ibid., p. 511.

59 *"I was never asked to play anyone"*: Ibid., p. 298.

59 *"Why did we ever bring this film here?"*: Mann, *Edge of Midnight*, p. 59.

59 *"I was considered an outsider"*: McFarlane, *An Autobiography of British Cinema*, p. 511.

59 *"The objective is to make a good film"*: "Away from the Kitchen Sink," *Billy Liar* Press Book, BFI.

61 *the producer deemed her breasts too small*: Tom Lisanti and Louis Paul, *Film Fatales: Women in Espionage Film and Television, 1962–73* (Jefferson NC: McFarland, 2002), p. 36.

62 *"When Julie Christie boarded that train"*: Walker, *Hollywood England: The British Film Industry in the Sixties* (London: Michael Joseph, 1974), pp. 289–90.

62 *"He had a clear vision"*: Author's interview with Ian Buruma.

64 *the first unapologetic, sexually active gay man*: Mann, *Edge of Midnight*, pp. 243–44.

65 *"It was probably the easiest part"*: McFarlane, *An Autobiography of British Cinema*, pp. 123–44.

65 *"I suppose John and I really bonded"*: Author's interview with Julie Christie.

65 *"Get your knickers off, darling"*: Julie Christie, letter to author re: JRS, June 27, 2017.

66 *As the British cultural critic Christine Geraghty put it*: Christine Geraghty, "Women and Sixties British Cinema," *The British Cinema Book*, Robert Murphy, ed. (London: British Film Institute, 2001 [2nd ed.]), pp. 104-105.

66 *"It's not at all what I myself liked"*: Author's interview with Christie.

66 *"one of my least favorite films"*: McFarlane, *An Autobiography of British Cinema*, p. 512.

66 *"a slashing social satire"*: Bosley Crowther, "'Darling' Is Selfish, Fickle and Ambitious," *NYT*, Aug. 4, 1965.

5. THE GAY METROPOLIS

68 *"Times Square is the magnet"*: John Rechy, *City of Night* (New York: Grove Press, 1963; fiftieth-anniversary ed., 2013), p. 31.

68 *"I felt like I'd found a home"*: Author's interview with Dotson Rader.

69 *"What are you doing here?"*: Ibid.

69 *"cheerful vulgarity"*: Jan Morris, *Manhattan '45* (New York: Oxford University Press, 1987), p. 38.

69 *"He was attracted to the dark side"*: Author's interview with Bob Thixton.

70 *"he never said no"*: Bailey email to author, Dec. 1, 2017.

70 *"an organized, multilayered . . . sub-culture"*: George Chauncey, "The Policed: Gay Men's Strategies of Everyday Resistance," in William Taylor, ed., *Invent-*

ing Times Square: Commerce and Culture at the Crossroads of the World (New York: Russell Sage Foundation, 1991), p. 317.

70   *"Faggots have a hard way to go"*: Herbert Huncke, *Guilty of Everything: The Autobiography of Herbert Huncke* (New York: Paragon, 1990), p. 43.

70   *"I never saw anything like it"*: Woody Allen, "Playing It Again," *New York*, April 6, 1998.

71   *"abrupt and candid overtures"*: Tennessee Williams, *Memoirs* (Garden City, NY: Doubleday, 1975), pp. 97–98.

71   *"Few civilians . . . ever dared intrude"*: Gore Vidal, *Palimpsest: A Memoir* (New York: Random House, 1995), pp. 99–100.

71   *"there were burglars and thieves"*: Anthony Bianco, *Ghosts of 42nd Street: A History of America's Most Infamous Block* (New York: Morrow, 2004), pp. 130–31.

72   *"Forty-second Street was dangerous"*: Patricia Bosworth, *Diane Arbus: A Biography* (New York: Knopf, 1984), p. 166.

72   *"A Study in Decay"*: Milton Bracker, "Life on 42nd St. A Study in Decay," *NYT*, March 14, 1960.

73   *"Most of the street hustlers . . . were nice guys"*: Author's interview with Rader.

73   *"I couldn't . . . get an erection on cue"*: Author's interview with Samuel Delany. See also Samuel R. Delany, *Times Square Red, Times Square Blue* (New York: New York University Press, 1999), pp. 14–16 and 32.

73   *"the usual seedy dudes, hustlers, etc."*: Jim Carroll, *The Basketball Diaries* (New York: Penguin, 1987 [paperback ed.]), p. 109.

74   *"my spare time was devoted to sex"*: Edmund White, *City Boy: My Life in New York During the 1960s and '70s* (New York: Bloomsbury, 2009), pp. 24 and 48.

74   *"the rise of organized young hoodlums"*: Quoted in Mack Friedman, *Strapped for Cash: A History of American Hustler Culture* (Los Angeles: Alyson Books, 2003), p. 117.

75   *"Growth of Overt Homosexuality in City"*: Robert C. Doty, "Growth of Overt Homosexuality in City Provokes Wide Concern," *NYT*, Dec. 17, 1963.

76   *"There was an inevitability about psychoanalysis"*: Anatole Broyard, *Kafka Was the Rage: A Greenwich Village Memoir* (New York: Vintage, 1997), p. 45.

76   *"This led to a superb article"*: Gay Talese, *The Kingdom and the Power: Behind the Scenes at* The New York Times (Cleveland: World Publishing; New York: Dell, 1998), p. 424.

76   *"the worst kind of* New York Times *article"*: Author's interview with Charles Kaiser.

76   *"This will ruin me"*: "CBS Reports: The Homosexuals," March 7, 1967, https://www.youtube.com/watch?v=zWNEdoXo0Yg.

77   *"the complete denial in the culture"*: Author's interview with Kaiser.

77   *"It is time to speak openly"*: Howard Taubman, "Not What It Seems," *NYT*, Nov. 5, 1961.

78   *"a homosexual daydream"*: Philip Roth, "The Play That Dare Not Speak Its Name," *NYRB*, Feb. 25, 1965.

78   *"It would . . . leave a cleaner smell"*: *Commentary*, May 1965.

78   *"I am . . . weary of* disguised *homosexual influence"*: Stanley Kauffmann, "Homosexual Drama and Its Disguises," *NYT*, Jan. 23, 1966.

79   *"The Homosexual in America"*: *Time*, Oct. 31, 1969.

79   *"Communists and queers"*: Ellen Schrecker, *Many Are the Crimes: McCarthyism in America* (Boston: Little, Brown, 1998), p. 148.

80   *Too many analysts . . . "violated basic norms of decency"*: Lewes obituary, *NYT*, June 28, 2020.

80   *"Relationship to Jim came to the same standstill"*: Oct. 28, 1953, handwritten diary entry in Anaïs Nin, *Trapeze: The Unexpurgated Diaries of Anaïs Nin, 1947–55* (Sky Blue Press, 2017 [Kindle ed.]).

81   *"The true degenerates"*: Ibid.

81   *"I've always leveled with you, Merle"*: Merle Miller, *On Being Different: What It Means to Be a Homosexual* (New York: Penguin, 2012 [paperback ed.]), pp. 19-20.

82   *"Baby, don't you ever forget"*: Author's interview with Rader.

82   *Duberman's own coming-of-age*: see Martin Duberman, *Cures: A Gay Man's Odyssey* (New York: Dutton, 1991).

83   *"The neighborhood freaked out"*: Martha MacGregor, "This Week in Books," *New York Post*, April 24, 1971.

83   *"I was astonished by its miserable state"*: Jamake Highwater, *Shadow Show: An Autobiographical Insinuation* (New York: Alfred van der Marck, 1986), p. 82.

84   *a review [that] "sent me reeling"*: Duberman, *Cures*, p. 258.

84   *"I got scared"*: Roy Newquist, *Conversations* (Rand McNally, 1967), p. 135.

85   *"Jerry is unforgettable"*: Kevin Kelly, "The Zoo Story," *Boston Globe*, Aug. 13, 1962.

85   *"What is a writer like you doing here"*: Newquist, *Conversations*, p. 137.

6. "A TOUCH OF THE FLICKS"

86   *"The film industry knows less about itself"*: *Variety*, March 27, 1946, quoted in Hortense Powdermaker, *Hollywood: The Dream Factory* (Boston: Little Brown, 1950; Mansfield Center, CT: Martino, 2013), p. 33.

86   *American companies were financing nearly 90 percent*: Alexander Walker, *Hollywood England: The British Film Industry in the Sixties* (London: Michael Joseph, 1974), p. 339.

86   *"the British make pictures"*: Author's interview with Glenda Jackson.

87   *"the sheer exuberance and inventiveness"*: JRS, "Blessed Isle or Fool's Paradise," *Films & Filming*, May 1963.

87 *"I hope so, sir"*: Kevin Brownlow, *David Lean: A Biography* (New York: St. Martin's, 1996), p. 479.

88 *"much of what is written about pictures"*: Joan Didion, "In Hollywood," in Didion, *The White Album* (New York: Simon & Schuster, 1979), p. 162.

88 *"The creative side is taking over"*: see "The Movies: The Big Flick Kick," *Look*, March 9, 1965.

89 The Sound of Music's *profits*: *Hollywood Reporter*, Oct. 24, 1967.

89 *"It's hard to convey now how much insecurity and anger there was"*: Mark Jacobson, "In Conversation: Paul Schrader," *Vulture*, Jan. 8, 2019, www.vulture.com /2019/01/paul-schrader-in-conversation.html.

90 *The code had been established in the early 1930s*: For a concise history of the Production Code, see Ben Yagoda, "Hollywood Cleans Up Its Act," *American Heritage* 321:2, Feb./March 1980.

91 *The biggest challenge yet came . . . with* The Pawnbroker: Leonard J. Leff, "Hollywood and the Holocaust: Remembering *The Pawnbroker*," *American Jewish History*, 84:4, 1996.

91 *Rosenblum constructed a series of "flash cuts"*: Ralph Rosenblum and Robert Karen, *When the Shooting Stops . . . the Cutting Begins: A Film Editor's Story* (New York: Da Capo, 1986), pp. 142–46.

92 *"there were stirrings of insurrection"*: For Valenti's account of replacing the Production Code with the ratings system, see Jack Valenti, *This Time, This Place: My Life in War, the White House, and Hollywood* (New York: Crown Archetype, 2007), pp. 302–306; also Vincent Canby, "Czar of the Movie Business," *NYT Magazine*, April 23, 1967.

93 *"freedom without discipline is license"*: Jon Lewis, *Hollywood v. Hard Core: How the Struggle Over Censorship Saved the Modern Film Industry* (New York: NYU Press, 2000), p. 140.

94 *"It is not a lie that destroys Martha"*: Vito Russo, *The Celluloid Closet: Homosexuality in the Movies* (New York: Harper & Row, 1981), p. 139.

95 *"There was a body of work emerging"*: Author's interview with Ronald Gregg.

96 *"coyly sensational exploitation"*: Russo, *The Celluloid Closet*, p. 131.

96 *"lots-of-people-screwing-lots-of-other-people novels"*: "William Sutcliffe's Top 10 Relationship Novels," *The Guardian*, Nov. 8, 2000.

97 Hardy . . . *"was such a visual writer"*: Ian Buruma, *Conversations with John Schlesinger* (New York: Random House, 2006), p. 93.

97 *"She's playing a modern girl"*: Ibid.

98 *"I didn't think Stamp was very good"*: Ibid., p. 94.

98 *"He wasn't the easiest man"*: "*Far from the Madding Crowd* Terence Stamp Interview," Studiocanal, posted Nov. 29, 2016, https://www.youtube.com /watch?v=WRVD0xe3fqc.

98 *"Terry had worked his butt off"*: Author's interview with Ann Skinner.

99 *"I didn't have any confidence"*: Author's interview with Julie Christie.

99 *"We threw our last dead sheep over a cliff"*: JRS to Hellman, Feb. 18, 1967, BFI.

100 *"Magnificence Is No Longer Enough"*: *NYT*, Nov. 5, 1967.

100 *In America . . . "they're much less polite"*: Len Richmond, "Films for the Madding Crowd," BBC Radio interview, March 8, 1977, transcript, p. 6, BFI.

100 *Margaret Booth . . . "was cutting the film to ribbons"*: JRS, "Introduction," 1998, p. vi, HELM.

101 *"a sort of grey-beige level of mediocrity"*: British Broadcasting Corp. interview with JRS, Aug. 4, 1970, p. 12, BFI.

7. THE NOVEL

102 *"It can be a cruel place, New York"*: Michael Shulman, "Robert De Niro Is Always Doing Something," *The New Yorker* online, Dec. 30, 2018.

102 *"Something snapped in the whole bottom half of him"*: JLH, *Midnight Cowboy* (New York: Simon & Schuster, 1965), p. 13.

104 *"an endless chain of people marching"*: Ibid., p. 45.

104 *"I'm gonna take hold o' this thing"*: Ibid., p. 103.

105 *a skinny, child-sized, "dirty, curly-haired, little blond runt"*: Ibid., p. 122.

105 *"like the progress of a lopsided wheel"*: Ibid., p. 123.

105 *"a big-eyed, handsome person, tall as a scarecrow"*: Ibid., p. 153.

105 *"There was an awareness entering him"*: Ibid., p. 149.

106 *"an urgent and sorrowful labor took place"*: Ibid., p. 147.

106 *"laboring like a broken grasshopper"*: Ibid, p. 164.

107 *"Locke cried out, but this time with pleasure"*: Ibid., p. 232.

107 *"You didn't kill him, did you?"*: Ibid., p. 237.

107 *"I'm no kind of a hustler"*: Ibid., p. 241.

107 *"He put his arm around him to hold him for a while"*: Ibid., pp. 252–53.

107 *"I met Joe Buck in my head"*: Jeannette Smyth, "From Cowboy to Witch," *Washington Post*, May 12, 1971.

107 "The tall, slim author sauntered in": Mary Daniels, "A Grown-Up Midnight Cowboy," *Chicago Tribune*, April 26, 1971.

107 *"Yes, Joe Buck is Jamie"*: Author's interview with Dick Duane.

108 *"I didn't want to write* Midnight Cowboy*"*: Jeffrey Bailey, "Interview with James Leo Herlihy," *The Advocate*, Aug. 25, 1976.

108 *"I really dig that character"*: Roy Newquist, *Conversations* (Rand McNally, 1967), p. 138.

108 *"The trick was adjusting your mind and therefore your entire attitude"*: JLH, *Midnight Cowboy*, p. 145.

110 *"When you do the street you think a lot about being a cowboy"*: Dotson Rader, *Gov't Inspected Meat and Other Fun Summer Things* (New York: David McKay, 1971), p. 68.

110 *"Are you a real cowboy?"*: Author's interview with Dotson Rader. He says Norman Mailer was so enamored with the cowboy hat that Mailer asked to borrow it for a costume party and never returned it. After the novelist's death, in 2007, his widow, Norris Church, returned the hat. Mailer had instructed her to do so because "I won't be needing it anymore."

110 *"The cowboy of American legend was a figure"*: Simon & Schuster 1965 publicity brochure, DEL.

110 *Williams described Brando as . . . a "regular midnight cowboy"*: Darwin Porter, *Brando Unzipped* (New York: Blood Moon Productions, 2006), p. 161.

111 *Grace Herlihy told her son . . . the book was pornographic*: JLH to Leo Lerman, Sept. 1, 1965, Lerman Papers, Columbia University archives.

111 *a capsule review and a quick kiss-off*: Martin Levin, "A Reader's Report," *NYT Book Review*, Aug. 22, 1965.

111 *"Do we still need another dumb brute hero?"*: Stanley Kauffmann, "Queer Lives," *NYRB*, Nov. 11, 1965.

111 *"an appalling story, told with great skill"*: Emile Capouya, "Love Is Where You Find It," *Saturday Review*, Aug. 28, 1965.

111 *"it was in the zeitgeist"*: Author's interview with Mart Crowley.

112 *"to write truthfully of what he knows"*: Stanley Kauffmann, "Homosexual Drama and Its Disguises," *NYT*, Jan. 23, 1966.

113 *"I can't get past the second page"*: Kaffe Fassett, *Dreaming in Color: An Autobiography* (New York: Stewart, Tabori & Change, 2012), p. 82.

8. THE PRODUCER

114 *"ignorance is a tremendous asset"*: "Dialogue on Film: Jerome Hellman," *American Film*, June 1978, p. 39.

114 *"I know what it's like to be lonely"*: William J. Mann, *Edge of Midnight: The Life of John Schlesinger* (New York: Billboard Books, 2005), p. 268.

114 *"He thought the idea was terrible"*: Ibid., p. 269.

115 *"I don't really like the material"*: Jerome Hellman in *Waldo Salt: A Screenwriter's Journey*, American Masters, outtakes, Sept. 22, 1988, Motion Picture Academy Film Archive.

116 *"a life-long depressive who expected everything to end badly"*: Jerome Hellman, "The Making of *Midnight Cowboy*: A Personal Memoir," unpublished manuscript, p. 1, HELM.

116 *"I always had my own struggle"*: Author's interview with Jerome Hellman.

117   *"It was a golden time in my life"*: Ibid.

117   *Joe Buck might be a great role for Elvis Presley*: Lee Langley, "Midnight Mirage," *Guardian Arts*, Sept. 4, 1969; columnist Mark Steyn said JRS told him the studio had proposed Sammy Davis Jr. for Ratso. See Steve Sailer, "Alternative History, Movie-Casting Division," Aug. 10, 2015, www.unz.com/steve/topics /movies/2015/08/10/.

118   *reaching out to [Levine, Stark, and] Landau*: JRS to Hellman, April 15, 1966, and Hellman to Peter Gregson, March 12, 1966, BFI.

118   *"The lunatics have taken charge"*: Steven Bach, *Final Cut: Dreams and Disaster in the Making of* Heaven's Gate (New York: New American Library, 1985), p.15.

118   *UA had one major advantage . . . it didn't actually own anything*: Ibid., p. 42.

119   *"We reached out to filmmakers"*: Author's interview with David Picker.

120   *"the action goes steadily downhill"*: Leonard Sloane, "Anatomy of a Movie: Still Risky," *NYT*, Aug. 3, 1969.

120   *a preliminary budget "not to exceed one million dollars"*: UA contract, Nov. 30, 1966, p. 3, HELM.

121   *"We enjoyed a gossipy meal"*: JRS "Introduction," 1998, p. v, HELM.

121   *Schulman . . . thought Joe Buck an uninteresting clod*: Hellman to JRS, April 28, 1966, HELM.

121   The Connection *was "exciting, dangerous, instructive, and terrifying"*: Jack Gelber obituary, *NYT*, May 10, 2003.

122   *they decided to hire him*: Jack Gelber contract, Sept. 1, 1966, HELM.

122   *"Now Joe," she pleads, "don't hold it against me"*: Jack Gelber, "The Midnight Cowboy," first draft, p. 65, NYU.

123   *"I know this is not going to work out"*: Ibid., p. 86.

123   *"If this doesn't work, then we have nothing"*: JRS to Hellman, Jan. 3, 1967, HELM.

123   *"I feel we are still far away from the character"*: JRS, "The Midnight Cowboy Notes on a Second Draft Script," July 18, 1967, p. 11, SALT.

124   *"we have no choice but to try again with a new writer"*: Hellman to Gelber, July 24, 1967, NYU.

124   *"if we didn't get a writer soon, John would walk out"*: Author's interview with Hellman.

124   *"Whenever John was up, he loved I was doing this movie"*: Ibid.

125   *Litto begged Hellman . . . "Read it"*: "Producing *Midnight Cowboy*: A Talk with Jerome Hellman," *Scenario*, Winter 1997, p. 94.

125   *"the same staccato, multilayered visual treatment"*: Hellman, "The Making of *Midnight Cowboy*," p. 12.

125   *"I kept staring at them without meaning to"*: Waldo Salt: A Screenwriter's Journey.

125   *"the screenplay seems to miss the exciting potential of the novel"*: Salt, "Notes on *Midnight Cowboy*," p. 1, SALT.

125 It *"tells the story of a young man's search"*: Ibid.

126 *"Much impressed Waldo Salt notes"*: JRS telegram to Hellman, Aug. 26, 1967, HELM.

126 *"I was depressed out of my skull"*: JRS audio interview with Richard Jewell and James Wagner, USC archive, April 9, 1974.

126 *"I wasn't a perfect producer"*: Author's interview with Hellman.

9. THE SCREENWRITER

127 *"A writer is someone to whom writing comes harder"*: Thomas Mann, "Tristan," in *Death in Venice and Seven Other Stories* (New York: Vintage Books, 1963), pp. 349–50.

127 *"the sort of man who carries his history in his face"*: *Waldo Salt: A Screenwriter's Journey Collection* outtakes, Academy of Motion Picture Arts and Sciences Film Archive, Hollywood.

127 *"the prettiest girls at Stanford were there"*: Waldo Salt, Marvin Borowsky Lecture in Screenwriting, transcript, Oct. 21, 1981, p. 13, SALT.

128 *"oh yes, an expensive record changer"*: *NYT,* Dec. 7, 1973.

128 *"Dialogue can drive people right out of the movie theater"*: Salt, Marvin Borowsky Lecture, p. 24.

129 *"We're all born with essential needs"*: *Waldo Salt: A Screenwriter's Journey.*

129 *Salt insisted she get the sole screenwriting credit*: Patrick McGilligan and Paul Buhle, eds., *Tender Comrades: A Backstory of the Hollywood Blacklist* (Minneapolis: University of Minnesota Press, 2012 [paperback ed.]), p. 637.

129 *Salt was a true believer*: see Larry Ceplair, "Mary Davenport Oral History," UCLA, Dec. 12, 1990.

130 *"it's like being on the battlefield"*: Ibid, p. 23.

130 *Jack Warner . . . ordered him to fire Salt immediately*: Salt, Marvin Borowsky Lecture, p. 22.

131 *"Hollywood was like a ghost town"*: Ceplair, "Mary Davenport Oral History," p. 29.

131 *"This committee has attacked my whole life"*: "Statement—Waldo Salt," n.d., SALT.

131 *"I was very young . . . but you could see it killing him"*: *Waldo Salt: A Screenwriter's Journey* outtakes.

132 *"he was cranky and difficult and erratic"*: Author's interview with Jennifer Salt.

132 *"a devastating revelation"*: Ceplair, "Mary Davenport Oral History," p. 38.

133 *"I am one of your greatest fans here"*: Peggy Phillips letter to Waldo Salt, Nov. 18, 1957, SALT.

133 *"All questions cheerfully answered"*: Waldo Salt to Kathryn (no last name), July 27, 1956, SALT.

133 *"This opportunity was very important"*: Ring Lardner Jr. in *Waldo Salt: A Screenwriter's Journey*.

134 *"My dad . . . thought every day was his birthday"*: Author's interview with Jennifer Salt.

134 *"if I go on this way . . . I cannot possibly survive"*: Davenport to Waldo Salt, n.d., SALT.

134 *"I think my mother was just completely shattered"*: Author's interview with Jennifer Salt.

135 *"three of the worst pictures ever made"*: *Waldo Salt: A Screenwriter's Journey*.

136 *"He didn't sound like the man I knew"*: Deborah Salt in *Waldo Salt: A Screenwriter's Journey* outtakes, Feb. 10, 1989.

136 *"He really did hit bottom"*: Author's interview with Jennifer Salt.

136 *"it really set me back on my heels"*: *Waldo Salt: A Screenwriter's Journey*.

137 *"Do you want to work with this guy?"*: interview with Waldo Salt, Aug. 31, 1973, USC.

137 *"Waldo seemed wise, intense, and biblical"*: Jerome Hellman, "The Making of *Midnight Cowboy*: A Personal Memoir," p. 14.

137 *"Why the fuck did you flash back here?"*: Salt, Marvin Borowsky Lecture, p. 28.

138 *"Writing doesn't take any time at all"*: Author's interview with Jerome Hellman.

138 *"It was a very difficult relationship"*: JRS in *Waldo Salt: A Screenwriter's Journey* outtakes, Sept. 22, 1988.

138 *"They could quickly have come to blows"*: Author's interview with Hellman.

138 Waldo *"always had a long-suffering smile"*: JRS in *Waldo Salt: A Screenwriter's Journey* outtakes.

138 *"a very strong, very powerful, and very moving book"*: Salt, Marvin Borowsky Lecture, p 24.

139 *"there should be conflict and mistrust"*: Waldo Salt, "Continuity Notes on Ratso-Joe Sequence," Nov. 29, 1967, SALT.

139 *"He's not ready for a commitment to anyone or anything"*: Ibid., p. 2.

139 *"Joe's illusions are . . . the absurd reality of our time"*: Waldo Salt, "Notes on *Midnight Cowboy*," p. 1.

139 *"a world of king-size illusion"*: Ibid., p. 2.

140 *"The Perry story is quite unnecessary"*: Waldo Salt, "Editing and Revision Notes for *Midnight Cowboy*," Jan. 11, 1968, SALT.

141 *"The memos are beautiful"*: Author's interview with Jennifer Salt.

142 *"Oh, shit, he's going to be a nightmare"*: Author's interview with Michael Childers.

142 *"They saw me as a toy boy"*: Ibid.

143 *"Is that a John Wayne western?"*: Ibid.

144 *"I kept him grounded"*: Ibid.

144 *Jacobs told him that the screenplay was a disaster*: Author's interview with Hellman.

10. FUN CITY

145 *"The question now is whether we can continue to survive"*: "John Lindsay's Ten Plagues," *Time*, Nov. 1, 1968.

145 *"It was extraordinary . . . A tough, torching script"*: David V. Picker, *Musts, Maybes, and Nevers: A Book About the Movies* (CreateSpace, 2013 [Kindle ed.]), pp. 61–62.

145 *"I was irritated to say the least"*: Ibid., pp. 62–63.

145 *"You learn to trust people until you know who you can't"*: Author's interview with David Picker.

146 *dinner with the young director Francis Ford Coppola*: Hellman to JRS, Feb. 7, 1967, BFI.

146 *seventy thousand tons of garbage*: Nat Hentoff, *A Political Life: The Education of John V. Lindsay* (New York: Knopf, 1969), p. 201.

147 *"It was a perfect storm"*: Author's interview with Kenneth T. Jackson.

147 *"I still think it's a fun city"*: *New York Herald Tribune*, Jan. 7, 1966.

148 *"The ordinary New York resident . . . is constantly on trial"*: Hentoff, *A Political Life*, p. 316.

148 *the specter of urban unrest*: for a summary of 1967 unrest, see Vincent Cannato, *The Ungovernable City: John V. Lindsay and the Struggle to Save New York* (New York: Basic Books, 2002), pp. 132–36.

149 *"This nation doesn't give a damn"*: Hentoff, *A Political Life*, p. 333.

149 *the orders to take up "hats and bats"*: Mark Reynolds, "Hats and Bats," in Paul Cronin, ed., *A Time to Stir: Columbia '68* (New York: Columbia University Press, 2018), pp. 274–75.

149 *"Artists have been breaking sex taboos"*: Robert Hofler, *Sexplosion: From Andy Warhol to A Clockwork Orange—How a Generation of Pop Rebels Broke All the Taboos* (New York: Harper Collins, 2014), p. xii.

150 *Myra's voice "was actually that of Anaïs Nin"*: Gore Vidal, *Palimpsest: A Memoir* (New York: Random House, 1995), p. 108.

150 *"I was sort of a crusader"*: Hofler, *Sexplosion*, p. 49.

151 *"New York went from hosting only two feature films . . . in 1965 to 366"*: Stanley Corkin, *Starring New York: Filming the Grime and the Glamour of the Long 1970s* (New York: Oxford University Press, 2011), p. 6.

152 *"He used to sit around with his pockets bulging"*: Author's interview with Jerome Hellman.

152 *Smaller, more mobile cameras and faster film stock*: Corkin, *Starring New York*, p. 5.

153 *"The movies have captured the soul of this city"*: Pauline Kael, "Urban Gothic," *The New Yorker*, Oct. 30, 1971, p. 113.

154 *Marion . . . was born outside Hollidaysburg, Pennsylvania*: For details of her early

years, see Marion Dougherty with Robert Roussel, *My Casting Couch Was Too Short* (Xlibris, 2015 [Kindle ed.]).

155   *"I think I understood about every third or fourth sentence"*: Ibid., p. 59.

155   *"Appealing, clean-cut American kid"*: Ibid., p. 347.

155   *"Marc Merson had simply erased my name"*: Ibid., p. 63.

155   *"eager, gifted, prominent-nosed, pompadour-haired kid"*: Ibid., pp. 65–66.

156   *"It was an actor in training"*: Ralph Senensky interviewed in *Casting By* documentary.

156   *"I was so bad I was physically sick"*: Jon Voight, ibid.

156   *"Hollywood had no idea what casting was all about"*: Marion Dougherty, ibid.

156   *"Lumet didn't want me"*: "Robert Redford: *The Old Man and the Gun* Interview" HWD, *Vanity Fair* online, Sept. 28, 2018.

157   *"Casting is a game of gut instinct"*: *NYT*, Dec. 8, 2011.

158   *She hired only women to work in her office*: Author's interview with Juliet Taylor.

158   *"Marion would say it's because we don't get paid enough"*: Ibid.

158   *"so you don't look too Jewish"*: Dougherty with Roussel, *My Casting Couch Was Too Short*, p. 95.

159   *Picker . . . learned not to mess with Marion Dougherty*: David V. Picker, *Musts, Maybes, and Nevers: A Book About the Movies* (CreateSpace, 2013 [Kindle ed.]), pp. 101–102.

159   *"Marion's phone was ringing off the hook"*: Author's interview with Taylor.

II. THE VOICE OF HIS GENERATION

160   *"Actors are a much hardier breed"*: Lillian and Helen Ross, *The Player: A Profile of an Art* (New York: Simon & Schuster), 1962, p. 297.

160   *"one of the most agile and subtly controlled comedians"*: Fremont-Smith, *NYT*, Oct. 17, 1966; and Kerr, Nov. 6, 1966.

160   *"Everything about him struck me"*: Jerome Hellman, "The Making of *Midnight Cowboy*: A Personal Memoir," p. 23.

161   "thatched-roof hair": "The Moonchild and the Fifth Beatle," *Time*, Feb. 7, 1969.

161   *"They were so young, so poor"*: Author's interview with Ron Hoffman.

161   *"two people who should not have had children"*: Meg Grant, "Just Dustin," *AARP The Magazine*, March/April 2009.

161   *"Those were unpleasant moments"*: Author's interview with Ron Hoffman.

162   *"It's like gym—nobody flunks"*: Author's interview with Dustin Hoffman.

162   *"I remember seeing a guy pissing on the tire of a bus"*: Author's interview with Dustin Hoffman.

162   *"Any actor who was around then was driven"*: Author's interview with Robert Walden.

163 *Duvall was a favorite of Meisner's, who called him "the next Marlon Brando"*: Judith Slawson, *Robert Duvall: Hollywood Maverick* (New York: St. Martin's, 1985), p. 15.

163 *"Barbra Streisand in drag"*: Richard Meryman, "Before They Were Kings," *Vanity Fair*, March 2004.

163 *"Be an actor? You're too homely"*: Author's interview with Ron Hoffman.

163 *"he's very hostile but talented"*: Author's interview with Dustin Hoffman.

163 *Dustin "had more girls than Namath ever had"*: "The Moonchild and the Fifth Beatle," *Time*, Feb. 7, 1969.

164 *"He liked to dance around the third rail"*: Walden email to author, Jan. 31, 2019.

164 *"There was dignity in being unemployed"*: Author's interview with Dustin Hoffman.

164 *"Marion got him every lead psycho part"*: Ibid.

165 *"his big nose . . . never seemed to get unstuffed"*: Arthur Miller, *Timebends: A Life* (New York: Grove Press, 1987), p. 373.

166 *"Suddenly you didn't have to look like Robert Redford"*: Author's interview with Walden.

166 *his dream role was to play Adolf Hitler*: *NYT*, July 14, 1968.

166 *how he lost his virginity at age sixteen*: *Columbia Daily Spectator*, April 25, 1968.

166 *"I'm not a celluloid fluke"*: Paul Wilkes, "The Burden of Making Dustin Shine," *New York*, Nov. 25, 1968.

166 *"He didn't sign up for any of that"*: Author's interview with Ron Hoffman.

167 *"I got so upset to prove them wrong"*: Marion Dougherty with Robert Roussel, *My Casting Couch Was Too Short*, p. 132.

167 *"this English fuck suddenly doesn't think I'm right"*: Hoffman speech at "John Schlesinger: A Life in Film," May 19, 2002, BAFTA Los Angeles Archive.

167 *"the Maxim's of the disenfranchised"*: Frank J. Prial, "When a Nickel Opened Doors," *NYT*, April 8, 2003.

168 *"I remember him saying, 'You fit in quite well'"*: Author's interview with Dustin Hoffman.

168 *"Hoffman started limping along Forty-second Street"*: Ian Buruma, *Conversations with John Schlesinger* (New York: Random House, 2006), p. 104.

169 *Hoffman . . . asked him if he thought he might get married*: Peter Biskind, "Midnight Revolution," *Vanity Fair*, April 2010.

169 *"See if you can get double"*: Author's interview with Dustin Hoffman.

169 *"I made you a star, and you're going to throw it all away?"*: Biskind, "Midnight Revolution."

169 *"I remember specifically watching one guy"*: Denis Hamill, "Hats Off to *Midnight Cowboy* at 25," *City Lights Magazine*, New York *Daily News*, Feb. 2, 1994.

170   *"We're always running scared—actors, writers"*: Author's interview with Dustin Hoffman.

170   *"They weren't all heroes—some of them were kapos"*: Ibid.

170   *"Once I figured it out, it was easy"*: Ibid.

12. THE GOLF PRO'S SON

171   *"All leading men and women should have something unpredictable"*: Elia Kazan, *A Life* (New York: Knopf, 1988), p. 146.

171   *Warren Beatty . . . "was desperate to play the part"*: AFI Seminar with JRS, Oct. 3, 1979, p. 2.

171   *The man who . . . jumped to the top of their list was Kiel Martin*: AFI Seminar with JRS, Oct. 27, 1998, p. 7.

172   *"I'm up for a big role," he told Voight*: Author's interview with Jon Voight.

173   *"How would you like to meet John Schlesinger?"*: Ibid.

173   *"No one starts at the top in the theater"*: Richard Meryman, "Before They Were Kings," *Vanity Fair*, March 2004.

173   *"We could sense Dad's severe disappointment"*: Jess Cook Jr., "Jon Voight: The Uneasy Winner," *NYT Magazine*, April 29, 1975.

174   *"Once I made the decision . . . I was at peace"*: Author's interview with Voight.

174   *"With Jon everything is up for question"*: Cook, "The Uneasy Winner."

174   *"He was so confident of his acting"*: Author's interview with Jennifer Salt.

174   *"I wasn't a man yet"*: Author's interview with Voight.

175   *"I can cry seventeen different ways"*: AFI Seminar with Voight, April 11, 1973, pp. 40–41.

175   *"Maybe I was really scared"*: Author's interview with Voight.

176   *"Voight and I saw each other every single day"*: Author's interview with Dustin Hoffman.

176   *"My God, the girls loved him"*: Peter Biskind, "Midnight Revolution."

177   *"I said, 'John, he's a brilliant actor'"*: Author's interview with Dustin Hoffman.

177   *Dougherty wrote "very possible" next to Voight's name*: *Midnight Cowboy* casting file, Dougherty Papers, MHL.

177   *"He just didn't seem to me . . . the physical image"*: Mark Shivas, "*Cowboy* Director Had a Blind Spot," *Sixteen*, April 12, 1970.

177   *"This boy is lonely, that's the essence"*: Author's interview with Voight.

178   *"How long's it been since you been on a horse, cowboy?"*: "*Midnight Cowboy*: Jon Voight Screen Test," Feb. 18, 1968, BFI.

179   *"You guys are making a terrible mistake"*: Marion Dougherty with Robert Roussel, *My Casting Couch Was Too Short*, p. 133.

179   *She told him that Sarrazin was too pretty*: Ibid.

179 *"I was devastated"*: Author's interview with Voight.

180 *"That was then . . . Now it's real"*: Jerome Hellman, "The Making of *Midnight Cowboy*: A Personal Memoir," p. 27.

180 *"Why are you going for that pretty boy"*: Author's interview with Michael Childers.

180 *"I found myself looking at Jon"*: Author's interview with Dustin Hoffman.

180 *"Okay, is this for real . . . ?"*: Author's interview with Jerome Hellman.

180 *"I didn't even want Jon Voight"*: Dougherty with Roussel, *My Casting Couch Was Too Short*, p. 134.

180 *he tore his phone off the wall*: Judy Klemesrud, "A Good Roommate Is Hard to Find," *NYT*, Dec. 20, 1970.

181 *"I didn't tell anybody I was an actor"*: *David Frost Show*, March 9, 1970.

181 *"He drove us all mad"*: JRS interview by Gene Phillips, *Film Comment*, May–June 1975.

181 *"Jon, I think you can take it up an octave"*: Author's interview with Voight.

182 *"He's not a coarse person"*: Ibid.

182 *"Every bum has a buddy"*: Rex Reed, "A 'Cowboy' Walks on the Wild Side," *NYT*, May 25, 1969.

182 *"He struggled with a lot of guilt"*: Author's interview with Jennifer Salt.

182 *"I believed in it so much"*: Author's interview with Voight.

13. THE ARMIES OF THE NIGHT

183 *"What the phuque am I doing?"*: JLH to MCR, Aug. 21, 1968, DEL.

183 *"To put it bluntly, I think you need ME"*: JLH to JRS, Feb. 10, 1968, BFI.

184 *John wrote back three weeks later*: JRS to JLH, March 1, 1968, Ibid.

184 *"I didn't like what was happening"*: Jeannette Smyth, "From Cowboy to Witch," *Washington Post*, May 12, 1971.

184 *"Have you seen what your country is doing?"*: Kay Bonetti, "Interview with James Leo Herlihy," April 1982 (Columbia, MO: American Audio Prose Library audiocassette).

185 *Their stated intention was to levitate . . . the 3.7-million-square-foot building*: see Norman Mailer, *The Armies of the Night: History as a Novel, The Novel as History* (New York: New American Library, 1968), pp. 117–25.

185 *"I like doing this"*: JLH to MCR, no date, DEL.

185 *"believed in technology . . . but also believed in LSD"*: Mailer, *The Armies of the Night*, p. 103.

185 *"Yesterday I had a most difficult day"*: JLH to MCR, Aug. 21, 1968, DEL.

186 *"I saw this whole new generation coming up"*: Smyth, "Cowboy to Witch."

186 *St. Marks Place was emerging as the eastern pole*: See Ada Calhoun, *St. Marks Is*

Dead: The Many Lives of America's Hippest Street (New York: W. W. Norton, 2016), pp. 127–39.

186 *in winter the plumbing froze*: Hannah Arendt, "Remembering W. H. Auden," *The New Yorker*, Jan. 20, 1975.

187 *"night-time was prime time on the Lower East Side"*: Joshua Furst, *Revolutionaries* (New York: Knopf, 2019), p. 69.

187 *"too many of them found permanent trouble"*: Pete Hamill, *Downtown: My Manhattan* (New York: Little, Brown, 2004), p. 210.

187 *Linda Fitzpatrick, an eighteen-year-old high school dropout*: See J. Anthony Lukas, "The Two Worlds of Linda Fitzpatrick," *NYT*, Oct. 16, 1967. Lukas expanded this account in *Don't Shoot—We Are Your Children!* (New York: Random House, 1968).

188 *"a violent experience, knives etc."*: JLH to MCR, n.d., DEL.

188 *"Manhattan today upsets me too much"*: Martha MacGregor, "This Week in Books," *New York Post*, April 24, 1971.

189 *"Not bad Greyhound bus terminal"*: JRS location memo, March 5, 1968, BFI.

189 *"We didn't take a day out of the schedule"*: USC Panel with JRS, Hellman, and Voight, Feb. 17, 1994, USC film archives. See also Hellman to Picker, March 7, 1968, "Attached is our budget," with bottom line total $2,041,560, BFI.

14. PREPARATION

190 *"John just had that glint in his eye"*: "Celebrating Schlesinger" featurette for *Midnight Cowboy* Collector's Edition DVD, 2006.

191 *"It had everything to do with wit"*: Author's interview with Ann Roth.

191 *"Edith Head . . . had an army of people under her"*: Author's interview with Isis Mussenden.

192 *"I outfitted everybody"*: Author's interview with Roth. The recounting of her outfitting of Hoffman and Voight is also from Author's interview.

194 *"It was an enormous influence"*: Author's interview with Mussenden.

194 *Holender had come to New York to create a new life*: The description of his life in Poland and New York is from author's interview with Adam Holender.

196 *John liked him right away*: Author's interview with Jerome Hellman.

197 *"It was a constant battle"*: Author's interview with Holender.

197 *his wife . . . told him he'd be crazy not to take the part*: Marion Dougherty with Robert Roussel, *My Casting Couch Was Too Short*, p. 135.

198 *"I was fairly naïve and inexperienced"*: Author's interview with Bob Balaban.

198 *"we wore hooded sweatshirts . . . you couldn't even see my face"*: Author's interview with Jennifer Salt.

199   *"Marion knew where the good New York actors were"*: Author's interview with Hellman.

199   *Lois Smith "gave a damn good reading"*: "Casting Cards Female (S–U)," Dougherty Papers, MHL.

199   *Vaccaro had been born in Brooklyn*: Author's interview with Brenda Vaccaro.

200   *a friend . . . told her she was "born to play Cass Trehune"*: John Stark, "Actress Sylvia Miles' Biggest Fan Is Sylvia Miles," *People*, Oct. 10, 1988.

200   *a horror flick called* Psychomania: Sylvia Miles, "Miles per Hour," *Soho Weekly News*, Jan. 17, 1980.

201   *"I was gonna get that part if it killed me"*: "After Midnight: Reflecting on the Classic 35 Years Later," 2004 documentary, *Midnight Cowboy* Collector's Edition DVD, 2006.

201   *"There was a lot of electricity in the air"*: Peter Biskind, "Midnight Revolution."

202   *"It's in the book"*: Author's interview with Dustin Hoffman.

202   *He also had acquired a set of false teeth*: Arthur Poster, "Dental Realism for Dustin Hoffman," *Journal of Dental Practice*, Oct. 1969. JRS and Hoffman were so impressed with Poster's work, they consulted him again in 1976 for the excruciating dental torture scene in *Marathon Man*.

202   *"I was so jealous of Dusty's ugly teeth"*: "After Midnight" documentary.

202   *"John, I don't even know what I sound like yet"*: Author's interview with Dustin Hoffman.

202   *"Is he gonna do that throughout the movie?"*: Ibid.

203   *Waldo "wasn't a prima donna about his lines"*: *Waldo Salt: A Screenwriter's Journey* outtakes, Sept. 28, 1988.

203   *"We transcribed what we recorded"*: JRS Interview with BBC, Aug. 19, 1994, BFI.

203   *"These guys were just beyond description"*: Waldo Salt, Marvin Borowsky Lecture in Screenwriting, transcript, Oct. 21, 1981, p. 22, SALT.

204   *Hoffman suggested adding a scene*: Douglas Brode, *The Films of Dustin Hoffman* (Secaucus, NJ: Citadel, 1983), p. 47.

204   *"we've got to have a scene where they're in bed together"*: Glenn Kenny, "John Schlesinger," *Premiere*, Oct. 2003.

204   *"He tests things, he goes that extra step"*: Biskind, "Midnight Revolution."

204   *"Jon was not a cool guy"*: Author's interview with Jennifer Salt.

204   *"Dustin was wonderful to work with"*: Author's interview with Jon Voight.

205   *"Quick—get in! We'll give you a ride"*: Daniel Chapman, "The Graduate Turns Bum," *Look*, Sept. 17, 1968.

205   *"She lifted up her T-shirt . . . 'Would you sign me?'"*: "Dustin Hoffman: *Larry King Live* (1994), Part 1 of 4," https://www.youtube.com/watch?v=gPUg1ssO0p0.

206 *"I don't think I could have dreamed that up"*: JRS Interview with BBC, Aug. 19, 1994, BFI.

206 *"You've got to see this!"*: *American Film*, Nov. 1987, p. 15.

206 *"the most extraordinary city in the world"*: Michael M. Riley, "I Both Hate and Love What I Do: An Interview with John Schlesinger," *Literature/Film Quarterly*, Spring 1978.

206 *"I tried to breathe into the film"*: Gene D. Phillips, *John Schlesinger* (Boston: Twayne, 1981), p. 126.

15. STOLEN SHOTS: THE NEW YORK FILM SHOOT

207 *"What if my mother sees my tits . . . ?"*: Author's interview with Brenda Vaccaro.

208 *John recognized . . . that Ratso was in good hands*: Author's interview with Jerome Hellman.

208 *"Jon is a tall fellow"*: Author's interview with Adam Holender.

209 *"What's my motivation?"*: Ian Buruma, *Conversations with John Schlesinger* (New York: Random House, 2006), p. 143.

209 *"This cabdriver tried to beat the signal"*: Author's interview with Dustin Hoffman. See also *Midnight Cowboy* draft script, Nov. 24, 1967, SALT.

210 *"It was the very essence of what I wanted to convey"*: Author's interview with Dustin Hoffman.

211 *"the rebirth of the Lower East Side"*: Charles G. Bennett, "Renewal Is Voted in East Side Area," *NYT*, July 23, 1965.

211 *"a fallow stretch of weed- and rat-ridden parking lots"*: Russ Buettner, "They Kept a Lower East Side Lot Vacant for Decades," *NYT*, March 21, 2014.

211 *the iconic still photograph of the two men in a doorway*: The site at 64–66 Suffolk Street was identified and photographed by Bob Egan for "25 Iconic New York City film locations," http://www.popspotsnyc.com/iconic_new_york_city_film _locations/. Egan also discovered the site across the street at 63–65 Suffolk where the iconic photo of Hoffman and Voight hovering in a blighted doorway was taken.

212 *"The absolute necessity to be authentically grungy"*: Lloyd Burlingame email to author, Jan. 23, 2018.

212 *"our young AD came unglued"*: Jerome Hellman, "The Making of *Midnight Cowboy*: A Personal Memoir," p. 40.

213 *He and John got along with a minimum of anxiety*: Author's interview with Burtt Harris.

213 *"We are ready for you, my queen"*: Author's interview with Dustin Hoffman.

213 *"Burtt was winging it"*: Author's interview with Holender.

213 *"John had expressed to me all his fears"*: Hostilities and discomfort between direc-

tor and crew were described in author's interviews with Hellman, Childers, and Holender.

214 *he grabbed a broom and smashed a series of lights*: JRS at USC panel, Feb. 17, 1994.

214 *he could "shoot this sucker with a couple of flashlights"*: Hellman, "The Making of *Midnight Cowboy*," p. 42.

215 *"The pressure was to do things faster"*: Author's interview with Holender.

215 *Balaban . . . says they shot his scenes in reverse chronological order*: Author's interview with Bob Balaban.

215 *"one of the most profoundly affecting and believable scenes"*: Hellman, "The Making of *Midnight Cowboy*," p. 50.

215 *Hughes took John aside and told him he was wearing false teeth*: Ibid., p. 49.

216 *"It was a pleasure to see two actors . . . feeding off each other"*: Author's interview with Holender.

216 *"We really did like each other"*: Author's interview with Dustin Hoffman.

216 *"That was something they did, not something I suggested"*: "Directing *Midnight Cowboy*: A Talk with John Schlesinger," *Scenario*, Winter 1997, p. 206.

217 "Mr. Hoffman, I paid for you!": Author's interview with Dustin Hoffman.

217 *"Well, you're pretty, I'll say that"*: "The Crowd Around the Cowboy," 1969 short film produced and directed by Jeri Sopanen, Criterion Collection, 2018.

218 *"I didn't like his fucking attitude"*: Author's interview with Vaccaro.

218 *"The pasties were driving me crazy"*: Ibid.

219 *"I think she should be fucked in fox"*: Author's interview with Ann Roth.

219 *As late as May 30 . . . Waldo was still producing new pages*: See Waldo Salt rewrites: "Notes on Cemetary (sp)," May 30; "Notes on Lunch Counter," May 30; revised pages for X-flat dialogue, July 18 and 20; revised opening scene, August 5. SALT.

219 *"Your scene isn't fucking working"*: *Waldo Salt: A Screenwriter's Journey* outtakes.

220 *"he was baggy-eyed and bloodshot"*: Author's interview with Jon Voight.

220 *"Joe's selfish . . . He's looking at Ratso as an inconvenience"*: *Waldo Salt: A Screenwriter's Journey*.

220 *"My dad had never had people who adored him"*: Author's interview with Jennifer Salt.

221 *Morrissey had the soul of a social worker*: Ultra Violet, *Famous for 15 Minutes: My Years with Andy Warhol* (New York: Harcourt Brace Jovanovich, 1988), p. 22.

221 *"everyone went to Max's"*: Andy Warhol and Pat Hackett, *POPism: The Warhol Sixties* (Orlando: Harcourt, 1980), p. 234.

222 *"John thought they were rather extraordinary freaks"*: Author's interview with Michael Childers.

222 *"There was always a party somewhere"*: Warhol and Hackett, *POPism*, p. 50.

222 *"We were seeing the future and we knew it for sure"*: Ibid.

222 *"Fame was the name of the game"*: Jean Stein, *Edie: An American Biography*, ed. George Plimpton (New York: Knopf, 1982), p. 197.

222 *"He'd just lick his chops and sit back and watch"*: Ibid., p. 204.

223 *"the spiritual father of AIDS"*: Ultra Violet, *Famous for 15 Minutes*, p. 2.

223 *"It's a bit like looking at a piece of art"*: Author's interview with Ronald Gregg.

224 *"The Iliad of the Underground"*: Jack Kroll, "Up from the Underground," *News-week*, Feb. 13, 1967.

224 *"What may be a provocative theme today"*: Picker to Canby, *NYT*, Jan. 5, 1967.

224 *"We were bitter at first"*: Ultra Violet, *Famous for 15 Minutes*, p. 114.

225 *"I was young . . . and very serious about my work"*: Author's interview with Paul Rossilli.

226 *Viva went around the . . . film set with a portable tape recorder*: Author's interview with Ann Skinner.

226 *"It was six days of wonderful mayhem"*: Author's interview with Burtt Harris.

226 *"The party scene got a little bit crazy"*: Author's interview with Vaccaro.

227 *"It fit perfectly into the film"*: Author's interview with Rossilli.

227 *"They're moving into our territory"*: Warhol and Hackett, *POPism*, p. 353.

228 *"We could have done it so* real *for them"*: Ibid.

16. NOSE CONES AND RATTLESNAKES: THE FLORIDA
AND TEXAS FILM SHOOTS

229 *"Do you really think anyone's going to pay money"*: Author's interview with Jon Voight.

229 *Manhattan had felt . . . like an oven with the dial turned to . . . broil*: JRS 1991 audio commentary, *Midnight Cowboy*, Criterion Collection Blu-Ray, 2018.

230 *"I loved the nose cones"*: Ibid.

230 *"Look, you guys don't understand. . . . they hate you"*: Adam Holender video essay with commentary, *Midnight Cowboy*, Criterion Collection Blu-Ray, 2018.

231 *Hoffman's nerves, like John's, seemed on edge*: Jerome Hellman, "The Making of *Midnight Cowboy*: A Personal Memoir," pp. 52–53.

231 *Hellman brought in a doctor to anesthetize his eyes*: JRS 1991 audio commentary.

232 *"I existed in the center of a big empty hole"*: Hellman, "The Making of *Midnight Cowboy*," p. 56.

232 *Big Spring . . . is located in the heart of West Texas*: See Bryan Mealer, *The Kings of Big Spring: God, Oil, and One Family's Search for the American Dream* (New York: Flatiron, 2018), pp. 36–38.

233 *"rodeo-type performers, gospel singers, a 45–50 year old Negro male musician"*: Ibid., p. 218.

233 *"none of the heavy hitters made the cut"*: Hellman, "The Making of *Midnight Cowboy*," p. 56.

233 *"people in town were scandalized and felt betrayed"*: Mealer, *The Kings of Big Spring*, p. 218.

233 *John . . . even had an underwater camera flown in*: John Neville, "Director Demands Reality," *Dallas Morning News*, Aug. 26, 1968.

234 *"It looked and sounded like Big Spring"*: Author's interview with Joel Mick.

234 *Carver wore a straw cowboy hat and a faded denim jacket*: Author's interview with Randall Carver.

235 *"They kept pulling my pants down further"*: Ibid.

236 *the house wasn't quite as empty as it looked*: For the rattlesnake story, see Hellman, "The Making of *Midnight Cowboy*," pp. 57–58.

236 *"the incompatibility of temperament"*: Waldo Salt Suit for Divorce, City of Juarez, Aug. 26, 1968, SALT.

237 *"everybody felt it would be best if he wasn't there"*: Author's interview with Jennifer Salt.

237 *"that was so humiliating I could not even discuss it"*: Ibid.

238 *Peckinpah said he wanted "the greatest rape scene ever"*: April Wolfe, "Rape Choreography Makes Films Safer but Still Takes a Toll on Cast and Crew," *L.A. Weekly*, July 11, 2017.

238 *"I felt a little raped"*: Ibid.

238 *"I needed to know that I had in fact been raped"*: Author's interview with J. Salt.

239 *Michael thought it could be a perfect metaphor*: Author's interview with Michael Childers.

239 *He told Burtt Harris to "get rid of them all"*: Panel discussion at USC, Feb. 17, 1994, USC.

240 *"He was red-faced and sweating and shaking"*: Author's interview with Voight, who described the scene.

17. IMAGES AND MUSIC

241 *Robertson "was a wonderful, talented editor"*: Author's interview with Irene Bowers.

242 *"Hugh Robertson was a catastrophe"*: Author's interview with Jerome Hellman.

242 *"an Englishman's view, not the real New York"*: Jim Clark, *Dream Repairman: Adventures in Film Editing* (Crockett, TX: LandMarc Press, 2010), p. 78.

242 *He later told . . . Marilyn Beck that the entire film shoot had been a disaster*: Marilyn Beck column, *L.A. Evening Citizen News*, April 15, 1970.

242 *"It was almost like a comedy routine"*: Author's interview with Adam Holender.

242 *"The more deeply John became involved"*: Jerome Hellman, "The Making of *Midnight Cowboy*: A Personal Memoir," p. 61, HELM.

242 *"the film editor's job can be a delicate psychological balancing act"*: Author's interview with Alan Heim.

243 *"I was forever touching up the corpses"*: Roy Perkins and Martin Stollery, *British Film Editors: The Heart of the Movie* (London: British Film Institute, 2004), p. 142.

243 *Many of them got their jobs through nepotism*: Declan McGrath, *Editing & Post-Production: Screencraft* (Cran-Pres-Celigny, Switzerland: RotoVision, 2001), p. 105.

243 *Clark had helped John turn it into a newsreel-style spectacle*: Perkins and Stollery, *British Film Editors*, p. 109.

244 *"Well, what are we going to do about this?"*: Clark, *Dream Repairman*, p. 124.

244 *"Little by little . . . we found a way"*: Ibid., p. 121.

245 *"These guys were high from morning til night"*: Jim Clark, "Notes re Cowboy" email to Hellman, July 24, 2003, HELM.

245 *"Clearly the white liberal period was over"*: Ibid.

245 *"Will it work? Will anyone want to see it?"*: Ibid.

246 *"I didn't save the film because it didn't need saving"*: Ibid., plus Clark, *Dream Repairman*, p. 78.

246 *"I will not see a first cut . . . without a temporary score"*: JRS to Neil Brand, May 15, 1996, BFI.

246 *In the pile of new albums . . . was Aerial Ballet*: Author's interview with Michael Childers.

247 *Fred Neil, an equally obscure New York singer-songwriter*: See the Fred Neil chapter in Richie Unterberger, *Urban Spacemen and Wayfaring Strangers: Overlooked Innovators and Eccentric Visionaries of '60s Rock* (San Francisco: Miller Freeman Books, 2000).

247 *"Fred had the flow"*: Bob Dylan, *Chronicles: Volume One* (New York: Simon & Schuster, 2004), p. 10.

248 *"an incredible swinging genius"*: Author's interview with John Sebastian.

248 *"Freddie would go to the club fucked up"*: Unterberger, *Urban Spacemen and Wayfaring Strangers*, p. 265.

248 *Cohen pleaded with him to come up with one more song*: David Browne, "The Echoes of His Mind Just Keep Reverberating," *NYT*, Nov. 24, 2006.

249 *"It has that Fred quality of uncertainty"*: Author's interview with Sebastian.

249 *"I'm going where the sun keeps shining"*: Fred Neil, "Everybody's Talkin'."

249 *"I could hear there was something special there"*: Author's interview with Rick Jarrard.

249 *Nilsson had been kicking around the L.A. music scene*: See Alyn Shipton, *Nilsson: The Life of a Singer-Songwriter* (New York: Oxford University Press, 2013).

250 *Jarrard . . . was sure he had another hit*: Author's interview with Jarrard.

251 *Even Bob Dylan showed up at Jerry's apartment*: Hellman, "The Making of *Midnight Cowboy*," p. 67, and author's interview with Hellman.

251 *"anybody can write a song like that"*: Eddi Fiegel, *John Barry: A Sixties Theme: From James Bond to* Midnight Cowboy (London: Constable, 1998), p. 226.

251 *"It was just impossible" to top "Everybody's Talkin'"*: John Barry interview in "Listen to the Movie," on *Teen Sounds*, Belgian TV pop music program, n.d., https://www.youtube.com/watch?time_continue=3233&v=vj9OZsfz5D0.

252 *songs that . . . "could embrace the various aspects of the New York scene"*: Fiegel, *John Barry*, p. 225.

252 *"I ran movies . . . I sold ice cream"*: Michael Schelle, *The Score: Interviews with Film Composers* (Los Angeles: Silman-James Press, 1999), pp. 6–7.

253 *"It's vulgar, it's wonderful!"*: Fiegel, *John Barry*, p. 7.

253 *"Goldfinger was John's big breakthrough"*: Author's interview with Jon Burlingame.

254 *"That harmonica theme was the soul of that character"*: Fiegel, *John Barry*, p. 227.

254 *Barry would later call . . . Schlesinger the most musically knowledgeable director*: John Barry interview in "Listen to the Movie."

254 *"essentially an A frame with a domed ceiling"*: For a description of the studio and Barry's creation of the *Midnight Cowboy* musical score, see Phil Ramone, *Making Records: The Scenes Behind the Music* (New York: Hyperion, 2007), pp. 136–40 (studio) and 226–30 (Barry).

255 *"My God! Where'd you get that music from?"*: Fiegel, *John Barry*, p. 226.

18. THE X RATING

256 *"We never saw a foot of dailies ever"*: Author's interview with David Picker.

257 *"We had zero money to do this"*: Author's interview with Adam Holender.

257 *Picker decided to invite the house—not just the top execs*: David Picker, *Musts, Maybes, and Nevers: A Book About the Movies* (CreateSpace, 2013), pp. 65–66.

257 *John gripped Jerry's arm tightly*: Jerome Hellman, "The Making of *Midnight Cowboy*: A Personal Memoir," p. 70, HELM.

258 *"It's a masterpiece"*: Picker, *Musts, Maybes, and Nevers*, p. 66.

258 *there was one infuriating problem*: The casting credit dispute is best recounted in Marion Dougherty with Robert Roussel, *My Casting Couch Was Too Short*, pp. 137–38, and in the *Casting By* documentary.

259 *"She said to me, 'Take it or leave it'"*: Author's interview with Jerome Hellman.

259 *"if ever a casting director earned a single-card credit"*: Hellman quoted in *Casting By*.

259 *"It just stuck in her craw for the rest of her life"*: Author's interview with Juliet Taylor.

259 *"I thought that was absolutely offensive"*: Author's interview with David Picker.

259 *"I am honored to say that John became a good friend"*: Dougherty with Roussel, *My Casting Couch Was Too Short*, p. 138.

260 *"Why'd you cut my best stuff out?"*: Author's interview with Dustin Hoffman.

260 *"He had a big black Cadillac and a driver named Joe"*: Author's interview with Ron Hoffman.

260 *"Dustin, when do you come into this movie?"*: Author's interview with Michael Childers.

261 *"Well, I think you'd better talk to him"*: Ian Buruma, *Conversations with John Schlesinger* (New York: Random House, 2006), p. 105.

261 *"He clearly was upset by something"*: Ibid.

261 *"people walked out in droves"*: "Dustin Hoffman: *Larry King Live, 1994*, Part 2 of 4," YouTube, https://www.youtube.com/watch?v=ViofIwot9BE.

261 *"the most veteran of audiences wound up in tears"*: "Home on the 42nd Street Range," *New York*, May 26, 1969.

261 to *"look like a respectable person"*: "Dustin Hoffman: *Larry King Live, 1994*, Part 2 of 4."

262 *"Oh my God, it's him"*: "The Moonchild and the Fifth Beatle," *Time*, Feb. 7, 1969.

262 *John and Jerry told versions of this story*: For one example, see Hellman letter to *LAT* reporter Amy Wallace, Aug. 12, 1999, where Jerry repeats the "cut one frame" claim and adds: "This we emphatically refused to do." JRS File, F 67, *Midnight Cowboy* Publicity, MHL.

262 *"the board came back with an R rating"*: Stephen Farber, *The Movie Rating Game* (Washington: Public Affairs Press, 1972), p. 85. Farber became a student member of the board the following year.

263 *"His mind was like a bear trap"*: Picker, *Musts, Maybes, and Nevers*, p. 19.

263 *"No one had won LBJ's trust and admiration more than Arthur Krim"*: Jack Valenti, *This Time, This Place: My Life in War, the White House, and Hollywood* (New York: Crown Archetype, 2007), p. 269.

263 *"an urbanely packaged man, with . . . the alertness of a fighter-pilot"*: Leonard Gross, "What's Blue at the Movies? Ask Dr. Stern," *LAT*, July 16, 1972.

264 *"Theirs is a choice born of fear"*: Aaron Stern, *Me: The Narcissistic American* (New York: Ballantine, 1979), p. 103.

264 Midnight Cowboy's *"homosexual frame of reference"*: Farber, *The Movie Rating Game*, pp. 85–86.

265 *"We watched the movie again and then everybody voted R"*: Author's interview with Stephen Farber.

265 *Farber and another former board member . . . wrote an op-ed piece*: Stephen Farber and Estelle Changas, "Putting the Hex on 'R' and 'X,'" *NYT*, April 9, 1972. Copies of letters to the *NYT* from Ernest Lehman, Sam Peckinpah, and Don Siegel, Stern's letter to Peckinpah requesting his support, and an exchange of letters between an apologetic Peckinpah and Farber are located in the "*Straw Dogs*—censorship" file in the Sam Peckinpah Papers at the MHL.

265 *"I once made the mistake of putting a psychiatrist in charge"*: Moira Hodgson, "Movie Ratings: Do They Serve Hollywood or the Public?" *NYT,* May 24, 1981.

265 *"a moment before the rating became a moral football"*: Kenneth Turan, "Why Joe Buck and Ratso Live On," *LAT,* Feb. 20, 1994.

266 *"a strong and at all times masterful story"*: James M. Skinner, *The Cross and the Cinema* (New York: Praeger, 1993), p. 174.

266 *"The quality was there, no question"*: Author's interview with Gabriel Sumner, who described UA's slow, careful marketing campaign.

267 *"They embraced like a pair of collaborationists"*: "Paul Krassner's Flicks and Kicks: Midnight Cowboy," *Cavalier,* n.d.

267 *"it turned out to be a really nice picture"*: Kay Bonetti, "Interview with James Leo Herlihy," April 1982 (Columbia, MO: American Audio Prose Library audio-cassette).

267 *"I wanted it out of the picture"*: Gregory King, "Herlihy's Modified Cowboy Rapture," *Variety,* May 4, 1971.

267 *"not a movie for the ages"*: Vincent Canby, "'Midnight Cowboy,'" *NYT,* May 26, 1969.

268 *"so extraordinarily good, and surprising"*: Archer Winston, "'Midnight Cowboy' at the Coronet," *New York Post,* May 26, 1969.

268 *"one of the . . . most melancholy love stories in the history of American film"*: Stefan Kanter, "Improbable Love Story," *Time,* May 30, 1969.

268 The *"spray of venom is just about overpowering"*: Pauline Kael, *New Yorker* capsule review. See also Ebert, July 5, 1969, at www.rogerebert.com/reviews/midnight -cowboy-1969; and Schickel review, quoted in Vito Russo, *The Celluloid Closet: Homosexuality in the Movies* (New York: Harper & Row, 1981), p. 82.

269 *"Schlesinger has understood the book"*: Stanley Kauffmann, "*Midnight Cowboy,* by John Schlesinger," *New Republic,* June 7, 1969.

269 *"It was a rare moment"*: "My Favorite Best Picture Oscar Winner," *The Guardian,* Feb. 20, 2017.

269 *"You've got to come down and see this"*: Author's interview with Childers.

269 *thirty-seven straight weeks at the Coronet*: *Variety,* April 15, 1970.

270 *"Dusty and the Duke"*: "Dusty and the Duke: The Life Styles of Two Very Different Heroes. Dustin Hoffman and John Wayne," photographed by John Dominis, *Life,* July 11, 1969.

270 *"an abundance of hair"*: Marilyn Bender, "There's a Show Outside, Too," *NYT,* Aug. 28, 1969.

19. THE MOVIE

272 *"a city of action, a place where things happen"*: James Sanders, *Celluloid Skyline: New York and the Movies* (New York: Knopf, 2001), p. 21.

273 *"Each of us had our own little play"*: Author's interview with Bob Balaban.

275 *Their domesticity comes to resemble a marriage*: For further exploration of this theme, see Caroline Madden, "The Queer Subtext of New Hollywood Era Biddy Movies," *Fandor*, June 28, 2018, https://www.fandor.com/posts/the -queer-subtext-of-new-hollywood-era-buddy-movies.

276 *Childers . . . argued it could easily turn viewers against Joe*: Author's interview with Michael Childers.

276 *John insisted that the scene remain*: Gene D. Phillips, *John Schlesinger* (Boston: Twayne, 1981), p. 123.

276 *"Dustin's a great comedian"*: "Midnight Cowboy Revisited," excerpt from 1994 documentary directed by Peter Fitzgerald, https://www.youtube.com/watch?v =BGR_mD9nW6g.

277 *"It's almost more comfortable for me to be Joe Buck"*: *David Frost Show*, Season 2, Episode 136, March 9, 1970, http://www.tv.com/shows/the-david-frost-show /march-9-1970-1272782/.

277 *"One thing I saw about Voight was the joy"*: Author's interview with Dustin Hoffman.

278 *"probably the most savage indictment against the City of New York"*: *Women's Wear Daily*, n.d.

279 *"John most admired humanist filmmakers"*: Author's interview with Ian Buruma.

279 *"These two actors . . . bring a level of sustained anguish"*: Lex Corbett, "The Inescapable Fever Dream of John Schlesinger's *Midnight Cowboy*," www .vaguevisages.com, Jan. 27, 2016.

280 *the movie isn't a story of liberation, pride, or self-esteem*: Mark Harris, "On the Fringe," *Midnight Cowboy*, Criterion Collection Blu-Ray essay, 2018.

280 *"Gay themes come without the slightest whiff of sensationalism"*: Matthew Kennedy, *Bay Area Reporter*, June 27, 2018, https://www.ebar.com/arts_&_culture /dvd//261802.

281 *"Bob and Paul really do have a chemistry"*: Vito Russo, *The Celluloid Closet: Homosexuality in the Movies* (New York: Harper & Row, 1981), pp. 81–82.

281 *"The film brought issues of male sexuality . . . to the fore"*: Gary Needham, "Hollywood Trade: *Midnight Cowboy* and Underground Cinema," in *The Hollywood Renaissance: Revisiting American Cinema's Most Celebrated Era*, ed. Peter Kramer and Yanni Tzioumakis (New York: Bloomsbury, 2018), p. 131.

282 *"The protagonists . . . may not necessarily have a sexual desire"*: Madden, "The Queer Subtext of New Hollywood Era Biddy Movies," *Fandor*.

282 *"I'm not concerned about gay lore"*: *The Village Voice*, June 30, 1975. It's worth noting that when ABC televised *Midnight Cowboy* in prime time in August 1974, it cut anything that even hinted at sexual contact—twenty-three minutes

in all. Still, Richard Glitter, director for standards and practices at ABC, insisted the movie's "integrity [was] preserved." See *Variety*, Aug. 28 and Nov. 6, 1974.

283 *loosely based on John Schlesinger's own two-year . . . affair with John Steiner*: Author's interview with Childers.

284 *"Gay characters . . . had to that point almost always been depicted as deviants"*: Ian Buruma, "*Sunday Bloody Sunday*: Something Better," for *Sunday Bloody Sunday*, Criterion Collection DVD, 2012.

284 *"alternative sexuality was taken for granted"*: Russo, *The Celluloid Closet*, p. 209.

284 *"Is this really necessary?"*: Murray Head at a BFI screening, Aug. 21, 2017.

284 *"I just thought it was a kiss and a very pleasant thing"*: Ibid.

284 *"I just closed my eyes and thought of England"*: Russo, *The Celluloid Closet*, p. 214.

285 *"they were obviously embarrassed"*: Ian Buruma, *Conversations with John Schlesinger* (New York: Random House, 2006), pp. 115–16.

285 *"probably the best thing I've ever done"*: Michael M. Riley, "'I Both Love and Hate What I Do': An Interview with John Schlesinger," *Literature/Film Quarterly*, Spring 1978.

285 "Midnight Cowboy . . . *captured the energy of America*": Author's interview with Glenda Jackson.

286 "Sunday Bloody Sunday *saved my life*": William J. Mann, *Edge of Midnight: The Life of John Schlesinger* (New York: Billboard Books, 2005), p. 374.

286 *"this film is not about the sexuality of these people"*: Michelle Wolfe and Alfred P. Kielwasser, eds., *Gay People, Sex, and the Media* (New York: Routledge, 2013), p. 28.

286 *"I think* Sunday Bloody Sunday *is a masterpiece"*: Roger Ebert, Jan. 1, 1971, https://www.rogerebert.com/reviews/sunday-bloody-sunday-1971.

20. EXPLOSIONS

287 *a different kind of revolution took place*: For a well-documented account of the Stonewall riots see Lillian Faderman, *The Gay Revolution: The Story of the Struggle* (New York: Simon & Schuster, 2015), pp. 171–86. She in turn relies heavily on two eyewitness *Village Voice* reports: Lucian Truscott IV, "Gay Power Comes to Sheridan Square," and Howard Smith, "Full Moon over Stonewall," July 3, 1969.

289 *"Homo Nest Raided"*: New York *Daily News*, July 6, 1969.

289 *Waldo Salt, whom John and Jerry had rewarded*: Hellman note to Morton Leavy, April 2, 1969. HELM.

289 *"This was a vast fortune for me"*: Kaffe Fassett, *Dreaming in Color: An Autobiography* (New York: Stewart, Tabori & Chang, 2012), p. 82, and letter to Hellman, Nov. 20, 1970, HELM.

289 *"Does anyone feel we should take back points? . . . "*: Author's interviews with Jerome Hellman and David Picker.

290 *"cult film . . . that rings true to the audience's vision"*: Pauline Kael, "The Bottom of the Pit," *New Yorker*, Sept. 27, 1969.

290 *"every studio in town was narcotized"*: Joan Didion, "In Hollywood," in *The White Album* (New York: Simon & Schuster, 1979), p. 159.

291 *"a kind of cinematic Guernica"*: Vincent Canby, "Real Events of '68 Seen in 'Medium Cool,'" *NYT*, Aug. 28, 1969.

292 *John Hinckley Jr. . . . had "absorbed the identity of Travis Bickle"*: "*Taxi Driver*: Its Influence on John Hinckley Jr.," http://law2.umkc.edu/faculty/projects/ftrials /hinckley/taxidriver.htm.

292 *"a crime-ridden . . . moral cesspool"*: J. Hoberman, "35 Years Later, *Taxi Driver* Still Stuns," *The Village Voice*, March 16, 2011.

293 *"my own reaction . . . was entirely negative"*: Hellman to JRS, Aug. 29, 1969, BFI.

293 *"After* Midnight Cowboy, *he'll be like Paul Newman"*: Rex Reed, "A 'Cowboy' Walks on the Wild Side," *NYT*, May 25, 1969.

293 *Voight yanked the wire from the wall*: Author's interview with Jon Voight.

294 *"He was looking for another challenging part"*: Author's interview with Jennifer Salt.

294 *"I'll spoil this"*: Author's interview with Voight.

294 *"Everybody made their own choices"*: Ibid.

295 *"I'm never gonna catch Joe Buck again"*: *David Frost Show*, Season 2, Episode 136, March 9, 1970, http://www.tv.com/shows/the-david-frost-show/march -9-1970-1272782/.

295 *"There was a tremendous amount of paranoia"*: Ibid.

295 *"I wasn't prepared to be a good partner"*: Author's interview with J. Salt.

296 *The blasts—there turned out to be three in all—were caused by dynamite*: For details, see Bryan Burrough, *Days of Rage: America's Radical Underground, the FBI, and the Forgotten Age of Revolutionary Violence* (New York: Penguin, 2015), pp. 100–113.

297 *one of the more thoughtful and articulate of the campus radicals*: The author, then a Columbia freshman, met Ted Gold in the fall of 1967 when Gold unsuccessfully sought to recruit him to join SDS.

297 *"biting her lip and looking glassy-eyed"*: New York *Daily News*, March 7, 1970.

298 *"they were getting their two favorites—a disaster and a celebrity"*: Douglas Brode, *The Films of Dustin Hoffman* (Secaucus, NJ: Citadel, 1983), p. 44.

298 *The mob then invaded city hall*: Homer Bigart, "War Foes Here Attacked by Construction Workers," *NYT*, May 9, 1970.

21. THE OSCARS

299   *"Hollywood lives at a considerable remove"*: John Gregory Dunne, *The Studio* (New York: Touchstone, 1979 [paperback ed.]), p. 8.

299   *The forty-second Academy Awards . . . had more than wealth and glamour on its mind*: Academy of Motion Pictures Arts and Sciences, "42nd Oscars Highlights," https://www.oscars.org/videos-photos/42nd-oscars-highlights.

300   *"He was so pessimistic about our chances"*: Author's interview with Michael Childers.

301   *"Midnight Cowboy is a wonderful picture, too"*: Author's interview with Hellman.

301   *"one of those almost unbearably classic movies"*: Vincent Canby, "Anne of the Thousand Days," *NYT*, Jan. 21, 1970.

302   *"a glorified vacuum . . . it's all so archly empty"*: Pauline Kael, "The Bottom of the Pit," *The New Yorker*, Sept. 27, 1969.

303   *"we decided that this was going to be our year"*: Aljean Harmetz, "How to Win an Oscar Nomination from 'Anne' to 'Z,'" *NYT*, April 5, 1970.

303   *"We used a different image with every full-page ad"*: Author's interview with Sumner.

304   *"He was very careful about choosing his words"*: Author's interview with Jennifer Salt.

304   *"a story about two fags"*: "A Candid Interview with John Wayne," *Playboy*, May 1971.

304   *"Damn, Hoffman and Voight were good"*: Randy Roberts and James S. Olson, *John Wayne: American* (New York: Free Press, 1995), p. 574.

305   *a $1.5 million diamond necklace*: Robert Osborne, *85 Years of the Oscar: The Official History of the Academy Awards* (New York: Abbeville Press, 2013), p. 208.

305   *"It was certainly a shock to Elizabeth Taylor"*: "Dialogue on Film: Jerome Hellman," *American Film*, June 1978, p. 45.

306   *"Oh, shut up, Bob Hope"*: Richard Zoglin, *Bob Hope: Entertainer of the Century* (New York: Simon & Schuster, 2014), p. 401.

22. FROM JIM TO JAMIE

307   *"The fact is this"*: Thomas Wolfe, *The Hills Beyond* (New York: Avon, 1944 [paperback ed.]), p. 176.

307   *"You're so sweet and generous"*: JLH to JRS, April 8, 1970, BFI.

307   *John wrote back eight days later*: JRS to JLH, April 16, 1970, BFI.

308   *"The name my soul hears . . . is JAMIE"*: JLH to MCR, n.d., DEL.

308   *Jamie was cagey about divulging*: Gregory King, "Herlihy's Modified 'Cowboy' Rapture," *Variety*, May 4, 1971.

309   *"When they dumped all this money on me"*: Martha MacGregor, "This Week in Books," *New York Post*, April 24, 1971.

309 "Midnight Cowboy *has made me too well known*": JLH to MCR, June 19, 1970, DEL.

309 "*I was in and out of communes*": *New York Post*, April 24, 1971.

310 "*It's a damned necessity people learn to live together*": *Chicago Tribune*, April 26, 1971.

310 "*Jamie was smoking too much*": Author's interview with Dick Duane.

311 "*I was resisting and I couldn't honestly go on*": Ibid.

311 "*this dainty quilted prison*": JLH, *The Season of the Witch* (New York: Simon & Schuster, 1971), p. 12.

311 "*the only place in the country*": Ibid., p. 13.

311 "*New York hell*": Ibid., p. 53.

312 *The novel* "*crosses the generation gap*": L. E. Sissman, "A Testimony," *New Yorker*, May 29, 1971.

312 "*Story of a 'now' child pure drivel*": *Philadelphia Express News*, May 9, 1971.

312 "*it's just a matter of where your head is at*": Christopher Lehmann-Haupt, "Everybody Turned On—Almost," *NYT*, April 8, 1971.

313 "*Most of the reviewers were terrified*": Kay Bonetti, "Interview with James Leo Herlihy," April 1982 (American Audio Prose Library audiocassette).

313 "*I made absolutely sure there was a film in it*": King, "Herlihy's Modified 'Cowboy' Rapture," *Variety*, Ibid.

314 "*I guess I don't like the life of the writer anymore*": Bonetti, "Interview with James Leo Herlihy."

314 "*Sex, in a word, is having a heyday*": Harold H. Hart, ed., *Sexual Latitude*, p. 11.

314 "*The time has come*": Ibid., p. 21.

314 a "*moral offense . . . against the dignity of man*": Lowen, p. 63; followed by quotations from Bettelheim, p. 241; Brown, p. 135, and Martin and Lyon, p. 155. A historical footnote: Martin and Lyon were married on June 16, 2008, in the first same-sex wedding in San Francisco after the California Supreme Court legalized same-sex marriage in the state.

315 "*Everybody would knock on the door*": Author's interview with Bob Thixton.

315 "*I suppose what made me so happy*": Lynn Mitsuko Kaufelt, *Key West Writers and Their Houses* (Englewood, FL: Pineapple Press, 1986), p. 77.

316 "*You could lay tripping on acid for hours*": Reader comments in Michael Snyder, "James Leo Herlihy: The Midnight Cowboy in Key West," April 29, 2010, Key West Literary Seminar, www.kwls.org/key-wests-life-of-letters/james _leo_herlihythe_midnight/.

316 "*a great fellow, much too generous*": McGuane email to author, May 19, 2018.

316 "*All the dopers would come on the bus*": Author's interview with Thixton.

316 "*I have nine canoes*": Cleveland Amory, "Tradewinds," *Saturday Review*, May 20, 1971.

317   *"what I've been trying to say . . . I'm a manic depressive"*: JLH to MCR, March 14, 1972, DEL.

317   *"I am swinging! . . . Please help me in this"*: JLH to MCR, n.d., DEL.

317   *"I was never so much concerned"*: JLH, "Arriving in Key West," draft, p. 4, DEL.

318   *"a terrible loneliness"*: Andrew Solomon, *The Noonday Demon: An Atlas of Depression* (New York: Scribner, 2015 [paperback ed.]), p. 203.

318   *"I had dinner with Tennessee one night"*: McGuane email to author, May 19, 2018.

318   Jamie was *"running, like, a flophouse"*: Author's interview with Dotson Rader.

318   *"I'm trying not to repeat the errors of Key West"*: Snyder, "James Leo Herlihy: The Midnight Cowboy in Key West."

EPILOGUE

319   *"An era can be said to end"*: "The Year It Came Apart," *New York*, Dec. 30, 1974, p. 30.

319   *"after knowing Rock intimately for a year"*: JLH to Bailey, Dec. 6, 1987, DEL.

320   *"I have a lot with a lot of different people"*: JLH to Bailey, May 30, 1982, DEL.

320   *"the fairy godmother . . . of women's erotica"*: Claudia Roth Pierpont, "Sex, Lies, and Thirty-five Thousand Pages," *The New Yorker*, March 1, 1993.

320   When she died, the New York Times *obituary listed*: Noël Riley Fitch, *Anaïs: The Erotic Life of Anaïs Nin* (Boston: Little, Brown, 1993), p. 411.

320   *"A strange case, so rare, of justice"*: Gunther Stuhlmann, "From Jim to Jamie: Tracing a friendship in Anaïs Nin's Diary," *Anaïs: An International Journal*, vol. 12, 1994, p. 124.

321   *"She could have run for president"*: "Interview with JLH," Fitch Papers, HRC.

321   *"It seems to me time that I had work to do"*: JLH to MCR, undated, DEL.

321   *"I haven't got a clue what to write anymore"*: JLH to Bailey, June 3, 1986, DEL.

321   *"my diaries were no longer performing a useful function"*: Jeffrey Bailey, "Interview with James Leo Herlihy," *The Advocate*, Aug. 25, 1976.

322   *"My best work as an actor"*: JLH journal entry, May–July 1992, DEL.

322   *"I like the wordlessness of the work"*: JLH to MCR, March 9, 1875, DEL.

322   *"Tennessee . . . was enormously considerate"*: Michael Snyder, "James Leo Herlihy: The Midnight Cowboy in Key West," April 29, 2010, Key West Literary Seminar, www.kwls.org/key-wests-life-of-letters/james_leo_herlihythe_midnight/.

323   *"choking on a Murine bottle cap"*: JLH to Bailey, April 1, 1983, DEL.

323   *"I do not have the faintest notion of what to do"*: JLH to Bailey, Aug. 11, 1986, DEL.

323   *"My closest friend here told me . . . he will be dying"*: JLH to MCR, n.d., GETTY.

324   first Broadway musical *"to deal matter-of-factly with homosexuality"*: Rich quoted

in Greg Varner, "James Kirkwood," Oct. 21, 2004, http://www.glbtqarchive
.com/arts/kirkwood_j_art_A.pdf.

324 *"The changes are profound and astonishing"*: JLH to Bailey, Feb. 11, 1992, DEL.

324 *"I have joined the ranks of the HIV-positive"*: JLH to Bailey, n.d., DEL.

324 *"I hope you won't be distressed"*: JLH to MCR, Nov. 14, 1992, GETTY.

324 *"My body has aged"*: JLH to Bailey, June 9, 1993, DEL.

325 *"The cup is before me"*: JLH journal entry, Oct. 19–20, 1993, DEL.

326 *"it left them stunned and depressed"*: Author's interview with Jerome Hellman.

326 *"'the last thing in the world you need'"*: Ibid.

327 *For Marion Dougherty's sixtieth birthday*: *New York Post*, Feb. 10, 1983.

329 *"I feel like he knew"*: Jenelle Riley, "Worth Her Salt," *Back Stage*, Aug. 5, 2010.

329 *"the finest white male singer on the planet"*: Alyn Shipton, *Nilsson: The Life of a Singer-Songwriter* (New York: Oxford University Press, 2013), p. ix.

330 *the "role Hoffman had been studying for"*: Jenny Thompson, "Dustin Hoffman's New York," Aug. 21, 2013, http://americanpast.blogspot.com/2013/08/dustin -hoffmans-new-york.html.

331 *The allegations . . . were "not reflective of who I am"*: *USA Today*, Dec. 14, 2017. See also: Steven Zeitchik, "John Oliver grills Dustin Hoffman about sexual harassment allegations," *Washington Post*, Dec. 5, 2017.

332 *"our greatest president"*: "Jon Voight Slams Media Lies," *Washington Times*, Dec. 26, 2018.

333 *"It was such a well-made film"*: Author's interview with Jon Voight.

333 WORK, LIVE, SHOP, PLAY, HERE: For the troubled history and rebirth of the site where the X-flat was located, see *NYT*: "Renewal Is Voted in East Side Area," June 23, 1965; "They Kept a Lower East Side Lot Vacant for Decades," March 21, 2014, and "Essex Crossing: A Renewal Project 60 Years in the Making," June 15, 2017.

333 *"own the dream"*: price list in www.242broomenyc.com, Feb. 17, 2019.

333 *"Signs of blight were everywhere"*: *The New Yorker*, Oct. 12, 2015.

334 *the most crime-ridden block per square foot*: Marc Eliot, *Down 42nd Street: Sex, Money, Culture, and Politics at the Crossroads of the World* (New York: Warner Books, 2001), p. 189. Eliot presents a thoroughly researched account of the renewal of the Times Square area between the 1970s and 2000.

335 *"Oh, why doesn't he just act?"*: Ian Buruma, *Conversations with John Schlesinger* (New York: Random House, 2006), p. 142.

336 *"John was a wonderful artist"*: Author's interview with Peter Bart.

336 *"Hollywood had changed"*: Author's interview with Michael Childers.

336 *The two men threw lavish parties*: For an authoritative account of the JRS-Childers party scene, see William J. Mann, *Edge of Midnight: The Life of John Schlesinger* (New York: Billboard Books, 2005), pp. 445–54.

337 *"the fit and the fashionable"*: Ibid, p. 447.

337 *"almost all of my films have gay characters"*: Boze Hadleigh, "Schlesinger Bloody Schlesinger," *The Advocate*, Dec. 5, 1988.

337 *"a significant landmark"*: Mann, *Edge of Midnight*, p. 528.

337 *"a garage sale of gay issues"*: Roger Ebert, March 3, 2000, www.rogerebert.com /reviews/the-next-best-thing-2000.

337 *"John made homosexual love look perfectly natural"*: Ian Buruma, "The Mind of a Misfit, Eye of an Outsider and Heart of a Family Man," *Daily Telegraph*, July 27, 2003.

338 *"We were lucky"*: "John Schlesinger, Joe Buck, and Ratso," *The New Yorker*, Feb. 28, 1992.

338 *"I was recently at dinner with a top studio executive"*: Ibid.

BIBLIOGRAPHY

SELECTED BOOKS

Albee, Edward. *The Zoo Story*. Samuel French acting ed., 1959.

Anderson, Sherwood. *Winesburg, Ohio*. Oxford: Oxford University Press (paperback ed.), 1997.

Bach, Steven. *Final Cut: Dreams and Disaster in the Making of* Heaven's Gate. New York: New American Library, 1985.

Bair, Deirdre. *Anaïs Nin: A Biography*. New York: G. P. Putnam, 1995.

Barstow, Stan. *A Kind of Loving*. London: Michael Joseph, 1960; London: Corgi, 1978.

Bell, Melanie. *Julie Christie*. London: BFI Palgrave, 2016.

Bianco, Anthony. *Ghosts of 42nd Street: A History of America's Most Infamous Block*. New York: Morrow, 2004.

Bieber, Irving, et al. *Homosexuality: A Psychoanalytic Study*. New York: Basic Books, 1962.

Biskind, Peter. *Easy Riders, Raging Bulls: How the Sex-Drugs-and-Rock 'n' Roll Generation Saved Hollywood*. New York: Simon & Schuster, 1997.

Bosworth, Patricia. *Diane Arbus: A Biography*. New York: Knopf, 1984.

———. *The Men in My Life: A Memoir of Love and Art in 1950s Manhattan*. New York: HarperCollins, 2017.

Braine, John. *Room at the Top*. London: Eyre & Spottiswoode, 1957; Harmondsworth, U.K.: Penguin, 1967.

Bram, Christopher. *Eminent Outlaws: The Gay Writers Who Changed America*. New York: Twelve, 2012.

Brode, Douglas. *The Films of Dustin Hoffman*. Secaucus, NJ: Citadel, 1983.

Brooker, Nancy J. *John Schlesinger: A Guide to References and Resources*. Boston: G. K. Hall, 1978.

Brownlow, Kevin. *David Lean: A Biography*. New York: St. Martin's, 1996.

Broyard, Anatole. *Kafka Was the Rage: A Greenwich Village Memoir*. New York: Vintage, 1997.

Burrough, Bryan. *Days of Rage: America's Radical Underground, the FBI, and the Forgotten Age of Revolutionary Violence*. New York: Penguin, 2015.

Buruma, Ian. *Conversations with John Schlesinger.* New York: Random House, 2006.

———. *Their Promised Land: My Grandparents in Love and War.* New York: Penguin, 2016.

Calhoun, Ada. *St. Marks Is Dead: The Many Lives of America's Hippest Street.* New York: W. W. Norton, 2016.

Cannato, Vincent. *The Ungovernable City: John V. Lindsay and the Struggle to Save New York.* New York: Basic Books, 2002.

Carroll, Jim. *The Basketball Diaries.* New York: Penguin (paperback ed.), 1987.

Chauncey, George. *New York: Gender, Urban Culture, and the Making of the Gay Male World, 1890-1940.* New York: Basic Books, 1994.

Clark, Jim. *Dream Repairman: Adventures in Film Editing.* Crockett, TX: LandMarc Press, 2010.

Corkin, Stanley. *Starring New York: Filming the Grime and the Glamour of the Long 1970s.* New York: Oxford University Press, 2011.

Cronin, Paul, ed. *A Time to Stir: Columbia '68.* New York: Columbia University Press, 2018.

Crowley, Mart. *The Boys in the Band.* New York: Samuel French, 1968.

Delany, Samuel R. *The Motion of Light in Water.* New York: Masquerade, 1993.

———. *Times Square Red, Times Square Blue.* New York: New York University Press, 1999.

Didion, Joan. *The White Album.* New York: Simon & Schuster, 1979.

Dougherty, Marion, with Robert Roussel. *My Casting Couch Was Too Short.* Xlibris, 2015 (Kindle ed.).

Duberman, Martin. *Black Mountain: An Exploration in Community.* New York: Anchor, 1973.

———. *Cures: A Gay Man's Odyssey.* New York: Dutton, 1991.

Dundy, Elaine. *Finch, Bloody Finch: A Biography of Peter Finch.* London: Michael Joseph, 1980.

Dunne, John Gregory. *The Studio.* New York: Touchstone (paperback ed.), 1979.

Dylan, Bob. *Chronicles: Volume One.* New York: Simon & Schuster, 2004.

Eliot, Marc. *Down 42nd Street: Sex, Money, Culture, and Politics at the Crossroads of the World.* New York: Warner Books, 2001.

Faderman, Lillian. *The Gay Revolution: The Story of the Struggle.* New York: Simon & Schuster, 2015.

Farber, Stephen. *The Movie Rating Game.* Washington: Public Affairs Press, 1972.

Fassett, Kaffe. *Dreaming in Color: An Autobiography.* New York: Stewart, Tabori & Chang, 2012.

Fazan, Eleanor. *Fiz and Some Theatre Giants.* Victoria, Canada: Friesen Press, 2013.

Fiegel, Eddi. *John Barry: A Sixties Theme: From James Bond to Midnight Cowboy.* London: Constable, 1998.

Fitch, Noël Riley. *Anaïs: The Erotic Life of Anaïs Nin*. Boston: Little, Brown, 1993.

Friedman, Mack. *Strapped for Cash: A History of American Hustler Culture*. Los Angeles: Alyson Books, 2003.

Furst, Joshua. *Revolutionaries*. New York: Knopf, 2019.

Gilliatt, Penelope. *Sunday Bloody Sunday: The Original Screenplay of the John Schlesinger Film*. New York: Dodd, Mead, 1986.

Gray, Beverly. *Seduced by Mrs. Robinson: How* The Graduate *Became the Touchstone of a Generation*. Chapel Hill: Algonquin, 2017.

Hamill, Pete. *Downtown: My Manhattan*. New York: Little, Brown, 2004.

Harris, Mark. *Pictures at a Revolution: Five Movies and the Birth of the New Hollywood*. New York: Penguin Press, 2008.

Hart, Harold H., ed. *Sexual Latitude: For and Against*. New York: Hart Publishing, 1971.

Hentoff, Nat. *A Political Life: The Education of John V. Lindsay*. New York: Knopf, 1969.

Herlihy, James Leo. *All Fall Down*. New York: E. P. Dutton, 1960; New York: Avon, 1977.

———. *Midnight Cowboy*. New York: Simon & Schuster, 1965.

———. *The Season of the Witch*. New York: Simon & Schuster, 1971.

———. *The Sleep of Baby Filberton and Other Stories*. New York: Dutton, 1959; reprinted as *Crazy October*. New York: Lancer, 1970.

———. *Stop, You're Killing Me*. New York: Simon & Schuster, 1970.

———. *The Story That Ends with a Scream and Eight Others*. New York: Simon & Schuster, 1967.

Herlihy, James Leo, and William Noble. *Blue Denim*. New York: Random House, 1958.

Highwater, Jamake. *Shadow Show: An Autobiographical Insinuation*. New York: Alfred van der Marck, 1986.

Hofler, Robert. *Sexplosion: From Andy Warhol to* A Clockwork Orange—*How a Generation of Pop Rebels Broke All the Taboos*. New York: HarperCollins, 2014.

House, Charles. *The Outrageous Life of Henry Faulkner: Portrait of an Appalachian Artist*. Knoxville: University of Tennessee Press, 1988.

Huncke, Herbert. *Guilty of Everything: The Autobiography of Herbert Huncke*. New York: Paragon, 1990.

Hurewitz, Daniel. *Stepping Out: Nine Walks Through New York's Gay and Lesbian Past*. New York: Henry Holt, 1997.

Kaiser, Charles. *1968 in America: Music, Politics, Chaos, Counterculture, and the Shaping of a Generation*. New York: Grove Press, 2018 (thirtieth-anniversary ed.).

———. *The Gay Metropolis 1940–1996*. Boston: Houghton Mifflin, 1997.

Kaufelt, Lynn Mitsuko. *Key West Writers and Their Houses*. Englewood, FL: Pineapple Press, 1986.

Kazan, Elia. *A Life*. New York: Knopf, 1988.

Kazin, Alfred. *New York Jew*. New York: Knopf, 1978.

Kramer, Peter, and Yanni Tzioumakis, eds. *The Hollywood Renaissance: Revisiting American Cinema's Most Celebrated Era*. New York: Bloomsbury, 2018.

Krassner, Paul. *Confessions of a Raving, Unconfined Nut*. Berkeley, CA: Soft Skull Press, 2012.

Kynaston, David. *Modernity Britain: Book Two, A Shake of the Dice*. London: Bloomsbury, 2014.

Lewes, Kenneth. *The Psychoanalytic Theory of Male Homosexuality*. New York: Simon & Schuster, 1988.

Lewis, Jon. *Hollywood v. Hard Core: How the Struggle Over Censorship Saved the Modern Film Industry*. New York: NYU Press, 2000.

Lisanti, Tom, and Louis Paul. *Film Fatales: Women in Espionage Film and Television, 1962–73*. Jefferson, NC: McFarland, 2002.

Locke, Michael, and Vincent Brook. *Silver Lake Bohemia: A History*. Charleston, SC: The History Press, 2016.

Lukas, J. Anthony. *Don't Shoot—We Are Your Children!* New York: Random House, 1968.

Mailer, Norman. *The Armies of the Night: History as a Novel, the Novel as History*. New York: New American Library, 1968.

Mann, Thomas. *Essays of Three Decades*. New York: Knopf, 1947.

Mann, William J. *Edge of Midnight: The Life of John Schlesinger*. New York: Billboard Books, 2005.

McCaffrey, Joseph A., ed. *The Homosexual Dialectic*. Englewood Cliffs, NJ: Prentice Hall, 1972.

McFarlane, Brian. *An Autobiography of British Cinema*. London: Methuen, 1997.

McGilligan, Patrick, and Paul Buhle, eds. *Tender Comrades: A Backstory of the Hollywood Blacklist*. Minneapolis: University of Minnesota Press, 2012 (paperback ed.).

McGrath, Declan. *Editing & Post-Production: Screencraft*. Cran-Pres-Celigny, Switzerland: RotoVision, 2001.

McKeen, William. *Mile Marker Zero: The Moveable Feast of Key West*. New York: Crown, 2011.

Mealer, Bryan. *The Kings of Big Spring: God, Oil, and One Family's Search for the American Dream*. New York: Flatiron, 2018.

Miller, Arthur. *Timebends: A Life*. New York: Grove Press, 1987.

Miller, Merle. *On Being Different: What It Means to Be a Homosexual*. New York: Penguin, 2012.

Morris, Jan. *Manhattan '45*. New York: Oxford University Press, 1987.

Morris, Willie. *New York Days*. Boston: Little, Brown, 1993.

Newquist, Roy. *Conversations*. New York: Rand McNally, 1967.

Nin, Anaïs. *The Diary of Anaïs Nin: Volume Five, 1947–1955*. New York: Harcourt Brace Jovanovich, 1974.

———. *The Diary of Anaïs Nin: Volume Six, 1955–1966*. New York: Harcourt Brace Jovanovich, 1976.

———. *Trapeze: The Unexpurgated Diaries of Anaïs Nin, 1947–55*. Sky Blue Press, 2017 (Kindle ed.).

Osborne, Robert. *85 Years of the Oscar: The Official History of the Academy Awards*. New York: Abbeville Press, 2013.

Perkins, Roy, and Martin Stollery. *British Film Editors: The Heart of the Movie*. London: British Film Institute, 2004.

Phillips, Gene D. *John Schlesinger*. Boston: Twayne, 1981.

Physique Pictorial, vols. I, II, and III. Cologne: Taschen, 1997.

Picker, David V. *Musts, Maybes, and Nevers: A Book About the Movies*. CreateSpace, 2013.

Porter, Darwin. *Brando Unzipped*. New York: Blood Moon Productions, 2006.

Powdermaker, Hortense. *Hollywood: The Dream Factory*. Boston: Little, Brown, 1950; Mansfield Center, CT: Martino, 2013.

Rader, Dotson. *Gov't Inspected Meat and Other Fun Summer Things*. New York: David McKay, 1971.

———. *Tennessee Williams: An Intimate Memoir*, London: Grafton, 1986.

Ramone, Phil. *Making Records: The Scenes Behind the Music*. New York: Hyperion, 2007.

Reay, Barry. *New York Hustlers: Masculinity and Sex in Modern America*. Manchester, U.K.: Manchester University Press, 2010.

Rechy, John. *City of Night*. New York: Grove Press, 1963. Fiftieth-anniversary ed., 2013.

Reid, David. *The Brazen Age: New York City and the American Empire: Politics, Art, and Bohemia*. New York: Pantheon, 2016.

Roberts, Randy, and James S. Olson. *John Wayne: American*. New York: Free Press, 1995.

Rosenblum, Ralph, and Robert Karen. *When the Shooting Stops . . . the Cutting Begins: A Film Editor's Story*. New York: Da Capo, 1986.

Ross, Lillian and Helen. *The Player: A Profile of an Art*. New York: Simon & Schuster, 1962.

Russo, Vito. *The Celluloid Closet: Homosexuality in the Movies*. New York: Harper & Row, 1981.

Sanders, James. *Celluloid Skyline: New York and the Movies*. New York: Knopf, 2001.

Schelle, Michael. *The Score: Interviews with Film Composers*. Los Angeles: Silman-James Press, 1999.

Schrecker, Ellen. *Many Are the Crimes: McCarthyism in America*. Boston: Little, Brown, 1998.

Shipton, Alyn. *Nilsson: The Life of a Singer-Songwriter*. New York: Oxford University Press, 2013.

Skinner, James M. *The Cross and the Cinema*. New York: Praeger, 1993.

Slawson, Judith. *Robert Duvall: Hollywood Maverick*. New York: St. Martin's, 1985.

Solomon, Andrew. *The Noonday Demon: An Atlas of Depression*. New York: Scribner, 2015 (paperback ed.).

Stein, Jean. *Edie: An American Biography*. Edited by George Plimpton. New York: Knopf, 1982.

Stern, Aaron. *Me: The Narcissistic American*. New York: Ballantine, 1979.

Stevens, Wallace. *Letters of Wallace Stevens*. Edited by Holly Stevens. Berkeley: University of California Press, 1996.

Talese, Gay. *The Kingdom and the Power: Behind the Scenes at* The New York Times. Cleveland: World Publishing; New York: Dell, 1998.

Taylor, William, ed. *Inventing Times Square: Commerce and Culture at the Crossroads of the World*. New York: Russell Sage Foundation, 1991.

Ultra Violet. *Famous for 15 Minutes: My Years with Andy Warhol*. New York: Harcourt Brace Jovanovich, 1988.

Richie Unterberger, *Urban Spacemen and Wayfaring Strangers: Overlooked Innovators and Eccentric Visionaries of '60s Rock*. San Francisco: Miller Freeman, 2000.

Jack Valenti. *This Time, This Place: My Life in War, the White House, and Hollywood*. New York: Crown Archetype, 2007.

Vidal, Gore. *The City and the Pillar*. New York: Vintage, 2003 (paperback ed.).

———. *Palimpsest: A Memoir*. New York: Random House, 1995.

Wakefield, Dan. *New York in the Fifties*. Boston: Houghton Mifflin, 1992.

Walker, Alexander. *Hollywood, England: The British Film Industry in the Sixties*. London: Michael Joseph, 1974.

Warhol, Andy, and Pat Hackett. *POPism: The Warhol Sixties*. Orlando: Harcourt, 1980.

White, E. B. *Here Is New York*. New York: Harper & Brothers, 1949.

White, Edmund. *City Boy: My Life in New York During the 1960s and '70s*. New York: Bloomsbury, 2009.

Williams, Tennessee. *Memoirs*. Garden City, NY: Doubleday, 1975.

Wolfe, Michelle, and Alfred P. Kielwasser, eds. *Gay People, Sex, and the Media*. New York: Routledge, 2013.

Wolfe, Thomas. *The Hills Beyond*. New York: Avon, 1944 (paperback ed.).

Zoglin, Richard. *Bob Hope: Entertainer of the Century*. New York: Simon & Schuster, 2014.

SELECTED ARTICLES, INTERVIEWS, AND WEBSITES

Bailey, Jeffrey. "Interview with James Leo Herlihy." *The Advocate*, Aug. 25, 1976.

Biskind, Peter. "Midnight Revolution." *Vanity Fair*, April 2010.

Bonetti, Kay. "Interview with James Leo Herlihy." April 1982. Columbia, MO: American Audio Prose Library (audiocassette).

Bowery Boys. "*Midnight Cowboy*: 25 Fascinating New York Details, in Celebration of the Film Classic's 50th Anniversary." Feb. 22, 2013. http://www.boweryboyshistory.com/2019/05/midnight-cowboy-25-fascinating -sleazy.html.

Bracker, Milton. "Life on W. 42nd St. A Study in Decay." *NYT*, March 14, 1960.

Cook Jr., Jess. "Jon Voight: The Uneasy Winner." *NYT Magazine*, April 29, 1975.

Daniels, Mary. "A Grown-Up Midnight Cowboy," *Chicago Tribune*, April 26, 1971.

"Dialogue on Film: Jerome Hellman," *American Film*, June 1978.

Doty, Robert C. "Growth of Homosexuality in City Provokes Wide Concern." *NYT*, Dec. 17, 1963.

"Dustin Hoffman: *Larry King Live, 1994*," YouTube, in four parts, https://www .youtube.com/watch?v=ViofIwot9BE.

"Dusty and the Duke." Photographed by John Dominis. *Life*, July 11, 1969.

Egan, Bob. "25 Iconic New York City film locations." www.popspotsnyc.com/ iconic_new_york_city_film_locations/.

Gross, Leonard. "What's Blue at the Movies? Ask Dr. Stern." *LAT*, July 16, 1972.

Harris, Mark. "On the Fringe." *Midnight Cowboy*, Criterion Collection Blu-Ray, 2018.

Harris, Mary. "Interview with James Leo Herlihy." Nov. 1971. Raleigh: North Carolina Museum of Art.

Hellman, Jerome. "The Making of *Midnight Cowboy*: A Personal Memoir." Unpublished manuscript, Jerome Hellman Papers.

"Interview with John Schlesinger." *American Film*, Nov. 1987.

Jon Voight Interview, *David Frost Show*, Season 2, Episode 136, March 9, 1970. http://www.tv.com/shows/the-david-frost-show/march-9-1970-1272782/.

Kael, Pauline. "The Bottom of the Pit." *The New Yorker*, Sept. 27, 1969.

———. "Urban Gothic." *The New Yorker*, Oct. 30, 1971.

Kauffmann, Stanley. "Homosexual Drama and Its Disguises." *NYT*, Jan. 23, 1966.

Kiefer, Christian. "Groggy from Stolen Phenobarbs: An Appreciation of JLH." *The Paris Review*, March 17, 2017.

Leff, Leonard J. "Hollywood and the Holocaust: Remembering *The Pawnbroker*." *American Jewish History* 84:4, 1996.

Madden, Caroline. "The Queer Subtext of New Hollywood Era Buddy Movies."

Fandor, June 28, 2018. https://www.fandor.com/posts/the-queer-subtext-of-new
-hollywood-era-buddy-movies.

Meryman, Richard. "Before They Were Kings." *Vanity Fair*, March 2004.

———"*Playboy* Interview: Dustin Hoffman." *Playboy*, April 1975.

Midnight Cowboy. Screenplay and accompanying articles: "Waldo Salt (1914–1987),"
"Producing *Midnight Cowboy*," "Directing *Midnight Cowboy*," and "My Father,
Waldo Salt." *Scenario: The Magazine of Screenwriting Art*, Winter 1997.

Mitzel, John. "Interview with James Leo Herlihy." *Gay Weekly*, Sept. 25, 1976.

"The Moonchild and the Fifth Beatle." *Time*, Feb. 7, 1969.

Reed, Rex. "A 'Cowboy' Walks on the Wild Side." *NYT*, May 25, 1969.

Richmond, Len. "Films for the Madding Crowd." BBC Radio interview with John
Schlesinger, March 8, 1977, transcript, BFI.

Riley, Michael M. "I Both Hate and Love What I Do: An Interview with John
Schlesinger." *Literature/Film Quarterly*, Spring 1978.

Roth, Philip. "The Play That Dare Not Speak Its Name." *NYRB*, Feb. 25, 1965.

Schlesinger, John. "Introduction." Jerome Hellman Papers.

Snyder, Michael. "James Leo Herlihy: The Midnight Cowboy in Key West." April
29, 2010, Key West Literary Seminar, www.kwls.org/key-wests-life-of-letters
/james_leo_herlihythe_midnight/.

Stuhlmann, Gunther. "From Jim to Jamie: Tracing a Friendship in Anaïs Nin's
Diary." *Anaïs: An International Journal*, vol. 12, 1994.

Turan, Kenneth. "Why Joe Buck and Ratso Live On." *LAT*, Feb. 20, 1994.

SELECTED FILMS

Documentaries

Casting By. Directed by Tom Donahue. HBO Documentary Films, 2013.

CBS Reports: The Homosexuals. March 7, 1967. https://www.youtube.com/watch?v
=zWNEdoXo0Yg.

Making the Boys. Directed by Crayton Robey. Warner Bros., 2011.

Midnight Cowboy. MGM, 2-Disc Collector's Set Edition DVD, 2006, includes
Audio Commentary by Jerome Hellman; "After Midnight: Reflecting on
the Classic 35 Years Later"; "Controversy and Acclaim," and "Celebrating
Schlesinger" featurette.

Midnight Cowboy, Criterion Collection Blu-Ray, 2018, includes 1991 Audio
Commentary by John Schlesinger and Jerome Hellman; video essay by Adam
Holender; "The Crowd Around the Cowboy," 1969 short film, and 2000
interview with Schlesinger for BAFTA Los Angeles.

Waldo Salt: A Screenwriter's Journey. Directed by Robert Hillmann and Eugene Corr.
American Masters. Public Broadcasting Service, 1990. Outtakes at Academy of
Motion Picture Arts and Sciences Film Archive, Hollywood.

Selected Films of John Schlesinger

Terminus (1961)

A Kind of Loving (1962)

Billy Liar (1963)

Darling (1965)

Far from the Madding Crowd (1967)

Midnight Cowboy (1969)

Sunday Bloody Sunday (1971)

The Day of the Locust (1975)

Marathon Man (1976)

Yanks (1979)

Honky Tonk Freeway (1981)

An Englishman Abroad (TV, 1983)

The Falcon and the Snowman (1985)

Madame Sousatzka (1988)

A Question of Attribution (TV, 1991)

Film and Television Adaptations of James Leo Herlihy's Work

Box 704 (1956), Kraft Television Theatre, based on Herlihy teleplay.

Blue Denim (1959), movie based on Herlihy-Noble stage play.

All Fall Down (1962), movie based on Herlihy novel.

Midnight Cowboy (1969), movie based on Herlihy novel.

Recorded Performances of James Leo Herlihy

"A Bunch of Lonely Pagliaccis," *Route 66* (1963), TV episode.

In the French Style (1963), movie.

Four Friends (1981), movie.

Other Films

The Shopworn Angel (1938)

Rope (1948)

Victim (1961)

The Children's Hour (1961)

Advise and Consent (1962)

The Pawnbroker (1965)

Blow-Up (1966)

Chelsea Girls (1966)

The Journey of the Fifth Horse (1966)

Reflections in a Golden Eye (1967)

Lonesome Cowboys (1968)

Easy Rider (1969)
Medium Cool (1969)
The Boys in the Band (1970)
Trash (1970)
Taxi Driver (1976)
Coming Home (1978)
I Shot Andy Warhol (1996)
Factory Girl (2006)

MUSIC

Fred Neil's original recording of "Everybody's Talkin'": *Fred Neil*, Capitol Records, 1967, also available on several compilation CDs.

Harry Nilsson's recording of "Everybody's Talkin'": first released on *Aerial Ballet*, RCA Records, 1968; also available on many Nilsson compilation CDs. There are two Nilsson recordings of "Everybody's Talkin'" on the original motion picture soundtrack album of *Midnight Cowboy*, first released by United Artists in 1969, reissued on compact disc by EMI-Manhattan Records, 1985. The album also includes John Barry's *Midnight Cowboy* theme. The latest reissue of the soundtrack is *Midnight Cowboy: Expanded Original MGM Motion Picture Score*, Quartet Records #QR435, produced by Chris Malone and Jose M. Benitez, 2020. It includes the essay "Musical Supervision: John Barry," by Jon Burlingame.

INDEX

A Note About the Author

Glenn Frankel worked for many years at *The Washington Post*, winning a Pulitzer Prize in 1989. He taught journalism at Stanford University and the University of Texas at Austin, where he directed the School of Journalism. He has won a National Jewish Book Award, was a finalist for the Los Angeles Times Book Prize, and is a Motion Picture Academy Film Scholar. He is the bestselling author of *The Searchers* and *High Noon*, and lives in Arlington, Virginia. Visit his website at www.glennfrankel.com.